MW00462655

THE BOOK OF

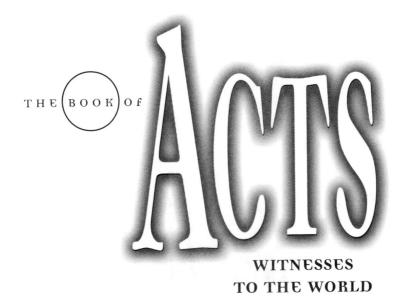

ACTS

WITNESSES
TO THE WORLD

Advancing the Ministries of the Gospel

AMG Publishers

God's Word to you is our highest calling.

TWENTY-FIRST CENTURY
BIBLICAL COMMENTARY SERIES®

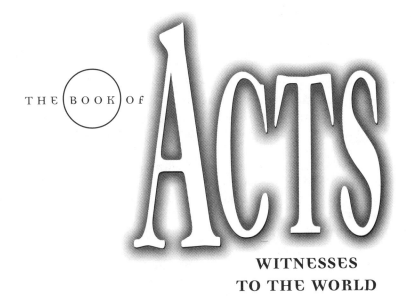

THE BOOK OF **ACTS**

WITNESSES
TO THE WORLD

STEVEN
GER

GENERAL EDITORS

MAL COUCH & ED HINDSON

The Book of Acts: Witnesses to the World
Copyright © 2004 by Scofield Ministries
Published by AMG Publishers.
6815 Shallowford Road
Chattanooga, TN 37421

TWENTY-FIRST CENTURY BIBLICAL COMMENTARY SERIES is a registered
trademark of AMG Publishers, Inc.

ISBN-13: 978-0-89957-818-7
ISBN-10: 0-89957-818-7

First Printing, January 2005
Cover Design by ImageWright, Inc.
Text Design by Warren Baker
Edited and proofread by Warren Baker, Patrick Belvill, and Weller Editorial
Services, Chippewa Lake, MI

Printed in Canada
20 19 18 17 16 15 –R– 8 7 6 5 4 3

To my wife, Adria Lauren, whose worth is far above rubies
and who reassuringly certified that my ramblings made sense;

and to my son, Jonathan Gabriel, our gift from God, who impatiently
waited for his Dad to get his nose out of this book to come play with him.

Twenty-First Century Biblical Commentary Series®

Mal Couch, Th.D., and Ed Hindson, D.Phil.

The New Testament has guided the Christian Church for over two thousand years. This one testament is made up of twenty-seven books, penned by godly men through the inspiration of the Holy Spirit. It tells us of the life of Jesus Christ, His atoning death for our sins, His miraculous resurrection, His ascension back to heaven, and the promise of His second coming. It also tells the story of the birth and growth of the Church and the people and principles that shaped it in its earliest days. The New Testament concludes with the book of Revelation pointing ahead to the glorious return of Jesus Christ.

Without the New Testament, the message of the Bible would be incomplete. The Old Testament emphasizes the promise of a coming Messiah. It constantly points us ahead to the One who is coming to be the King of Israel and the Savior of the world. But the Old Testament ends with this event still unfulfilled. All of its ceremonies, pictures, types, and prophecies are left awaiting the arrival of the "Lamb of God who takes away the sin of the world!" (John 1:29).

The message of the New Testament represents the timeless truth of God. As each generation seeks to apply that truth to its specific context, an up-to-date commentary needs to be created just for them. The editors and authors of the Twenty-First Century Biblical Commentary Series have endeavored to do just that. This team of scholars represents conservative, evangelical, and dispensational scholarship at its best. The individual authors may differ on minor points of interpretation, but all are convinced that the Old and New Testaments teach a dispensational framework for biblical history. They also hold to a pretribulational and premillennial understanding of biblical prophecy.

The French scholar René Pache reminded each succeeding generation, "If the power of the Holy Spirit is to be made manifest anew among us, it is of primary importance that His message should regain its due place. Then we shall be able to put the enemy to flight by the sword of the Spirit which is the Word of God."

The book of Acts represents the biblical transition from Judaism to Christianity. It is the biographical account of the earliest Christians and the record of their evangelistic endeavors. Its initial setting, as Steven Ger so effectively demonstrates, is thoroughly Jewish. But as the story develops, so does the outreach of Christianity into the Gentile world of the Roman Empire of the first century A.D.

Acts also represents a *balanced eschatology.* The early Christians believed the "last days" had been initiated at Pentecost. Yet, we find in Acts a "tempered imminence." The expectation of Jesus' imminent return was balanced by His commissioning the disciples to evangelize the world. Thus, in the Acts of the Apostles we find a thorough going effort to preach the gospel, win the lost, and build the Church. Luke continues to calculate the tally of the number of converts until he is unable to count them. At the same time, it is clear that these early followers of Christ were expecting His return at any moment. In retrospect, this is probably why they were so successful. The Church today would do well to maintain the same dual emphasis.

Contents

Foreword

We easily identify with the people in Acts because Luke never allows us to forget their humanity. It is impossible to confuse Peter or Paul with fictional characters. No ancient novelist would ever create men whose lives were characterized by such dramatic contradictions: the brash and blustering everyman who blossoms overnight into an elder statesman; a movement's most infamous persecutor who develops into its most prominent advocate. Luke has drawn two millennia's worth of readers into the overlapping apostolic "adventures" of these two first century Jewish men who, while so dissimilar, shared a common vision and served the same Messiah.

While Acts is the definitive account of the early church's expansion, it was not Luke's intention to provide a comprehensive report on the apostolic mission to Israel and the Roman world. To do so would have taken an entire series of sequels to his original gospel. At its present length, Acts already approaches an ancient scroll's maximum length of between thirty-two and thirty-five feet.[1]

Luke provides considered selections, chosen from the vast historical panorama of early church history. The majority of the apostles barely make a cameo appearance within the narrative. Nor does Luke mention their eventual destinations or destinies. Even Peter disappears from the narrative after fifteen chapters.

In a series of vignettes, or "postcards," some historical, some biographical, still others theological, Acts reveals the successes and defeats, the conquests and tragedies of the original band of Jesus' followers. In Acts we are able to share in the joy, the loss, the rejection, the confident assurance, the jealousy, the setbacks, the frustration, the passionate debate and the ultimate triumph of these pioneers of the Jesus movement. These are ordinary people who, through the power and enablement of the Holy Spirit, accomplish extraordinary things in the name of their Messiah. In less than one generation, three decades, this initial cohort of Christians boldly "turned the world upside-down" (17:6)!

The existing literature on Acts is voluminous, and new works are regularly being added. I have introduced nothing in this commentary that has not been previously written about Acts, most likely with superior style and scholarship. Nevertheless, commentaries on Acts written from the perspective of and with the sensitivities peculiar to a Jewish Christian are in the distinct minority. Most of the Acts narrative, however, deals with specifically Jewish issues, questions, concerns and controversies, which arose as the church expanded from its initial Jerusalem borders and Hebrew boundaries. These issues and questions are not often examined through Jewish eyes or explained using Jewish categories. I believe that providing such a basic cultural insight facilitates understanding in the study of this foundational work.

I am a fourth-generation Jewish believer, nurtured in the faith from birth, whose family found our Messiah, beginning with my great-grandmother, over three quarters of a century ago. This project is an outgrowth of that legacy, and I pray that this Jewish Christian perspective may prove of value in studying Acts.

As I cannot be your personal study partner, I submit this volume as my surrogate to accompany you on your sojourn through the world of the nascent church. The following are the modest study notes of this particular "Hebrew of Hebrews;" the views of a messianic Jew as he ponders the book of Acts.

Steven Ger
Sojourner Ministries
Dallas, Texas

Background of Acts

The book of Acts grants readers a unique and fascinating glimpse into the world of the early church. We peer through the corridors of two millennia and see the still vivid foundations of our own faith. Beginning in Jerusalem, Acts shows us the road we believers have traveled to arrive at our present state. All that we, the contemporary church, are today, we owe to the pioneers to whom its author, Luke, introduces us. Luke continues to perform an inestimable service for contemporary believers by unveiling the historical, social, cultural, political and religious milieu of the first three decades of church history.

Indeed, Acts is, at its most basic, a book of history. Yet for so many of us, the mention of any sort of history book immediately brings to mind dry, dusty tomes filled to overflowing with infinitely irrelevant data from some unrelated, bygone age.

Acts is not that sort of history book. In many ways, Acts is the singularly most earthy and accessible book in the entire New Testament. It is in its own distinct category. It is not chock full of challenging, doctrinal propositions, as are the epistles. It is not composed of enigmatic, apocalyptic imagery, as is the book of Revelation. Nor does it consist of the biography, teaching and parables of the crucified and resurrected God-man, as do the Gospels. Nonetheless, Acts provides the necessary context for the New Testament and is the connecting bridge that links this collection of gospels, epistles and apocalypse together.

Acts is unique. It is story—a simple story about regular human beings who are just like us. They share our same hopes and similar fears, our worst biases and best qualities. In fact, Acts is, essentially, *our* story. It is your legacy and mine. It is the record of our brothers and sisters who came before us, blazing a revolutionary, messianic trail from Jerusalem to "the ends of the earth."

Authorship of Acts

The traditional claim that Luke wrote Acts has been essentially uncontested throughout the book's history. There is clear internal evidence that Luke is the author of Acts.

First, the same individual wrote Acts who penned the Gospel of Luke. The prologues of both books are linked to one another (Acts 1:1 refers back to Luke 1:1-4) and both prologues designate the same person, Theophilus, as the book's intended recipient.

Second, Acts was written by one of Paul's traveling companions, as is evidenced by the famous "we" passages (16:10-17; 20:5-15; 21:1-18; 27:1—28:16) when, at certain points, the author changes narrative voice from third to first person. Luke was one such companion of Paul and is mentioned in three of Paul's letters (Col. 4:14; Philem. 24; 2 Tim. 4:11). Aside from Luke, Acts notes another eight companions: Silas, Timothy, Sopater, Aristarchus, Secundus, Gaius, Tychicus, and Trophimus. Each of these men, however, is mentioned at some point within the context of the "we" passages, eliminating from consideration all but Luke. Luke alone is not referenced by name anywhere within the "we" passages.

Third, it is an indisputable fact that Luke, as an eyewitness and participant, demonstrates exceptional familiarity with Roman law and government. He is unfailingly accurate in his use of the proper political terminology for each Roman official in every Roman province he mentions. This is no small accomplishment, as titles, offices and terminology frequently shifted from time to time, province to province and, often, from one administration to another.[1]

For example, in Cyprus, Luke recognizes Sergius Paulus as proconsul; in Philippi, which is accurately recognized as a colony, the leaders are called *strategoi* (magistrates); in Thessalonica, the leaders are called *politarchs*; in Malta, the leader is called the *protos* (chief man); in Ephesus, Luke deftly differentiates between *Asiarchs* (religious administrators), the *grammateus* (town clerk) and proconsuls.[2]

Therefore, we are on extremely safe ground when we assert Luke to be the author of Acts.

Luke the Man

Aside from what facts may be gleaned from the Acts "we" passages and his triple mention within Paul's epistles, as noted in the above discussion, very little is known about Luke as an individual.

Based upon Luke's literary skill and vocabulary usage, there is no question that he was extremely well educated. It comes then as no surprise that Paul identifies Luke as a "beloved physician" (Col. 4:14). In the realm of the Roman Empire, there were only three major medical schools where Luke may have studied. The three celebrated university towns of the ancient world were Athens (in Greece), Alexandria (in Egypt) and Tarsus (in Asia Minor, specifically, Cilicia, Paul's hometown). (A fourth possibility is the small Greek isle of Cos, which had both hospital and medical school.)[3] Precisely at which of these three eminent sites of learning Luke studied is a point open to speculation (and imagination as well, if he was educated in Tarsus and, if so, whether he was there concurrent with Paul's five year residency, from AD 37–42 [Acts 9:30—11:26]). Of course, in his medical capacity, Luke could verify the many healing miracles of which he was an eyewitness.

There is an ongoing debate over whether or not Luke was Jewish. While the overwhelming consensus has always been that Luke was a Gentile, the New Testament does not explicitly reveal Luke's nationality. However, in Paul's letter to the Colossians, Luke is listed separately (4:14) from Paul's list of Jewish coworkers (4:10–11). While this is the sole New Testament hint that Luke was a Gentile, on the surface this passage would seem to be conclusive.

There is, however, at least an adequate case to be made for Luke having been Jewish—not a native of Israel, but a Hellenistic (Greek) Jew of the Diaspora (if so, he would be the earliest recorded "Jewish doctor"). First, beneath the surface of Luke's superb mastery of Greek literary style, there are indications that, while the author wrote in Greek, he might have been thinking in Hebrew. This is indicted by the presence of Hebraisms (Hebrew word order, phrases and terminology) scattered throughout the Greek text. An alternative but less satisfying way to explain the presence of such Hebraisms in Acts is that they derive from the original Jewish sources, either written or oral, which Luke translated as he compiled his account.

Second, Luke's exquisite knowledge of Jewish theological issues and sectarian parties, familiarity with the Temple, acquaintance with Jewish holidays and marked concern for Jerusalem go beyond that of merely a historian's reporting of the facts. It is difficult to explain Luke's Jewish expertise and concern by simply citing the two years he spent in Israel, from AD 57–59 (Acts 21:8—27:1) or imagining the quantity of time he spent personally with his friend, Paul, that noted "Hebrew of Hebrews."

Third, Luke deftly weaves quotations and allusions from the Hebrew Scripture throughout his book. His fluency and familiarity with the Law, Prophets, and Writings (the Jewish divisions of the OT) reveal a mind saturated in the contents of the Old Testament. Luke's facility with the Hebrew Scripture indicates comprehensive study. Such sophistication simply cannot have been developed over a limited period.

A probable way to satisfactorily synthesize the evidence, pro and con, concerning Luke's Jewish or Gentile status, would be to posit that prior to becoming a Christian, Luke was either a God-fearer, a Gentile worshiper of the God of Israel, or a "proselyte of the gate," a near convert to Judaism. This would explain Paul having listed him separately from the Jewish Christians, Luke's familiarity with Judaism and the Temple as well as his facility with the Hebrew Scripture. In addition, it would clarify the profound interest in God-fearers that Luke demonstrates throughout Acts.

Date of Composition

As indicated in the prologue of Acts, Luke's gospel must necessarily have been written prior to Acts. Since Acts is the sequel to Luke's gospel, most scholars hold that one should assign a date for the creation of Acts only after first determining a date for the writing of the gospel. This methodology, while logical, is not the only approach to dating Acts. To reverse this equation is equally justified, as the following will demonstrate.

In Luke's gospel, Jesus graphically predicts the coming destruction of Jerusalem (19:43–44, 21:20–24). The Romans fulfilled his prophecy in AD 70. Due to extreme bias against accepting the validity of any predictive prophecy, even that which originated with Jesus, many scholars assign a date after AD 70 to Luke's gospel. This would allow Luke to portray Jesus as predicting something that, by the author's time, had already occurred.

Yet presuppositions against the possibility of Jesus' prophetic ability cannot be allowed to take precedence over documentary data. There is no reason other than bias against predictive prophecy to accept this late date for the composition of Luke's gospel, and so this late dating must be rejected. Therefore, there is no compelling rationale for first assigning a date to the composition of Luke's gospel prior to assigning a date to Acts. Indeed, it is easier to first date the creation of Acts and then move backward in time to date Luke's earlier composition of the gospel.

A logical starting point in assigning a date to Acts is the last recorded event, which was Paul's two-year long imprisonment in Rome. This two-year term began in the first few months of AD 60. Counting ahead two years makes AD 62 the earliest possible date of composition. This much is certain. What remains controversial is the indeterminate range between the earliest possible date and the latest likely date of composition.

It is possible that the Acts narrative deliberately ends as it does through Luke's own creative design. Many commentators presuppose that it was his calculated intention to complete the account with Paul's arrival in Rome. Therefore, Acts could have been composed at any point before Luke's death. If this view is correct, then one may comfortably date the composition of Acts anytime between AD 63 and AD 85 or possibly even later, since the date of Luke's death is unknown.

However, ending Acts with Paul under Roman house arrest seems an extremely unsatisfying manner in which to conclude this majestic chronicle. For Luke to have known the outcome of Paul's "appeal to Caesar" (Acts 25:11) and not have recorded it for his readers, effectively leaving them up in the air concerning Paul's fate, is simply not credible, especially since Luke expends the final quarter of the book on Paul's arrest and trial.

A more persuasive case may be made for a date of composition no later than AD 64. There is compelling evidence that the window between AD 62 and the latest possible date is extremely narrow, for the following reasons.

First and foremost, when read at face value, Acts seems to bring readers up to date with Luke's own contemporary circumstances. In other words, there was nothing more to write. Paul still awaited trial, and the church continued expanding, unabated and unopposed. Any additional chapters would necessarily have had to wait until history unfolded with the occurrence of new events.

If Acts had been written later than AD 64, it is inexplicable that Luke would fail to mention Paul's trial, his release from Roman imprisonment, the first Roman persecution of Christians under Nero beginning in AD 64, the death of Peter that same year, or the death of James, the brother of Jesus, two years earlier. If Acts had been written after AD 70, it is unfathomable that Luke would avoid mention of Paul's death in AD 68 or the Roman destruction of Jerusalem and the Temple in AD 70. The fact is that Luke makes no reference to any of the crucial events that concerned the church after AD 62.

Second, the sole theological controversy Acts records is the debate over Gentile inclusion. This debate was only active through the fifth decade of the first century. It was finally settled in AD 49 at the Jerusalem Council (Acts 15). By AD 70, Gentile inclusion was universally accepted and this issue no longer controversial. Whether a Gentile needed to first become Jewish before becoming a Christian was hardly a concern for believers after AD 70 and an unlikely topic on which to expend so much precious scroll space.

Third, throughout Acts, the Roman Empire shows no animus toward the church and is still impartial, in fact, almost disinterested, concerning the nascent Christian movement. Time and again, the Romans do not comprehend the nature of the Jewish accusations brought against the church or the ferocity of those accusations. These accusations are of a religious, not political nature. Indeed, in most instances within the early years, Rome treated Christianity as one more incomprehensible Jewish sect among many. This was no longer the case after AD 64, when the Roman Empire began to view Christians as a political and cultural threat.

A fourth reason to assign Acts an early date is Luke's expenditure of a great deal of narrative energy in demonstrating Christianity's Jewish roots and association with the nation of Israel. Following the initial outbreak of Israel's revolution against Rome in AD 66, it would no longer have been prudent to press the fledgling faith's association with Israel as dynamically as Luke does in his narrative.

Finally, Acts obviously does not rely on Paul's epistles as a source of biographical information about Paul. Luke makes no attempt to correlate his account of Paul's life with the apostolic correspondence. Therefore, Acts had to have been written before Paul's letters had been collected as Scripture and widely circulated. Peter's final epistle, written in AD 64, recognizes the circulation of Paul's epistles and their Scriptural authority (2 Pet. 3:16).

For these reasons the composition of Acts may confidently be dated between AD 62 and 63.

Luke's Sources

During Luke's extensive travels in Paul's company, Luke himself was a personal eyewitness to the events he recorded in Acts. In addition to his European travels, Luke also spent two unintentional years living in Israel (21:8—27:1). Upon their return from the third missionary journey, Paul was arrested in Jerusalem and imprisoned in Caesarea for approximately two years, from the spring of AD 57 through the summer of AD 59. Luke remained at liberty in Israel throughout this period.

While Paul was enjoying the Roman procurator's "hospitality," it is impossible not to envisage Luke traveling among the churches strewn throughout Israel, researching his two books. Luke would have had ample time and opportunity to gather eyewitness accounts and personal stories from many of Jesus' original followers and members of the early church. In addition to what he had already learned of the early days of the church from Paul's unique perspective during their travels together, Luke's list of additional possible interviews staggers the imagination.

Certainly, Luke would have spent time with James, the brother of Jesus and leader of the Jerusalem church (21:18–19). There were many members of Jesus' family who would still have been available with whom to speak.

Mary was, perhaps, still living, and Jesus' siblings, including Jude, may also have been available.

Some of the twelve apostles may still have been serving in Israel, and most of those who were elsewhere, including Peter and John, would have likely returned to Jerusalem over the course of two years for at least one pilgrim festival. Furthermore, the apostles' wives and families may not have always accompanied them on their journeys and may have been available.

Some of the original Hellenistic Jewish deacons (6:5) may have still been in Israel. Luke certainly spent time with Philip, who lived in Caesarea (21:8–10).

In addition, whether they first met during this time in Israel or later as coworkers in Rome (Col. 4:14; Philem. 24), Luke and Mark were well acquainted. There is no question that in writing both Luke's gospel and Acts, he was reliant on Mark's written testimony (the gospel of Mark) as well as oral reminiscence of his early Christian experiences.

The gospels and Acts are strewn with the names of additional individuals with whom Luke may have had opportunity to speak and get their personal accounts: Mary Magdalene (Luke 24:10), Mary, Martha and Lazarus (Luke 10:38–42), the unnamed lame beggar (Acts 3:2), Nicodemus, Joseph of Arimathea (Luke 23:50), Tabitha (Acts 9:40), Aeneas (Acts 9:33), Rhoda (Acts 12:13), Agabus (Acts 21:10), the priests who came to faith (Acts 6:7); Cleopas and his Emmaus companion (Luke 24:18); Bartimaeus (Luke 18:35); Zaccheus (Luke 19:2) and additional dozens.

Indeed, one may only speculate on how many of the five hundred witnesses of Jesus' resurrection (1 Cor. 15:6), or of the seventy emissaries Jesus had appointed (Luke 10:1), or the "Pentecost three thousand" (Acts 2:41) were subject to Luke's careful investigation. Both of Luke's volumes teem with concern for the "personal touch." In Acts alone, Luke references over one hundred people by name! This conscientious historian records for posterity all the protagonists, antagonists, minor characters, and bystanders.

Luke's time in Israel also accounts for his tremendous attention to geographical detail. As Paul's missionary companion, Luke's ability to conjure up the geographic details that characterize his European travelogues is not at all surprising. Yet it is his strikingly vivid rendering of Galilee, Jerusalem, the Temple, Samaria and Israel's coastal cities that reveal Luke's first hand knowledge of Israel.

Purpose of Acts

Perhaps as many as a dozen plausible reasons have been proposed over the centuries to explain the occasion of Luke's writing of Acts. Countless students have valiantly, but futilely, applied themselves to the task of narrowing down the list to one overarching purpose. Yet to limit Luke to only one purpose does injustice to his broad and monumental work. Although addressed to only one individual, his patron, Theophilus, it must be recognized that Luke wrote with multiple purposes in mind. It is possible to ascertain, upon analysis of the Acts narrative, four particularly compelling purposes.

Historical Purpose

The primary purpose of Luke's work is historical. It is the sequel to his gospel, which was the chronological account of Jesus' earthly ministry, and Acts resumes with the record of Jesus' continued ministry through the agency of His apostles (1:1). Luke wrote this account to carefully and systematically trace the growth and geographical expansion of the church over its first three decades (2:47; 5:14; 6:7; 9:31; 12:24; 16:5; 19:20). While acutely selective in his choice of material, Luke provides every necessary historical highlight to understand the development of the church from its origins in Jerusalem through its climactic extension to Rome.

Theological Purpose

Luke's purpose went far beyond the historical. Another purpose Luke has is theological in nature. He wrote Acts to validate that Christianity is the legitimate development of God's plan and program for both Jews and Gentiles as engineered by the Holy Spirit (1:5-8; 2:1-47; 5:1-11; 6:5; 8:14-17; 10:44-47; 13:1-4; 19:1-7). Luke reveals the continuity between what God had promised to Israel through covenant and prophecy and what the church has received.

Luke also carefully demonstrates that God's promises to Israel have not been exhausted by the initiation of the church age. Although only a Jewish remnant has currently accepted their messiah and at present the nation stands in opposition to him, at some point in the future Israel will acknowledge Jesus as their Lord, savior and king (3:21).

Acts, however, is not a theological treatise. It must always be remembered while studying Acts that Luke is not concerned with developing doctrine. This is a book of historical descriptions, not propositional prescriptions. His intent was not to make normative for all believers through all time the unique and unrepeatable experiences of Pentecost, Saul's Damascus Road encounter, or to standardize various apostolic decisions, miracles and judgments.

As a historian, Luke is concerned with the practical application of these new and unprecedented theological developments. He defines the nature, structure, and practices of this new community of believers. He describes the relationship of this community to its adherents, to the unbelieving and often hostile Jewish community, to the Temple, in Judaism in general, and to the power of the Roman Empire. Finally, he relates the only major theological controversy to arise within the first three decades of the Church, that of Gentile inclusion into the church on an equal basis with Jews.

Chronology of Acts and History Immediately Following

Event	Chapter	Date
Christ's Ascension	Acts 1	May, AD 33
Pentecost	Acts 2	May, AD 33
Peter and John arrested	Acts 3–4	Summer, AD 33
Apostles arrested	Acts 5	AD 34
Deacons Appointed	Acts 6	Winter, AD 35
Death of Stephen	Acts 7	Spring, AD 35
Samaritans believe	Acts 8	Summer, AD 35
Saul's Commission	Acts 9	Summer, AD 35
Saul's Damascus Ministry	Acts 9	AD 35–37
Saul returns to Jerusalem, sent to Tarsus	Acts 9	Fall, AD 37
Peter meets Cornelius	Acts 10	AD 40
Paul in Antioch	Acts 11	AD 42
Death of James and Herod Agrippa	Acts 12	AD 44
Saul and Barnabas in Jerusalem	Acts 12	Fall, AD 47
First Missionary Journey	Acts 13–14	Spring, AD 48–Fall, AD 49
Jerusalem Council	Acts 15	Late AD 49/Early AD 50
Second Missionary Journey	Acts 16–18	Spring, AD 50–Fall, AD52
Third Missionary Journey	Acts 18–21	Spring, AD 53–May, AD 57
Paul imprisoned	Acts 22–26	June, AD 57–Summer, AD 59
Voyage to Rome	Acts 27	Summer, AD 59–March, AD 60
Paul's Roman imprisonment	Acts 28	March, AD 60–Spring, AD 62
Death of James		Spring, AD 62
Death of Peter		Summer, AD 64
Death of Paul		Early AD 68
Jerusalem Destroyed		Summer, AD 70

Apologetic Purpose

Luke also writes with an apologetic purpose in mind. He proves that, while the Jewish leadership consistently opposed the Christian movement from the start, the Roman civil authorities demonstrate no such antagonism (13:12; 16:39; 18:15–17; 19:37–40; 24:23; 25:19–25; 26:31–32; 28:30–31). Although Judaism viewed Christianity as an ominous and menacing sect, the Roman Empire perceived no such threat from the burgeoning movement, despite the fact that its founder had been executed as a criminal by Rome.

Luke assembles a thorough stream of evidence to establish that Christianity was not a political movement, but primarily a religious one; a movement with a profound Jewish heritage and deeply rooted in Hebrew Scripture. Therefore, by highlighting Christianity's Jewish association, Luke sought to demonstrate that the new faith should share Judaism's status as a recognized, legally accepted religion within the Empire.

Biographical Purpose

Luke's final purpose is a biographical one. In Acts, Luke firmly associates Paul's apostolic ministry with the apostolic ministry of Peter. By developing this strong literary connection between Peter and Paul, Luke demonstrates the full apostolic authority of Paul. Time and again, example upon example, the record of Acts reveals that whatever Peter was empowered to do, Paul was so empowered as well. Luke carefully presents these two men as absolute equals in supernatural ability, apostolic gifting and divine commission.

Theme and Structure of Acts

The theme, or "big idea," of Acts emanates from the crucial opening passage in the book, which contains Jesus' commission to his apostles, "you will be My witnesses in Jerusalem, and in all Judea and Samaria, and to the ends of the earth" (Acts 1:8). This central idea combines each of Luke's four purposes into one coherent whole: identifying message (witness of Jesus, i.e., the gospel), messenger (the apostles) and location of delivery (Jerusalem, Judea and Samaria, the ends of the earth).

With adroit literary skill, Luke uses this divine apostolic commission to organize his book in two major ways: geographical and biographical.

Luke's geographical structure arranges the book according to the location of the gospel's delivery, from Jerusalem (1:1—8:4) to Judea and Samaria (8:5—12:25) and to the ends of the earth (13:1—28:31).

Luke's biographical structure neatly divides the book into two parts, which are mirror images of each other (1:1—12:25 and 13:1—28:31). While the second half of Acts is longer in *verbal* content than the first (more chapters and verses), Luke has arranged both halves to be equal in *chronological* content. Luke has broken his coverage of the first twenty-nine years of church history into two equal parts consisting of fourteen-and-one-half years apiece.

Additionally, each fourteen-and-one-half year historical period has its own "leading man," the principal apostle with whom the narrative is concerned throughout that period; first Peter, then Paul.

Peter's Ministry and Paul's Ministry in Acts

Ministry	Peter	Paul
Commissioned apostles	To Jews (and also witnessed to Gentiles)	To Gentiles (and also witnessed to Jews)
Healed a man lame from birth	3:1–11	14:8–10
Unusual means of healing/exorcism	5:15–16	19:11–12
Jewish opposition	5:17	13:45
Opposed a sorcerer	8:18–24	13:6–11
Raised the dead	9:36–41	20:9–12
Conferred the Holy Spirit through laying on of hands	8:14–25	19:1–10
Miraculously released from prison	12:1–19	16:16–34
Both were erroneously worshiped	10:25	14:11–13
Both rendered swift judgment	5:1–11	13:6–11
Angelic visitation	12:7–11	27:23–24
Both heard the voice of God	10:13–16	9:4–6
Both preached to Jews and Gentiles	11:2–9; 10:34–43	9:20–29; 13:1 — 28:31
Both filled with the Spirit	2:1–4; 4:8	9:17; 13:9
Both preached with boldness	4:13, 31	9:27–29

He further subdivides each fourteen-and-one-half year period into a twelve-and-one-half year and a two-year period. The two-year periods bracket the Acts narrative. The story begins with the first two-year period (1:1—8:4) and takes place solely in Jerusalem, the birthplace of the church. Luke expends seven chapters relating this defining stage in the church's history. The two-year period that concludes the book (28:14–31) takes place solely in Rome, the geographic goal of Paul's apostolic witness. Luke summarizes this final stage in only half a chapter.

The core of the book takes place within the two twelve-and-one-half year periods and chronicles the gospel's transition from Jerusalem to Rome. It also shifts the apostolic focus from Peter to Paul. The key word in Acts is "witness" (Greek verb, *martureō*; Greek noun, *martus*), which is used twenty-one times to describe the ministry of the apostles.

Outline of Acts

I. The Jerusalem Witness (1:1—8:4)
  A. Acts 1:1-26 Beginning in Jerusalem
    1. Prologue (1:1-3)
    2. The Promise of the Father (1:4-5)
    3. Commission (1:6-8)
    4. Ascension (1:9-11)
    5. Return to Jerusalem (1:12-14)
    6. Choosing the Twelfth Apostle (1:15-26)
  B. Acts 2:1-47 Birth of the Church
    1. Coming of the Spirit (2:1-4)
    2. Results of the Coming of the Spirit (2:5-13)
    3. Peter's Witness (2:14-36)
    4. Response: Jewish salvation! (2:37-42)
    5. The First Church (2:42-47)
  C. Acts 3:1-26 Miracle in the Temple
    1. The Healing (1-11)
    2. Peter's Witness (3:12-26)
  D. Acts 4:1-31 Those Irrepressible Apostles
    1. Response to Peter's Witness (4:1-4)
    2. The Trial (4:5-12)
    3. Response to Peter's Witness (4:13-22)
    4. Prayer of Apostles and God's Response (4:23-31)
  E. Acts 4:32—5:42 Opposition from Within and Without
    1. Glowing Update on the Church (4:32-37)
    2. Sin in the Church Camp (5:1-11)
    3. Witness of the Apostles with Power (5:12-16)
    4. Opposition to the Witness of the Apostles (5:17-26)
    5. The Trial (5:27-42)
  F. Acts 6:1—8:4 The Witness of Stephen
    1. Commissioning of Deacons (6:1-7)
    2. The Ministry of Stephen (6:8-10)
    3. The Arrest of Stephen (6:11—7:1)
    4. The Defense of Stephen (7:2-53)

Section 1

The Jerusalem Witness

Acts 1:1 — 8:4

CHAPTER 1

Beginning in Jerusalem
Acts 1:1-26

Preview:
Together, the gospel of Luke and the book of Acts comprise about twenty-five percent of the New Testament. Luke's writings have made a significant contribution to the church's collection of Holy Scripture. In this initial chapter of his second volume, Luke prepares his readers for the major events still to come. This chapter records a summary of the last conversation between Jesus and His apostles prior to His ascension and the selection of a replacement to fill the apostolic position vacated by Judas.

Prologue (1:1-3)

Luke begins Acts with a prologue that connects this book with his gospel, his "first," or former, "account." Luke meant for the book of Acts to be the sequel to his gospel, the next installment in a two-scroll series. In fact, Acts might be thought of as *Luke, Book II*. Long before Hollywood had conceived its first blockbuster sequel there was Luke, continuing his own gospel blockbuster, which just happened to be the greatest story ever told.

In his opening words, Luke briefly summarizes the contents of his previous work, his gospel, an account of "all that Jesus began to do and teach." In using the term, "began," Luke affirmed that what he had reported in his gospel was only the beginning, the "first stage" of Jesus' work. In the book of Acts, the story of Jesus continues as He works, now in His resurrected state, through His apostles and His church, His body. Luke's purpose in Acts is the same as was for his gospel: to convey accurate, systematic, chronological and historical information about his subject.

In the first two verses, Luke introduces the main players in the narrative. The three protagonists are Jesus, the Holy Spirit and the apostles. Luke emphasizes in Acts 1:2 Jesus' specific choice of these individual men (as recorded in Luke 6:13–16) and His personal invitation for them to carry out their commission as His witnesses. Ultimately, what Luke relates throughout twenty-eight chapters is the continuing work of the risen and exalted Messiah, Jesus, carried out by his apostles, with the guidance and through the power of the Holy Spirit. Jesus and His apostles are organically interconnected to one another, bonded by the agency of the Spirit.

Theophilus. As in the preface to his gospel, Luke once again addresses his work to the enigmatic Theophilus. Outside of Luke's parallel prefaces, no mention of this individual is made, either within the New Testament record or outside of it. However, the preface to Luke's gospel provides some insight, if not into the identity of Theophilus, at least into his background (Luke 1:4).

The name Theophilus itself means either "lover of God" or "beloved of God." Luke uses the standard first century historical format in addressing his intended audience. Theophilus was perhaps Luke's benefactor, and was most likely a Roman official of notable rank. Luke addressed his patron with the term *kratistos*, "most excellent," which was a formal Roman designation of honor. Luke also applies this designation in Acts to Felix (Acts 23:26; 24:3) and Festus (Acts 26:25). Additionally, an example of parallel usage occurs where Josephus prefaced his writing with the same term of honor when addressing his patron, Epaphroditis.[1]

It may be presumed that Theophilus was a believer who, although he had received some Christian instruction, was in need of a broader education in the foundational history of his faith (Luke 1:1–4). Furthermore, it is probable that prior to becoming a Christian, Theophilus had been a God-fearer, a Gentile who worshiped the God of Israel. This might explain Luke's preoccupation in Acts with God-fearers (Acts 10:2, 22, 35; 13:16, 26, 43, 50; 17:4, 17; 18:7).

Although solely addressed to Theophilus, Acts was clearly not meant to be sequestered away in Theophilus' private library. Luke clearly intended for this work to instruct other believers and to be widely circulated among them as well as the general public.

In Acts 1:3, Luke provides a brief summary of Jesus' post-resurrection ministry to his apostles. The foundational task Jesus had to accomplish was to convince His apostles that He was alive. To this end, Luke records that Jesus had to furnish to them "many convincing proofs," from the Greek *tekmeriois*, to forever remove all doubt that He was resurrected in a physical, tangible, yet glorified body. The New Testament books are painstakingly careful to continually emphasize that Jesus was physically resurrected. There is to be no misunderstanding concerning His resurrection appearances. This was no ghost or spirit, no mass vision or hallucination. Jesus rose from the dead corporeal, touchable (John 20:27), and capable of eating and drinking (Luke 24:42–43; Acts 1:3).

Acts 1:3 is the only place where the forty-day length of his post resurrection ministry is recorded. Jesus did not appear continuously for forty consecutive days, but rather at intervals. The exact number of appearances Jesus made to His disciples is not recorded, but from the gospel records we know there were at least ten separate appearances over the forty-day period, if not more.

Luke relates that the main subject of Jesus' teaching over the course of forty days during those appearances was "the kingdom of God" (1:3). This was the major topic of discussion between Jesus and the apostles and provides a major theme of the apostolic message in Acts. However, before launching into a discussion of what is meant by the kingdom of God and related teachings of Jesus, a brief overview of the name Luke used to refer to each of Jesus' specially selected students, the main protagonists of Acts, the term, "apostle," is in order.

Apostle. The term "apostle," which appears some thirty times in Acts, is a transliteration of the Greek, *apostolos*. A key term in Acts, *apostle* is primarily used throughout the New Testament in a specialized sense to mean, "commissioned one," with the commissioning having been done by Christ. Thus, an apostle is a commissioned representative of Christ who is empowered by His delegated authority.

The New Testament teaches two extremely restricted views of the apostolic office. There were two classifications of apostle. The first category was the more restrictive. This is the primary category of apostle, and membership was limited to the Twelve. In Acts, the term almost always refers to the Twelve (1:26; 2:37, 42, 43; 4:33, 35, 36, 37; 5:2, 12, 18, 29, 40; 6:6; 8:1, 14, 18; 9:27; 11:1). The Twelve were personally selected by Jesus to be His representatives, authoritative witnesses of His ministry, and provide the founding leadership for His church. In the impending kingdom, their leadership responsibilities will include ruling over the twelve tribes of Israel (Matt. 19:28).

This foundational commission to rule Israel is why in verses 15–26, at the dawn of their mission, selecting a replacement for Judas' abandoned slot was essential. In other words, it was not because the apostolic slot was empty, per se, that there was a need to replace Judas. Otherwise, a continuous stream of votes would eventually need to be taken upon the death of each apostle. Rather, it was necessary for the empty apostolic slot to be filled because the unimaginable had occurred: one of the twelve apostles had abandoned his present *and future* position of responsibility. As the kingdom of God was imminent, the apostles wanted to ensure that they all stood ready to fulfill their commissioned roles.

The concept of a perpetual apostolic succession cannot be derived from the Acts narrative. By definition, only those who had seen Jesus could ever be apostles. It was not an office that could ever be passed down to the next generation. The apostolic office of the Twelve terminated with their deaths.

The final division of Acts (chaps. 13—28) focuses on those who are members of the remaining apostolic category. This second classification of apostle was more inclusive, but possessed requirements that were no less stringent. Luke does not supply a complete list of this group of apostles, but it includes James (the brother of Jesus), Barnabas and Paul.

From Paul's first letter to the Corinthians, we learn that the essential requirement for this level of apostleship is to have actually seen the resurrected Lord Jesus (1 Cor. 9:1). Paul gives us a comprehensive list of those who have witnessed the resurrected Christ (1 Cor. 15:5-8). We can infer from Paul that while the capacity of this category of apostle is seemingly not restricted to twelve, it is limited to a set number of individuals to whom Christ personally appeared. Moreover, Paul is clear that in addition to the unprecedented fashion by which he has witnessed the resurrected Christ (Acts 9:3-8), he is the very last (and least) one of this group to do so (1 Cor. 15:8-9). Paul is adamant that, by definition, there can never be any other apostles after him.[2]

There is one final delimiter Paul gives concerning this category of apostle. This is the ability to perform "the signs of a true apostle," i.e., signs, wonders and miracles (2 Cor. 12:12). Like identifying "calling cards," these signs were the divine validation, the credentials of those with genuine apostolic authority.

In addition to serving as commissioned witnesses of the Lord Jesus' resurrection, the apostles also provided the leadership of the community of faith, overseeing its growth and radical expansion outward from Jerusalem. Finally, Paul refers to apostleship as being one of the gifts of the Spirit (1 Cor. 12:28; Eph. 4:11).

The Promise of the Father (1:4-5)

Luke's gospel ended with the ascension (Luke 24:50-51), and this is also the event with which Luke begins his sequel. What Luke provides in the first eleven verses of Acts is a rough summary of his gospel ascension account (Luke 24:44-53). The narrative story of Acts picks up in Acts 1:4, with Jesus gathered together with His apostles immediately prior to His return to heaven. If Jesus' passion and resurrection occurred in the year AD 33, as is likely, then some precision may be exercised on the date of this event. The ascension of Jesus most probably occurred on Thursday, May 14, AD 33, ten days prior to the Jewish festival of Pentecost.

The Greek term *sunalizō*, which most translations render as "gathering them together," appears in the New Testament only here in Acts 1:4. A better translation may well be, "eating together with." As mentioned previously, one of the "convincing proofs" of Jesus' bodily resurrection was His ability to eat. However, whether the apostles are gathered together on the Mount of Olives with Jesus for instruction alone or instruction accompanied by a meal does not affect the point the passage, which is the content of Jesus' final commission to His apostles.

Foundational to the commission is Jesus' command for the apostles to "sit tight" in Jerusalem and wait an indeterminate amount of time for what Jesus called, "the promise of My Father." Luke quotes this same phrase of Jesus' in the parallel account of the commission at the end of his gospel (Luke 24:49). In addition to what Jesus may have taught his apostles during His post-resurrection ministry, he had discussed this promise some forty-three days earlier at the Passover Seder he shared with them on the evening of His betrayal, His "Last Supper." At that meal, he had revealed to His apostles that the Holy Spirit, the *paraklētos*, the "Comforter," would be coming to empower them (John 14:16, 26; 15:26; 16:7, 13).

Continuing His commission, Jesus then revealed to His apostles that they were about to enter into a major period of transition. A new age was about to dawn which would be defined by a new ministry of the Holy Spirit, that of Spirit baptism. This new age would be characterized by great acts of the Spirit. The expectation of the Holy Spirit, *Ruach Hakodesh* in Hebrew, was a key concept in first century Judaism, and the apostles would have been eager for this particular promise of the Father to be kept.

Jesus refers back to the ministry of his cousin, John the Baptist (Luke 3:16) to contrast water baptism with the impending baptism with, or by means of, the Holy Spirit. In total, Luke refers to John's ministry of water baptism eight times in Acts (1:5, 22; 10:37; 11:16; 13:24–25; 19:3–4), usually in contrast to Spirit baptism. The example in Acts 1:5 is typical. John's water baptism, done for the purpose of ritual purification to signify repentance, is contrasted with baptism with the Spirit for the enablement of ministry and the establishment of a holy lifestyle.

This promise of Holy Spirit baptism will be fulfilled at Pentecost in Acts 2:1–4. Before we continue, a brief discussion of baptism is in order.

Baptism. Baptism is simply a transliteration of the Greek word *baptisma*. The parallel Hebrew term is *mikvah*. The first century world of the Bible knew of three different types of Jewish ritual *mikvah*, or baptism: baptism as practiced within Judaism, the baptism of John, and Christian baptism.

Ritual baptism was an essential practice of first century Judaism. Observance of ritual baptism was standard practice for ritual cleansing from any state of impurity and served as a preparatory ritual for observance of holy days and entrance to the Temple. Additionally, baptism or mikvah, along with circumcision (for men) and the offering of a sacrifice, was one of three ritual components that were integral for Gentile conversion to Judaism and their initiation into the people of Israel. This conversion ritual also included an element of purification as a Gentile entered the water in a state of uncleanness and rose up cleansed and reborn, no longer identifying with his former pagan status but as a Jewish proselyte.

John's ministry was so characterized by ritual baptism that he was popularly nicknamed "the Baptist." John's baptism was neither for the purpose of ritual cleansing nor for the purpose of Gentile conversion. Both the New Testament (Matt. 3:1–11; Mark 1:4–5; Luke 3:7–14) and Josephus[3] record that John's innovative emphasis to this ancient Jewish ritual was its focus on the personal repentance and future commitment to righteousness of the Jewish people desiring to be immersed. Those whom John baptized were then identified as his disciples. The reason for John's innovative baptismal emphasis was his overwhelming concern to prepare Israel for the coming Messiah and the kingdom He would establish (Matt. 3:11–12; Mark 1:7–8; Luke 3:15–18; John 1:15–31). Jesus' early ministry was also characterized by this same baptism of repentance (John 3:22).

Following Israel's visitation by the Messiah and His exaltation, the early church quite naturally incorporated the common ritual of baptism, adapting it for the purpose of initiation into the community of faith and identification with the resurrected Founder of that community. Christian baptism incorporated John's innovative emphasis on repentance and commitment and combined it with the purifying conversion ritual of Judaism.[4]

Commission (1:6–8)

This next section contains a profound question asked of Jesus by the apostles. This question and how it is answered (or is not answered) uncovers an essential interpretive issue that colors the entire book of Acts. What is this weighty question? The apostles inquired as to whether it was at this time that Jesus would be restoring the kingdom to Israel.

Kingdom. This question about the kingdom was the most logical one they could have asked. After all, Jesus had primarily been teaching them about the coming kingdom of God over the past forty days (1:3). Furthermore, throughout their three years together, Jesus' preaching was continually characterized by such kingdom-oriented instruction. Even the model prayer, which Jesus had taught to his disciples, contained a phrase entreating God to establish His kingdom, "Your kingdom come" (Matt. 6:10; Luke 11:2).

In fact, during their last Passover meal together, on the evening of His betrayal, Jesus had made two specific promises concerning the coming kingdom. First, Jesus promised that He would not eat another Passover meal until the festival was fulfilled in the kingdom (Luke 22:16–18). Second, Jesus promised his apostles that in the kingdom, they would sit upon twelve thrones, judging the twelve tribes of Israel (Luke 22:30). In fact, what had immediately precipitated this promise was the disciples' argument over which of them was to be the most respected leader in the future kingdom (Luke 22:24)!

There is no question that both Testaments of the Scripture present and confirm the reality of the future restoration of Israel as a nation. The coming messianic age will be characterized by the physical, actual rule and reign of the Messiah, Jesus. His throne will be that of His ancestor, King David, and as the kings of Israel did in ancient days, Jesus will rule from Jerusalem.

In the next verse, Jesus' answer indicates that He accepted the question as a logical one but would not provide specifics. Jesus does not brush off the question; He treats it with a serious, yet mysterious, answer. By telling them that it was not for them to know "the times or epochs which the Father has fixed by His own authority, He indicated His agreement with His students that the issue was "when," and not "if" the kingdom is restored to Israel. It was simply a matter of divine timing, which just happened to be none of the apostles' business.

The word translated "times," is *chronous*, and expresses a quantitative aspect of time, the length of a period. The word translated "epochs," *kairous*, indicates a specific time span, definite period or season. It was not for the apostles to know how far in time the kingdom still was or on what eventual date it would arrive. The kingdom would assuredly come, but at an unknown future time. That knowledge was reserved only for the Father (Matt. 24:36).

Over the forty days Jesus had been teaching them, the apostles had finally become apt and capable pupils. Having sat at the resurrected Messiah's feet for those forty days, having been granted a measure of the Holy Spirit (John 20:22), and having spent over three years in His company exposed to Jesus' teaching, life and example, the apostles could not have received a better education.

Jewish rejection? There are some who believe that the Jewish people have forfeited God's promises of a glorious future kingdom as a result of their rejection of Jesus. They believe those promises of land possession, numerous descendants and multiple blessings made to Abraham, Isaac, Jacob and their progeny have now somehow morphed into spiritual promises which have transferred to the church. These people believe that God is through with the Jews; that He has broken off His relationship with them. His concern has now been transferred to the church. What this concept practically means, for most of the people espousing it, is that God has abandoned the Jews and is now working exclusively with the Gentiles.

Yet the entirety of the Jewish people did not reject the Messiah. If they had, there would be no book of Acts at all! Every one of the protagonists in this book is a Jew who accepted Jesus as Messiah. The first Gentile believer does not even enter into the historical account for seven years, a full ten chapters into the narrative. From Acts chapter one through twenty-eight, thousands of Jews responded to the gospel. Moreover, we Jews are still responding to Jesus to this very day. The ancient promises of God's kingdom program, His glorious restoration of Israel, have merely been postponed, not abandoned.

Spirit and kingdom. Another reason the apostles would have asked their question is that the Davidic Kingdom, the kingdom of God, is linked five times in the Hebrew Scriptures with the return of the Holy Spirit, the Shekinah glory of the Lord, to Israel (Is. 32:15–20, 44:3–5, Ezek 39:28–29, Joel 2:28—3:1, Zech 12:10—13:1). In fact, Acts 1:6 begins with the Greek, *men oun,* translated "so." This "so" connects the apostle's question with Jesus' statement about Spirit baptism in the previous verse. The outpouring of the Spirit was an integral component of what the prophets had written concerning the institution of the messianic kingdom. In other words, the outpouring of the Holy Spirit is clearly in the context of Israel's national restoration. Since the apostles were conscious of the connection between the messianic kingdom and the baptism of the Spirit, they were asking whether, as a result of this coming Spirit baptism, all Israel would finally be saved.

The apostles were soon to learn that the corporate salvation of Israel would not be accomplished in short measure but was dependent on a still future outpouring on Israel just prior to the return of Christ and the establishment of the kingdom (Acts 3:19-21; Rom. 11:25-27).

However, what Jesus indicated in telling his apostles to wait for the baptism of the Holy Spirit was that the Spirit's outpouring was not dependent on the establishment of the kingdom. Indeed, the events of Pentecost demonstrate that one component of the future kingdom program, the outpouring of the Holy Spirit, was delivered to them. The Spirit is a down payment, an earnest (Eph. 1:13–14), of the glorious future inheritance of the kingdom to come. Nevertheless, what a down payment He is!

Acts 1:8 begins with a strong contrast, *alla*, a big "but," as Jesus changed the subject from Israel's future kingdom to the present responsibilities of the apostles in Israel. Jesus, referring back to His subject of Spirit baptism (1:4–5), prepares His apostles for the awesome power they would presently receive (in 2:1–4). It was by means of this power that they would be enabled to carry out Jesus' orders.

The apostolic commission is to be Jesus' witnesses. Consequently, the concept of witness becomes a key, perhaps the key word, in the book of Acts (1:22, 2:32, 3:15, 5:32, 10:39, 41, 13:31, 22:15, 26:16). The word translated witness, the Greek *martus*, means "One who testifies, bears witness, declares, confirms." Indeed, this witness would be discharged by the entire church, even unto death (7:60; 22:4).

Although Acts 1:8 does not specify the proposed content of the apostolic witness, the parallel passage at the conclusion of Luke reveals the specifics. The apostles were commissioned to witness of the ministry of Jesus: His life, death, resurrection and exaltation, "and that repentance for forgiveness of sins would be proclaimed in His name to all the nations, beginning from Jerusalem" (Luke 24:46–47).

The phrase, "you shall be my witnesses," recalls the use of that same phrase by God in the nation of Israel's commission, as the corporate servant of the Lord, to proclaim that He is the only legitimate means of deliverance, the sole savior of His people (Is. 43:12) and God's repeated use of the phrase "you shall be my witnesses" in Israel's related commission to testify among the idolaters that the Lord is the only God (Is. 44:8).

Jesus specifies where they will receive the Holy Spirit, Jerusalem, and vaguely alludes to when, "not many days from now." Significantly, there is no mention made of *how* the apostles will receive the Holy Spirit. No conditions whatsoever are placed on the apostles in preparation for the upcoming baptism of the spirit. There are no instructions, no uncertainties, no last minute provisos. The baptism of the Spirit will not in any way depend upon the apostles' faith, attitude or behavior. The Spirit will be the certain and sovereign gift of God to His children (Luke 11:13).

Jesus provides broad geographic parameters for this commission to witness. Indeed, it is these geographic designations that provide Luke's structural outline of his Acts narrative, as noted in the introduction. Jesus' commission begins in Jerusalem, extends through the rest of Israel, Judea and Samaria, and eventually reaches "the ends of" or "the remotest part" of the earth.

Jerusalem. The city of Jerusalem is mentioned 670 times within the Hebrew Scriptures. From the time of David, it has had an unparalleled grip on the heart and imagination of the Jewish people. Jerusalem is the historic and eternal capital of the Jewish people. By the time of the events of Acts, Jerusalem had been the Jewish capital for over a thousand years. From antiquity, Jews have considered Jerusalem to be the center, the very "navel" of the earth (Ezek 5:5; 38:12). Jerusalem has always been the political, economic, military, social and religious heart of the Jewish nation and leadership.

Jerusalem played a role in Jewish history from the beginning. It was known in the time of Abraham as Salem (Gen. 14:18) and is the location of Mount Moriah, where Abraham almost sacrificed Isaac (Gen. 22). Jerusalem was conquered from the Jebusites by David and chosen to be his capital over 3000 years ago (2 Sam 5:7; 1 Chr. 11:5). Jerusalem was thereafter popularly known as "the city of David." David relocated the sacred ark of the covenant to Jerusalem (2 Sam. 6:12) and his son, Solomon, built the Temple on Mount Moriah to house the ark (1 Kin. 6:1).

Solomon's Temple, along with the entire city, was destroyed by Nebuchadnezzar, the king of Babylon, in 586 BC (2 Kin. 25; 2 Chr. 36; Jer. 39). When Israel returned from exile at the end of the sixth century, the Temple was modestly rebuilt (Hag. 1:14). Five centuries later, Herod the Great elaborately renovated and enlarged the Temple and the Temple Mount. In addition, he reconstructed and extensively modernized the entire city of Jerusalem, recreating a city of sufficient architectural splendor to rival any other in the entire Roman Empire.

The Hebrew Scripture eloquently conveys the key role Jerusalem plays in biblical theology. The Psalms record God's specific choice of Jerusalem as His holy city (Ps. 2:6; 9:11; 74:2 78:68; 87:2; 102:16; 132:13). The prophets affirm that salvation will spread to the Gentiles from Jerusalem (Is. 37:32; 52:7; Joel 2:32; 3:16; Obad. 1:17; Zeph. 3:14) and that the Gentiles will pilgrimage to Jerusalem to worship God in the Temple (Is 2:2-4; 18:7; Mic. 4:2, 7; Zech. 14:16-19).

Even for those Jews living outside of Israel, Jerusalem remained a central focus of religious consideration as well as of sentiment. Annual pilgrimages were made to Jerusalem, up to three times per year, to observe the Feasts of Passover, Pentecost and Tabernacles. The Temple was also the only authorized location where one could present required sacrifices to the Lord. Even the obligation of the annual Temple tax focused an entire people's attention on the city.

In the gospels, Jesus mentions Jerusalem on some fifteen occasions, mostly in reference to His upcoming rejection and suffering. The climax of each gospel account occurs with Jesus' rendezvous with His destiny. As He lamented, despite all the rich theological significance of the city to the Jewish people, Jerusalem is also the city which kills its prophets (Luke 13:33). The gospel records make it clear that Jerusalem was also the center of Jewish opposition to Jesus.

Following their receipt of the Holy Spirit at Pentecost, the apostles continued their Jerusalem residence. These former Galileans made the holy city their new center of ministry from which the gospel witness would advance. However, the Acts narrative reveals that Jerusalem would remain the center of opposition for Jesus' disciples.

Included in the designation of Judea were also Galilee and the rest of Israel. Samaria was the region in Israel populated by followers of a hybrid religion hostile to Judaism and to the Jewish people.

The "remotest part of the earth," or "ends of the earth," is the Greek phrase *heōs eschatou tēs gēs*. This was a Jewish idiom for Gentiles, originally derived from the parameters of the Servant of the Lord's mission as relayed in Isaiah 49:6. Jesus, the definitive "Servant of the Lord," delegated His commission to His apostles through His Great Commission.

What they most likely understood by the phrase, "ends of the earth," based on the context of the first fifteen chapters of Acts, was the entire realm of the Diaspora; that they were being commissioned to take the gospel to every Jewish community both inside and outside of the land of Israel. Their minds may have automatically focused on another passage from Isaiah, where God announced to the ends of the earth the "good news" that salvation had come specifically to Israel (Is. 48:20).

Ascension (1:9–11)

At the conclusion of His commission, Jesus' physical work on earth was completed. He would thereafter be working through the apostles and His church. As also recorded in Luke's parallel gospel account (Luke 24:51), Jesus was then lifted up and disappeared into a cloud. It is unclear whether this is an ordinary cloud or if Luke wishes his readers to associate this cloud with the Shekinah glory. It is possible he is relating the cloud to God's manifest presence in the wilderness following the exodus (Ex. 13:21; 16:10) or means for us to correlate Jesus' disappearance in the cloud with Moses' disappearance in the cloud surrounding Mount Sinai at the giving of the Law (Ex. 24:15–18). Jesus ascension also has precedent in the account of Elijah's ascension (2 Kin. 2:11).

As the apostles stared into the sky, perhaps they remembered that Jesus had previously alluded to His ascension (John 3:14, 6:62, 20:17). Shortly after this, Peter would associate the ascension with Jesus' exaltation, as He took His rightful and deserved place at the right hand of God (Acts 2:33–36; 5:31). The author of Hebrews would assert a similar point (Heb. 1:3; 8:1; 12:2).

The apostles' stunned reverie is interrupted by two angels, dressed in the white attire that the messengers of God are usually described as wearing (Matt. 28:3; Mark 16:5; Luke 24:4; John 20:12). The angels tell the apostles to stop looking up into the sky, for Jesus went up and He would not immediately be coming back down again. They affirmed that at such time when Jesus returns, though, it will likewise be from the midst of a cloud in the sky (Dan 7:13; Matt. 24:30; Mark 13:26; Rev 1:7).

Although the angels did not specify the location of Jesus' return, the traditional Jewish expectation for the Messiah's appearance has been the Mount of Olives (Zech 14:3–5). For millennia, devout Jews have been buried on the Mount of Olives in order to be in "prime real estate" in anticipation of the Messiah's coming and for the associated resurrection of the dead. Today the hill is literally studded with thousands of ancient and modern graves. According to Zechariah's prophecy, when Jesus returns at the end of the age, the Mount of Olives will split open from east to west, creating an avenue of safety for the residents of besieged Jerusalem.

Return to Jerusalem (1:12–14)

Following this stunning turn of events, the apostles return to Jerusalem. Luke specifies that the Mount of Olives is a Sabbath day's journey in distance from Jerusalem, a distance of about six tenths of a mile, in other words, not far at all.[5] Luke provides a roll call of the apostles in 1:12. The list is identical to the one in his gospel (Luke 6:14–16) with the exception of one missing apostle, Judas Iscariot.

The apostles make their way home to an upper room. This is the same upper room where they had observed the Passover with Jesus at His last supper (Mark 14:15; Luke 22:12) and where He had appeared to them (John 20:19, 26). This home seems to have been their headquarters following Jesus' death and resurrection.

Luke reveals that the apostles were not the only inhabitants of the house. They were joined by Jesus' family, specifically His mother and brothers. This is the final New Testament mention of Jesus' mother, Mary. Not only has James come to faith by this time but also Jesus' other brothers, all of whom had, throughout the gospels, been antagonistic toward His ministry (John 7:5). The New Testament records a specific post-resurrection appearance of Jesus to his brother James (1 Cor. 15:7). Perhaps all of Jesus' brothers came to faith as a result of the resurrection. Both James and Jude authored the divinely inspired letters that bear their names within the New Testament canon. Of the brothers, only James plays a prominent role in the Acts narrative, eventually exercising leadership in the Jerusalem church.

Present in the house as well were an unspecified number of women. Luke does not provide a list of which specific women were present, although the list probably included Mary Magdalene, who had been the first to see the resurrected Christ (John 20:18), Mary, James' mother (Mark 16:1), Salome (Mark 16:1), Joanna (Luke 8:3), Susanna (Luke 8:3), Mary and Martha (John 12:2–3), Jesus' aunt Mary (John 19:25), as well as the wives of some of the apostles. It is unusual in first century literature to see the participation of women highlighted.

This earnest group devoted themselves to intense and energetic prayer. Following the ascension of their Messiah, what more appropriate response could there have been? The likely main topic of their prayer was the coming baptism of the Holy Spirit, the "promise of the Father" (Acts 1:4–5). Luke relates that they were unified in their prayers, "of one mind."

Choosing the Twelfth Apostle (1:15–26)

At some point during the ten days between the ascension and Pentecost, the entire group of Jerusalem believers is assembled in the upper room. While the figure that Luke provides of one hundred twenty people is a great number to be packed into a first century upper room, it must be remembered that this number was much less than the sum total of believers at this time. This group would have included many of Jesus' followers who had made the pilgrimage to Jerusalem to celebrate the upcoming festival, Pentecost, or Shavuot, as was the custom of devout Jews throughout Israel. However, given Paul's account of the post-resurrection appearances of Jesus (1 Cor. 15:5–7), including an appearance to five hundred believers at one time, there necessarily must have been at least three hundred eighty additional believers in Jesus who were unaccounted for. Perhaps they had remained in Galilee and elsewhere, for whatever reason, being unable (or afraid?) to make the festival pilgrimage that year.

Peter, having emerged as the leader of the apostles, rose to address the assembled believers concerning the choice of a replacement apostle for Judas.

Peter. Peter's Hebrew name was Simon, or Simeon, which means "hearing" (Acts 15:14). Jesus gave him the nickname of "Rock," *Petros* in Greek, *Kepha* in Aramaic (John 1:42; Matt. 16:18–19). He and his brother Andrew, also an apostle, had been fishermen, originally from Bethsaida in Galilee (John 1:43). The brothers were among the first apostles called by Jesus to follow Him (Luke

5:1–11). Prior to following Jesus, both brothers were disciples of Jesus' cousin, John, called the Baptist.

Peter was married (Mark 1:29–31; 1 Cor. 9:5), and during the events related by the gospels, Peter lived in Capernaum (Mark 1:29) in a large home which, evidently, was within close proximity of the synagogue (Mark 1:29; Luke 4:38). Jesus often stayed with Peter's family, even healing Peter's mother-in-law (Luke 4:38–39). Jesus also made use of Peter's fishing boat from which to preach (Luke 5:1–3).

Peter was the natural leader of the apostles and is always listed first, indicating his priority (Matt. 10:2; Mark 3:16; Luke 16:14; Acts 1:13). He also was one of Jesus' three most intimate friends, along with James and John (Mark 5:37; 9:2; 14:33). However, all four gospels record Peter's infamous triple denial of Jesus on the evening of his betrayal (Mark 14:29–31; Luke 22:33–34; Matt. 26:33–35; John 13:37–38). Yet Peter was the first apostle to have seen the resurrected Christ (Luke 24:34; 1 Cor. 15:5), and following His resurrection, Jesus specially commissioned Peter to shepherd the church (John 21:15–17).

The narrative of Acts 1–15 presents Peter as the undisputed leader of the nascent Jerusalem church. Although Paul refers to Peter as the "apostle to the Jews" (Gal. 2:7–8), Peter's ministry knew no such ethnic boundaries (just as Paul, the "apostle to the Gentiles," ministered with great success within the Jewish community). He was the apostle with the responsibility of the "keys to the kingdom" of God (Matt. 16:19). In this position, Peter was the mediator by which pioneer groups of Jews (Acts 2:41), Samaritans (Acts 8:17) and Gentiles (Acts 10:44) first passed through the "gate" of the church into Christ's salvation.

Peter's first, second and final use of his "keys" were immediately followed by the divine confirmation of the Holy Spirit. In his appointed leadership role in the early church, Peter could be loosely described as functioning as a sort of head rabbi who made legal decisions and executive judgments (binding and loosing [Matt. 16:19]). Peter's authority was dazzlingly authenticated by his unique exercise of extraordinary supernatural power (Acts 5:15).

Although Peter is the main figure within the first two divisions of Acts, following his appearance at the Jerusalem Council of Acts 15, the apostle disappears from Luke's narrative. Based on evidence from Peter's two letters, Paul (1 Cor. 9:5), and church tradition, it is thought that much of the remainder of Peter's apostolic commission was spent as an itinerant missionary.

Peter based his argument for the necessity of replacing Judas on Scripture. He first affirmed that Judas' betrayal was a fulfillment of Scripture. In Acts 1:16, Peter matter-of-factly attests to the dual authorship of Scripture, mentioning by name both divine and human authors, the Holy Spirit and King David.

Although Judas was one of the Twelve, had been intimately associated with Jesus for three years, and even held the privileged position of treasurer, he had betrayed the Messiah. Before Peter continues his line of reasoning, Luke inserts a parenthetical explanation for his readers as to the dour fate of Judas.

Luke records that Judas had acquired a field with the thirty pieces of silver he had received as the reward for his betrayal. However, this is seemingly in contradiction to Matthew's parallel account (Matt. 27:3–10), which states that the priests were the ones who had purchased the field. The question as to which party, the priests or Judas, actually purchased the field can be solved with an eye to Jewish custom.

Matthew records that Judas, feeling remorse, returned the money to the priests immediately prior to hanging himself. However, according to Jewish law, wrongfully gained money had to be returned to the donor. Yet Judas died before the priests could return the money to him. Therefore, the "blood money" had to be spent, in the name of the donor (dead or alive), to purchase something for the common good. The priests purchased a field, in Judas' name, to serve as a cemetery for the destitute. The field's name will be discussed momentarily.

As to Judas' death, there is yet another seeming contradiction that must be reconciled between Matthew's account and Luke's. (Two thousand years later, and Judas is still making trouble.) Matthew is clear that Judas hung himself (27:5), but Luke records that Judas fell headlong, bursting open on impact and having his intestines gush out.

Interestingly, and a bit morbidly, there are two options as to how Judas' body fell and split open thereafter. The first possibility is that after hanging himself, the branch from which he hung broke, causing him to fall and his body to split open.

An alternative option is that His body was discovered hanging from a tree. Dead bodies were considered to be defiling and were not permitted to remain in Jerusalem overnight. Therefore, someone cut him down, tossed his body up and over the walls of Jerusalem, and upon impact in the Hinnom valley below, the body split apart.[6] The second option, while more imaginative, still seems the more likely, as it would better explain how someone who had hanged himself could fall "headfirst," as is specified by Luke (Acts 1:17). However the two "death of Judas" passages are reconciled, it was bad news for Judas!

Having explained the gruesome death of Judas, Luke specifies how, following the spread of the story of Judas through the Jerusalem grapevine, the field purchased by the priests in his name with the "blood money" acquired the grisly name of the "Field of Blood," in Aramaic, *Hakeldama*.

As the narrative returns to Peter, he is quoted as citing two passages of Scripture, psalm 69:25 and 109:8, to support his argument that Judas must be replaced. Peter did not argue that these passages were prophecies fulfilled by Judas; rather, Peter is pointing out the applicability of these two imprecatory psalms to their current situation, linking Scripture to contemporary circumstances through one point of similarity. These psalms, written by David about the king's adversaries, could certainly be applied to the adversary of the son of David. The psalms' original point about the abstract unrighteous could certainly be applied to one specific, reprehensible individual.

Peter proposes restrictive criteria for the apostolic replacement. Judas' replacement must have been an eyewitness not only of Jesus' resurrection, but also of the entirety of Jesus' ministry from His baptism by John through His recent ascension. This would have narrowed down considerably the field of the one hundred twenty people assembled.

From the group, only two men met the necessary criteria. The first man was Joseph, who was known by two additional names. His nickname was "Barsabbas," which is Aramaic for "son of the Sabbath." Perhaps this was his actual last name, or maybe this man really enjoyed his day off! He also had a Roman name, Justus. However, by whichever name one wishes to call this fellow, this is the only mention of him in Acts or the New Testament.

The second man was Matthias. Apparently, both men were equally qualified to fill the position, so the apostles sought the Lord's divine guidance. In their prayer, they recognize that God had already made His choice; He only needed to reveal whom it was He had chosen to replace Judas.

They then drew lots to determine God's decision. The Hebrew Scriptures document that the casting of lots was a common Jewish method of determining God's will (Lev. 16:8; Josh. 14:2; Neh. 10:34; 11:1; Prov. 16:33; 1 Chr. 24:7; 25:8), and was even shown to be effective with Gentiles under certain unique circumstances (Jonah 1:7).

Two stones, each stone having one of the candidate's names inscribed on it, were placed in a metal pot or some other sturdy vessel. The vessel's sturdiness was essential because the stones were then shaken up inside. God's choice was determined when one stone either was allowed to pop out or was removed by hand. Whichever candidate's name was written on that stone was God's selection.

Matthias, and not Joseph, was recognized as God's choice to replace Judas, and he was numbered among the Twelve. However, Matthias is not mentioned by name again in Acts or the New Testament. However, the term "the twelve" (which included him) continues to appear.

Following the baptism of the Holy Spirit at Pentecost, this method of determining God's will was no longer necessary. This is the final recorded instance of this method being utilized by the church.

Apostolic error? Some believe that the eleven apostles erred in choosing Matthias to replace Judas. The assumption is that Paul was God's choice to fill the apostolic void, and that the apostles "jumped the gun" with a hasty selection. There are two arguments that mitigate that opinion.

First, by Peter's discriminating criteria for the apostolic replacement (1:21–22), Paul simply did not qualify. He was never an eyewitness of Jesus' ministry. He was only a witness of the resurrected Christ through unique revelation and, therefore, qualified only for membership within the second apostolic classification.

Second, Luke provides no indication within the account that Peter or the apostles are in error. Just the opposite is true. There is every reason to accept that this was the proper method of determining God's choice, considering that the Holy Spirit had not yet been outpoured. The apostles had prayed for guidance and asked God to reveal which man he had already appointed for the vacancy. The entire testimony of the book of Acts is that God was very much in control of and actively directing the ministry of His church.

Another point to acknowledge is that, based on Peter's word choice of *anēr*, "man," the apostolic replacement for Judas had to be male. The numerous female followers of Jesus were ineligible for the office. Since that time, based largely upon an application of this grammatical point, paired with Jesus' original choice of His twelve apostles, the official position of most churches throughout church history has been that the priesthood and the pastorate are thereby exclusively limited to men.

However, Jesus imposed one additional restriction on his choice of apostles, which never seems to enter into the contemporary discussion. Jesus not only limited his apostolic choice to men, but He restricted His choice to ethnically *Jewish* men. It might prove interesting if any of the major denominations were to add that particular criterion to their list of ministerial qualifications. That would certainly narrow the field of potential candidates for ministry!

Conclusion

This chapter contains the crux of what separates Christianity from all other world religions. Unlike other religions, which revere their founders' life work and venerate their tombs, the tomb of our founder is empty. Our founder's work will never be completed; His death merely ended the initial stage of His ministry. Acts continues the mission of the resurrected, ascended and exalted Lord of all.

Study Questions:

1. What is an apostle?

2. Why or why not does Acts teach a literal future kingdom for Israel?

3. What is the importance of Jerusalem for Jews? For Christians?

4. List five facts about Peter.

5. What languages were spoken in first century Israel?

6. Why or why not was Matthias the right choice to replace Judas?

CHAPTER 2

Birth of the Church
Acts 2:1–47

Preview:

The early church did not have long to wait for the impending events that Jesus, in His final commission, had prepared them to expect. He had told them to anticipate the outpouring of the Holy Spirit, which would be characterized by their being baptized in the Spirit. As a result of that Spirit baptism, they would then receive power to proclaim their witness. In this next chapter, Jesus' promises were fulfilled. Ten days following Jesus' ascension, while in the Temple courts at the festival of Pentecost, the apostles were baptized with the Holy Spirit and boldly proclaimed before the assembled nation of Israel that Jesus is both Lord and Christ.

Ten days following the ascension of Jesus, the festival of Pentecost had arrived. Luke begins this chapter with a bold proclamation that during this year's celebration of Pentecost, the festival had been fulfilled. In Acts 2:1, he purposely chose the term *sumpleroō*, which means to "completely fulfill," indicating that what he is about to relate is the prophetic consummation of this biblical feast.

Pentecost. The Feast of Pentecost, or the Hebrew *Shavuot*, marks the anniversary of the giving of the Law to the Jewish nation and celebrates the theophany, or God's appearance, at Mount Sinai. Following the events of this chapter, Pentecost will also forever mark the granting of the Spirit to Jewish believers and celebrate their indwelling on Mount Moriah, the Temple Mount.

Pentecost is one of the "big three" pilgrimage festivals when, as during Passover and Tabernacles, every Jewish male is commanded to worship at the

Temple in Jerusalem (Deut 16:16). In Deut. 16:9–10, the holiday is designated as *Hag Hashavuot*—"The Festival of Weeks." This name, *Shavuot*, was so designated because seven weeks, or fifty days, are counted down from the week of Passover until the arrival of this holiday. *Pentekostē*, Greek for the number fifty, was used interchangeably with the Hebrew *Shavuot*.

Pentecost is also called *Hag Hakatzir*, the Feast of Harvest (Ex. 23:16). This day marks the end of the barley harvest, which began at Passover, and the initial ripening of the wheat harvest. During the week of Passover, a sheaf of barley was selected from the first fruits of that year's crop. This sheaf is called the "omer" and is offered at the Temple. From the point of that offering, a countdown period of fifty days begins, called "counting the omer."

This particular Jewish festival is unique, as it is the only one without a precisely fixed date. The date must be re-determined each year (Lev. 23:15–16). The Jewish sages have always hated ambiguity and so, not surprisingly, the issue of this holiday's date generated quite a controversy. This was particularly true in the century prior to the birth of Jesus, although the controversy was still alive at the time of Acts. It is not surprising that the Pharisees and the Sadducees, so frequently at odds, bitterly disagreed over the method of determining this date.

The controversy arose over the interpretation of one disputed phrase, "the day after the Sabbath" (Lev. 23:15). The Sadducees celebrated Pentecost on the fiftieth day from the first Sunday of Passover week, interpreting the word 'Sabbath' in its normal sense, "Saturday." According to this method, Pentecost would always fall on a Sunday. Therefore, although the specific day of the week, Sunday, was always fixed, the calendar date would shift from year to year.

Although not specified in Scripture, Pentecost also came to be commemorated as *zman mattan toratainu*, "the season of the giving of our Torah," the day on which the Torah was given to Israel. In fact, the central Scripture reading for this holiday is the passage that records God's giving the Torah to Israel and entering into the Mosaic Covenant with them at Mount Sinai (Ex. 19–20). The events described within this passage of Exodus, and those events that immediately follow, provide the foundation for what will be fulfilled in Luke's narrative.

When Moses returned, he condemned the nation for their grievous sin. In holy indignation, he destroyed the two stone tablets containing the Ten Commandments (Ex. 32:19). He instructed his own tribe, the Levites, to kill the idolaters. The Levites struck down three thousand Israelites before God mercifully restrained them from decimating the nascent nation (Ex. 32:26–28).

The events of Pentecost described by Luke in this chapter, some fifteen hundred years after the Sinai experience, are the God-directed sequel to the foundational events related by Moses.

Coming of the Spirit (2:1–4)

Luke records that at about nine o'clock on the morning of Pentecost, the twelve apostles were gathered together in one place. There is some disagreement, however, regarding exactly where the "one place" was in which they were gathered and in which the awesome manifestations of the Spirit's visitation are experienced.

The traditional interpretation has presumed that they are still in the same house that contained the upper room, in which the dealings described in the previous chapter took place. This is the immediately previous referent of location and would seem a logical assumption. Indeed, Acts 2:2 uses the term "the house" to describe their location. However, if this is the case, and the "one place" of Acts 2:1 is the upper room, it is difficult to explain why Luke provides no transitional description which maneuvers the apostles out of the house, through the city streets and into the Temple complex, where they are positioned by Luke in Acts 2:5.

A more likely interpretation of the "one place" where they are assembled is the Temple courts. The term "the house" was customarily used in reference to the Temple (Acts 7:47). Furthermore, where else would every Jew in Jerusalem be on this festive day of pilgrimage and celebration, but gathered in the Temple courts awaiting a wonderful communal festival meal, an international Jewish picnic. Most likely, the apostles, together with the other one hundred and eight believers, were in the area of the Temple known as Solomon's Portico, or Colonnade, a favorite spot of Jesus' (John 10:23) and, later in Acts, of the apostles (Acts 3:11; 5:12).

Another interpretive disagreement stemming from these opening verses is the identity of the recipients of the supernatural manifestation of tongues in Acts 2:1–4. To which group does the "all" of Acts 2:1 refer? As with the location, there are two choices here as well.

The traditional understanding has been that the recipients of the gift of tongues were the full company of the one hundred twenty believers. While this is possible, it is difficult to reconcile with the internal evidence of the passage. Luke seems to indicate that the supernatural empowerment that morning was only granted to the twelve apostles.

First of all, the antecedent group, or previous referent, were the Twelve (Acts 1:26). It must be remembered that what Luke originally wrote had no chapter divisions or headings, and what he mostly likely meant by "all" was the newly reconstituted group of the Twelve, his previous subject.

Second, the tongues-speakers were identified in the text as Galileans (Acts 2:7). This clearly referred to the apostles, who were all Galileans, and not the larger group, who probably hailed from a variety of locations in Israel. Furthermore, Peter, with the eleven other apostles, responded to their being singled out by the crowd as drunkards (Acts 2:14). In the next verse, Peter specified that "these men" were not drunk. Since the group of the one hundred and twenty contained both men and women (Acts 1:14), and Peter assuredly did not mean to say that "the men were not drunk but the women were," then only the apostles could have received the gift of tongues in Acts 2:1–4.

Third, Luke indicates throughout the Acts narrative that the gift of tongues was given for the purpose of authenticating the apostolic calling, office and witness. Each of the four recorded instances of tongues speaking in Acts served this authenticating purpose, either through the apostles' exercise of the gift at Pentecost (as in 2:1–4) or through "echoes" of the initial Pentecost experience as each new group category believed the apostolic message and received the Spirit (8:14–17; 10:44–47; 19:1–7).

Acts 2:2–4 describes strange, supernatural manifestations that suddenly and rapidly envelop the disciples. As the apostles were gathered among the relaxed and joyous crowds in the Temple complex, a noise resembling a violent wind, one that was heard but not felt, suddenly filled the Temple. In the Hebrew Scripture, wind, *ruach*, the same Hebrew word used for "spirit," is a common symbol of the Holy Spirit. One prominent example is the reassembling and resuscitation of the valley of dry bones in Ezekiel 37, where the wind represents the Spirit of God, the prophesied instrument of Israel's national restoration.

This was followed by a supernatural pyrotechnic display. A sizable mass of something resembling fire appeared, clearly visible yet not physically felt, which then began swiftly dividing and cutting itself up in pieces, distributing one "tongue" of fire to rest upon each of the apostles. The Holy Spirit had dramatically arrived.

Luke's description of this manifestation resembles the description of God's Shekinah glory manifest on Mount Sinai (Ex. 19:18) and filling the Temple upon its dedication (2 Chr. 5:14). The Holy Spirit was once again gloriously manifesting Himself in the midst of Israel.

Philo, the first century Jewish historian, in describing the giving of Torah at Mount Sinai, emphasized both the fire of God and the language of God in communicating His will to His people.

And a voice sounded forth from out of the midst of the fire which had flowed from heaven, a most marvelous and awful voice, the flame being endowed with articulate speech in a language familiar to the hearers, which expressed its words with such clearness and distinctness that the people seemed rather to be seeing than hearing it.[1]

This was a direct fulfillment of John the Baptist's prophecy that the Messiah would baptize with the Holy Spirit as well as with fire (Matt 3:11). This also fulfilled Jesus' promise, given some seven weeks earlier on Passover at the Last Supper, that He would send the Comforter, the Teacher (John 14:26; 16:7–15). Additionally, this was the empowering event that Jesus had told His apostles to anticipate (Acts 1:4–8).

The pouring out of God's Holy Spirit on Pentecost would have been profoundly appreciated by Jewish recipients. The anniversary of the divine gift of Torah was the most eloquent of moments for the revelation of the divine Spirit. This was indeed the logical sequel to the Sinai experience. The God who came near on Sinai had now come ultimately near as He indwelled believers with His Spirit.

The Spirit's presence at Pentecost was marked by three similar signs also experienced at Sinai: violent wind, fire, and supernatural sounds. In Acts 2:1–3, Luke described the wind and the fire. In 2:4, Luke will begin his description of the "supernatural sounds" of this Pentecost.

The result of this outpouring of the Spirit was the apostles' newly acquired supernatural ability to communicate "with other tongues;" in known, intelligible spoken languages. What Luke means when he relates that "the Spirit gave them utterance," is not that the Spirit Himself is speaking, but that He is providing their ability to speak. From this point on, the apostles would be empowered to be the witnesses whom Christ had commissioned.

On this Pentecost, it can be said that there was indeed something new under the sun! Those Pentecost worshippers were witness to the birth of the church, the beginning of a new era. From this point on, all believers would be permanently indwelt by the Spirit, forever united with Christ and each other.

Filling and baptism. The "filling" of the Spirit is not synonymous with the "baptism" of the Spirit. Although Luke combined them in Acts 2:4, these are actually two distinct ministries of the Holy Spirit. Although only the "filling" of the Spirit is specifically mentioned here, the "baptism" of the Spirit was also simultaneously taking place. Luke does not use the specific technical term, "baptism of the Spirit" in Acts 2:4 to describe these events, substituting instead a description of the apostles being "filled" with the Spirit, which emphasizes the controlling aspect of the Spirit's ministry.

However, this event would subsequently be recognized by the apostles as the fulfillment of what Jesus had promised would take place within a few days' time (Acts 1:5) as well as the inauguration of the Spirit's ministry of baptism, indwelling and filling (Acts 11:15–16).

The filling of the Spirit refers to being under the control of the Spirit (Eph. 5:18), resulting in a holy lifestyle of mature spirituality as well as empowerment for ministry (Acts 2:4; 4:8, 31; 9:17; 13:9). In Acts, the primary ministry the Spirit is shown empowering is that of evangelism, witnessing of the Messiah. It is a repeatable event (Acts 4:8, 31; 6:3–5; 7:55; 9:17; 13:9, 52) that both Old and New Testament believers experienced, although it was much rarer in the Old Testament (Ex. 31:3; 35:30–34; Num 11:26–29; 1 Sam. 10:6–10). Believers cannot generate the filling of the Spirit, but they can and should purposely yield themselves to the filling of the Spirit (Eph. 5:8). The primary result of the Spirit's filling in Acts is empowerment for effective ministry.

In contrast, the primary result of the baptism of the Spirit in Acts is organic union with Christ and His Church (1 Cor. 12:13). It is a onetime, nonrepeatable event in which each new believer is supernaturally united with Jesus and joined together with every other fellow believer. This organic union occurs at the moment of trusting Christ as Messiah (Rom. 8:9; 1 Cor. 12:13). This is not an experience one can either yield to or resist. One cannot actively trigger spirit baptism; one may only be the recipient of the sovereign work of God. The ongoing consequence of Spirit baptism is that believers subsequently experience the unending, continual indwelling of the Holy Spirit (John 14:16; 1 Cor. 6:19).

Scripture records three atypical examples of Spirit baptism occurring at a significantly later time than initial belief. All fall within the Acts narrative (Acts 2:1–4; 8:17; 19:6). These instances, however, serve respectively to authenticate the ministry of the apostles (2:1–4), authenticate Samaritan salvation (Acts 8:17), and authenticate the ministry of Paul (Acts 19:6).

Tongues. The word that is translated "tongues" in Acts 2:4 and 2:11 is *glōssa*, the common Greek word for the physical organ of speech. It is also used metaphorically for speech, or language, itself. That *glōssa* is used in the sense of "language" in Acts 2 is confirmed by Luke's alternate use of the Greek term *dialektos*, "known language" or "dialect," in Acts 2:6 and 2:2.8. Further confirmation that known languages are being described is Luke's description of the tongues to be *heterais*, "of a different and distinguishable kind."

Therefore, as described in Acts, tongues has long been understood to be recognizable languages supernaturally granted to serve as authenticating confirmation of the apostolic message.[2] Without exception within Acts, this authenticating confirmation provided by the four recorded episodes of tongues speaking is before a Jewish audience (Acts 2:4–11; 8:17; 10:46; 19:6). Later, Paul elaborates that the gift of tongues was the fulfillment of the prophet Isaiah's depiction of an authenticating sign for the Jews (Is. 28:11; 1 Cor 14:21–22).

Since every person in the Temple crowd, including the apostles, could normally converse in Aramaic, Hebrew or Greek (and most were conversant in two out of the three languages), then the purpose of speaking in tongues at Pentecost could not have been to facilitate communication between the apostles and the crowd. The apostles' speaking in a multiplicity of languages would neither have added to their efficiency nor the crowd's edification. The gift of tongues at Pentecost had the sole purpose of serving as a colossal beacon to the gathered multitude that God Himself wanted their attention. There was something vital of which He wanted them to be aware.

In the entire narrative of Acts, it is only in the apostles' initial ministry to the Jews (Acts 2:1–4), Samaritans (Acts 8:17), Gentiles (Acts 10:44), and transitional believers (Acts 19:6) that the phenomenon of tongues is experienced. This is strong indication that, at least within Acts, tongues was a sign given by God to authenticate a new work of salvation (Heb. 2:4). It was, therefore, limited to the initial outpouring at Pentecost plus the three separate "echoes" of Pentecost that follow, as old boundaries were newly broken through by the Spirit. It is of note that in none of these four special instances was the gift of tongues an indication of a "second" or "additional" Spirit baptism," or a "second work of grace."

Results of the Coming of the Spirit (2:5–13)

As Pentecost was a pilgrimage festival, the Temple was filled to overflowing with huge crowds of pilgrims from all over Israel and the Diaspora as well as the cosmopolitan residents of Jerusalem. Due to the difficulties and expense of travel to Jerusalem, particularly for those who lived outside the land of Israel, vast numbers of Jews stayed in Jerusalem for the fifty-day period between Passover through Pentecost. This was the only two-month period in the year when the holy city would be packed with so many people. Therefore, this period was particularly strategic for facilitating the news of Jesus' crucifixion and resurrection as well as for the apostolic witness.

Luke described the wind and fire as occurring with such rapidity that by the time anyone other than the apostles or their comrades noticed them and turned their heads to look, they were already gone. Yet if most of the Temple crowd missed the initial rush of the Spirit's coming, the result of His visitation, the empowered apostolic utterance, was inescapable.

Whatever it was that the apostles were so animatedly and enthusiastically proclaiming, the crowd recognized them as being Galileans. In first century Israel, Galilee was considered to be the boondocks of Israel, and Galileans were considered to be uneducated, country bumpkins, with strong, guttural accents (Matt. 26:73; Mark 14:70; Luke 22:59). Apparently, whether speaking in tongues or not, the apostles retained their accents! The crowd would naturally have wondered how they were able to speak so many foreign languages with such fluency.

There is an ancient rabbinic legend in the midrash, which states that as God gave the Torah to Israel at Mount Sinai, all nations throughout the world simultaneously heard God's voice in their own languages. Similarly, on Mount Moriah that morning, as Peter and the apostles preached, Jews from all the nations heard the word of the Lord in their own languages. This, however, was no legend.

The crowd contained representative Jews from a variety of Diaspora nations and regions. Luke's selected representative list of visitors sweeps like a compass around Jerusalem, the geographic center of the Jewish Diaspora as well as the Roman Empire,[3] from east to north to west to south, and includes visitors from the regions of Persia (Acts 2:9), Asia Minor (Acts 2:9–10), North Africa (Acts 2:10), Europe (2:10–11) Arabia (Acts 2:11), and, of course, Israel (Acts 2:9). When Luke mentions the Roman contingent, however, he pauses to particularly specify that this group contained both Jews and proselytes, Gentiles who had converted to Judaism (Acts 2:10). Perhaps Luke is foreshadowing the eventual climax of the Acts narrative in Rome, or it is possible that members of this Roman contingent, subsequent to Pentecost, were the founders of the Roman church.

Having listened for some time now to the apostles' dazzling display of linguistic fluency, the crowd was, by now, thoroughly confused and simply did not know what to think. Luke writes that they were "amazed and greatly perplexed." In other words, they were flummoxed, and the crowd's response was mixed. One group responded with intense curiosity. They seem to have recognized that there was a miracle occurring right before their eyes, or ears in this instance, and they pondered its meaning and significance (Acts 2:12).

A second group exhibited an opposite response. They scoffed and mocked the apostles, accusing them of being too enthusiastic in their consumption of new, or sweet, wine. In other words, they accused the apostles of being drunk (Acts 2:13). "Sweet" or "new" wine was the very sweet and highly intoxicating batch of wine that had not yet completed the fermentation process. Drunkenness was frowned upon in ancient Jewish culture, so an accusation of drunkenness, particularly so early in the morning and in the Temple on the festival day, would have been a particularly derisive accusation.

Peter's Witness (2:14–36)

Peter, serving as the spokesman for the apostles, who are standing with him in solidarity, will deliver a brief message that will generate profound results. With this evangelistic sermon to his Jewish brethren, Peter will, for the first time, use his keys to the kingdom (Matt. 16:19) to unlock the door of Christ's salvation and open the fount of the Holy Spirit for the Jewish people.

Now That I Have Your Attention (2:14–21). Like many good sermons, this one begins with a small joke. After having called for the close attention of the crowd, his first concern is to deny the accusation of drunkenness that had been levied at the apostles. His argument was that they could not possibly be drunk, as it is too early in the morning, only 9:00 AM. In Jewish culture, Jews reserved their drinking for the evening, seldom drinking at any other time of day. Furthermore, 9:00 AM was one of the three appointed Jewish times of prayer, when the morning sacrifices were being offered. In other words, regardless of reasons of propriety, Peter reminded the crowd that no Jewish bars were open for business yet, and, even so, they would be closed on this great holiday!

Having told the crowd what *was not* transpiring, Peter followed this good-hearted denial by telling them what *was* going on. He immediately launches his opening argument with a supporting Scripture.

Peter's text is Joel 2:28–32 (Joel 3:1–5 in the Hebrew Bible). He explained that the apostles' extraordinary abilities manifested that morning were "what was spoken of through the prophet Joel" (Acts 2:16). He goes on to quote the remainder of Joel's prophecy, making a slight adjustment, however, with the insertion of the pregnant phrase, "in the last days" (Acts 2:17). This insertion supplies the eschatological context of the quotation for Peter's audience. "The last days" is an ambiguous phrase used in the prophets to reference the "day of the Lord," or its immediate aftermath (Is. 2:2; Mic. 4:1).

It seems abundantly clear from Peter's use of Joel's prophecy that he was stating that "the last days" had in some way been inaugurated on that very day. Peter's insertion of the phrase "the last days" corresponds to the usage of the phrase by the author of Hebrews (1:2), which indicates that Peter was not the only member of the early church who believed that "the last days" had indeed begun.

Peter's use of the Joel quotation can be divided into three parts. The first part (Joel 2:28–29) concerns the outpouring of God's Spirit on all flesh, which will result in supernatural prophetic abilities, without respect of age or sex or class distinctions (Acts 2:17–18). Based on the new and revolutionary insight concerning Gentile salvation which Peter gleans later on in the Acts narrative (Acts 10:34), it seems a safe assumption that when he quotes the portion of Joel which mentions God's Spirit being poured out "on all flesh," what Peter actually has in mind is Jewish flesh and not all mankind.

The second part (Joel 2:30–31) concerns the associated supernatural, astronomical and geological signs which will follow the spiritual outpouring (Acts 2:19–20). This portion describes events that will occur in the great Tribulation, just prior to the establishment of the messianic kingdom. The phrase, the "day of the Lord," is a common term used in the Bible for the Tribulation.

The last division of Joel's prophecy (Joel 2:32) is the evangelistic promise of salvation, "everyone who calls on the name of the Lord will be saved" (Acts 2:21). In the original Hebrew quote from Joel 2:32, the Hebrew word for Lord is *YHWH*, the ineffable covenant name of God. The Greek translation of this word is *kurios*. By applying to Jesus this same word used for God, Peter is identifying Jesus with YHWH. Peter clarified that from now on, Jesus is the One whom Peter is calling Lord. Peter's understanding is that Jesus freely exercises God's authority. From the initial recorded sermon, the apostolic witness was that Jesus was to be identified with the Lord God Himself. Jesus rules with God and possesses divine authority over salvation and deliverance from sin.

Use of Joel. How Peter used Joel's prophecy in his sermon has engendered some debate. There are two interpretations that bear consideration.

The first interpretation cautiously posits that Peter was using the Joel prophecy in an analogical sense. In other words, when Peter said, "this is what was spoken of," what he actually meant was "this is *like* what was spoken of," or "this is a *similar* event," or "this is an *illustration* or *application* of what was spoken." This interpretation's obvious level of caution seems warranted, since none of the specific prophetic events which Joel described (the moon turning crimson, the sun blackening, etc.) actually occurred that Pentecost. Joel's prophecy describes the final outpouring of the Spirit on the nation of Israel just prior to the inauguration of the messianic kingdom, yet the messianic kingdom was observably not dawning in the Temple that Pentecost morning while Peter was preaching.

Furthermore, the one supernatural event that did occur at Pentecost, specifically the apostles speaking in tongues, is not at all addressed within Joel's prophecy. Nor does Joel's prophecy address the birth of the church. According to this interpretation, Peter was pointing out that what they were experiencing was an outpouring of God's Spirit, just as Joel wrote about, but it was not actually the specific event of which Joel wrote.

One further line of argument for this position is that Peter did not specifically state something to the effect of "and so is fulfilled Joel's prophecy." Peter instead chose alternate terminology to introduce the prophecy *(touto estin to eirēmenon)*, and did not use the standard language of a prophecy "fulfillment formula."

However, the lack of an introductory "fulfillment formula" is not a compelling point, for there are a variety of introductions for quotations of Hebrew prophecy within Acts.[4] Indeed, a contemporary parallel with the linguistic formula Peter used for prophetic fulfillment has been found within the Dead Sea Scrolls (1QHab).[5]

Nonetheless, it seems that by quoting Joel, Peter intended more than to draw a similarity or a comparison. This analogical interpretation is ultimately unsatisfactory. It simply does not acknowledge the plain, straightforward fashion in which Peter declares, "This *is* what was spoken." Peter did not say it was something, "similar to," "an illustration of" or "like" that of which Joel wrote. Rather, Peter said, "this is what was spoken of."

This leads then to the preferable second interpretation, that of an "initial fulfillment" of Joel's prophecy. This position asserts that what Peter believed was that the preliminary stage of Joel's prophecy was being fulfilled right then and there, as he was speaking. Thus, Peter argued for a preliminary, partial fulfillment of Joel's prophecy. This position is perhaps less cautious than the above analogical view but is more faithful to the context of Peter's message. There is merit in taking Peter's declaration of prophetic fulfillment at face value. Some have described Peter's use of Joel 2 as the launching of the New Covenant, but not as a fulfillment in the normal sense.

However, this preliminary fulfillment is only in reference to the first portion of the prophecy which deals with the Holy Spirit's outpouring (Acts 2:17–18). That morning's Pentecost experience was indisputably an outpouring of the Holy Spirit. In addition to Joel, several of the Hebrew prophets also wrote of a future age when God's Spirit would be liberally poured out (Is. 32:15; 44:3; Jer. 31:31–33; Ezek. 39:29, etc.). Yet Peter did not state that these numerous prophetic expectations had been completely fulfilled at Pentecost. Nor does he state that there should be no expectation of a great deal more of the Spirit to be forthcoming in the future when Israel corporately repents and God inaugurates Israel's kingdom.

What Peter appears to have been declaring is that, in a limited sense, the "spigot" of the Holy Spirit had been opened. The Pentecost experience was merely a "down payment" on Joel's prophecy, a "taste" of God's future blessings; a foretaste of the eventual outpouring of the Spirit upon all Israel. There is a much more extensive fulfillment of this prophecy still to be "tapped" at a later date. In no way does an initial fulfillment drain or exhaust the ultimate, future fulfillment of this prophecy. This was only "stage one!" Yet for Peter, even a limited fulfillment of the prophetic outpouring of the Spirit was still a revolutionary event; a paradigm shift in the history of God's relationship with Israel.

This partial fulfillment also indicates the inaugural stage of the New Covenant prophesied by both Jeremiah and Ezekiel (Jer. 31:31-37; Ezek. 11:14-21; 36:22-38) At Jesus' last supper, the Passover Seder which He shared with His disciples on the evening of His betrayal, Jesus affirmed that His death would be the catalyst which would launch the New Covenant. That evening, with the breaking of unleavened bread and drinking of wine, He established the ordinance of the Eucharist as a memorial to His impending sacrifice and the inauguration of a new era. That new era commenced as the New Covenant began to be fulfilled with Jesus' distribution of His Spirit on Pentecost.

This view is careful to recognize that there has been no fulfillment, in any sense, of any portion of the second segment of Joel's prophecy (Acts 2:19-20). These astronomic cataclysms are to occur immediately prior to the inauguration of the messianic kingdom. It was obvious to every Jew standing in the Temple that sunny May morning that these signs and wonders were still to be fulfilled. Yet the promise of these cataclysms, cited by Peter, would have been compelling incentive to urge the assembled crowd to positively respond to their messiah.

Jesus is Messiah (2:22-32). As the initial evangelistic sermon in Acts, indeed, as the first sermon Luke reports, Peter's message is foundational to the book and sets the stage for every other sermon that follows in the narrative. Peter straightforwardly witnessed that Jesus was the Messiah of Israel.

After getting the crowd's attention by quoting Joel to establish that the last days had begun, Peter commenced his witness of Jesus. Knowledge of Jesus was widespread in Israel and Peter, capitalizing on this common knowledge, began by discussing the public ministry of Jesus. He argued that Jesus was openly authenticated as God's anointed choice through His performance of miracles, wonders and signs (Acts 2:22). These miracles, wonders and signs provocatively demonstrated God's power and validated to Israel that Jesus was God's messenger who spoke God's message. This point is central to Acts and variations of the phrase "wonders and signs" will appear throughout the narrative (Acts 2:19, 22, 43; 4:30; 5:12; 6:8; 7:36; 8:6; 14:3). Peter's use of the phrase "wonders and signs" would have reminded his audience of Moses (Deut. 34:10-12). Later, in his follow-up Temple sermon in the next chapter, Peter will be much more explicit in his connection of Jesus to Moses (Acts 3:22-23).

Peter's message immediately moved to Jesus' execution. Peter pointed out that Jesus' death did not take God by surprise, making reference to God's "foreknowledge" (a theological concept Peter also mentions in 1 Peter 1:2, 20).

Then, in one brief sentence, Peter cogently answered the profound question of who was responsible for the death of the Messiah. From one perspective, Jesus was delivered over to His death by God Himself. It was an inevitable part of His predetermined plan from the beginning.

The sermons of Acts, whether from Peter, Stephen or Paul, are studded throughout with harsh accusations that the Jews have murdered their Messiah. These accusations are similar in style and tone to others found throughout the Hebrew prophets and always have the intent of calling the nation to repentance, that they may be forgiven their grievous sins and be saved. Additionally, the sermons in Acts are addressed to that particular generation of Jews who rejected their Messiah.

Even so, these verses have been used for two millennia by Jew-haters, both within and without the church, by both the ignorant and the educated, as prooftexts that label all Jews throughout time as "Christ-killers." These charges of deicide and bloodguilt have caused the Jewish people to experience unimaginable persecution and suffering, often at the hands of Christians and to the shame of the Church. It is essential to remember that according to Scripture, not only Jews were responsible for the death of Christ; the Romans also shared responsibility. Indeed, the entire world, all humanity shares in the blame and, ultimately, God Himself was responsible for the predetermined death of His Son.

Peter was not pointing his finger at either the Jews or the Romans; rather, he was pointing his finger toward the resurrected Christ. However, the responsibility for Jesus' death pales in comparison to the power of His resurrection. The agony of death was terminated for Jesus by the superior power of God, who "raised Him up again" (Acts 2:24).

Peter's reference to the resurrection leads him to his second use of prophetic Scripture in support of his argument. Peter's quotation is from Psalm 16:8–11, a messianic psalm written by King David approximately one thousand years earlier.

The specific circumstances attending David's composition of this psalm are unknown. However, it begins with David's plea for God's preservation of his life (Ps. 16:1). It continues with praise of God's mercy (Ps. 16:2) and goodness (Ps. 16:3, 5–7) and comments on the hopelessness of others foolish enough to worship other gods instead of the one true God (Ps. 16:4).

David concludes the psalm with a confirmation of confidence in the Lord's sustenance of his flesh and his soul, both in the present and beyond death (Ps. 16:8–11). It is this concluding section, specifically 16:8–11, to which Peter made reference.

Peter manifestly affirmed the prophetic aspect of David's writing. Without mincing words, Peter reminded his audience of David's prophetic capacity

(Acts 2:30) and argued that David, both king and prophet, actually had written the psalm in the first person voice of the Messiah, his descendent. Furthermore, when Peter introduced the passage with "for David says of Him" (Acts 2:25), he was not just stating that David was writing prophetically, personifying the future Messiah. He was also making the astonishing claim that David, writing one thousand years earlier, was consciously aware that his subject was the Messiah's resurrection.

Peter boldly and confidently argued that David could not possibly have been writing about himself. David died, was buried, and most assuredly had not been resurrected. In fact, his prominent tomb was just down the road in the city of David (Acts 2:29). Anyone in Jerusalem could see this for a fact. Coincidentally, according to a commonly accepted Jewish tradition, David's death was on Pentecost. (The ancient tomb of David, located in the city of David [1 Kin. 2:10] was destroyed by the Romans a few decades later, in AD 70. To date, the exact site of the tomb's ruins still remains a mystery, although the general area is known. One fact is certain, however; the location of the authentic site is over a mile away from the traditional site, conveniently located directly beneath the traditional "upper room" and regularly visited by contemporary tourists!)

God had established an indissoluble covenant with David in which David was promised that one of his descendants would forever rule over Israel (2 Sam. 7:12–13; Ps. 132:11; Ps. 89:3–4). Peter's point is that the Holy Spirit enabled David to look ahead into the future and understand precisely how God's Davidic Covenant promise of an eternal throne was to be fulfilled. God showed David that an eternal throne and an unending dynasty required an immortal descendant. David had been allowed to see the future Anointed One, the Messiah, the One who would neither decompose nor be abandoned to the abode of the dead (Greek *Hades*, Hebrew *Sheol*). After resting in the grave and abiding in *Hades*, the Messiah, paradoxically, would still live forever. To fulfill the Davidic Covenant, this Son of David would of necessity need to be resurrected.

Son of David. In first century Israel, the title "son of David" conveyed a potent political charge. It was widely understood to refer to an idealized political revolutionary who would cast off the shackles of Roman oppression, judge the wicked and purge evil from the midst of Israel. Israel enthusiastically anticipated that the dynasty of David would be restored and the kingdom of Israel made glorious. This expectation, based on the Hebrew prophets (Jer. 23:5–8; Is. 11:1–16), is widely espoused throughout first century Jewish literature, including the Dead Sea Scrolls.

Jesus conducted His ministry amidst this whirlwind of amplified Davidic anticipation. In fact, one of the foremost messianic titles ascribed to Jesus in the New Testament is "Son of David." This designates Jesus as the recipient of all the promises God had made to David concerning the future and eternal government of one of his descendents. It specifies Jesus to be a royal, majestic messiah who is entitled by birthright to rule and reign over all Israel.

During Jesus' earthly ministry, while He certainly accepted this title as applicable to Himself (Matt. 9:28; 20:32; Mark 10:49), He abjectly refused to be drawn into either political intrigue or revolutionary activity. While Herod the Great feared the one who was born "king of the Jews" (Matt. 2:2), and although He was crucified as "king of the Jews" (Luke 23:38), Jesus forcefully proclaimed that His kingdom, at least for the present time, was "not of this world" (John 18:36).

According to the teaching of the apostles, the Son of David concept is primarily applicable to Jesus' future function as king of the earth, as He reigns from His father David's throne in Jerusalem. Although the particular title "Son of David" is never actually articulated within Acts, the concept is specifically linked to Jesus by both Peter (Acts 2:30) and Paul (Acts 13:23). The Son of David concept was an important theological component within the presentations of both apostles when addressing a Jewish audience.

Peter's citation of Psalm 16:8–11 in Acts 2:25–31 is one of the clearest examples in the New Testament of the specific fulfillment of messianic prophecy. There is no other way to interpret Peter's affirmation. Empowered and infused with the Holy Spirit (Acts 2:1–4), Peter could not have been mistaken in his interpretation, neither could he have been creatively or imaginatively appropriating the psalm to fit his theological purpose. With vibrant confidence, he preached that morning to thousands of his people that one of the most exalted and revered figures in their history, David, in one of the most sacred portions of the Hebrew Scripture, the Psalms, had prophesied that the Messiah would be resurrected.

Having established his point concerning the necessity of the Messiah's resurrection, Peter spelled out exactly of whom David wrote. He doesn't just reveal that it was Jesus; rather, Peter frontloaded the word order of his pronouncement to emphatically emphasize that it was "this Jesus," *touton ton Iēsoun*, whom God resurrected.

At this point, Peter then revealed the stunning connection between himself and Jesus; the connection which would explain why he and his companions had been so powerfully visited by the Holy Spirit. There in the Temple courts, to an audience of thousands, Peter identified himself and his companions as personal eyewitnesses of Jesus' resurrection.

Application (2:33–36). Wrapping up his sermon, Peter advanced to the practical application. He explained that this resurrected Jesus, God's anointed one, was now exalted in glory at the right hand of God. "The right hand of God," was an expression commonly understood to refer to the presence of God Himself. The concept originated in Psalm 110:1, the next Scripture that Peter cites. Jesus used the comparable "the right hand of power" in reference to Himself (Matt. 26:64; Mark 14:62), and it was a frequently employed phrase within the New Testament to emphasize Jesus' exaltation (Acts 2:33; 7:55–56; Rom. 8:34; Col. 3:1; Heb. 10:12; 1 Pet 3:22).

Peter bolstered his claim of Jesus' exaltation by once again relying on a prophecy of David (Acts 2:34–35). Psalm 110:1 is the most frequently cited messianic prophecy in the New Testament. Peter stands firmly within Jewish tradition in interpreting this passage as referring to the messiah. It has a long pedigree of being so interpreted within rabbinic literature (albeit, never with reference to Jesus). Peter demonstrated that Jesus' exaltation fulfilled this prophecy.

There are three individuals referred to within this psalm. There are the two individuals who are called "Lord," and there is the author, David. In English translation it is more difficult to perceive the messianic dynamic of the psalm than in Hebrew, primarily because David, in reference to these two individuals, used two different words, both of which are translated "lord." The first "Lord," is the name *YHWH* and refers to the covenant making God of Abraham, Isaac and Jacob. The second "Lord" is the Hebrew *adonai*. This second "lord," *adonai*, is the individual whom David called "my Lord."

If the first "Lord" refers to God and the second "Lord" is David's lord, then, obviously, neither of these "lordly" individuals could have been David. Indeed, it was universally accepted that David had neither been resurrected nor had he ascended into heaven. This raises the question, if God is the first Lord, and David is the "my" of "my Lord," then just who is David's Lord? Jesus Himself had vexed the Pharisees by posing this perplexing issue (Matt. 22:44–45). Certainly, while he lived, David had no mortal lord. As the undisputed sovereign of all Israel, his only Lord was God Himself.

The answer to this prophetic riddle, Peter reveals, is, of course, Jesus. He announced to the "whole house of Israel," that through God's exaltation of Jesus they might be supremely confident that "this Jesus," whom the Jewish nation had crucified, had been exalted by God and proclaimed to be "both Lord and Christ."

What Peter meant in his climactic disclosure that God had made Jesus both Lord and Christ, or Messiah, was that Jesus' true identity has now finally been revealed. The Jewish people had believed Him to be a mere man, indeed, one worthy of an ignoble execution. However, now, through His exhibition of power in His resurrection and glorious exaltation to the right hand of God, it was clear that Jesus is the reflection of God's essential nature. He is, therefore, supremely worthy of both titles, "Lord" and "Christ."

Christ. The term, Christ, is a transliteration of the Greek word *christos* which means "anointed one." A word with the identical meaning is "messiah," which is likewise a transliteration of the Hebrew word *mashiach.* In the Hebrew Scripture, it generally signifies one who, upon assumption of a sacred office, is specially consecrated (set apart for God) by anointing with oil. This was performed, for example, upon installation of prophets, priests and kings (Ex. 28:41; 1 Sam. 9:15–16; 10:1; 16:3, 12–13; 1 Chr. 29:22).

What was the Jewish expectation of the Messiah? Contrary to what many understand, in first century Judaism, there was no monolithic perception concerning the coming Messiah. The Messianic ideal in the first century was by no means static and was still in development. Within this state of flux, the scope of messianic expectation stretched over a broad range of possibilities.

There existed the portrait of messiah as the idealized Davidic king who would be God's conquering warrior, vanquishing nations and establishing the primacy of Israel. There was the portrait of the messiah as an ultimate priestly leader who would die on behalf of his people. There was an imaginative dual rendering, of two separate but related messiahs; one messiah destined to die, and one destined to conquer. Then there was the mysterious and enigmatic super-human figure, mystically elevated to a semi-divine status. Finally, there is even indication, in certain limited circles, that there was no specific messianic hope at all.

"Christ," or "Messiah," is Luke's most frequently used title for Jesus, occurring some twenty-five times in Acts. Roughly half of these are direct quotations from Peter or Paul's sermons in which Christ is used as Jesus' title, i.e., "Jesus the Messiah." The other half are Luke's narrative descriptions of the church's evangelistic efforts to persuade people that Jesus is the Christ, the Jewish messiah. In both usages, the testimony of Acts is vividly clear that Jesus is the fulfillment of Jewish messianic expectation, and then some! Although He shattered the confines of pre-existing descriptive categories, the Messiah whom God sent to His people turned out to be a much more spectacular figure than anyone had previously imagined.

Response: Jewish salvation! (2:37–42)

The response to Peter's passionate message was unprecedented. Luke reports that the Temple crowd was "pierced to the heart;" that they were experiencing the throws of severe emotional turmoil. Their turmoil had been precipitated by their having heard "this," the immediately preceding referent, Peter's accusation that they had crucified the Messiah, God's anointed One. The crowd earnestly implored Peter to tell them what they should do, how they might atone for this devastating error in judgment.

Peter responded with a forceful exhortation, telling the crowd that there were two things that they must do, two actions that they must perform in sequence, first one and then the other. First, it was necessary for the Jewish people to repent.

The Greek word that is translated repentance is *metanoia*, which means "to change one's mind." Peter, however, was most likely not speaking Greek that morning in the Temple, but Hebrew. The Hebrew word for repentance is *shuv*, which, although similar to the Greek, *metanoia*, indicates an even more dramatic image, that of completely turning oneself around. Whether drawn from Hebrew or Greek Scripture, biblical repentance calls for a vivid change, a complete reorientation of one's perspective. In the case of Peter's exhortation to his Jewish audience that morning, that change of perspective, that reorientation, was to be about Jesus.

Repentance in Acts is the possession of utter confidence that Jesus is the Messiah. It is only that basic, uncomplicated belief which results in the forgiveness of sin. This is the sole New Testament requirement for the salvation of both Jews and Gentiles (Acts 3:19; 5:31; 8:22; 10:43–44; 11:19; 13:24; 17:30; 19:4; 20:21; 26:18–20; John 3:16, 36; Rom. 11:6; Eph. 2:8–9). That Jesus is God's exalted representative, the One authorized to forgive sin, the Messiah, is a simple, although not simplistic, belief. It is an uncomplicated, liberating truth that is perceivable to all and receivable by all.

The second required action that Peter enumerated was baptism. Repentance must immediately be followed by water baptism in the name of Jesus. Although this water baptism would resemble the customary Jewish ritual, this was not to be just another basic repeatable washing as per Jewish custom. Neither was this baptism to be identified with John's baptism of repentance, although they shared certain characteristics.

This baptism would publicize their repentance, their change of mind and orientation, in the sight of all Israel. Baptism would publicly identify the penitent with Jesus and all his followers. Baptism would also serve to publicly disassociate them from the Jewish leadership that had rejected Jesus. This was the opportunity for new believers to make their "official pledge of allegiance to Jesus."[6] Peter was not calling for a simple, "every-head-bowed-every-eye-closed-raise-your-hand" type of response. Rather, he called for the most public of identifications with the Messiah imaginable. Conveniently, there were multiple public *mikvah* pools just outside the Temple where the baptisms could be performed, that very day!

The grammatical construction of Acts 2:38 is complicated and has led to differences of opinion as to the connection between water baptism and the forgiveness of sin. The specific question is which of Peter's two exhortations, to "repent" or to "be baptized," is linked to the forgiveness of sin.[7] The issue relates to whether Peter is affirming that water baptism is necessary for the forgiveness of sins.

There are some who would link the forgiveness of sin to the exhortation to be baptized. In this view, the Greek word *eis*, translated "for," would indicate that forgiveness of sin was the *result* of baptism. However, this would make salvation the result of works. This position is theologically supported nowhere else in the New Testament and is contradicted in the numerous passages listed above concerning the sole New Testament requirement of faith for the salvation of both Jews and Gentiles.[8]

A second view is that while the exhortation to be baptized is linked with the forgiveness of sins, the *eis* should be interpreted to mean that one is to be baptized *because* of, or as a result of, sin having been forgiven. In contrast to the first view, which places forgiveness of sin as a result of baptism, this interpretation affirms the reverse, that baptism is a result of forgiveness. This interpretation is popular in evangelical circles[9] and is in theological agreement with the passages that teach salvation by faith alone, not by faith plus baptism. However, there is scant grammatical evidence for an interpretation of *eis* meaning "because of."[10]

A third view is simply that Acts 2:38 connects baptism with repentance so intimately as to make the former a reflection of the latter. In other words, water baptism is a physical action that reflects and corresponds to the spiritual reality of repentance.[11] The term *eis* indicates that forgiveness of sin is the sole result of repentance. Repentance, however, would necessarily be reflected in the act of water baptism. Peter, then, was not saying that the physical act of baptism results in forgiveness of sin, but rather, that baptism is the closely related physical sign of the spiritual reality of repentance, which results in forgiveness. Thus, Peter's teaching parallels John the Baptist's marked correlation of baptism with repentance (Matt. 3:11). Although an appealing interpretation, it is one that is difficult to articulate.

A final and superior view is one which is based upon the grammatical construction of the verse as well as the theological testimony of the New Testament concerning salvation by faith alone. In this interpretation, repentance is linked with the forgiveness of sin based upon grammatical agreement in both gender and number (both are second person plural). The *eis* indicates that forgiveness of sin is the result of repentance. This makes the command to be baptized (third person singular) a parenthetical idea. The verse could then be paraphrased as follows, "Repent for the forgiveness of your sins, and be baptized."

In this analysis, the forgiveness of sin, engendered by repentance, provides the foundational basis for baptism. This avoids both making forgiveness the result of baptism and the unconventional use of *eis*. This view appreciates that, throughout the remainder of Acts, Peter only associates repentance or belief with the forgiveness of sin, making no mention of baptism as a condition of forgiveness (3:19; 5:31; 10:43)

While this is an attractive and theologically sound position, it must be recognized that a detailed interpretation of the grammar of the Greek text is necessary to arrive at this destination.[12] The linguistic intricacies of this position, however, do not disqualify it from serious consideration and acceptance.

Although God's promise extends to *many* Jews, Peter also indicates that it does not extend to *every* Jew, specifying only those Jews whom God has sovereignly chosen, "as many as our God will call to Himself" (Acts 2:39).

Peter's sermon was not yet finished. He continued on to "round two." Unfortunately, Luke only summarized the remainder of the message. The apostle's concluding exhortation was a call to separation from the "perverse," or "crooked" generation. The word Peter used to describe that particular generation of Israel was *skolios*, from which we derive the medical condition scoliosis, the curvature of the spine. It means to be "twisted," "crooked," or "perverse." This is the sole use of this word in Acts, but Peter applies it in his first epistle to certain unsavory employers (1 Peter 2:18), and in his gospel, Luke quotes John the Baptist as promising that the "the crooked will become straight and the rough roads smooth" (Luke 3:5; Is. 40:4). Paul echoes Peter's usage in Acts 2:40, contrasting the church with the "twisted generation" in which they lived (Phil. 2:15).

Peter's point was for his audience to save themselves, not primarily from the fires of hell and eternal damnation (although that is implied), but from the excruciating and cataclysmic judgment coming upon this particular generation of the nation of Israel which had rejected the Messiah. This divine judgment had been central to the witness of John the Baptist, who repeatedly warned his audience of "the wrath to come," which would imminently descend upon Israel (Matt. 3:7). Jesus further clarified that the coming judgment was to be inflicted upon the specific generation of Israel which had rejected Him (Luke 11:50–51; Matt 23:35–36) and would result, in part, in the destruction of the Temple (Matt 24:2).

The biblical record indicates that a generation had a duration of forty years. This was the length of time it took for the torch of the Egyptian Exodus generation to be passed to their children, the generation raised in the wilderness (Num. 32:13). Approximately forty years after John's initial warnings and the commencement of Jesus' public ministry, the Romans decimated Jerusalem and completely demolished the Temple.

It is abundantly apparent that Peter's message got through to the crowd. On the day of Pentecost, three thousand Jews responded in repentance. They were then baptized in the numerous mikvah pools located at the southern end of the Temple. There are archaeological estimates of possibly two hundred of these baptismal pools at the foot of the Temple Mount, of which dozens have already been uncovered.[13]

The First Church (2:42-47)

In this section, Luke reports that in the early church, the spectacular results of Peter's evangelism were followed through with exemplary discipleship and fellowship. Following their Pentecost experience, these believers were "enthusiastic" in the original, truest sense of the word, that of "having god within" or being "possessed by god," from the Greek *entheos*.

Luke is not as concerned with providing specific details (what was taught, what they prayed, how they ate together, etc.), as he is in communicating the atmosphere of love and mutual devotion which characterized the early church. He simply reports that they "continually devoted themselves" to the apostolic teaching and fellowship, *koinōnia*, as characterized by sharing common meals and praying together.

The content of the apostolic teaching to which they were devoting themselves was what Jesus had taught the apostles during His time with them. There was a vast repository of Jesus' teaching which the apostles would have shared, called forth from memory with the Holy Spirit's enablement.

There is a question as to whether the "breaking of bread" refers to the Eucharist or the eating together of actual meals. It is probable that both are in view. The agape feasts of the early church were real meals that also included the regular celebration of the Eucharist. Then, as now, Jewish people exhibit fellowship through their eating together. Indeed, in this particular Jewish Christian home, Bible study is often characterized by such "fellowship." As the mishnah teaches, "without food, there is no Torah study and without Torah study there is no food (Avot 3:17)!

Apparently, the believers still attended formal worship services in the Temple and synagogue. The definite article precedes the plural form of the Greek word for prayer, *proseuchē*, which should be translated, "the prayers," indicating not just the practice of occasional prayer, or a prayerful state, but rather, their continued participation in the formal, corporate times of prayer practiced within Judaism. This will be illustrated in Acts 3:1.

Miracles in Acts by the Apostles and their Associates

Miracle	Agent(s)	Result	Acts
Tongues	Apostles	Authentication/Salvation	2:1–41
Lame man healed	Peter	Authentication/Salvation	3:1–11
Death of Ananias and Sapphira	Peter	Authentication/Organizational Purity	5:1–11
Aeneas healed of paralysis	Peter	Authentication/Salvation	9:32–35
Dorcas raised from the dead	Peter	Authentication/Salvation	9:36–41
Various	Peter	Authentication/Salvation	5:15–16
Elymas blinded	Paul	Authentication	13:6–11
Lame man healed	Paul	Authentication	14:8–10
Demons exorcized	Paul	Authentication	16:16–18
Eutychus raised from the dead	Paul	Authentication	20:7–12
Paul bitten by viper	Paul	Authentication	28:3–5
Publius' father healed	Paul	Authentication	28:8
Various	Paul	Authentication/Salvation	19:11–12
Various	Paul	Authentication	28:8–9
Various	Paul/Barnabas	Authentication/Salvation	14:3
Various	Paul/Barnabas	Authentication/Salvation	15:12
Various	12 apostles	Authentication/Salvation	2:43
Various	12 apostles	Authentication/Salvation	5:12
Various	Stephen	Authentication	6:8
Various	Philip	Authentication/Salvation	8:6

Luke then related that the early Jerusalem church was characterized by the sharing of possessions. This was a display of biblical "common-ism," not communism. Members of the church sold and distributed property from time to time as other members experienced need. The early Jerusalem church clearly valued people over possessions and, at least for a time, modeled the ideal community as envisaged in the Mosaic command, "there shall be no poor among you" (Deut. 15:4). Their behavior must have been motivated in part by their expectation of the imminent return of Christ and the establishment of His kingdom. This was a reasonable way to live for a community of faith that believed they were living in "the last days" and that the current age was drawing to a close.

This behavior was not meant as prescriptive for every church, but merely as descriptive behavior of the earliest church. Luke's use of the imperfect tense of the verb *pipraskō*, "to sell" (Acts 2:45) indicates that what he had described was the previous and not the current Jerusalem church practice. Such "common-ism" was apparently a short-lived, localized practice. The remainder of the Acts narrative fails to record any other local church structured in this way except that of Jerusalem, and only then within the early years. Sooner or later, perhaps after a famine or two, the members of the Jerusalem church ran out of property and possessions to distribute and became an especially impoverished community (Acts 11:28–29; 24:17; Rom. 15:26; Gal. 2:10).

Luke concludes his description with strong confirmation of the Jewish character of the early church. First, He made reference to their faithful Temple attendance. Indeed, as resident Jews of Jerusalem, it would seem obvious that they would have frequented the Temple. The Jewish believers attended the Temple for times of corporate teaching (2:46; 5:12), customary daily prayer (3:1), and national worship (2:1; 20:16; 21:26).

Second, He reiterated that they habitually ate together, enjoying each other's company and carrying on a joyous, ongoing, perpetual progressive dinner from one home to another. Even today in Israel, as in other ethnic cultures set around the Mediterranean, very little happens apart from food. As we say, where you have two Jews you have at least four plates of food!

Finally, Luke reports that the early church experienced no problems with the surrounding community. The Jewish community did not yet feel threatened by the presence of the church in their midst. In fact, the community responded favorably and added to the membership of the church. The believers' zeal for the word of God and love for one another must have been positively contagious.

This concludes the first of seven progress reports on the church that Luke relates throughout the narrative (2:47; 6:7; 9:31; 12:24; 16:5; 19:20; 28:30–31).

Conclusion

One must agree with Luke's assessment that Pentecost was indeed prophetically fulfilled by these events (Acts 2:1). The response to the spiritual manifestations of the morning of Pentecost and Peter's powerful message was that three thousand Jewish people came to faith in their Messiah. While it would be imprudent to suggest that God employs a "holy calculator," this account would suggest that through Pentecost, He had balanced His "Book of Life." Fifteen hundred years following God's capital judgment at Sinai of three thousand rebellious Israelites, He graciously restored another three thousand Israelites to eternal life. The Law kills, but the Spirit gives life (2 Cor. 3:6).

This Temple Mount sequel to the Mount Sinai experience was necessary because the account recorded in Exodus leaves no doubt that external experiences - even the most awesome ones such as the miraculous escape from Egypt and the thunderous voice of God himself shaking Mt Sinai - ultimately do not change lives. Lives can only be transformed from the inside out.

Ultimate life change that results in obedience can only be accomplished by the Lord taking up permanent residence in His temple. Not the Temple in Jerusalem, which no longer stands, but that temple which is each one of us frail, imperfect men, women and children. Individual Jews and Gentiles alike are transformed into a community of saints by the receipt of a gift—the indwelling Torah.

Pentecost reminds us that God has personally engraved His righteous standards on our hearts (Jer. 31:31) by His Spirit. He has given His Spirit to permanently indwell us, enabling immediate and direct access to the Father. He has provided the perfect Intercessor: a great high priest, Jesus, the incarnation of Torah (John 1:1). Unlike Moses or the Levitical priests, this intermediary is no mere "middleman"; He is the *"God-man!"* God's presence was manifest on Sinai within an ominous and distant cloud. On Pentecost, God gave us His Spirit so that His presence can be more intimate than the very air we breathe. We now have the eternal, abiding presence of Immanuel, *God with us.*

Study Questions:

1. Describe how the Jewish feast of Pentecost was fulfilled in Acts 2.

2. Who spoke in tongues in Acts 2:1–13? What is the basis of your answer?

3. Why and how did Peter quote from Joel in his Pentecost sermon?

4. According to Peter, who was responsible for killing the Messiah?

5. Based on Peter's sermon, why is Jesus the Messiah?

6. Define the word "christ."

7. What was the first century Jewish expectation of Messiah?

8. What did Peter mean by repentance?

CHAPTER 3

Miracle in the Temple
Acts 3:1–26

Preview:
Immediately following his report of the numerous miracles being performed through the apostles, Luke provided the details of one quite unforgettable example. Peter's healing of a lame man is nothing short of spectacular and provides Peter an opportunity to once again preach a powerful message of salvation to the assembled masses in the Temple courts.

The Healing (3:1–11)

As this chapter opens, two of the apostles, Peter and John, were on their way to the Temple to observe the afternoon prayers that accompanied the "evening" sacrifices, which began around 2:30 PM.

Jews attended mandatory corporate prayer in the Temple or synagogue twice daily, at 9:00 AM (the third hour, according to the Roman calculation), and at 3:00 PM (the ninth hour). These prayer times roughly corresponded to the morning and evening sacrifices.[1] It was also customary to add an optional home prayer service at noon (the sixth hour). Even today, it is Orthodox Jewish practice to pray together in a morning service, called in Hebrew *Shacharit*, an afternoon service, called *Mincha*, and an evening service, called *Ma'ariv*.

Regular Temple attendance would have been a normative custom for the apostles, who were devout Jews. It is clear from Acts that the first generation of believers, all of them Jewish, saw no inconsistency with their new faith in maintaining their ancient Jewish customs such as circumcision, traditions such as Sabbath observance, and practices such as keeping kosher (Acts 2:46; 3:1;

5:21–25, 42; 10:14). The early church was, at this point, simply one more Jewish sect among many others, thriving among a people who were seemingly prone to sectarianism. The sole feature distinguishing the church from all other contemporary Jewish parties was their belief that Jesus of Nazareth was the Messiah.

It is telling that the maintenance of Jewish custom and tradition as described in Acts is not qualified by Luke as something negative, ill advised, or unenlightened. Rather, such practices were normative within the early church. This remains the case throughout the rest of the narrative. The only aspects of the church's Jewish culture that later required adaptation were those which interfered with the incorporation of Gentiles into the church and their acceptance as equals, such as strict adherence to kosher food regulations.

It must be remembered that in first century Israel, Judaism was not only a religious system, but a national way of life, the ancient law of the land. It would have been exceedingly difficult to extricate religious responsibilities from national duties or even from simple cultural expression.[2]

In this account, Peter is the major figure. Although presented in the gospels as one of the three central apostles most intimate with Jesus (along with the other "son of thunder," John's brother, James, and the ubiquitous Peter), John is relegated to a minor role in the Acts narrative. Here he appears as Peter's apostolic "sidekick."

As they entered the Temple, they encountered a familiar figure, a lame beggar, in his customary spot. Every resident of Jerusalem would have known the face of this beggar; after all, he was forty years old and had been lame all his life. He would, therefore, have occupied this extremely prime begging location every day for many years. He would have been simply unavoidable as the heavy traffic passed proceeded on their way to pray.

Beautiful Gate. Luke records that the beggar had stationed himself at the Temple gate that was called "Beautiful." There is some difficulty in identifying which gate this actually was, as Luke is the only ancient writer who records this "nickname." There are three candidates for the "Gate called Beautiful," each option being an eastern Temple entrance.

First, one popular identification is the towering, gleaming, bronze Nicanor Gate, which was inside the Temple proper and led from the Court of Women into the Court of Israel. However, equating this with the Nicanor Gate does not seem likely, considering the Herculean efforts it would have taken to deposit the lame beggar at its threshold. To reach the Nicanor Gate, he would have first had to have been carried up a flight of steps into the initial precinct of the Temple complex, the Court of the Gentiles, then carried up another flight of steps which led from the Court of the Gentiles to an elevated terrace, which led through the "Corinthian" Gate into the Court of Women, and then carried through the Court of Women to the staircase leading up to the Nicanor Gate. Furthermore, one may imagine the havoc and the disruption to the daily Levitical service that would ensue having a handful of beggars constantly lying underfoot upon the central Temple staircase.

Another popular identification with the "Beautiful Gate" is the enormous "Corinthian," or "eastern" gate previously noted, situated one flight up from the Court of the Gentiles, which led from the elevated terrace into the Court of the Women. Alfred Edersheim describes this gate in detail.

> "But far more magnificent . . . was the . . . *eastern* gate (italics original), which formed the principal entrance into the Temple. The ascent to it was from the terrace by twelve easy steps. The gate itself was made of dazzling Corinthian brass, most richly ornamented; and so massive were its double doors that it needed the united strength of twenty men to open and close them."[3]

However, the difficulty with accepting this identification is similar to that of the Nicanor Gate. It would have still entailed a tremendous effort for the lame beggar to be set down there. If either this or the Nicanor Gate is meant, then it certainly seems that whatever daily alms were collected were certainly earned in sweat equity!

This leaves the final, least mentioned, yet most likely possibility; that of the Shushan Gate, which was located on the Temple's eastern outer wall, roughly where in the area where the "Eastern" or "Golden" Gate is today. This gate was not inside the Temple complex, as were the previous two examples. Rather, the Shushan Gate was an outer entrance into the Temple, which led from the Kidron Valley into the Temple complex, specifically into Solomon's Portico in the Court of the Gentiles.[4] Therefore, when the lame man was healed, he entered the Temple from outside with Peter and John, only getting as far as the initial, outer Court of the Gentiles before the amazed crowd surrounded them.

In Jewish culture, then as now, a high value was placed upon charitable acts. In fact, the Hebrew word for charity, *tzedakah*, is a word often translated "justice" or "righteousness." In Jewish society, one never made a professional career of begging unless there was absolutely no alternative. Therefore, this lame man, whose handicap was congenital, would not have gone hungry. In fact, he had selected one of the most prime Jerusalem locations in which to beg; at the entrance to the Temple, where the religious sensitivities of passersby would be most heightened. As he saw Peter and John passing by, he made his usual request for *tzedakah*. He was, however, neither aware of to whom he had addressed his request nor what manner of "charity" they would be extending.

Peter took a moment to make personal contact with the beggar, commanding him to look at him and John. The man eagerly complied, believing that his paying attention to these men would elicit a particularly generous gift. Typically, people would simply toss coins at beggars, paying them money but no heed, indeed not usually giving them a second glance.

Also of interest is the fact that Peter and John did not run back to the other believers and ask if someone would sell a piece of property in order for them to put together a "benevolence" package for the lame man. Instead, the apostles powerfully demonstrated the strength of their faith and the capacity of their Messiah.

Without explanation, warning or fanfare, Peter commanded the lame man to walk. Reminiscent of the dramatic Hebrew prophets of old, Peter asserted the authority of Jesus, assumed the realization of the healing, and demanded the man stand up.

His command was made "in the name of Jesus the Messiah, the Nazarene." This specification indicated that Peter was careful to stress that he himself did not possess the authority to heal. The phrase, "in the name," invoked twenty three times in Acts, should not be confused with a magical incantation. It simply means "by means of the authority." Peter identified that the source of this unparalleled authority was Jesus Christ. Throughout the Acts narrative, the extent of the authority of Jesus is demonstrated by the degree of power exercised in His name. Luke reveals that Jesus' exercise of power is unlimited. Yet only God possesses unlimited power. Therefore, to invoke the name of Jesus is to call upon God Himself.

The healed man responded with an aggressive move of his own. He leaped upright and neither wobbled nor fell down. For the first time in his life he enjoyed what had heretofore been forbidden him, to walk into the Temple of God. Grabbing hold of Peter on one side and John on the other, he walked through the Beautiful Gate, now seen from the new unique upright (and not sideways) angle, and he entered the Court of the Gentiles. He not only walked through the court, but also vigorously leapt about the colonnaded Portico of Solomon, praising God for his healing and glorying in the exercise of heretofore-unused muscles, putting them through the paces of new physical maneuvers!

As the gathered worshippers stared at this one particularly exuberant worshipper and realized exactly how awesome the sight was which they beheld, they could also not help but notice the apostles on either side of him, firmly held in his grateful grasp throughout his athletic display (Acts 3:11).

Solomon's Portico. Solomon's Portico, or Colonnade, was a two-hundred-twenty-five yard long, covered, columned walkway that ran along the entire eastern outer wall of the Temple in the Court of the Gentiles. Edersheim portrays the massive scope of this meeting area, as well as the additional porticos which buttressed the Temple's outer walls:

> "These . . . were among the finest architectural features of the Temple. They ran all round the inside of its wall, and bounded the outer enclosure of the Court of the Gentiles. They consisted of double rows of Corinthian pillars, all monoliths, wholly cut out of one block of marble, each pillar being thirty-seven and one half feet high."[5]

Solomon's Portico was a popular place in the Temple complex for teaching, debate and, indeed loitering, both in winter, because it was roofed and sheltered from the bitter winds on three sides, and in summer because of the shade it provided and the cool temperature of the marble columns.

Peter's Witness (3:12–26)

His Accusation (3:12–16)

Peter capitalized on this opportunity to once again witness of the Messiah. He explained that neither he nor John had the power to heal the man. Rather, the man had been healed by means of the authority of Jesus the Messiah.

As the prayer service was mainly composed of men (not many women being at liberty to leave the preparation of their family's evening meal to attend a prayer service in the city center), Peter begins with the formal address, "men of Israel." This formality will contrast with his later use during his conclusion of the familiar "brethren."

The "God of our fathers" was a familiar phrase recited during the Jewish prayer services and is found within the collection of Jewish prayers called *The Amidah*, or *The Eighteen Benedictions*. The phrase would also be recognized as originating from the Hebrew Scriptures in the passage which records God's reply when asked by Moses how to identify Him to the Israelites (Ex. 3:13).

In his opening statement, Peter identified Jesus as the covenant God of Israel's prophesied "Servant of the Lord" (Is. 42:1-6; 43:8-13; 49:1-13; 50:4-9; 52:13—53:12; 61:1-3). The people would have been greatly familiar with the "servant of the Lord" complex of prophecies, which cover the mission, humiliation and eventual exaltation of God's servant. Peter referenced these prophecies not only to focus on Jesus rejection, but also to establish that God had subsequently exalted His Servant.

The term "Holy One" comes from the David's prophecy, "nor will you allow Your Holy One to undergo decay" (Ps 16:10), which Peter previously cited in his initial sermon to refer to Jesus' resurrection. The term "Righteous

One," comes from Isaiah's "Servant of the Lord" complex, specifically the "suffering servant" passage which states "the Righteous One, My Servant, shall turn many to righteousness, seeing that he bore their sins" (Is. 53:11).

Israel had chosen to ask freedom for the murderer, Barabbas, and had given Jesus over to execution. Peter used a unique phrase for Jesus in Acts 3:15, calling him the "Prince of life," *archēgon tēs zoēs*. Peter's emphasis was that Jesus was the originator, the pioneer, the leader, the source, the champion, the very author of life. Jesus was the template for a perfect humanity. Yet when given the choice, Israel chose an eradicator of life over the originator of life!

Nevertheless, God had other plans and raised Jesus from the dead. Peter proclaimed that he and John were eyewitnesses of that resurrection. He goes on, however, to state that although they were witnesses of Jesus' resurrection, the crowd that day was eyewitness to His resurrection power and authority! This was an undeniable, very public miracle.

His Exhortation (3:17–26)

Having demonstrated that the authority of Jesus, whom the Jews rejected, was the responsible party in this man's healing, Peter moves to a passionate exhortation. Having begun his address with the formal, "Men of Israel," Peter now addressed the crowd as family, using the intimate, "brothers."

Peter explains that the crowd's guilt, and that of the leaders of Israel, in rejecting and condemning the Messiah; their abject failure to recognize God's Holy and Righteous servant, the prince of life, was the result of ignorance. However, ignorance was no excuse. They were still collectively and individually responsible.

Peter's point has strong Scriptural support. As Hosea wrote, "my people are destroyed for lack of knowledge" (Hos. 4:6). The good news, however, is that from the beginning, God has always extended an opportunity to atone for sins which were committed unintentionally (Num. 15:22–31). As Jesus said on the cross, "Father, forgive them, for they know not what they do" (Luke 23:34).

Peter goes on to state that although the Jewish people acted in ignorance, God acted with knowledge; foreknowledge, to be exact. The Messiah's rejection by Israel and crucifixion were always part of God's eternal plan. The Hebrew Scriptures are replete with messianic prophecies not only of exaltation and victorious rule, but also of humiliation, suffering, and death. Although God holds the Jewish people responsible for their actions, in one sense they were merely pawn-like participants in God's cosmic predetermined and pre-announced program.

Therefore, Jewish people must repent and return. Peter repeats the solution to Israel's problem which he initially proclaimed in his earlier sermon at Pentecost (Acts 2:38). The Jewish people must exhibit repentance. They must change their mind about Jesus.

Not only must Israel's mind and perception about Jesus change, their allegiance must also be changed. Israel must demonstrate a return to God through joining the messianic movement, the church. They must turn around and march again in cadence with God's drumbeat. Peter insisted that Israel's faith was askew; something was desperately wrong. Their Messiah, Israel's centerpiece, their foundation, was missing.

Peter promised that upon this repentance and return would be three formidable results. First, the immediate fruit of repentance would be forgiveness. Any Jewish person could have his sins "wiped away," blotted out, rubbed out, erased, simply by accepting God's provision of the Messiah.

Second, when the Jewish people have been forgiven as a result of their repentance, "times of refreshing" will be granted by God. The phrase "times of refreshing" does not refer to various periods of spiritual revival within the church age. Rather, these "times of refreshing" are specifically described as being the result of corporate Jewish repentance. Therefore, the "times of refreshing" must refer to the establishment of the messianic kingdom (Ezek 37:21–28; Hos. 11:9–11; 14:4–7; Amos 9:11–15 Zech. 12:10–14).

The third result of Jewish repentance is the return of Jesus, the second coming. The return of Jesus firmly establishes the identity of "times of refreshing" with the messianic kingdom, because the "times of refreshing" and the return of the Messiah are grammatically connected by the *kai*, "and" of Acts 3:20,[6] making them simultaneous events. Therefore, the cumulative fruit of individual Jewish repentance would be the messianic king's return to establish the era of His sovereign rule, the "times of refreshing." In other words, Jesus will not return until Israel repents. Jesus is, after all, Peter pointed out, "the Christ appointed for you," with reference to the Jewish people.

Peter goes on to relate these two events to "the restoration of all things," which had been prophesied in the Hebrew Scripture. The "all things" are not limited just to spiritual blessings. "All things" means all things. This is the long anticipated "age to come" (Is. 11:1–12), the coming kingdom which will be the final realization of all the promises God had made to the Jewish people through the prophets.

Jesus Himself referred to this restoration in the gospel of Matthew as the time of the coming physical kingdom when He would rule from Jerusalem on the throne of His father David, His twelve apostles seated at His side on thrones of their own.

"Truly I say to you, that you who have followed Me, in the restoration when the Son of Man will sit on His glorious throne, you will sit upon twelve thrones, judging the twelve tribes of Israel" (Matt. 19:28).

The Messiah will not return from heaven "empty handed." The kingdom will come with the coming king.

Peter now knows what must first proceed the answer to the apostles' previous question of when exactly it would be that Jesus would restore the kingdom to Israel (Acts 1:6). Prior to this restoration must come Israel's corporate repentance.

Needless to say, Peter's line of reasoning should be common knowledge to contemporary students of the Scripture.

Peter then advances from the messianic prophecies of Isaiah to that of Moses. Peter quotes Moses' promise to Israel that the Lord would raise up a prophet like himself from among the people of Israel (Deut. 15–18). Peter's point is simple. Moses had made a messianic prophecy. Jesus fulfilled it. Jesus was the prophet like Moses. This was not Peter's innovation, but an established association that had been made by the Jewish people throughout Jesus' ministry (John 6:14; 7:40).

Jesus' ministry shared certain unique features with Moses. Moses had been distinct from all other prophets because only with Moses had God spoken "face to face" (Deut 34:10) and "mouth to mouth" (Num. 12:8). Jesus exhibited similar intimacy with the One He called "My Father."

The common twenty first century contemporary Jewish interpretation of these verses is that the prophet like Moses referred to the successive line of prophets in Israel who followed Moses. Yet this is not what the passage plainly teaches, and it is not the interpretation that was held in the first century.[7]

Peter presses his point by highlighting the warning which accompanied Moses' prophecy (Deut 18:19). Obedience to the prophet like Moses would be so crucial, of such utmost importance to God, that those who neither recognize this prophet nor obey him will suffer the severest penalty. God's harshest judgment will fall upon those who willingly disregard this singular prophet.

Peter moves from messianic prophecy to the Abrahamic Covenant to argue that the nation of Israel, as heirs to the Abrahamic Covenant and the natural recipients of God's prophesied promise, should have, of all people, recognized their Messiah. This has been the paradox of Jewish evangelism since the time of Peter and his apostolic comrades. Those to whom the gospel was intended, those who should have most enthusiastically embraced their Messiah, for the most part did not do so.

Nonetheless, it is essential to remember that a significant remnant of Israel did respond as expected. Thanks to that remnant, the contemporary church stands today. The gospel has always been "to the Jew first" (Rom. 1:16), which means not only their priority in evangelism, but that the good news has obvious resonance and particular applicability to Israel. Although the entire world will enjoy the benefits of the Covenant God made with Abraham, the promises of the Abrahamic Covenant are especially Israel's to receive as the direct heirs of Abraham (Gen. 12:1–3; 15:18–21; 17:1–8; 22:18). The promise of Messiah is Israel's inheritance.

The Jewish people are God's evangelistic priority. God sent His Servant, Jesus, "to the Jew first." His salvation first went to Israel (Matt. 10:6; 15:24; John 4:22; Rom. 1:6) Jewish salvation should likewise always be the evangelistic priority of the church. The reason for this is that the Bible teaches that the inauguration of the coming messianic kingdom is dependent on Jewish response. This is supported not only by Peter's declaration in verses 19–20. Jesus Himself promised that the world would not see Him again until the moment the inhabitants of Jerusalem cry out, "*Baruch ha ba b'shem Adonai*," "blessed is He who comes in the name of the Lord!" (Matt. 23:39). To this must be added the testimony of Paul that "the Deliver will come forth from Zion" (Rom. 11:26)

Conclusion

There are some who see in this speech Peter's extending an offer of the kingdom to Israel. This view is unacceptable, as the kingdom was never Peter's to offer. Jesus had already formally and conclusively offered Israel the kingdom with Himself as king (Matt. 4:17). Subsequently, Jesus was definitively rejected (Matt. 2:22–37; John 19:15, etc.). Peter's audience could not have been given the opportunity to reject the kingdom. By the time Peter's sermon was delivered, the rejection of the kingdom by Israel was already a *fait accompli*.

Therefore, Peter's purpose was not to once again offer the already postponed kingdom to Israel, but to relay the circumstances under which that delayed kingdom can finally be established. The prerequisite for the kingdom to come was Israel corporately hailing her messianic king. Peter provides a rousing incentive for Israel to repent and claim Jesus for their own. What Peter offered to Israel that afternoon was not a kingdom, but their Messiah. As the next chapter records, his offer generated the positive response of five thousand Jewish men.

Study Questions:

1. What were the three standard times of Jewish prayer?

2. Why or why not did the church abandon Jewish customs?

3. According to Peter's sermon, what will be the results of Israel's corporate repentance?

4. Describe the "prophet like Moses."

5. Was Peter offering the kingdom to Israel? Why or why not?

CHAPTER 4

Those Irrepressible Apostles
Acts 4:1–31

Preview:

The previous chapter's evangelistic sermon is interrupted with the arrest of Peter and John. After spending the night in prison, they are brought before the Great Sanhedrin, the same court that had sentenced Jesus to death. Peter and John take this opportunity to "speak truth to power," witnessing to the leaders of Israel and accusing them of repeatedly standing in opposition to God. Compared to God, the seemingly powerful Sanhedrin is shown an impotent force. Having misused and abused its authority, it stood squarely in opposition to God's will.

Response to Peter's Witness (4:1–4)

Just as Peter had been speaking of the rebelliousness and wickedness of Israel, as if on cue, a large group of Jewish leaders stepped forward to interrupt the Temple "revival meeting." Peter's message was cut short by those same ignominious leaders who, through their treatment of Jesus, had led their people into God's judgment. Apparently, these leaders did not appreciate the theological thrust of Peter's message. Luke describes them as hostilely bursting upon Peter and the crowd gathered around him.

Priests. Luke mentions three separate factions within this group. Since they possess the authority to interrupt Peter's instruction, the priests whom Luke mentions are most probably the twenty-four "leading," or "chief" priests.

Josephus estimates that the population of the first century priesthood was over twenty thousand.[1] Therefore, the priests were divided into twenty-four divisions, with each priest serving for one week, twice each year (1 Chr. 24:7–19). Accordingly, on any given week, hundreds of priests might be serving within the Temple.

In addition to this semi-annual rotation, every priest served in the Temple during the three weeks of the great annual pilgrimage festivals: Passover, Pentecost and Tabernacles. Consequently, each priest spent approximately five weeks every year in Temple service. As a means of support during the remainder of the year, most priests engaged in either a trade or the teaching of Torah.

While on the topic of priests, a word about Levites is in order. Levites, like priests, derived from the tribe of Levi, however, without the specificity of being direct descendants of Aaron. The Levite males, like priests, also served in the Temple, but in a supportive capacity. They functioned as Temple musicians, maintenance workers, and Temple Guards. There were even more Levites than priests, so most of them served in the Temple only briefly during the course of a year, if at all, supporting themselves as craftsmen or scribes.[2]

Captain of the Temple Guard. Another member Luke mentions is the captain of the Temple guard, in Hebrew, *ish har habeit,* "the man of the Temple Mount." This individual functioned somewhat like a chief of the Temple police department. He was second only to the high priest in the authority exercised within the Temple complex and could even stand-in for the high priest, as an "understudy" of sorts, in the case of an emergency.

Sadducees. The third faction Luke includes in this trouble-making delegation is the Sadducees. Since both the chief priests and the captain of the Temple guard were members of the Sadducean party, Luke must simply be referring to additional Sadducean minions, aristocratic ruffians who were spoiling for trouble.

The Sadducees were a particular sect, or party, within first century Judaism. Their membership was largely derived from the wealthy Jewish aristocracy. As the party of the aristocracy, they comprised the upper echelon of power in Israel. To maintain their powerful status, however, they also were, by necessity, extremely cozy with the Romans.

The majority of Sadducees were either priests or Levites. This did not in any way mean, though, that the majority of common, ordinary priests and Levites belonged to the Sadducees. The general population of the priesthood shared neither wealth nor power and did not gravitate toward the party of Roman accommodation.

Parties within first century Judaism were never exclusively of a political nature. In fact, politics were only a reflection of deep theological distinctions. Unique to the Sadducees in Judaism was their limited acceptance of what could be considered divine revelation. They believed that only the Torah, the

Law of Moses, was the divine word of God, rejecting the authority of the Hebrew Prophets and the Writings (Psalms, Proverbs, etc.). Not surprisingly, the Sadducees vehemently rejected the Jewish oral law and traditions of the Pharisees.[3]

They also rejected doctrines that arose from a source outside the Torah. Among these rejected doctrines were those of resurrection, angelic or demonic beings, and the immortality of the soul. Consequently, in their theological system, there was no eternal reward or punishment since the immortal soul was a fiction. Predictably, they also emphasized human responsibility over divine sovereignty.[4]

Josephus portrayed the Sadducees as abrasive louts. Although they were from among Israel's wealthy aristocracy, Josephus records that they were a rude, argumentative and thoroughly disagreeable lot.

> "But the behavior of the Sadducees one towards another is in some degree wild; and their conversation with those that are of their own party is as barbarous as if they were strangers to them."[5]

Of course, this report may be somewhat tempered when it is remembered that Josephus was a Pharisee, but needless to say, the Sadducean party neither attained widespread popularity with Israel's general populace nor garnered their affection.[6]

Luke portrays this gathering of Sadducees as being greatly disturbed. What had worked them into such an indignant fury was that these uneducated men, these Galileans, had invaded Sadducean turf. Without any authorization from the Temple leadership, this man Peter was teaching unacceptable theology to the assembled crowd. How dare this man teach on the resurrection, and specifically on the resurrection of the discredited and humiliated Jesus! This heated topic was all too familiar to these Sadducees, for these were the same men who, just a few months earlier, had instigated Jesus' crucifixion.

By this time it was reasonably late in the afternoon, so Peter, John and the healed man, held as "exhibit A," were placed under arrest in the prison chambers within the Temple compound. The apostles would be placed on trial the following day, ostensibly on the accusation of sorcery (Acts 4:7). According to Jewish law, no trials were conducted after sundown, so they would have to be held until the morning.

The Trial (4:5–12)

The following day the Sanhedrin, Israel's Supreme Court, convened in judgment of the prisoners. This is the first of four trials before this judicial body recorded in Acts. In this instance, it was only Peter and John who were on trial, but soon the entire group of the Twelve will be brought before the Sanhedrin (Acts 5:27), followed by Stephen (Acts 6:12) and Paul (Acts 22:30).

The Sanhedrin (4:5). According to the Mishnah,[7] the Sanhedrin was a judicial council composed of seventy-one of the wisest and best educated men in Israel. The Greek word, *sunedrion,* simply means council. The Sanhedrin functioned as both a "Supreme Court" and a legislature; subject, of course, to the pleasure of the Herodian kings and, ultimately, to Rome. Its power to govern fluctuated depending upon which Herodian king or which procurator held political office at any given time.

As best as can be established historically, the origin of this council dates to the return of the exiles from Babylon, although the rabbinic literature posits its origin in the seventy elders who assisted Moses (Num. 11:16–24).[8]

In the first century BC, under Roman occupation, the judicial authority and legal powers of the Sanhedrin were greatly expanded, and they were entrusted with basic functions of government for the nation, including the judging of criminal cases, as in Acts 4–5. The Sanhedrin's authority was limited in but one area, that of capital punishment, to which they had to defer to the Roman procurator's authority. The one exception to this limitation was if someone was guilty of defiling the Temple; for example, if a Gentile transgressed the Temple barrier that separated the Court of the Gentiles from the Court of the Women.

Membership incorporated an assortment of the most prominent members of the parties of the Sadducees, including the high priest, who served as president, the twenty-four chief priests (the "rulers" of Acts 4:5), as well as members of the priestly aristocracy. Additionally, membership included the leading Pharisees, (the "elders" of Acts 4:5).

The scribes, listed in Acts 4:5, were the legal experts and guardians of the sacred oral traditions (Matt. 7:29; Mark 1:22). This group was composed of members of both the Sadducean and Pharisaic parties. The gospels depict the scribes as some of the most aggressively antagonistic opponents of Jesus (Matt. 27:41; Mark 2:6, 16. 3:22; 11:18; 14:1; 15:31; Luke 6:7; 11:53). Their status and position of influence within the Jewish community had been severely jeopardized by Jesus' claim to an unprecedented and authoritative interpretation of the Torah. Jesus, therefore, had posed a direct challenge to scribal authority (Matt 5:21–48; Mark 1:22; 7:1–23). The scribes used what power they still possessed to terminate Jesus' ministry, utilizing "extreme prejudice."

The composition and nature of the Sanhedrin was never static. From all historical indications, from time to time, depending upon political circumstances, the power within the council would shift from the Sadducees to

Pharisees and back again as one party or the other jockeyed for a majority. In Acts 23:6–9, we will see how Paul, in his youth a veteran observer of the Sanhedrin's inner workings, leverages this two-party composition to his advantage.

On this particular occasion, which had more of the character of an inquiry than a trial per se, it is possible but unlikely that the entire seventy-one member court convened, although there were at least twenty-three judges in attendance since that was the necessary number for a quorum. Trials were conducted in a semicircle so that the judges could see one another. As rabbinic and legal students were regularly invited to attend the Sanhedrin's proceedings, it is possible that one particular student, Saul of Tarsus, was in attendance for these proceedings.

While Saul's presence is a matter of speculation, Luke does specify that in attendance at this trial were many prominent Saducean priests, including the two most powerful elements, the high priest, Caiaphas, and his father-in-law, Annas.

The High Priest (4:6–7). As the president of the Sanhedrin and the leading religious figure, the high priest was the most powerful man in Israel next to the king and the Roman procurator. In the Hebrew Scripture, the high priest inherited his critical position, and the appointment was for a lifetime. In the first century, however, the high priest was appointed by Rome. Serving at the pleasure of Rome, the high priest's function had become more political than theological. Not only did he serve as intermediary between Israel and God, he also was to represent Rome's interests toward Israel.

To ensure political survival, the high priest had to become a wily politician. Under Roman rule, the position had become a revolving door. high priests were frequently appointed and routinely demoted according to the whims and moods of the procurators. Josephus records twenty-eight appointments in the century between 37 BC and AD 70.[9]

Josephus Caiaphas was the appointed high priest from AD 18–36, and was therefore in office throughout both Jesus' ministry (Luke 3:2) and the events of Acts 1:1—9:2. His ability to remain in that office indicates his exceptional political skills and diplomatic ability in managing his dual constituencies of Israel and Rome.

Caiaphas was the son-in-law of the former high priest, Annas. Annas officially served as high priest from 6 BC–AD 15. Yet Annas held power for far longer than his official twenty-one year tenure. Over the five decades that followed his being deposed from office, five of Annas' sons, one grandson, and his son-law, Caiaphas, each served a term of various lengths as high priest. During the Roman occupation, Annas' family was a veritable high priestly dynasty. This aristocratic family was by far the most powerful and influential in Israel throughout the first century.

The Annas Dynasty of High Priests	
Annas (Acts 4:6)	6 BC–AD 15
Eleazar (son of Annas)	AD 16–17
Josephus Caiaphas (son-in-law of Annas, Acts 4:16)	AD 18–36
Jonathan (son of Annas, Acts 4:16)	AD 36–37
Theophilus (son of Annas)	AD 37–41
Matthias (son of Annas)	AD 42
Ananias (not part of dynasty, but in office Acts 23:2; 24:1)	AD 47–59
Ishmael (not part of dynasty, but in office, Acts 25:2)	AD 59–61
Annas (son of Annas)	AD 62
Matthias (son of Theophilus, grandson of Annas)	AD 65–66

With the continual reinstallation of family members, Annas himself never truly ceded the reins of high priestly authority. For decades, he retained power and remained the recognized high priest in the Jewish community. With such frequent leadership turnover, Annas' presence provided valuable stability and continuity.

Luke astutely recognized that although Caiaphas was high priest, it was his father-in-law, Annas, who wielded the true power behind the priestly robes. He even reported John the Baptist's ministry as originating during the high priesthood of both Annas and Caiaphas (Luke 3:2). Later, Luke specifies Annas' central role in Jesus' ersatz trial (John 18:13; 24).

Annas has the dubious distinction of being the entrepreneur responsible for expanding commercial activities within the Temple. Providing the ancient equivalent of "one stop shopping," Annas, and his familial successors in office, intensified the scope and variety of financial transactions within the outermost Temple Court, the "Court of the Gentiles." This consequently enriched the Temple treasury as well as the personal coffers of the chief priests. The Pharisees infamously called this "the bazaar of the sons of Annas."

Although displeased by this invasion of profiteering into the Temple, the Pharisees allowed it to continue. Jesus, however, exhibited no patience with this dishonorable activity and overthrew this bazaar when he cleansed the Temple. This dramatic action is of such strategic importance in Jesus' ministry that it is reported by all four gospel writers (Matt. 21:12–13; Mark 11:15–17; Luke 19:45–46; John 2:14–17).

Speaking Truth to Power (4:8–12). At this, Peter, filled with the Holy Spirit, accepted the opportunity to be a witness for Jesus in front of the entirety of Israel's leadership. Shaking off worry and putting on valor, sustained by Jesus' promise that when brought before the Jewish authorities the Holy Spirit would prompt a spontaneous defense (Luke 12:11–12), Peter began to preach.

He immediately pressed the offensive. Since he has been brought before the Sanhedrin to determine by whose authority a miracle had been performed, He would address their concern. Since the Sanhedrin demanded a name, then they were going to get one.

Peter, standing in the midst of the most powerful men in Israel, announced that the authority behind the healing was none other than Jesus of Nazareth, the Messiah. Peter reminded the Sanhedrin that this particular name should sound familiar to them. It should "ring a bell," for only recently, it was this same assembly who handed Him over to the Romans for crucifixion.

Peter, who only recently had denied Jesus, preached the most daring speech of his life before the assembled leadership of Israel. In an instant, Peter had put the entire Sanhedrin on trial, accusing them of murdering their Messiah. Peter drew a contrast between the purposes of the Sanhedrin and that of God. This murderous council had done their worst to Jesus, having Him executed. However, God had other plans, raising Jesus from the dead. They had rejected Him, yet God had exalted Him. The resurrection had proven that behind the authority of Jesus was the power of God.

Peter then advanced to his closing argument, drawing support from a passage of Scripture that would have been extremely familiar to his Jewish audience. He identified Jesus as "the stone" which, although rejected by the builders, nonetheless becomes the chief cornerstone (Ps. 118:22). It would have been obvious to the Sanhedrin that Peter was associating them with the foolish builders. Jesus quoted this passage as well, with reference to Himself (Luke 20:17).

Psalm 118 was part of a collection called the "Psalms of Hallel," which consisted of Psalms 113–118. "Hallel" is the Hebrew word for praise, and this collection of psalms was sung on every Jewish holy day, especially the three major pilgrim festivals of Passover, Pentecost and Tabernacles. Needless to say, this psalm was embedded in the memory of every Jewish family. In addition to the "rejected stone" passage, Psalm 118 also is the textual source of the crowd's shouts of "hosanna" and "blessed is he who comes in the Name of the Lord" accompanying Jesus' Triumphal Entry (Mark 11:9; John 12:13).

Peter's impromptu case against the Sanhedrin's for rejecting the Messiah now drew to a close. In no uncertain terms, Peter argued that they had consistently set themselves against God. The most formidable and learned body in Israel had opposed God and rejected His Messiah. That was particularly bad news for them because, in the exact words of Peter, "there is salvation in no one else; for there is no other name under heaven that has been given among men by which we must be saved" (Acts 4:12).

This declaration teaches in indisputable terms that Jesus is God's exclusive means of salvation, or deliverance. Along with Jesus' own statement referencing His being the way, truth and life and no one coming to God except through Him (John 14:6), this is without question the most audacious statement of the exclusivity of Jesus imaginable. Jesus is not one way, or a way to God; He is the only way. No one, no Jew, no matter how observant, can be saved apart from Jesus, without exception. Consider that Peter was addressing the most "orthodox," stringently observant Jews of his day; the most punctilious, devout, and educated adherents to the Torah of their generation!

Those ecumenists of our age who, in the name of tolerance and open-mindedness, believe that there are many pathways to God, patently demonstrate their acute ignorance of Peter's declaration. Theological pronouncements simply do not get narrower or more restricted than Peter's does in this passage. Furthermore, ecumenists demonstrate not only ignorance but also contempt for the record of Acts and the gospels. One is hard pressed to explain the compulsion of the apostles to witness to their Jewish brethren if it was an unnecessary exercise. Their continued efforts, which repeatedly resulted in rejection, imprisonment, torture and finally execution, become an exercise in base masochism if they had not been convinced of the exclusivity of Jesus.

Indeed, the apostolic witness throughout the narrative of the book of Acts is placed squarely in opposition to every major religious alternative of the first century. Whether it was idolatry, sorcery, Greek philosophy, the pantheon of Greco-Roman gods and goddesses, or Judaism itself, each is weighed in the balance against the gospel and found wanting.

Nor can one explain the necessity of Jesus' willing sacrifice if his death were to serve as just another option in the religious smorgasbord of pathways to God. Jesus prayed three times to "let this cup pass" from him, if only it were possible (Matt. 26:39). Jesus would have been an unhinged messiah, indeed, if He willingly went to His death believing that Abraham, Moses, Buddha, Mohammed, Krishna, etc., were all acceptable spiritual alternatives. Jesus did not die just to provide one more alternative option on God's spiritual buffet. Either he is the only way to God's presence, or He is no way at all. The fact of salvation through Jesus necessarily excludes the possibility of salvation by any other means.

Response to Peter's Witness (4:13–22)

Although Luke did not report his words, he indicates that John also addressed the court. The Sanhedrin reacted in amazement at the apostles' confident witness. It was not every day that Israel's Supreme Court was accused of murder and of standing in opposition to God!

Luke specifies that what really perturbed the Sanhedrin was being insolently addressed by untrained, unpolished, Galilean-accented provincials. It was not that Peter and John were illiterate, for most Jewish men received a basic education through lifelong involvement in community synagogues. The basis for their exasperation was that the apostles were laymen, not "yeshiva boys," completely devoid of recognized theological training. They should have known better than to presumptuously preach their sectarian drivel to the "teachers of Israel." The Sanhedrin had also made the same churlish allegations against Jesus during His ministry (John 7:15). As was the case with the apostles, the Sanhedrin's' disdain for Jesus' lack of formal rabbinic training overcame their ability to appreciate His authoritative theological interpretations.

The members of the Sanhedrin were speechless, winded, and finding themselves in a real predicament. The healing of the man who stood before them, "exhibit A," was the undeniable handiwork of God and a publicly witnessed fact which had effectively made heroes of both Peter and John in the eyes of the Jewish people. Still, the court obstinately refused to give credence to this obvious miracle or the Source claimed as its origin. The prisoners were sent out of the chamber so that the court could privately strategize their response.

One must assume that in the absence of the apostles and the healed man, the only way Luke was privy to the discussion at this closed meeting was through one of those men present in the chambers at the time. There are three obvious candidates who might have been present at this trial. Both Nicodemus, *the* teacher of Israel (John 3:1) and Joseph of Arimathea (Luke 23:50) were members of the Sanhedrin as well as secret believers in Jesus. Additionally, as previously noted, Saul of Tarsus may have been a student observer in the gallery (Acts 8:1).

In light of the tremendous growth of the church that resulted from the miracle and Peter's sermon, the council resolved to cut the movement off at the knees, to nip it in the bud. When the prisoners were returned to the chamber of judgment, they were commanded to completely desist from both teaching about or speaking of Jesus. They threatened Peter and John, as well as the healed man, to keep their mouths shut or face punitive measures. The court was determined to suppress the whole matter and hoped that this was the last that would be heard from these Jesus fanatics.

There was no discussion by the court of the merits of Peter's testimony. Whether or not he had spoken truthfully was apparently not open to debate. The judges even refused to speak the name of Jesus, using the euphemism, "this name." For almost two thousand years, the phrase "this name" and "this man," have been commonly used by Jews who cannot bring themselves to utter Jesus' name.

Peter and John did not hesitate to inform the Sanhedrin that this ruling was one by which they could not abide. If the Sanhedrin were previously amazed by the confidence of the apostles, they had not seen anything yet! Peter and John informed the council that, in keeping with the court's established pattern, the Sanhedrin had again ruled in opposition to God. Furthermore, by imposing this ruling, they had placed the apostles in the position of having to choose to obey either them or God. Peter threw the ball back into the court's court by asking the spiritual judges of Israel, learned and wise men all, to state their position on "whether it is right in the sight of God to give heed to you rather than to God (Acts 4:19).

The apostles' response had reduced the Sanhedrin to toothless threats, at least for the moment. As there was no finding of wrongdoing, the Sanhedrin had no legal basis for punishing them. Furthermore, the account of the previous day's miracle by now had spread throughout the entire city, sparking massive worship. The Jewish leadership found itself opposed to God; while the common people were worshipping Him for His miracle, the Sanhedrin were trying to suppress knowledge of the miracle's source.

Prayer of Apostles and God's Response (4:23–31)

Upon their release, Peter and John ran to tell the other apostles and the church what had happened. This report of opposition from such "high places" motivated all of the apostles to pray together. Their prayer begins with a citation of Psalm 146:6, an affirmation that God is the powerful creator of all and, therefore, is the supreme authority (the Greek *despotēs*, from which we derive "despot"). He is the ultimate "friend in high places."

Of additional theological interest is that Acts 4:25 references the dual authorship of Scripture, noting that King David wrote by means of the Holy Spirit. An additional point of interest is the allusion within the prayer to Jesus as Isaiah's "Servant of the Lord" (Is. 53), emphasizing the prophetic aspect of His suffering and death.

Their prayer concludes with a request for God to regard their perilous situation, give them continued confidence to be witnesses of the Messiah, and authenticate their witness with further miracles.

God confirmed his receipt of their prayer requests by shaking the ground underneath them as He did at Mount Sinai when He gave the Torah to Moses (Exodus 19:18). Immediately, the apostles were freshly infused with the Holy Spirit empowering further bold witness.

Conclusion

The critical encounter in this chapter between the leadership of the church and that of Israel sets in motion a chain of events, which, over the next few chapters, will eventually propel the apostolic witness into the midst of hostile territory. Yet first the church must experience even greater opposition from the enemies of their gospel witness. The Sadducees are not yet through with the apostles and will again rear their petulant heads in the next chapter to antagonize the church and oppose the work of God. We have as yet only witnessed the initial stage of their persecution.

Study Questions:

1. List five facts about priests and Levites.
2. Who were the Sadducees and what were their beliefs?
3. What was the purpose and composition of the Sanhedrin?
4. Describe the state of the high priesthood in the first century.
5. Why were the apostles arrested and brought to trial?
6. What were the "psalms of Hallel?"
7. Defend why Jesus is God's exclusive means of salvation.

CHAPTER 5

Opposition from Within and Without
Acts 4:32–5:42

Preview:

In this section, for the first time, Luke presents opposition to the church from within, the sin of Ananias and Sapphira. Luke's readers will learn through this episode that the church has never been perfect, even from its earliest days. God is not mocked (Gal. 6:7), and His judgment of sin always "begins in the household of God" (1 Peter 4:17). Once the apostles successfully deal with the internal threat, renewed external opposition breaks out. The Sadducees, on the lookout for an opportunity to renew their persecution of the fledgling church, seize their chance. It is only through the intervention of a Pharisee, Gamaliel, that the apostles survive.

Glowing Update on the Church (4:32–37)

Within the first year following the crucifixion, there was a multitude of believers within the church. Although Luke never provides a cumulative total, it is possible to estimate the approximate size of the church by adding the number of new believers noted in the periodic summaries supplied to this point throughout the narrative.

The story of Acts begins with the hard minimum of five hundred believers to whom Jesus had appeared at one time (1 Cor. 15:6). Whether this appearance occurred in Jerusalem or Galilee, this minimum number does not necessarily include the believing multitudes scattered throughout Israel and

Samaria, as recorded by the gospels (John 4:39–41; 7:31; 8:30; 10:42; 11:45; 12:11, 42).

To this original five hundred, Luke adds three thousand (Acts 2:41) and another five thousand men (Acts 4:4), making for a minimum of eighty-five hundred believers. With the addition of the families of the five thousand men of Acts 4:4, an estimate can be made of twenty-three thousand five hundred believers (or more). Even if two-thirds of the three thousand Pentecost believers are subtracted on the assumption that they were pilgrims and subsequently returned to their home nations, it can be confidently assumed that there were in Israel by this point over twenty-one thousand followers of Christ. No wonder it took the apostles years to venture forth from their Jerusalem home base. Leading a burgeoning movement of that size entailed intensive ministry!

To provide a sense of comparative scale, in the first century, according to Josephus, only an estimated six thousand men officially belonged to the Pharisees.[1] The Sadducees, being far less popular, were an even smaller party. Already the new messianic movement had vastly dwarfed both opposition parties, a fact that would not sit well with either faction for long.

Luke begins this section with an update on the church similar to the one he gave in Acts 2:42–47. The members are unified and generous to one another. The apostles' prayer for boldness at the conclusion of the last section had been manifestly answered.

God provided for the Jerusalem church's needs through voluntary gifts, which from time to time were brought to the apostles. They, in turn, distributed aid to those members in need. At a later point, this taxing benevolence ministry will need to be delegated to alternate leadership (Acts 6:1–6).

Barnabas. Luke chose this point in the narrative to introduce a Jewish believer, a Levite named Joseph, who will figure prominently later in the narrative. He was nicknamed "Barnabas," Aramaic for "son of exhortation" or more likely, "son of encouragement," by the apostles, signifying their impression of him. In Jewish culture, the term "son" was often used to indicate character modeled or essential nature. "Son" functioned in a way equivalent to our contemporary slang usage of the title, "mister." For example, today an entertainer may be referred to as "Mr. Excitement!" or "Mr. Las Vegas!" or we may use the phrase, "no more Mr. Nice Guy," all of which are indicative of character or nature. Perhaps if Barnabas lived today he might be known as "Mr. Encouragement."

Over the course of his narrative, Luke recorded quite a bit about Joseph Barnabas, mentioning him twenty-four times. Barnabas also rates five mentions in Paul's epistles (1 Cor. 9:6, Gal. 2:1, 9, 13, Col. 4:10). Although now living in Jerusalem, he was a Diaspora Jew, originally from the island of

Cyprus. According to an ancient church tradition recorded by Eusebius (who cited the earlier Clement of Alexandria), Barnabas was one of the seventy disciples sent out by Jesus (Luke 10). He is called an apostle by Luke (Acts 14:14), indicating that, like all within this secondary category of apostle, he had been a personal eyewitness of the resurrected Messiah.

Additional biographical information includes his being the cousin of John Mark and his mother, Mary (Col. 4:10). He is also described as a "good man," habitually controlled by the Spirit (Acts 11:24). When the going gets tough during the persecution of Acts 8, Barnabas does not flee Jerusalem, as did many other Hellenistic Jewish believers. He also had the trust of the Twelve, who sent him as their representative to investigate Gentile salvation in the church at Antioch (Acts 11:19–24). He became Paul's friend and advocate (Acts 9:27), seeking Paul out in Tarsus to invite him to share Barnabas' pastoral responsibilities in Antioch (Acts 11:25–26). Their partnership continued through a missionary journey to the Gentiles (Acts 13–14) but dissolved (amicably, it is assumed) over a dispute concerning John Mark (Acts 15:36–39).

Luke introduced Barnabas here to highlight his model behavior in contrast to the behavior exhibited immediately following in the story of Ananias. Barnabas is reported to have sold a large tract of land and given all of the proceeds to the apostles for distribution to the needy. Luke did not specify whether the field Barnabas sold was in Jerusalem or his native Cyprus. Interestingly, according to the Torah, priests and Levites were forbidden to own land (Num. 18:20–23, Deut. 10:9). Apparently, following Israel's return from exile, for some reason this regulation ceased to be applied, as indicated by the extreme wealth and fabulous Jerusalem mansions of many of the Sadducees,[2] most of whom, like Barnabas, were from the tribe of Levi.

Sin in the Church Camp (5:1–11)

As noted above, Barnabas' behavior stands in sharp contrast to that of a married couple Luke introduces, Ananias and Sapphira. This couple also sold land and voluntarily brought the proceeds to the apostles, in a parallel description to that of Barnabas' gift. Luke even uses his exact same phrase, "laying it at the apostles' feet." There was one critical difference, however. Unlike Barnabas, this couple grossly misrepresented their gift, holding back a portion of the proceeds for themselves.

As with the infamous sin of Achan, who had also kept back wealth for himself and consequently was sentenced to death (Josh. 7:1–26), the sin of Ananias and Sapphira would receive a penalty of equal severity. Luke ensured that his readers would make the connection with Achan by using the same verb found in the Septuagint account, *nosphizō*, "to misappropriate for oneself." This is the first recorded internal threat the church faced and, as such, would stand as an example that no sin is ever truly concealed from the eyes of God. In the words of the Torah, "be sure your sin will find you out" (Num. 32:23).

As Ananias brought his offering to the apostles, Peter supernaturally perceived his deception and challenged him. Peter told him that in lying to the church, he had actually lied to the Holy Spirit. He accused him of having been controlled not merely by his "sin nature" but by the angelic arch adversary, Satan himself! Peter's point was that Ananias had been "Satanized" from within, that Satan had "filled" Ananias' heart and taken control of his actions. This stands in strong contrast to the ideal of believers being filled with the Spirit (Eph. 5:18).

Peter pointed out the awful irony that this had been an unnecessary sin. No one had compelled Ananias to sell his land, and after selling the land, He was under no obligation to donate even one drachma to the church, much less the entirety of the proceeds. This grievous violation could have been completely avoided. While Satan may have exercised influence, Ananias himself was still responsible for this sin. Ananias had birthed this sin within his heart, then nurtured it and brought it to fruition.

An important feature of the story is the progression within Peter's accusation that Ananias, while lying to the apostles, had actually lied to the Holy Spirit. Furthermore, having lied to the Holy Spirit, he had actually been lying to God Himself. This passage is clear in its identification of the Holy Spirit with God. Lying to the Holy Spirit is lying to God. One cannot lie to an impersonal force, but only to a "person."

The Holy Spirit Is a Person

Reference	Activity
Acts 5:3	The Spirit is lied to
Acts 5:9	The Spirit is tested
Acts 5:32	The Spirit bears witness
Acts 7:51	The Spirit is resisted
Acts 8:29; 10:19; 13:2	The Spirit gives orders
Acts 16:7	The Spirit refuses permission
Acts 28:25	The Spirit speaks

In the midst of Peter's accusation, Ananias, whose name means "God has given," had his life "taken away" by God and immediately expired. He literally dropped dead. Luke describes this using the word *ekpsuchō*, the common medical term for death. As Arnold Fruchtenbaum remarks, at that movement, Ananias was "souled-out."[3]

This transaction had not occurred in Peter's private "pastoral study," but publicly, during a house church meeting. The young men of the congregation wrapped Ananias in a burial cloth and immediately began preparing his body for burial. The corpse could not be left overnight within the city of Jerusalem but had to be buried before sundown according to Jewish law, based on Deut. 21:23.

Three hours later, Ananias' wife, Sapphira, walked into the meeting, blissfully unaware of the unfortunate event that had transpired. Peter gives her an opportunity to come clean and tell him the truth. Withholding any information of her husband's fate, Peter allowed Sapphira to speak for herself, absent the potentially corrupting influence of her husband. He was not trying to entrap her but rather give her an opportunity to be honest with him.

However, she did not avail herself of this gracious opportunity. Sapphira, whose name means "beautiful," did not acquit herself "beautifully" before the apostles and her church family. Peter suddenly and dramatically pronounced that, for the past three hours, Sapphira had unknowingly been a widow. However, she would not be so for long. It was obvious to all present that she was an equal part of the conspiracy with her husband and shared full responsibility with him for having "tested" the Holy Spirit, i.e., having challenged His authority. This accusation is yet further confirmation that the Holy Spirit is no mere impersonal force.

In the same manner as had her husband, Sapphira fell down dead at Peter's feet. The young men, who had just returned from burying Ananias, now performed a second funeral, taking her corpse out to bury her with her husband. To quote Fruchtenbaum once again, Ananias and Sapphira were truly "slain by the Spirit."[4]

In the Torah, the death penalty was intended as a deterrent to restrain future acts of evil (Deut. 21:21). In this instance, the deterrent seems to have been quite effective. Peter had used his apostolic authority "to bind and to loose," to legislatively forbid and permit certain activities (Matt. 16:19; John 20:23). As in the episode with Achan, sin was "purged" from the camp. The result of this regrettable episode was that the entire church and the surrounding Jewish community took note of God's judgment and felt justifiable fear. Apostolic authority was affirmed and the faith community's sanctity safeguarded.

Of interest is that Acts 5:11 contains the first technical use of the word *ekklēsia* as a term for the church. This word simply means "assembly," and is commonly used in the Septuagint as a translation of the Hebrew *qahal*. From this point in the New Testament, *ekklēsia* will be the preferred term to describe the assembly of believers in Christ.

Witness of the Apostles with Power (5:12–16)

Another result of the purging of sin from the church seems to have been an increase in miracles. These "signs and wonders" were likely occurring during the regular public assemblies of the church community in the Temple at Solomon's Portico. Luke once again specifies that only the apostles were performing these signs and wonders, thus emphasizing God's authentication of their authority.

Among the apostles, Peter's healing ability is singled out as particularly unusual. Even his shadow had healing ability! Luke's report indicates that whether the problem was medical or demonic, all were healed, comprehensively and consistently. No one came away from the apostles disappointed.

What had happened to Ananias and Sapphira had given the Jewish community "the creeps," and many were keeping their distance and thinking twice before associating themselves with the church. Nevertheless, the general population thought highly of the church, and although they were hesitant to join, the church still experienced continual growth, expanding beyond the city borders of Jerusalem into the surrounding communities of Judea.

Opposition to the Witness of the Apostles (5:17–26)

The progress of the church movement was not proceeding unnoticed, however. The high priest (probably Annas is still meant, but possibly Caiaphas) and the Sadducees once again initiate persecution of the church leadership. In contrast with the apostles, who are "filled" with the Spirit, Annas and his minions were controlled or "filled" by jealousy. The Sadducees' obsession with maintaining control of Israel's religious proclivities was apparently unquenchable. This time, all of the apostles are arrested and imprisoned, not within the Temple, as Peter and John had been, but in a public jail.

However, during the evening, an angel released the apostles from prison, charging them to go back to the Temple the next morning and preach. Daybreak found the apostles once again at their posts at Solomon's Portico in the Temple. Simultaneously, the convening Sanhedrin sent to the prison to summon the apostles to appear before them.

An almost comic situation ensued, as Luke contrasts the apostles' active preaching with the passivity of the Great Sanhedrin sitting and waiting expectantly for prisoners who have somehow vacated their jail cells. Officers report to the court that although the prison doors were locked, they could find no one inside. This indicates that the rescuing angel was polite enough to go back and relock the doors following the apostolic prison break.

To say the least, this news proved "greatly perplexing" to the captain of the Temple guard and the chief priests. As a writer, Luke occasionally exhibits a flair for understatement. Before the Sanhedrin had a chance to wonder what was next, they learned that that the apostles had been located back in the very same area where they had been arrested the previous day!

By this time, the apostles had drawn quite a crowd. The Jewish people assembling at the Temple in preparation for mandatory 9:00 AM prayers would have been surprised to again see the apostles out and mobile as free men. They were even more surprised to learn how that freedom was regained, as the apostles relayed the previous evening's supernatural adventure.

At this point, the captain of the Temple guard and his officers entered Solomon's Portico. Afraid of provoking a riot in the Temple, one in which they would have likely served as the focal point of the violence, they politely, genteelly, and discretely, interrupted the reunion and rearrested the apostles. It is interesting to note that when the apostles are grilled by the Sanhedrin in the subsequent passage, no mention is made or interest shown as to how the apostles managed to pull off such a "Houdini." Apparently, they were afraid of the answer they might have received.

The Trial (5:27–42)

Peter's Witness (5:27–32)

Once again, Peter and John, this time in the company of their apostolic comrades, stand in the midst of the Sanhedrin's semicircle of judgment. The trial begins with an interrogation by the high priest, who reminded them of the Sanhedrin's' strict orders (*paraggelia parēggeilamen*, "a command we commanded"), to desist their public preaching of Jesus (Acts 4:17–18). Annas cannot even bring himself to articulate the name of Jesus, again employing the euphemisms, "this name" and "this man." Not only had the Sanhedrin's directive been disobeyed and their threats ignored, but the forbidden Jesus was now a topic of conversation throughout the entire city of Jerusalem and its suburbs.

Furthermore, the court seems surprised and perturbed that the apostles were squarely laying the responsibility of the Messiah's death upon the Jewish leadership. They finally seem to understand that the apostles had taken with gravity the Jewish leadership's own words, "His blood be upon us and our children" (Matt. 27:25)

Peter, as usual the apostolic spokesman, made no attempt to deny Annas' charge. In fact, he repeats what he had previously told them, that being obedient to God necessarily meant that they must disobey the Sanhedrin's ungodly directive. The apostles had no intention on playing for the losing team on this issue. They had made a "ruling" of their own, that the Sanhedrin stood in opposition to God. There really was no choice but to disobey the leadership and continue their witness of Jesus.

Furthermore, Peter affirmed Annas' concern of being accused of the responsibility for Jesus' death. In fact, Peter aggressively spelled out the indictment, saying, "Jesus, whom you violently murdered," in the most heinous fashion, by crucifixion. The specific word for cross, *stauros*, is never used in Acts, studiously avoided by both Peter (Acts 2:23; 5:30; 10:39) and Paul (Acts 13:29). To hang from a tree was the most cursed way to die in Jewish law (Deut. 21:22–23; Gal. 3:13). In this instance, Peter substituted a euphemism, the word *xulon*, meaning, "tree, wood, or stake."

Although the Jewish leadership had murdered Jesus, God had glorified him through His resurrection and ascension, and exalted Jesus by seating Him at God's right hand. As a result of this exaltation, Jesus is the Prince (see Acts 3:15) and Savior, granting repentance to Israel and remission of their sins.

Peter concluded his statement with confirmation that he and his companions were eyewitnesses of Jesus' resurrection and ascension. In the spirit of the Torah's prescription of establishing a matter by the mouths of two or three witnesses (Deut. 19:15), Peter presented not only himself and his fellow apostles as witnesses, but also the Holy Spirit Himself. Jesus had pledged that one of the Holy Spirit's ministries would be bearing witness (John 15:26). Furthermore, believers in Jesus were in possession of the Holy Spirit as a result of their obedience to God in accepting the Messiah.

Once again, in this chapter, the Holy Spirit's personality is highlighted. An impersonal "force" cannot serve as a witness.

Peter's final claim would have been disconcerting to the Sanhedrin. In stark contrast to the church, the Sanhedrin did not possess the Holy Spirit, because in rejecting their Messiah, they had been disobedient to God.

According to Jewish oral tradition, the presence of the Shekinah glory of God was absent from the second Temple. The Holy Spirit, the *Ruach Hakodesh*, had departed from Israel with the last of the prophets, Malachi. The *Ruach Hakodesh* would eventually return, however, when Messiah appeared. Even so, rabbinic literature taught that theoretically, on rare occasions, the Holy Spirit would still rest upon the most pious, exceptionally holy of individuals.[5]

A Rabbi's Intervention (5:33–39)

Needless to say, Peter's incredibly bold claim enraged his audience. Luke describes them as being *dieprionto,* "sawn asunder," beside themselves with fury. Although Peter had delivered essentially the same message he preached at Pentecost, the Jewish leadership had not responded with the same repentant attitude as the common people. Rather, the leadership responded with the basest of hostility and rage, calling for the apostles' immediate execution.

The escalating rage of the mob was defused by the intervention of the great rabbi, Gamaliel. He sent the accused outside the chamber, out of sight, to enable the Sanhedrin to avoid a hotheaded decision and arrive at a rational one. There was no legal basis to execute the apostles. The death penalty could not be invoked over the simple disobedience of one edict of the court.

Gamaliel. Gamaliel, whose name means, "God is also for me," was the most prominent and respected member of the Pharisees. He was the foremost rabbi of his generation and part of an elite group of Torah scholars whom Luke refers to as *nomodidaskalos,* "teachers of the law" (Luke 5:17; Acts 5:34). Gamaliel was a student of famous rabbi, Hillel, and was the leader of the "school of Hillel," which promulgated the great rabbi's teachings. One of Gamaliel's most infamous students was Saul of Tarsus (Acts 22:3).

His memory is venerated in the Mishnah. He was the first of only seven rabbis throughout Jewish history who received the honorific title, *rabban,* which means "our teacher," (as opposed to rabbi, "my teacher.") As the Mishnah records, "When Rabban Gamaliel the Elder died, the glory of the Torah came to an end, and cleanness and separateness perished."[6]

Following this brief study of the most celebrated Pharisee, it is appropriate to define and highlight the Pharisaic sect as a whole.

Pharisees. The Pharisees were the most culturally conservative of the major Jewish religious parties. The Hebrew term, *parashim* means, "separated ones," and so, the Pharisees can be characterized as a dedicated group of Jews who had taken a passionate, proactive stance against the propagation of Greek culture, *Hellenism,* and other corrupting aspects of the surrounding culture.

Concerning specific doctrines, Jesus and the apostles were theologically closer to the Pharisees than they were to the rival parties of Sadducees, Essenes and Zealots. The Pharisees believed in the resurrection of the dead, the immortality of the soul, eternal reward and eternal punishment, and angelic and demonic activity. They also carefully held in balance divine sovereignty and human responsibility.[7] They also affirmed that the entirety of Hebrew Scripture (the Law, the Prophets and the Writings) was divine revelation.

In fact, the Pharisees were more accurately characterized by their commitment to the Mosaic legislation, Torah, and not by the specific doctrinal positions that they held. Their zeal to maintain a purity of practice in regard to the Mosaic Law led them to develop a complex and comprehensive legal system based on the Torah and its contemporary application to every aspect of life, however minute. This system of practices and traditions, called in the Mishnah, "a fence around the Torah,"[8] was an oral law which regulated every facet of their lives and to which they rigorously adhered.

During the three decades of Israel's history covered by the Acts narrative, Pharisaic Judaism was the de facto Judaism of the common people. It was not so much that the ranks of Pharisaic membership were swollen beyond measure, for, to the contrary, Josephus estimates no more than six thousand actual, "card-carrying" devotees.[9] Rather, Israel's commonly accepted religious norms were, to an enormous extent, dictated by the Pharisees. The Pharisees were so well respected, and their ideology and piety had so captured the religious sensitivities of the people that the Pharisees effectively defined what the commonly accepted standards were for Judaism. That most Jews could never live up to those high and elusive standards, however, is why Pharisaic membership remained so exclusive.

The Pharisees are alternatively presented in the gospels as Jesus' allies and archenemies. On the one hand, the Pharisees invited Jesus to be their guest at dinner parties (Luke 7:36; 11:37; 14:1) and they warned him of a plot against his life (Luke 13:31). On the other hand, Jesus accused them of hypocrisy (Luke 11:37–52) and the Pharisees, in turn, ardently opposed Jesus and conspired against him (Matt. 12:14; Mark 3:6; John 11:57). In the first few chapters of the book of Acts, the Pharisees are portrayed as taking a neutral stance on the church, as epitomized in this chapter by the position of their leader, Gamaliel. Beginning in chapter eight, following shortly after this incident, one of Gamaliel's brightest pupils, Saul of Tarsus, will categorically reject his rabbi's sage and cautious counsel.

Gamaliel advises the Sanhedrin not to act rashly. If the Jesus movement is not of God, it will die out, and conversely, if God is behind it, no one can fight against it. While this was good advice at the time, it is not universally true, as many movements and organizations that are arguably not of God have exhibited remarkable longevity.

Gamaliel lists two examples of political movements that temporarily burned brightly but eventually collapsed. He first notes the revolutionary movement of Theudas, a historical unknown,[10] and the tax revolt that erupted in AD 6, led by Judas of Galilee.[11] Josephus notes that the origin of this revolt was the obligation to pay taxes (apparently an evergreen topic). The struggle gradually evolved over the next several decades into the Zealot movement, which eventually provoked Israel's great revolt against Rome in AD 66.

Release and Rejoicing (5:40–42)

Josephus records that the Pharisees generally tended more toward mercy than severity in their judgments and subsequent punishments.[12] That Gamaliel's wise counsel won the day was a positive development for the disciples who otherwise might have fallen victim that day to mob justice.

Therefore, instead of executing the apostles, the Sanhedrin punished the apostles for disobedience by having them flogged. Most likely, each apostle received the infamous thirty-nine stripes. The Torah commanded disciplining the guilty with no more than forty stripes (Deut. 25:3). It was Jewish custom to administer one less stripe than the maximum (forty minus one), to avoid inadvertently exceeding the maximum allowable penalty, because of the possibility of losing count.

The Mishnah records in some detail the specific procedures that were set in place for the flogging of criminals. First, an estimate was made of the man (or woman's) physical capacity to withstand the punishment without expiring or being irreparably injured. If the guilty party's constitution seemed fragile, then the thirty-nine lashes were reduced, depending upon the mercy of the court. The victim then had both hands tied on either side of a pillar and his shirt torn off, baring his chest and back. He was then forcefully whipped thirty-nine times with a triple strap of cowhide.

If the court overestimated the amount of pain the victim could withstand, and the victim were to die while undergoing this torture, the flogger was completely exempt from liability of murder. If while undergoing the whipping, however, the victim happens to urinate or defecate, the punishment was mercifully cut short.[13] Josephus records that the Sadducees, who held power in the Sanhedrin, were particularly ruthless in the administration of punishment.[14]

Assuming that the apostles were all healthy, vigorous men at this point, they would have received thirteen lashes on the chest and twenty-six on the back that day. This was the first occasion, but not the last, that the apostles would have to physically suffer for Jesus. Incidentally, Paul notes that he had experienced this particular torture on five separate occasions (2 Cor. 11:24).

The Sanhedrin reaffirmed their order to cease witnessing of Jesus and released the apostles. However, as Luke's readers project what actual credence will be given to the Sanhedrin's order, the immediate future does not necessarily bode well for the apostles.

The apostles exhibit a counter-intuitive reaction to their beatings. Instead of licking their wounds and skulking home, tails between their legs, the apostles rejoiced. They wore their suffering on behalf of the name of Jesus as a badge of honor. Not surprisingly, they kept right on teaching and preaching that Jesus was the Messiah. This untoward encounter with the Sanhedrin did not slow them down at all. In fact, their zeal was renewed, and both publicly and privately, in the Temple courts and in people's homes, they continued their bold witness.

Conclusion

The encounter with the Sanhedrin provides an important example for believers of any age. The apostolic model was to live in obedience to municipal authority up to the point where that obedience would contradict a divine instruction. God's authority, by definition, trumps even the most exalted of legislative authorities.

Their arrest, imprisonment and punishment did not take the apostles by surprise. Jesus had predicted that the Jewish leadership would treat his apostles no differently than their fathers had treated the prophets of old.

> I am sending you prophets, wise men and scribes; some of them you will kill and crucify, and some of them you will scourge in your synagogues, and persecute from city to city, so that upon you may fall all the righteous blood shed on earth, from the blood of righteous Abel to the blood of Zechariah . . . Truly I say to you, all these things will come upon this generation. Jerusalem, Jerusalem, who kills the prophets and stones those who are sent to her (Matt 23:34–37a).

Jewish tradition viewed both the coming of Messiah and of the Holy Spirit as being dependent upon the rise of a sufficiently worthy generation. What has become clear thus far in the narrative is that within the same generation of Israel is a faithful Jewish remnant willing to accept their Messiah and receive the Holy Spirit, and a faithless majority who will cause God's wrath to fall upon the nation.

Study Questions:

1. Provide an estimate for the number of believers within one year of the crucifixion.
2. List five facts about Barnabas.
3. What was the sin of Ananias and Sapphira and why was it handled as it was?
4. Why were the apostles rearrested?
5. List the evidence in Acts 5 that the Holy Spirit is a person.
6. Who was Gamaliel?
7. Who were the Pharisees and what were their beliefs?

CHAPTER 6

The Witness of Stephen
Acts 6:1–8:4

Preview:

This section, occurring in the early months of AD 35, highlights the brief but extremely influential ministry of Stephen. We are also briefly introduced to Saul, a young rabbi whose life and ministry will eventually dominate the remainder of the Acts narrative. Acts 6–7 provides crucial historical information without which Luke's readers could not understand the author's transition midway through the narrative from a focus on Peter to a spotlight on Paul and from the land of Israel to the "ends of the earth." Stephen's abbreviated ministry serves as the connecting link between these two towering apostles and the scope of their commissions.

Commissioning of Deacons (6:1–7)

This section highlights the church's second internal problem. This difficulty, however, arose as a result of God's blessing. The church had continued to grow large enough that, by this point, almost two years after Pentecost, internal factions had begun to appear and coalesce. The Greek or *Hellenistic* Jewish believers from the Diaspora had begun to resent the native, Hebraic Jewish believers. Discontented "murmuring" and "secret whispering," *goggusmos*, against the Hebraic Jews began to spread throughout the Hellenistic Jewish community.

Hellenistic Jews. Hellenistic Jews were Jewish immigrants to Israel. These were ethnic Jews who, having lived outside of Israel for decades or even generations, had now returned to live in Jerusalem. The Hellenists were, to some extent, culturally distinct from native Judeans, for example, worshiping in separate Greek-speaking synagogues as opposed to synagogues that conducted their services in Hebrew. In addition, although the pervasive influence of the mainstream Greco-Roman culture would have been inescapable for either native or immigrant Jews, the lifestyles of the Jewish immigrants reflected an elevated level of Greek cultural absorption.

This assimilation included much more than which community primarily spoke Aramaic and which community primarily spoke Greek. To thrive within the Roman world, both groups would have had to demonstrate proficiency in the Greek language, although the Hellenists would be more fluent as Greek was their mother tongue. To whatever extent, the acculturation created a divergence in education, outlook and worldview, and generated for the Greek Jews heightened levels of artistic, theatric, athletic and philosophic interests. This was at the root of the notable distinction between the native and immigrant communities reflected in Luke's narrative.

There are a particularly large number of Hellenistic widows due to the custom of many Jews of the Diaspora of returning to Jerusalem later in life so as to be buried in the holy city. There was a Jewish belief that in the last days, when the resurrection occurred, the first to rise would be those buried in the soil of Jerusalem. Those bodies buried outside of Israel, would first have to burrow underground however many hundreds or thousands of miles back to Israel to enjoy the resurrection. Needless to say, this immigration pattern would have left an inordinate number of widows to attend to. (This is the origin of the custom, still practiced by Jews today, of being buried together with a packet of soil from Israel.)

The combined testimony of the Law and the Prophets is that widows and other needy parties should be cared for by the community of faith (Deut. 10:18; 14:29; 24:19; 26:12–13; 27:19; Is. 1:17, 23; Jer. 7:6; Mal. 3:5). The early church had faithfully continued this tradition of benevolence, as earlier indicated by Luke (Acts 2:44–45; 4:32–35). Even so, the reason for the Hellenists' complaints was the perception that favoritism was being shown to the Hebraic widows to the neglect of the Hellenistic widows. The Greek Jewish community felt overlooked.

The Twelve did not allow this resentment to fester. They immediately called an "all church" congregational meeting and unveiled their plan to delegate the administration of the church's benevolence ministry to seven men whom they would commission for the task. This would allow the apostles to concentrate on their primary responsibilities, prayer and teaching the word of God.

This episode is Luke's recounting of the origin of the office of deacon. Although technically the noun *diakonos*, "deacon," is not used in this passage, the verb form *diakoneō,* "to serve," does appear. As in Moses' day, the people were entrusted with selecting their own leadership (Deut. 1:13), under the guidelines of the apostles and subject to their ratification. Unlike at the selection of Matthias, which occurred prior to the outpouring of the Spirit, there was no casting of lots. The apostles relied on the internal prompting of the Holy Spirit to guide the selection. The qualifications for this task were few but notable: men, with good reputations, wisdom and temperaments controlled by the Holy Spirit (Acts 6:3).

The apostolic plan was well received, and seven men were chosen, all possessing Greek, not Hebrew names. This strongly indicates that they were all Hellenistic Jews, representatives of the affronted Greek community. These men could be trusted by all parties to be fair in carrying out their duties and to take equal care of every widow.

Stephen is listed first, given priority and a more detailed description due to the primary role he played in the Jerusalem church. Luke characterized Stephen as being "full of" or alternately, "controlled by" the Holy Spirit, wisdom, faith, grace and power. Although a deacon and not an apostle, he became the church's first martyr, the ultimate witness. His death resulted in the spread of the gospel as the church dispersed from Jerusalem.

Philip was listed second because of his importance in the narrative. An additional deacon of note is Nicolas from Antioch, who before following Jesus had become a proselyte, a Gentile convert to Judaism. The city of Antioch and Gentile proselytes will be of great importance later in the Acts narrative.

The apostles prayed and laid hands on the seven, thereby publicly transferring a measure of apostolic authority to the men. This will enable the seven to be recognized by the church community as apostolic representatives, or delegates. The laying on of hands was the ancient Jewish method of commissioning to an office. This ordination procedure dates back to Moses and Joshua (Num. 27:22–23) and continues in the ordination of contemporary rabbis.

Luke adds a new wrinkle to the second of his church progress reports strewn throughout the narrative (2:47; 6:7; 9:31; 12:24; 16:5; 19:20; 28:30–31). The church in Jerusalem continued to attract new membership, including a surprising number of priests who had become believers. These priests were very likely Sadducees. This is Luke's way of foreshadowing the accusations about to be made against Stephen in the following chapter. There is no way to explain the attraction of so many priests to the faith if the allegations against Stephen were accurate.

The Ministry of Stephen (6:8-10)

Luke reveals that Stephen's ministry was not limited to the distribution of benevolence. In fact, Stephen is never actually shown to be "waiting on tables." Stephen's ministry is described in similar terms to that of the apostles, characterized by the habitual performance of signs and wonders. He is one of only two non-apostles whom Luke reports exercised this ability (the other being Philip, in Acts 8:6), received through apostolic commissioning.

Stephen was primarily an evangelist and took his witness into the various Hellenistic synagogues. Luke notes his debates about Jesus' messianic identity with the members of one particular synagogue, the "Synagogue of the Freedmen," which was composed of Jews who were either formerly Roman slaves or the free children of Jewish slaves. Archeologists have claimed to have located the ancient dedicatory inscription for this synagogue.[1]

Stephen debated with four international factions within this one synagogue: Cyrenian Jews from Libya, Alexandrian Jews from Egypt, Cilician Jews, and Jews of various provinces in Asia Minor. Since a faction of Cilicians are mentioned, it is possible that this was also the synagogue of Saul of Tarsus, although this is merely enjoyable speculation, as is the possibility that he and Stephen had debated one another concerning Jesus at this time.

Synagogues. The term synagogue is a transliteration of the Greek "*sunagōgē*," which means "assembly," a word interchangeable with the other Greek word for assembly, "ecclesia," which we generally translate as "church." As with the development of the term, "church," the word synagogue originally referred to the gathering together of Jews, but eventually became understood as referring to the meeting place itself.

The origin of the synagogue is murky. It is generally accepted as having arisen during the Babylonian exile, circa 586 BC, as a stopgap measure to keep Judaism alive absent the destroyed Temple. The local synagogues served as localized community centers for prayer and Torah study. At the conclusion of the exile, the returnees established local synagogues in Israel, and those who remained in the Diaspora continued regular meetings in their synagogues. It had proven a useful institution as a supplement to formal Temple worship.

Immigrants from various cities or regions would naturally congregate together and form culturally similar sub-communities of worship. It is claimed that there were four hundred eighty synagogues established throughout Jerusalem, and even if this figure is exaggerated, many of these were clearly established by homogeneous communities (see Acts 6:9). As "birds of a feather flock together," there were synagogues tailored for every community and socio-economic distinction.

Even today, within large Jewish communities, there will usually be several synagogues from which to choose. In fact, there is a story told about two Jews, Manny and Abe, who were sailing onboard a ship in the middle of the ocean. Suddenly the ship sinks. Just as they are about to drown, Manny and Abe see an island and swim ashore. There they remain, isolated on this island for many years. Finally a passing ship discovers them, and they are rescued. The captain comes ashore, curious to see how they had survived on the island all these years. The captain is amazed to see that Manny and Abe have built from palm fronds, sticks, etc., three separate huts. The captain asks if these structures were their homes. Manny and Abe reply that these huts were actually synagogues. "My goodness," the captain answers, "But why in the world would two men need three synagogues?" Manny and Abe reply, "One synagogue is for Manny, who is an Orthodox Jew, and one synagogue is for Abe, who is a Reform Jew." "What about the third synagogue?" asks the captain. Manny and Abe respond, "That synagogue is the one neither of us would be caught dead in!"

Over time, the local synagogue became as central to the Jewish community in Israel as the Temple itself, and even more so within the Diaspora. Synagogues served not only as community centers, but also as places of worship, prayer and preaching. They provided gathering places for the celebration of social occasions and the debating of contemporary and political issues. In addition, and perhaps most critically, synagogues functioned as schools for the theological education of Jewish adults, children and prospective proselytes. Whenever possible, synagogues were situated near water to facilitate Jewish ritual baptism (*mikvah* in Hebrew and *baptisma* in Greek).

It is difficult to overestimate the significance of the synagogue within the first century. Luke mentions the synagogue nineteen times in Acts, which indicates the incontrovertible role the institution played not only in Jewish cultural life, but also as a medium for the propagation of the gospel. Indeed, one may only speculate at the magnitude of the task the apostles, Paul in particular, would have faced in sharing the gospel without the multitude of previously established synagogues strewn throughout the Roman Empire.[2]

In the Diaspora, it would not be unusual for an inn to be located within close proximity to the local synagogue. One may speculate that itinerant missionaries, such as Paul and Barnabas, might have availed themselves of such convenient lodging as they traveled throughout Jewish population centers.

The Arrest of Stephen (6:11–7:1)

When Stephens's opponents could not prevail in debate, they resorted to bribery and the invention of spurious charges. Stephen is accused of blaspheming both God and His servant, Moses. The basis for their accusation, as seen from the content of Stephen's sermon, was Stephen's sweeping implication that following the resurrection and exaltation of Christ, the Law of Moses had been rendered inoperative by the New Covenant. Needless to say, if obedience to the Torah's legal code were no longer obligatory, the convoluted oral law of the Pharisees would then be completely dispensable. This further implied that the Temple worship of God was no longer necessary or relevant. While radical teaching, this did not qualify as blasphemy under Jewish oral law. According to the Mishnah, blasphemy was the improper utterance of the covenant name of God, *YHWH*.[3] However, it may be that at this time there was a broader definition of blasphemy, as expressed in the Torah.

> The person who sins defiantly . . . blasphemes the Lord, and that person must be cut off from his people. Because he has despised the word of the Lord and broken his commandment, that person must surely be cut off; he is guilty" (Num. 15:30).

The accusations against Stephen were particularly inflammatory. This time a believer was not just preaching the resurrection, the doctrine which had earlier set off the Sadducees. Stephen's emphasis was also on the termination of the law, the Pharisees' hot button. A mob formed, rushing Stephen and dragging him into the Temple and before the Sanhedrin, which had already unambiguously warned the believers to discontinue their witness or face severe penalty.

Combining the initial incendiary accusations against Stephen with those raised before the Sanhedrin, a total of four false charges were brought forth. He was accused of blasphemy against Moses (Acts 6:11), blasphemy against God (Acts 6:11), threatening the Temple (Acts 6:13–14) and challenging the Torah (Acts 6:13–14).

These accusations, which concerned the foundations of Judaism itself — God, Moses, Torah and Temple — had broad appeal; there was something here to inflame everyone equally. The Sadducees would react to the Temple accusation, the Pharisees to the one concerning Torah, and the accusations regarding God and Moses would likewise enrage both groups. The allegations made against Stephen read like a greatest hits list for Jewish heresies. Furthermore, within a nation that would not have grasped the concept of "the separation of church and state," Stephen's aberrant teaching would strike the people not only as theologically scandalous but also downright unpatriotic.

In the past, there had at least been accuracy in the accusations against the apostles. In this case, Stephen's teaching was inflammatorily misrepresented, even though, according to Jewish law, the crime of false witness warranted the death penalty.[4] Luke explicitly affirmed the falsehood of these witnesses.

These witnesses had clearly either misunderstood or purposely distorted Stephen's words. If there was a kernel of truth to these accusations against Stephen, Luke did not record it.

What Luke did record within the content of Stephen's defense before the Sanhedrin, however, reveals a committed Jew with high regard for both Moses and the Temple, yet with an appropriately realigned perspective relative to the Messiah's accomplishments regarding salvation. Stephen's public preaching probably had a great deal in common with the argument of the book of Hebrews: contending Jesus' superiority to every revered Jewish institution, including Moses, Torah and the Temple. Jesus Himself claimed to be greater than the Temple (Matt. 12:6). Stephen probably cited his Lord's claim as well as Jesus' prophecy of the Temple's imminent destruction (Luke 21:6), which had also been twisted out of context by the false witnesses who had accused Jesus (Mark 14:58). Stephen stood in good company.

As the assembled Sanhedrin gave their attention to Stephen's defense, Luke records that they all witnessed Stephen's face begin to glow, perhaps reminiscent of Moses, whose face brilliantly reflected his encounter with God at Sinai (Ex. 34:29–30).

The Defense of Stephen (7:2–7:53)

What is recorded here reads much like a replay of Jesus' trial before the Sanhedrin two years earlier. Many of the same cast of characters is assembled; in particular, Josephus Caiaphas, the high priest, who had presided at Jesus' trial. As required by Jewish law, Caiaphas gave Stephen ample opportunity to refute his accusers but Stephen chose not to respond directly to a single allegation.

In his speech, Stephen turned the tables on his accusers. Instead of offering a good defense, his strategy was to put forth a great offense. That may well be good tactics in sports, but it did not work out too well for Stephen. However no one could accuse Stephen of not "going for broke" in his final address. Unlike Jesus, who at his trial "as a lamb led to slaughter, opened not his mouth" (Is. 53:7), Stephen would, for the last time, demonstrate his oratorical skills to an audience who would hang on every word and feel each lash of his rhetorical whip.

Stephen's sermon stands alone among the other recorded messages in Acts. It is the longest speech in the book, and it is the only sermon that does not present some sort of gospel presentation. Upon first reading, Stephen's sermon appears to consist of not much more than a collection of tedious excerpts of memorable moments in the history of the Jewish nation. However, Stephen's discourse is profoundly sophisticated. When one reads between the lines and follows the inexorable flow of his relentless logic, what is discovered is no history lesson but the initial systematic theological presentation of the universal applicability and intent of the gospel, solidly rooted in the Old Testament. Unlike Peter and Paul, who in their sermons use the Hebrew Scriptures to support their arguments, for Stephen, the Hebrew Scriptures are his argument.[5]

Abraham: God Covenants with a Gentile in a Foreign Land (7:2-8)

In his opening words, Stephen calls for the lending of ears; not those of "friends" (rare in that crowd, as will be seen) or Romans (this is the assembled leadership of Israel), but of his "countrymen." He addresses the court as "brothers," a warm reference to fellow Jews, and "fathers," a respectful reference to the members of the Sanhedrin. However, the kindred spirit implicit in Stephen's opening appeal for the attention of His "family" will gradually give way throughout the course of this message to his impassioned denunciation of the leadership assembled in judgment.

In this speech, Stephen did not mount a defense; he assembled a prosecution. His overarching argument was that those very aspects of Judaism that he is accused of threatening, Torah and Temple, were never the true heart of the Jewish religion. These components, although important, were added after God had already laid the basis of Jewish identity. The true foundation of Jewish destiny had always been God's love and gracious provision for His children. Yet these beloved children, almost from the beginning, were consistently unable to recognize their Father's provision when it arrived.

Stephen introduced his case with "exhibit A," a familiar phrase from Jewish liturgy, "our father Abraham." Although highlighting the original Jewish "father," Abraham, this initial portion of Stephen's argument also focused on the actions of the ultimate Jewish Father, God. Stephen began by citing God's call of Abraham; a divine invitation to a Gentile within a foreign land (Gen. 11:31—12:3).

Stephen noted Abraham's migration from Babylonia to Haran. Upon his father's death, Abraham moved to Canaan, the land God had promised to Him. Yet God made His promise of the land at a time when Abraham neither owned the most minuscule tract of Israel nor possessed an heir to inherit the land (Gen. 12:7; 13:15; 15:2, 18; 17:8). God had not given Abraham during his lifetime even one footstep's worth of the land of Israel. As Stephen later notes, the patriarchs even had to purchase the land for their own tombs (Acts 7:16)! Furthermore, God told Abraham that before his descendents could inherit their promised land, they would first leave and be enslaved by a foreign nation for a duration of four centuries (Gen. 15:13–14).

In spite of Abraham's not yet owning the land and his progeny's dire future, God confirmed the Abrahamic Covenant promises by instituting the sign of circumcision, the foundation of Jewish identity and basis of the relationship between God and Israel (Gen. 17:9-14). Stephen quickly bypassed Abraham's son, Isaac, and grandson, Jacob, to highlight his great-grandson, Joseph.

Joseph: The Rejected Becomes the Exalted Savior (7:9-16)

Stephen noted that so powerful was the Jewish patriarchs' jealousy and hatred of their brother Joseph that they sold him into Egyptian slavery (Gen. 37:25-36). Stephen's audience would have appreciated that for fifteen hundred years in the Jewish imagination, Egypt was the archetypical dominion of Gentile oppression. Yet there in the midst of Egypt was God, watching over Joseph and orchestrating the circumstances of his exaltation in the Egyptian government (Gen. 39-41). Although Joseph had been rejected by his own family, he had been accepted by foreigners in a foreign land and exalted by God's hand.

Stephen then relates the circumstances of the famine which forced the patriarchs to journey to Egypt for food on two occasions. Stephen highlights that it was only on the patriarchs' second Egyptian visit that they were able to recognize their brother, Joseph (Gen. 42-45). Another of Stephen's themes now emerges; the rejected one, now exalted, becomes the savior of those who had rejected him.

Stephen's argument is that the patriarchs did not recognize their brother the first time that they saw him. The sons of Israel only perceived that their own brother was their savior on his second appearance before them. The parallel Stephen drew is clearly seen. The first time the descendents of the sons of Israel saw Jesus, they likewise did not recognize Him. Unfortunately, the vast majority of the Jewish people will not perceive that Jesus is their Messiah until His glory is eminently manifest upon His return.

Stephen goes on to note that the Jewish patriarchs, with their father, Jacob, moved their families to Egypt to be with Joseph (Gen. 46:26-27). In Acts 7:14, there is discrepancy as to the exact number of the Jewish population migrating to Egypt. Although the Masoretic text of our contemporary Hebrew Bible lists a total Jewish population of seventy (Ex. 1:5), Stephen listed seventy-five. There are two solutions to reconcile this discrepancy. The first is to assume that in addition to the seventy of Exodus 1:5, Stephen was also including Joseph's five grandsons (Gen. 50:23). The second solution simply assumes that the Bible from which Stephen quoted derived from a different textual source. Stephen most probably was quoting the Septuagint, which twice records the number seventy-five (Gen. 46:27; Ex. 1:5). The possibility also exists that he used an alternate Hebrew text, for example, the version of Exodus 1:5 found in the Dead Sea scrolls, which also records the number seventy-five.[6]

Stephen then makes mention that the burial of the Jewish patriarchs was in Shechem. Historically, Shechem had been one of Israel's very significant cities, but in the first century, it was the center of Samaria. The reference to Shechem, in the midst of Samaritan territory (which was almost as ghastly as if it had been in Gentile country), foreshadows the next major division in Acts, the mission to Judea and Samaria (8:4—12:25). Immediately following Stephen's martyrdom, Luke travels with his readers directly to Samaria.

Two additional confusing discrepancies arise in Acts 7:16. First, although Stephen states that the patriarchs were all buried in Shechem, the Hebrew Scriptures record that Joseph was buried in Shechem (Josh 24:32), while Jacob was buried in Hebron (Gen. 50:13). Second, Stephen states that Abraham purchased a tomb in Shechem from the sons of Hamor. However, Abraham had actually bought a tomb from the Hittites in Hebron (Gen. 23:15–20). It was Jacob who had bought land in Shechem from the sons of Hamor (Gen. 33:19; Josh. 24:32). While it is possible that Stephen was citing the many popular patriarchal stories in contemporary circulation, it is most probable that Stephen simply spliced together two separate patriarchal stories into one condensed account.[7] All in all, that these discrepancies still remain intact without having been reconciled by Luke as he compiled Acts is strong testimony to a remarkably faithful account of Stephen's actual words.

Moses: The Rejected Becomes the Deliverer (7:17–40)

Stephen transitions to Moses, another rejected one who, following God's exaltation, became the deliverer of those who had rejected him. During their Egyptian sojourn, the people of Israel had greatly multiplied. At some point, a new and different kind (Greek *heteros*) of Pharaoh arose, perhaps indicating a change of dynasty (Ex. 1:8, Septuagint). This king enslaved the Hebrews and commanded that their newborn male infants be left outside to die of exposure.

In defiance of Pharaoh's decree, Moses' parents nursed him at home for three months and then set him adrift on the Nile River. He was found and adopted by Pharaoh's daughter and received the thorough education of an Egyptian prince (Ex. 2:1–10). Although the Hebrew Scripture does not comment on Moses' education, it is remarked upon by Luke's contemporaries, Josephus[8] as well as Philo, who records Moses' instruction in the subjects of arithmetic, geometry, music, literature, astronomy, writing, philosophy and more.[9]

At the age of forty, Moses decided to identify with his people, Israel, instead of the Egyptians (Heb. 11:24–26), realizing that God had made him the deliverer of his people. Moses' intervention in an Egyptian's physical abuse of a fellow Hebrew ended with Moses killing the Egyptian and hiding his body (Ex. 2:11–12). He believed that Israel would understand that He was the instrument God was going to use to deliver them from bondage and that they would welcome him in his role as their deliverer. However, Moses was mistaken. Israel neither understood his intentions nor accepted him as their deliverer.

The day following Moses' murder of an Egyptian, he tried to reconcile two of his people who were fighting. However, the instigator of the conflict challenged Moses' authority and right to interfere, asking Moses who appointed him "ruler and judge" over the Israelites (Ex. 2:13–14). God, of course, had appointed Moses to be ruler and judge of Israel, but ironically, the Hebrews rejected his leadership the first time it was offered. The very ones Moses attempted to help, his own nation, resolutely rejected their deliverer.

Moses realized that, apparently, the murder he had done in secret was already common knowledge. Fearful of Egyptian retribution and rejected by his own people, Moses fled Egypt for Midian, taking a wife from and raising his family among the Gentiles.

Forty years later, at the age of eighty, Moses encountered God in a flaming thorn bush at Mount Sinai (Ex. 3:2).[10] God identified himself to Moses as the covenant God of the Hebrew patriarchs (Ex. 3:6). Yet again God had revealed himself far outside the boundaries of the land of Israel. God commanded the terrified Moses to remove his sandals because he was standing on "holy ground" (Ex. 3:5). Stephen's point was that God had never been limited to the specific geography of Israel. Any land in which God's presence was manifest should rightfully be considered holy territory.

Moses was reassured that God Himself had appointed Moses as ruler and judge of Israel, despite the inability of the Jewish nation to recognize his authority as their redeemer (Ex. 3:7–10). Moses returned to Egypt and delivered Israel from Egyptian bondage. As in the account of Joseph and his brothers, it was not until Moses' second appearance to the Jewish people that they finally recognized Moses' authority as God's agent of redemption. The rejected one, now exalted, had become the deliverer of those who had rejected him.

Stephen's insinuation was that history was once again repeating itself. Israel had held true to the established pattern of not immediately recognizing their own savior. Jesus, too, was disowned by his people (Acts 3:13) although He was appointed by God to be the ultimate "ruler and judge," not just of

Israel, but of the world (Acts 10:42; 17:31). As with Joseph and Moses, when Israel sees Jesus at His second appearing, the rejected one, now exalted, will become the deliverer of those who had rejected him.

Stephen reminded his audience that Moses, the same man who had been rejected by Israel, was also the potent instrument of the plagues against Egypt, the parting of the Red Sea, and the miracles in the wilderness. In addition, Moses, this onetime rejected deliverer, had admonished his people to be vigilant in watching for another prophet to arise from Israel in the unspecified future who would exercise similar leadership and miraculous abilities. When this prophet appeared, Israel must obey him or face the harshest of consequences (Deut. 18:15–19).

Stephen's argument was that it should have been obvious, especially to the Torah scholars, that Jesus was the prophet of whom Moses spoke since Jesus' display of "wonders and signs" closely paralleled that of Moses. Nevertheless, not only had this generation of leadership disregarded the prophet like Moses, they had murdered him. Peter made the same argument (Acts 2:22; 3:22–23) with far less subtlety but far more effectiveness than did Stephen (unfortunately for Stephen).

Stephen continued, pointing out that Moses, the onetime rejected deliverer, was also the one whom God chose to transmit the Torah, the divine words, to the nation of Israel on Mount Sinai. Yet after everything Moses had done for the Israelites, while he was on Mount Sinai communing face to face with God, his people rejected him for a second time.

Moses, up on Mount Sinai, was out of sight and out of mind, and the Israelites disowned his leadership by constructing and then worshiping a golden calf (Ex. 32:1). Moses was betrayed even by his own brother, Aaron, the designing engineer of the idol. It would not have been necessary to point out to the Sanhedrin that Aaron was also the original high priest.

It was one thing to reject a former prince of Egypt, a murderer. It was quite another to reject the individual whom God had used to direct ten devastating plagues, a parting of the sea and the awesome spectacle of God's thunderous appearance on Sinai at the giving of the Torah (Ex. 19—20). By rejecting Moses, God's provision for Israel, the Jewish people had also rejected God. They were guilty of breaking the commandment not to revile God or curse God's appointed ruler (Ex. 22:28).

The sad irony of Stephen's situation was that he stood on trial before the descendents of the prototypical, greatest challengers of Moses and violators of Torah! When it came to rejecting God and His divine provision, no one took second place to the exodus generation of Israelites, except, perhaps, for the generation of Israelites who had rejected their Messiah.

Israel's Chronic Idolatry (7:41–43)

The golden calf episode was just the beginning. Almost as soon as they had settled into the promised land, the Jewish people wasted no time in violating the injunctions of Torah against idolatry (Deut. 4:19; 17:2–5). In fact, Israel was plagued throughout its history with a propensity for idolatry. Their record was one of almost continual unfaithfulness and rejection of God (Ps.106:36–43; 2 Kin. 17:16–17; 21:3, 25; 23:5; 2 Chr. 33:3–5; Jer. 19:13).

Stephen asserted that God had "delivered Israel up" to their iniquity, and he cited the prophet Amos to support his denunciation that at various times the Israelites had worshiped the stars, planets and a menagerie of pagan deities (Amos 5:25–27). These repugnant foreign gods included Moloch, the worship of whom required the sacrifice of human children (Jer. 32:35; 2 Kin. 23:10).

Again, ironically, Stephen was accused of blaspheming God by the descendents of a nation for whom idolatry had been almost a national pastime.

The Temple (7:44–50)

Thus far, Stephen had discussed Moses, Torah and God. He next transitioned to dealing with the Temple. However, to arrive at the Temple, Stephen first had to discuss the Tabernacle. While Israel was still sojourning in the wilderness of Sinai, God had commanded Israel to build the Tabernacle. Israel was to design the Tabernacle according to God's exact specifications. It was designed to be mobile so that it could accompany the Israelites on their wanderings, before possession of their land, and also afterward.

The Tabernacle was utilized from the time of Moses through David, who asked to build a permanent house, a Temple, for God. The portable Tabernacle was replaced when David's son Solomon built the Temple. Stephen did not belittle the Temple in contrast to the Tabernacle; after all, he alluded to the fact that, as God Himself had provided Moses with the Tabernacle blueprints, He had done the same for King David with the Temple blueprints (1 Chr. 28:19).

However, Stephen argued, in contrast to David and Solomon's intent, God's presence could not be confined to merely dwelling in the Temple. God is not and never has been confined to one location, even the Temple. The Lord and creator of the entire universe "does not live in houses made by human hands" (Acts 7:48). In making this assertion, Stephen implied no criticism of the Temple. There was nothing derogatory in his contention; in fact, Solomon made the same point (1 Kin. 8:27; 2 Chr. 6:16) as did the prophet Isaiah (Is. 66:1–2), and the apostle Paul in his address to the Athenians, referencing the Parthenon, yet another magnificent temple (Acts 17:24).

In no way does Stephen's sermon provide support for the false accusation of his having threatened the Temple. Stephen did not reject Temple worship but simply argued that the Temple must be held in proper perspective. Just as Tabernacle worship had been divinely instituted and yet replaced, with God's sanction, by Temple worship, the possibility existed that the Temple might also be an impermanent institution. Since the biblical record teaches that God's program changes and develops over time, at some point God might have other plans. The uncomfortable question Stephen raised was whether or not the nation of Israel would be alert when God instituted those plans.

Stephen's Accusation (7:51–53)

Stephen then reached the passionate climax of his message by directly addressing the Sanhedrin. There is a sudden shift of tenses, from dispassionate third person to fervent second person, as Stephen pronounced his own verdict over his accusers.

Using the graphic and colorful terminology of the Hebrew prophets in whose sandals he now stood, Stephen accused the Sanhedrin of being "stiff-necks" (Ex. 32:9, 33:3, 5; 34:9; Deut. 9:6; 10:16) who were "uncircumcised in heart and ears" (Lev.26:41; Deut.10:16; Jer 4:4; 6:10; 9:26; Ezek. 44:7), guilty of continually resisting the Holy Spirit (Is. 63:10). As F.F. Bruce comments,

> "While they were circumcised in the literal sense, in accordance with the Abrahamic institution, their unresponsiveness and resistance to God's revelation were such as might have been expected from Gentiles to whom he had not made known his will."[11]

Surprisingly, up to this point in his defense, Stephen had avoided explicitly mentioning Jesus. Only now did Stephen introduce Him, not by name but by title, the "Righteous One," of Isaiah's suffering servant passage: "the Righteous One, My Servant, shall turn many to righteousness, seeing that he bore their sins" (Is. 53:11). It was God's prophesied "Righteous One," the Messiah, whom the Sanhedrin had rejected, although He was their deliverer. Stephen condemns the court as both betrayers and murderers. It would have been insufficient to label them as mere "Judases," for Judas was only guilty of betrayal, not murder. The Sanhedrin, however, was guilty of both.

This heinous rejection was consistent with Israel's treatment of God and his representatives throughout its history. The Hebrew Scripture testifies to this pattern:

> The LORD, the God of their fathers, faithfully sent His messengers, because He had compassion on His people and on His dwelling place; but they mocked the messengers of God, despised His words and abused His prophets, until the wrath of the LORD arose against His people beyond all remedy (2 Chr. 36:15–16).

You build the tombs of the prophets and adorn the monuments of the righteous, and say, 'If we had been alive in the days of our fathers, we would not have joined with them in murdering the prophets.' So you testify against yourselves, that you are sons of those who murdered the prophets. Fulfill, then, the measure of your fathers' sins. You serpents, you brood of vipers, how will you escape the sentence of hell?" (Matt. 23:29–33).

A prophet cannot die outside of Jerusalem (Luke 13:33).

Finally, the book of Hebrews also bears witness to the persecution of Israel's prophets:

> . . . Others were tortured, not accepting their release . . . and others were mocked and scourged, chained and imprisoned. They were stoned, sawn in two, tempted, and executed by the sword " (Hebrews 11:35b-37a).

Stephen intensified his charges. After denouncing the entirety of the Jewish leadership for rejecting Moses, the prophets, the Messiah and God Himself, the straw that finally broke the proverbial "camel's back" was Stephen's accusation that they were in flagrant violation of the Law of Moses. Israel, to whom the Torah had been divinely administered by Moses through the agency of God's angels,[12] was without excuse. Those who had so diligently strived, with greatest stringency, to obey the Torah, whom, of all people, should have known better, had unfalteringly misunderstood God's purposes. It was not Stephen who was guilty of blasphemy, but the Great Sanhedrin.

The Death of Stephen (7:54–60)

The Sanhedrin and the masses assembled to view the trial could take no more. They had heard all they needed to render judgment. Luke describes them as being *dieprionto*, "sawn asunder," beside themselves with fury, the same term he used in describing the Sanhedrin's reaction to Peter's message (Acts 5:33). However, unlike the previous occasion, this time there was no sage mediating force like Gamaliel's counsel to calm the mob's passionate reaction or stay their violence. The crowd's anger bubbled up frighteningly until, like ferocious carnivores, they all began "gnashing their teeth" at Stephen, biting loudly and vigorously.

In contrast to the rising fervor of the mob, Stephen was at peace, "full of," controlled by, the Holy Spirit. While the mob fiercely glowered at him, his attention was on heaven. He was granted a vision, seeing the Shekinah glory and the exalted Jesus, the "Son of Man," standing at the right hand of God.

Stephen does more than relay the heavenly vision he experienced. He was also dramatically echoing Jesus' last words to the Sanhedrin at His trial, "But from now on the Son of Man will be seated at the right hand of the power of

God" (Luke 22:69, also Matt.26:64; Mark 14:62). As these words had occasioned the Sanhedrin's verdict of blasphemy against Jesus, Stephen's vision would now do the same.

The picture of Jesus at God's right hand is an allusion to Psalm 110:1. In that psalm, quoted earlier by Peter on Pentecost (2:34), David described the messiah as a royal figure who intimately sat in God's presence, enthroned at his side, and sharing in his reign. This is the usual description of the exalted Jesus (Psalm 110:1; Rom.8:34; Eph. 1:20; Col. 3:1; Heb. 1:3; 13; 8:1; 10:12; 12:2; 1 Pet. 3:22). Stephen's vision is the only time in Scripture that the exalted Jesus is portrayed as standing at God's right hand. It is likely that the vision of Jesus standing is indicative of His reception of Stephen, the first believer martyred in His name.

Son of Man. The enigmatic title "son of man," the Aramaic *bar enash*, was Jesus' preferred messianic self-designation. His use of this term for Himself is studded throughout the gospels. The phrase is often used in the Hebrew Scripture as an alternate means to simply indicate a human being, someone in possession of the character of humanity.

However, "son of man" was not universally used this way in Scripture. Jesus did not wish to merely indicate that he was a human being, a "regular Joe." Jesus used this phrase as an allusion to the vision of the Hebrew prophet, Daniel, of a divinely exalted figure, "one like a son of man," coming with "the clouds of heaven" (Dan. 7:13–14). This mysterious figure receives authority over God's kingdom from the "Ancient of Days," God Himself.

Stephen's vision thrusts the mob's passion over the edge. They screamed and covered their ears so as not to hear even one more word. They had had enough, and their homicidal intentions could no longer be held in check. The Sanhedrin did not pause for a discussion, a verdict, or a vote. The Sanhedrin was allowed to exercise capital punishment for an offense against the sanctity of the Temple, and Stephen's words had been struck them as offensive, indeed. As one, the mob rushed Stephen and drove him out past Jerusalem's city limits where they could legally execute him. On the one hand, this could be considered a crime of passion, yet on the other hand, there was enough premeditation by the mob to know enough not to have assuaged their murderous intent within the Temple courts.

The Mishnah records the procedure for an execution by stoning. The mob would have dragged Stephen to the edge of the city, stripping him of most of his clothing.[13] One of the false witnesses would have thrown him over the edge of a minimum twelve-foot deep precipice and down into a valley which served as the place of execution. The possibility always existed that, at this point, the fall would break the condemned's neck and kill him. The other false witnesses were to be the first to throw the stones (Deut.13:9-10; 17:6-7).[14] Peering down from the edge of the precipice, the witnesses, followed by the mob, would have hurled large stones down upon Stephen, aiming as accurately as they could for his heart. Death occurred when the weight of the stones, combined with the force with which they were hurled down from the precipice, had sufficiently crushed the body's bones and organs.

In order for their throwing arms to achieve the full range of motion necessary to perform their murderous deed, the mob would have had to take off their outer cloaks. Luke records that in attendance, accepting the cloaks of the stone throwers, was Saul of Tarsus. Luke's passing mention of Saul's presence at Stephen's execution foreshadows the critical role Paul will play in the second half of the Acts narrative and also highlights the fact that Stephen is the personal and theological link between Peter and Paul.

Luke did not specify Saul's age, recording only that he was a *neanias*, "young man," setting a possible range of between twenty-four and forty years.[15] It is reasonable to assume that at the time of Stephen's stoning, Saul was at or nearing thirty years of age. This conclusion is derived from the consideration of several factors, including the level of authority Saul will soon wield as the high priest's energetic agent of church persecution, his singleness, his lengthy and vigorous missionary career and his probable death in AD 67-68.

Although leaving their cloaks with Saul indicates that he held some recognized position of authority with the Sanhedrin, it does not signify that he was a member, as some enjoy speculating. Saul was in attendance at Stephen's execution in his capacity as a leading rabbinical student of Gamaliel, and his holding of the cloaks no more makes him a member of the Sanhedrin than a schoolboy's banging of erasers makes him the teacher. Later in Saul's life, when listing his Hebrew pedigree, conspicuously absent from his detailed list is any mention of membership in the Sanhedrin (Acts 22:3; 26:4-5; Rom. 1:1; 2 Cor. 11:22; Phil. 3:5-6).

As the stones began to impact their target, Stephen called out to Jesus, "Lord Jesus, receive my spirit," in words reminiscent of Jesus' own prayer to His Father on the cross (Luke 23:46). However, in this instance, Stephen addressed Jesus as the one who would receive his Spirit. It is unimaginable to come away from the words of this martyr's prayer and blithely regurgitate the ignorant blather that there is no indication that Jesus is God in the book of Acts.

According to Jewish custom, before stoning, the condemned was either to confess his sin or simply pray, "May my death atone for all my sins."[16] Stephen, however, knelt down and prayed again to Jesus, this time shouting to heaven, perhaps to be heard by the false witnesses, Israel's leadership, the mob and the young man standing over their discarded robes, "Lord, do not hold this sin against them." Again, Stephen's last words were reminiscent of Jesus' on the cross (Luke 23:34).

Luke then uses a biblical euphemism for Stephen's death, simply reporting that "he fell asleep." At his death, Stephen's spirit was immediately welcomed into Jesus' presence, but one day, at the resurrection, his body will awaken in a glorified state.

Jesus had prophesied that His disciples would suffer, be rejected and possibly even executed because of their allegiance to Him (Luke 9:23–24; 12:8–12; 21:12–19). As the first martyred believer, Stephen proved to be the ultimate witness (Greek *martus*) of His messiah. As one scholar cogently noted,

> Yet because he acknowledged Jesus before others and lost his life for Jesus' sake, he saved his life and was acknowledged by the Son of Man (Luke 9:23–24; 12:8).[17]

Introduction of Saul's Persecution (8:1–4)

Jewish law prohibited the public mourning of someone executed by stoning.[18] However, certain "devout men" (see Acts 2:5), sympathizers who disagreed with Stephen's murder, prepared his body for a Jewish funeral and passionately mourned him. Perhaps they had been present at his trial, but were unable to impede the mob's frenzy. Their "loud lamentation" indicates that, at least for these few, Stephen's message hit home.

Luke notes that Saul heartily agreed with Stephen's execution, using the word *suneudokeō* to indicate that the execution brought Saul "pleasure" or "satisfaction." Assuredly, his safeguarding of the mob's cloaks publicly broadcast his approval. It is likely that Saul had debated Stephen about the Messiah in one of the Hellenistic synagogues and wound up on the losing end of the argument (Acts 6:9).

Luke portrays Saul as the chief architect and perpetrator of this persecution. It was Saul's brainchild, and he approached his self-appointed task with imposing zeal. Unlike Gamaliel, Saul did not perceive the church as primarily a political movement to be tolerated until otherwise indicated. Rather, Stephen's speech helped Saul to realize that the followers of Jesus were propagating dangerous doctrines that would essentially undermine traditional Judaism as he knew it. No tolerance or compromise could be extended.

Saul ravaged the church, wreaking devastation and inflicting ruin. While believers were worshiping, Saul would raid the house churches and arrest everyone, both men and women. The inclusion of women in this persecution was unprecedented. Previously, only men were arrested, specifically the apostles. By contrast, no one was exempt from Saul's fury.

Further on in the narrative and years later, Paul relates further details of his previous acts of persecution (Acts 22:19; 26:11). In these passages, it is revealed that Saul also arrested believers while they were in the synagogue. This clearly indicates the early church's attempt at continued participation within the larger Jewish community and their initial rejection by the leaders of that community.

Saul's ruthlessness was not in keeping with Josephus' characterization of the Pharisees as more prone to mercy in their punishments than the Sadducees.[19] It was obvious that Saul chose to ignore his teacher Gamaliel's prudent advice.

This persecution marked the alliance of the Pharisees and the Sadducees who, for the first time united together to destroy the Jerusalem church. The church was being forced into a new Diaspora, as many believers fled from Jerusalem, leaving behind a decimated flock. From this point on, the majority of the believers would be scattered, far from the apostles and apostolic authority. Incidentally, this dispersion is the stated reason why James and Peter will eventually write their epistles (James 1:1; 1 Pet. 1:1).

Many scholars assume that Saul's persecution was only directed against the Hellenistic believers. This arises from a misunderstanding of Stephen's basic argument and an exaggerated dichotomy between the theological positions of the Hellenists and the native Jews.

These scholars reason that the persecution erupted as a direct result of Stephen's position, which they misinterpret as attacking the sacred institutions of the Mosaic Law and the Temple. Since Stephen was a Hellenist, the persecution was limited to the Hellenistic Jewish believers. These would naturally have been suspected of sharing his theologically radical perspective. Conversely, it was widely known that the apostles, all native, "home-grown" Jews, while preaching the resurrected Christ, continued to observe traditional Jewish practices. Therefore, it is presumed, the persecution targeted the Hellenists and exempted the more traditionalist, native Jews.

While there is some merit to this opinion and it would satisfactorily explain why the apostolic leadership are neither molested nor forced to flee Jerusalem (Acts 8:1), this explanation is not probable.

Nowhere does the text indicate that the need to escape Jerusalem was limited to the Hellenists. The only specific believers we are told did not flee were the twelve apostles. It is unwarranted by the text to presume that only the Hellenists were targeted. One should also exercise caution in assuming that the apostles were somehow exempt from persecution, a conjecture unconfirmed by the text.

However, there are two probable explanations as to why the apostles were able to remain in Jerusalem. First, it may well be that the public humiliation of the apostles' miraculous escape from prison (Acts 5:19–21) and the challenge to the Sanhedrin's authority this represented was one embarrassment that the leadership did not want repeated. Essentially, the apostles had made such a sufficient impression upon the Sanhedrin that no one was willing to lay a finger on them, although that restraint will prove short-lived.

Second, the apostles' ability to remain in Jerusalem may imply a change in the Sanhedrin's strategy. The Sadducees, who had earlier taken the initiative in arresting the apostles and bringing them to trial, had gotten nowhere in suppressing this movement. Now that the Pharisees were taking the initiative, under Saul's leadership, and combining their efforts with the Sadducees, their approach may have been to attack the church's grass roots, the common people. The sect of the Nazarenes would be derailed if enough followers could be induced, by whatever means necessary, to renounce the movement and desert the apostolic leadership.

However, the church was scattered but not defeated. They were simply forced to adapt a change of strategy; to break new demographic ground in witnessing of Jesus. As seed was scattered in Jesus' famous parable (Matt. 6:26; 13:3–4, 18; 25:24, 26; Luke 8:5; 12:24), this persecution resulted in the seed of the gospel being scattered as the church was strewn throughout Judea, Samaria, the rest of Israel and even into neighboring countries (Acts 11:19).

Conclusion

There is no correspondence between the relatively small amount of space devoted to Stephen in the Acts narrative and his importance to the witness of the early church. Unlike the trial of Jesus, which was held in the dead of night and with only a limited number of leaders convened, Stephen's trial transpired in the light of day before the full assembly of the Sanhedrin. Stephen's execution by Israel's leadership, therefore, should be considered an official, national rejection of Jesus.

Although Jerusalem would continue to be the geographic center of the church for decades to come, the Acts narrative now enlarges its scope as it traces the spread of the gospel into previously uncharted territory. Stephen's polarizing polemic against behaving as if the God of the universe was confined to the Temple or the geographic borders of the holy land had set the stage for the expansion of the church beyond the land of Israel.

Study Questions:

1. Who were the Hellenistic Jews?

2. List five facts about Stephen.

3. Describe the function of the synagogue.

4. List the charges against Stephen and why his preaching was so inflammatory.

5. Summarize Stephen's defense and his accusation against the Jewish leadership.

6. Describe Stephen's execution.

7. Why was Saul so zealous in persecuting the church?

Section 2

The Judean and Samaritan Witness

Acts 8:5 — 12:25

CHAPTER 7

The Witness of Philip
Acts 8:5-40

Preview:

In this chapter, Luke highlights the witness of Philip. This is not the apostle Philip, but rather Philip the deacon, second on the appointed list of deacons after Stephen (Acts 6:5). As was Stephen, Philip was both a deacon and an evangelist (Acts 21:8) as well as a close associate of the apostles, wielding their delegated authority (Acts 6:6). As an apostolic associate, Philip's ministry was likewise characterized by signs and wonders (Acts 8:6). Although he would later settle in Caesarea and raise a family (including four daughters who possessed the gift of prophecy [Acts 21:8-14]), Philip's initial pioneering ministry crossed two ethnic boundaries; one large boundary, the Samaritans, and one small boundary, an Ethiopian Jewish proselyte.

Philip in Samaria (8:5-13)

Samaritan Salvation (8:5-8)

Forced from Jerusalem by the persecution of Saul that began in the early months of AD 35, Philip was sent by the apostles as their pioneer witness to Samaria. After Jerusalem and Judea, Samaria was the next geographic area that Jesus had specified in His final commission (Acts 1:8). In addition, a beachhead of Samaritan allies had already been established by Jesus Himself (Luke 17:15-18; John 4:7-42), and it was an appropriate time to strengthen their number. Luke notes that Philip "went down," the customary description for the descent from the mountains of Jerusalem.

Samaria was the region of Israel situated between Galilee on the north and Judea on the south. Sebaste, the Old Testament city of Samaria, was the main city in the region, but as it was predominantly populated by Gentiles, it is more likely that what Luke meant by "the city of Samaria" was Neapolis, originally identified in the Hebrew Scripture as the city of Shechem. Shechem was the key spiritual center for the Samaritans due to its historic and religious significance (see discussion on Acts 7:16).

Historically, the Samaritan inhabitants appeared when the remnant of the decimated northern kingdom of Israel, allowed to remain in their land following their conquest by Assyria, fused together with an assortment of Gentile populations transplanted into Israel by Assyria. Scripture records that when the initial transplanted Gentile populace began to worship their own national gods instead of the God of Israel, the Lord sent a pride of lions to destroy them. When the now reduced population complained to Assyria that they were being eaten by lions, the Assyrian king sent a Levitical priest to instruct them in the Jewish religion, eliminating their lion crisis (2 Kin. 17:24–33).

Thereafter, the Samaritans began incorporating the worship of the Lord with their continued idol worship. Over time a syncretized, hybrid religion developed, known as Samaritanism. Although the Samaritans worshiped the one God, revered Moses and observed Sabbath, circumcision and the Torah, they were viewed as heretics by the Jews and were accorded no better than semi-Gentile status. Although half-Jewish, the Samaritans were treated as virtual pariahs. The Jews allowed no contact with the Samaritans and in many cases, went out of their way to avoid their territory (John 4:9).

The Samaritans, for their part, returned the sentiment. Strong animosity existed between the two communities almost from the beginning. When the Jews returned to Jerusalem from the Babylonian exile, the Samaritans ostensibly offered their help in rebuilding the Temple. Their assistance was rebuffed by the Jews, however, because of the Samaritan's hybrid religion Thereafter, the Samaritans made every effort to hinder the rebuilding of the Temple and the walls of Jerusalem (Ezra 4:1–24; Neh. 6:1–19).

During the first century AD, relations between the Jews and Samaritans were extremely tense and great hostility was exchanged. The Jews had earlier demolished the Samaritan's holy temple on Mount Gerizim. Later, the Samaritans exacted their revenge by smuggling in dead bodies into the Jerusalem Temple in the middle of the night. Leaving the bodies strategically strewn about the Temple to be discovered at daylight, they successfully defiled the entire Temple complex.[1]

Thereafter, the Jews strictly prohibited the Samaritans from worshiping at Jerusalem. Samaritans were also forbidden to intermarry with Jews or to have any social contact with them.

When Philip arrived in Samaria, the miraculous signs he performed, both in healing the sick and exorcising demons, notably got the attention of the Samaritans and resulted in the population's rejoicing over God's power.

Simon (8:9–13)

While Luke was on the subject of God's power, he introduced his readers to a particular Samaritan, a self-aggrandizing magician named Simon, whose "stage name" was "the Great Power of God." Apparently, Simon was a real showman, whose abilities entertained and impressed members of all social classes, convincing them that he was indeed the personification of God's power. However, when Simon encountered the genuine "great power of God" through Philip's ministry, Simon became a believer in Jesus, yielding to a force greater than himself.

Unlike the somewhat comparable "great and powerful wizard of Oz" of later fiction, Luke gives no indication that Simon's "astonishing magic arts" could be attributed to his practicing the "art" of legerdemain. On the contrary, Simon's amazing abilities seem to derive from sorcery. The Hebrew Scriptures recognize the genuine sorcery of the Egyptian magicians opposing Moses (Ex.7:11, 22; 8:7), and Jewish legends are chock full of various Jewish sorcerers, some of whom performed their magic through the power of Beelzebul, Satan. Jesus Himself was accused of such sorcery (Luke 11:15). Later in Acts, Paul will also encounter a sorcerer, Elymas (Acts 13.6–11).

Not only Simon, but also a great number of Samaritans believed in Jesus and were water baptized. Philip's proclamation of the gospel would have been heavily centered on Jesus being the fulfillment of the coming prophet like Moses (Deut. 18:15–19, see also Peter's use in Acts 3:22–23 and Stephen's in Acts 7:37). As did the Sadducees, the Samaritans rejected the Prophets and the Writings as divine Scripture, accepting only the Torah, the five books of Moses (albeit a doctored and appended version, edited to reflect Samaritan doctrinal particularities). Furthermore, Philip, like Stephen, would have likely rejected the Jewish oral law, making his message that much more appealing. Philip's evangelism, coupled with the attention-getting miraculous signs he performed in their midst, resulted in a great number of Samaritans coming to faith.

In addition, Luke describes Philip's presentation as having included the kingdom of God, correcting the Samaritan belief in a future Samaritan kingdom, not a Jewish kingdom. As Jesus taught the Samaritan woman, "salvation is from the Jews" (John 4:22). God's program included only one kingdom and one king to rule over it. That king, Jesus the Messiah, happened to be Jewish.

The question of whether Simon was a genuine believer is ultimately unanswerable based on the context of Luke's brief account. As described by Luke, it would seem that he became an authentic follower of Christ, publicly identifying with Jesus through baptism along with the other new believers. Although his later behavior casts a flicker of doubt on his salvation (Acts 8:18–24), there is no indication that Simon does not receive the same Spirit baptism as the other believers at the Samaritan "Pentecost" (Acts 8:17).

F.F. Bruce is convinced that Luke knew much more about Simon than he records in this passage (although contra Fitzmyer)[2], pointing to the inordinate attention paid to Simon in early Christian literature, where he is known as the Gnostic magician and arch foe of Peter, "Simon Magus."[3]

It is impossible to tell if any of these legendary accounts of Simon's later career contain even a granule of truth. If no record of these later accounts existed, it is doubtful whether anyone would dispute the face value account of Simon's conversion. However, granting that Simon was a genuine believer, it is obvious that he possessed an immature faith which was superficially grounded in miracles and displays of power. He became close to Philip, perhaps to ascertain Philip's power source.

The Apostles in Samaria (8:14–25)

For Samaritans to come to faith was not exactly unprecedented (see Luke 17:15–18; John 4:1–42); nonetheless, it was an unexpected, although joyful, surprise. Even though the Samaritans were related to the Jewish people genealogically and theologically and were circumcised, they were not considered Jews. According to Jewish opinion, Samaritans existed in a sort of netherworld, hovering somewhere between Jews and Gentiles. Philip sent for the apostles to come to Samaria and grant their endorsement of this new work of God.

Samaritans Receive the Spirit (8:14–17)

It was going to take persuasive testimony to convince everyone back in Jerusalem to accept their new Samaritan brethren. The Torah legislates that matters are to be established by two or three witnesses (Deut.19:15), and Peter and John arrived to investigate and offer Philip their apostolic approval. For the second time Peter used his keys to the kingdom, this time to publicly open the door of salvation to the Samaritans.

There is a subtle irony in John's presence in this apostolic delegation. On a previous occasion, John and his brother James had asked permission of

Jesus to rain down fire and brimstone on the Samaritans (Luke 9:54). Yet now he and Peter would receive the Samaritans as their brothers. Incidentally, Acts 8:14 is Luke's final mention of John by name within the Acts narrative.

Although the Samaritans had believed in Jesus and publicly professed their allegiance to Him through water baptism, no Samaritan had yet received Spirit baptism. That Luke actively points out this fact is clear indication of its exceptional nature. To have believed in Jesus and not to have simultaneously received the Holy Spirit was a conspicuous anomaly, one that can only be explained by the uniqueness of the new Samaritan believers themselves.

An authenticating sign was necessary for both the apostles and the Samaritan believers. Both parties needed assurance that God had truly received the Samaritans. From the time of Jesus' commission, the apostles had ministered in an exclusively Jewish context, and they required confirmation that Samaritans were to be treated on equal basis with Jewish believers. Similarly, the Samaritans, so long reviled by the Jews, required reassurance of their salvation by a Jewish Messiah.

Peter was the apostle to whom Jesus had delegated the authority to open the gates of salvation, "the keys of the kingdom." Therefore, he would also be the means by which the Holy Spirit was initially mediated to each new people group. He and John prayed for the Samaritans to receive the Spirit, and as the apostles subsequently laid their hands on the believers, a second Pentecost ensued.

As was experienced by the Jewish believers at the fulfillment of Pentecost (Acts 2:1–41), the Samaritan believers likewise received the baptism of the Holy Spirit. Although Luke does not specify how the receipt of the Spirit was manifest, the Samaritans' baptism of the Spirit was most likely visibly and audibly evidenced by their speaking in tongues. This was the first of three "echoes of Pentecost" that occur in Acts (Acts 2:1–4). Even so, although the end result of Spirit baptism was the same as at Pentecost, the means of the Samaritans receiving the baptism were different. Unlike the spontaneous Spirit outpouring at Pentecost, in this instance, the baptism required the formal laying on of the apostles' hands. From this point forward all Samaritans who believe in Jesus will receive the Spirit immediately without the agency of the apostles.

Simon's Simony (8:18–25)

Considering Simon's personal history of sorcery, the spectacular result produced by the apostles' laying on of hands was extremely appealing. He must have believed that the Samaritan "Pentecost" was quite a show, as indicated by his subsequent assumption that Peter and John were some variety of "super-magicians." While Luke is silent as to whether or not Simon himself had received Spirit baptism, there is nothing in the text that suggests he was only a witness and not a participant.

Simon naturally assumed, based upon his prior dabbling in pagan spirituality, that this supernatural power was a transferable commodity and offered the apostles money if they would share a portion with him. (This is the origin of the term "simony," to purchase ecclesiastical office.) Perhaps Simon desired to return to his former identity as "the Great Power of God."

Peter's reaction was both swift and severe; plainly speaking, he let Simon "have it." Fortunately for Simon, his sin did not achieve the caliber of Ananias and Sapphira's! Nonetheless, Peter assuredly dealt Simon a formidable curse when he told him, "May you and your silver both be destroyed!" Peter, clearly shocked at the audacity of Simon's request, informed Simon in no uncertain terms that apostolic authority could not be purchased; the gift of God, the "dynamo of Christian life,"[4] was not a commodity to be sold.

Peter's insightful diagnosis was that Simon's heart was not right toward God. Simon was enslaved to sin, "in the bondage of iniquity," and could be graphically characterized as living in a spiritual state of bitter vomit or bile, *cholē*, "the gall of bitterness." Peter's prescription was that Simon must repent of this evil contemplation and his materialistic perception of God. If it was possible for Simon to repent, Peter promised that it was certain God would forgive him. Note that Peter did not prevail upon Simon to trust Christ; Simon's faith is assumed.

Simon's response is feeble, ambiguous, and ultimately unsatisfying. Lacking confidence to pray to God himself, he fearfully requested that the "super-powerful" apostles pray for him. Although Simon's genuine fear of Peter's curse was evident, his genuine repentance was not so apparent. Regrettably, at this point Simon drops out of the Acts narrative to be heard from again only through intriguing Christian legends.

Peter, John and Philip concluded their ministry in Samaria by strengthening the foundational grassroots of the Samaritans. In the past, the apostles had gone out of their way to bypass the villages of Samaria (Matt. 10:5; Luke 9:56), but this time they passed directly through each population center on their way, preaching the Samaritan circuit as they returned to Jerusalem.

Philip's Witness to the Ethiopian Proselyte (8:26–40)

Luke returned Philip again to center stage, relaying the evangelist's divine commission not to continue on through Samaria with the apostles to Jerusalem. An angel commanded Philip to change direction and head southwest along the particular fifty-odd mile road that descended from Jerusalem to Gaza, one of the five ancient cities of the Philistines. Although some translations take "desert" to refer to the road, it probably referred to the ruins of the old city of Gaza, destroyed in 96 BC, through which the road passed on its way to the new city of Gaza, which was further down the road on the Mediterranean coast.[5]

While making his way down the road, Philip noticed a royal Ethiopian official traveling in his chariot, or carriage, from Jerusalem to Gaza, the direction Philip was walking. In biblical times, what was called Ethiopia was actually the kingdom of Nubia, immediately south of Egypt and west of the Red Sea, roughly in the northern region of today's nation of Sudan and northwest of modern Ethiopia. As the king was viewed as a holy figure too sacred for the menial running of government, Ethiopia was a matriarchy, ruled by the queen mother, the *Kandake*, "Candace," a royal title analogous to "Pharaoh."

While never relating the official's name, Luke does report that the Ethiopian (*aithiops*, "burnt-face") held the high and influential position of treasurer in the *Kandake's* court. He is designated by Luke as a *eunouchos*, a "eunuch." The use of this term is commonly understood to mean that the official was a castrate. Eunuchs were commonly employed in the ancient Near Eastern world as servants of female royalty, to facilitate a closer working relationship than would otherwise be possible with non-eunuchs. However, the term *eunouchos* does not have to imply emasculation.[6] It was often used in the ancient Near East as a governmental title denoting high military and political officials.[7] It is possible that this is what Luke meant to convey by the term.[8] However, whatever conclusion is drawn, this is one private area that ultimately must remain enigmatic.

Additional uncertainty is cast concerning the Ethiopian's religious identity. Luke never so specifies, but the Ethiopian was evidently either Jewish or some degree of proselyte, a Gentile convert to Judaism.[9] In order to weigh the evidence in favor of one status or another, it is first necessary to discuss the various levels of Jewish proselytism.

In first century Judaism, there were three degrees of Jewish proselyte, each directly corresponding to a level of interest in Judaism. The first level was that of *phoboumenos ton theon* "God-fearer," or the equivalent *sebomenou ton theon*, "worshipper of God." These were not actual proselytes, or converts, but Gentiles who worshiped the God of Israel without adopting Jewish customs or practices. The second level is that of "proselyte of the gate," a Gentile who not only worshiped the Lord but also adopted certain modified Jewish practices, excluding circumcision. The third level was that of full proselyte, *proselutos*, a Gentile who completely accepted the Torah, fully identified with the Jewish people, and took on their customs and practices, including circumcision. For obvious reasons, this third category was dominated by females and the second category dominated by males.

As the Ethiopian was returning from having worshiped at the Temple during one of the three big pilgrimage feasts, most likely Passover,[10] and was reading his own personal scroll of Isaiah in the Septuagint's Greek (the translation Luke cites in Acts 8:32–33 and Philip's native tongue), it is most likely that he was either Jewish, a full proselyte, or a proselyte of the gate.

The first option, and one seldom considered, is that he was an Ethiopian Jew. In discussing this section of Acts, most commentators have ignored the historical existence of large communities of Jews in North and East Africa. As early as the seventeenth century, the West had knowledge of a huge community of African Jews along the Nile, south of Sudan in modern Ethiopia, the *Beta Esrael*, "House of Israel," (commonly called "Falashas") who exhibited Jewish customs dating from the time of Israel's monarchy. One of the most fascinating chapters in modern Jewish history is the exodus of this community in a succession of dramatic airlifts from Ethiopia to the state of Israel and their subsequent grant of Israeli citizenship in the latter part of the twentieth century.[11]

The Beta Esraels' folklore asserts that they are the descendants of a Jewish delegation led by the offspring of Solomon and the Queen of Sheba ([1 Kin. 10:1–13] whose kingdom most likely was actually across the Red Sea from Ethiopia in southern Arabia, although Josephus affirms Ethiopia).[12] The legend goes on to claim that this delegation transported the Ark of the Covenant with them for safekeeping in Ethiopia. Remarkably, the Ethiopian royal dynasty claims the same origin, and indeed the Ethiopian church claims to still have the ark in its possession![13] While one would imagine that where there is smoke, there is fire as well, there is presently no compelling historic or biblical evidence to elevate these accounts from the level of folklore.

Notwithstanding legends of Solomon and Sheba and the Ark of the Covenant, there has been a demonstrable and continuous Jewish presence in Ethiopia and surrounding African nations from antiquity. In fact, the entire period of Second Temple Judaism was characterized by aggressive missionary activity. Often overlooked is the fact that both Christian and Jewish missionary outreaches proceeded from Israel not only northward and westward to the familiar Asia Minor and Europe, but south and east to Africa as well. As Jesus remarked to the Pharisees, "you travel around on sea and land to make one proselyte" (Matt. 23:15). From Israel to Ethiopia is a jaunt across the Red Sea or a negotiable trip over land through Egypt. It is not unreasonable to conjecture that the Ethiopian's ancestors were proselytes who had converted to Judaism generations prior to his birth.

Another reasonable possibility is that this Ethiopian official was a full proselyte to Judaism. This not only accounts for his worship in Jerusalem and his possession of the Isaiah scroll, but it fits the context of Luke's orderly and progressive outward expansion of the gospel, from Jews (Acts 2:1–41), to Samaritans (Acts 8:5–25), to proselytes (the eunuch) and finally to Gentiles (Acts 10:1–48). Of course, if he were a literal eunuch, a castrate, this possibility would be ruled out.

A proselyte of the gate is the most likely option, but only if *eunouchos* is taken to mean that he was a literal eunuch. In that case, being a proselyte of the gate would be his only available conversion option. According to the Torah, his emasculation would have prohibited him not only from becoming a full proselyte,[14] but also from entering into the Temple to worship (Deut. 23:1). This, however, would not prevent his entry into the outer Court of the Gentiles.

There are some who have inaccurately concluded that the eunuch was actually the first Gentile Christian. This conclusion, however, is inconsistent not only with the contextual evidence but also with the entire narrative flow of Acts. Luke's narrative construction is geared to the climactic encounter between Peter and Cornelius as the new door of Gentile salvation is opened immediately following Saul's commission to the Gentiles. The text of Acts itself identifies Cornelius as the first Gentile believer (Acts 10:45—11:2). If the Ethiopian was the first Gentile convert, whose conversion predated that of Cornelius by five years, then why was the church so flummoxed by Cornelius and not by the Ethiopian? It is highly improbable that his conversion somehow "flew under the apostolic radar." Would an African Gentile's conversion not rock the boat as violently as would that of a Roman Gentile? To suggest any Gentile conversion predating that of Cornelius does injustice both to Luke's graceful presentation and to historical truth.

However, the eunuch was not the first proselyte to come to faith in Jesus. At least one other Jewish proselyte had previously come to faith by this time, Philip's deacon colleague, Nicolas of Antioch (Acts 6:5), and there were probably others as well in the Temple crowd at Pentecost (Acts 2:10). There are three possibilities as to why Luke chose to include the conversion of this particular proselyte, "proselyte of the gate" (or less likely, Jew) at this specific juncture.

First, Luke intended for the timing of the Ethiopian official's conversion, wedged between the Samaritans and Saul's Gentile commission, to reinforce Acts' theme of an ever-expanding progression of the gospel from Jews to Gentiles and to foreshadow the gospel's climactic achievement of reaching "the ends of the earth." While Jews popularly considered Rome to be "the ends of the earth" to the west, Ethiopia was likewise considered to be "the ends of the earth" to the south.

Second, instead of focusing on the Ethiopian's proselyte status, Luke was focusing on the Ethiopian's racial identity as a black man. This theory, like the first, demonstrates the expanding outreach of the gospel's acceptance, from Semitic Jews and proselytes to Samaritans to African proselytes to Gentiles.

The third and most probable option is that the Ethiopian was a literal eunuch and therefore not a full convert to Judaism but rather a proselyte of the gate. In this instance, Luke is reinforcing the incremental expansion of the gospel's witness, from Jews and full proselytes, to Samaritans, to "half-proselytes," to Gentiles, with the additional overtone of the church's acceptance, without qualification, of one whom Judaism considered to be "damaged goods" and unfit for full community entry.

As Philip noticed the Ethiopian, the Holy Spirit spoke to Philip, directing him to approach, *kollaō*, literally "be glued to," the carriage. Acts 8:29 is yet another indication in the text that the Spirit is a person, not a force. As Philip broke into an athletic trot beside the royal carriage, he noticed that the Ethiopian was engrossed in study, reading aloud in Greek from a scroll of Isaiah. In the ancient world, reading "was almost invariably done aloud."[15] (A royal charioteer handled the horses, of course. The Ethiopian was not reading while driving!)

Philip recognized the passage being read and asked the official if he could use a study buddy. The official politely invited Philip to come up into the carriage and study the Scripture alongside him.

Luke identifies the particular Scripture by citing the Septuagint translation of Isaiah 53:7–8, part of the "suffering servant" passage (Isaiah 52:13—53:12) The official had not merely been reading these two verses, but the larger context as well. This passage is, without a doubt, the clearest messianic prophecy in the Hebrew Scripture. The Ethiopian asked Philip a timeless question still being asked today. It is one of the finest leading questions in the entire book of Acts, second only to the Philippian jailer's "What must I do to be saved?" (Acts 16:30). The eunuch asked Philip, "Of whom does the prophet speak?"

The ancient rabbinic literature strongly attests that it was the overwhelming consensus of the Jewish rabbis that Isaiah's suffering servant passage (Isa. 53) spoke of the Messiah. This near monolithic consensus remained the case until the eleventh century innovation of the renowned rabbi, Rashi, who identified the suffering servant not as the messiah but as corporate Israel, most likely in reaction to the evangelistic use of the prophecy by Christians[16] (Isaiah 53 has been excised from the synagogue's liturgical cycle of public readings.) This corporate interpretation is the current popular consensus (for much the same reason as it was originally innovated), but many Jewish circles still hold the more traditional view. It is the paradoxical tragedy of the Jewish people that the majority are unable to perceive that the prophet spoke of Jesus.

Regardless of the rabbis, it is incontestable that one particular rabbi, Jesus, explicitly identified Himself as the prophetic fulfillment of the Isaiah 53 passage, the one who would suffer, be treated with contempt and be "numbered with the transgressors" (Mark 9:12; Luke 22:37). His identification with the suffering servant is also implicit in foretelling His death and resurrection (Matt. 26:2; Mark 9:31; 10:33; Luke 24:7)), and in his silence before Pilate (Mark 15:5).

In the passage, Isaiah described the Messiah as despised and rejected, forsaken of men, a man of sorrows, without esteem (Is. 53:3). This servant of the Lord was to be rejected by the people of the Lord. Through the suffering of this Messiah, intercession would be made on behalf of all people. This passage stands as a Scriptural monument to Messianic suffering.

The Messiah would have no attractiveness or impressive appearance (Is. 53:2), and Israel would believe that His sufferings were brought on as a consequence of His own sin (Is. 53:4-5). The Messiah would be cruelly pierced through and crushed, chastened and scourged. Yet through His suffering, He paradoxically heals them, bearing Israel's sorrows (Is. 53:5-6). It is for their transgressions and iniquities that He willingly will suffer, not for His own (Is. 53:4).

In Is.53:5 comes the disclosure that the Messiah would not merely suffer, but would die. Despite Israel's sin and disobedience, God would divert the just punishment for the nation's iniquity toward the Messiah (Is. 53:5-6). Although innocent of any violence, rebellion or sin, the Messiah would be killed in the prime of life. Like a perfect, unblemished lamb slain at Passover, He would shed His blood for the redemption of the chosen nation. The ultimate personification of goodness would bear the ultimate punishment, His sacrifice to go largely unrecognized by His own people.

This sacrifice, however, would be central to the divine master plan. It would be the Lord's sovereign aim for His Messiah to be crushed. This was to enable the Servant to do the unprecedented - render Himself as the ultimate and final guilt offering (Is. 53:10). The Messiah would die, yet through His sacrifice make perfect intercession for all sinners by carrying their sins (Is. 53:12). He is called the Righteous One who, by bearing the penalty for the sins of others, has justified His people. As the reward for His suffering and death, His self-sacrifice, He will be exalted and glorified. The murdered Messiah must be raised up (Is. 53:10-12).

Philip used the suffering servant prophecy, and most likely the entire "Servant of the Lord" complex of messianic prophecies (Is. 42:1-6; 43:8-13;

49:1–13; 50.4–9; 52:13—53:12; 61:1–3), to witness of the good news that Jesus was God's promised Messiah. The passage would have been of particular significance for the eunuch, having recently celebrated the Passover. Evidently, Philip's preaching was effective, for the moment the carriage passed in sight of water, the official asked if Philip knew of any reason to prevent immediate baptism. The official desired to publicly pledge allegiance to his messiah

At some point in the past, the Ethiopian had responded to a Jewish missionary and joyfully discovered the God of Israel. To remain simply a "God-fearer" was insufficient for the Ethiopian; rather, he accepted the full weight, responsibility and privilege of Jewish identity as a proselyte (or, if he was a castrate and thereby prohibited from full proselyte status, a proselyte of the gate). At the time of his conversion to Judaism, he would have willingly submitted himself to the *mikvah*, ritual baptism. Upon emerging from the waters of the mikvah, the Ethiopian would have been considered as having a new identity; no longer a Gentile, now a Jewish proselyte. As he had joyfully responded to news of Israel's God, the Ethiopian now responded to Israel's Messiah and would naturally seek baptism to reflect his new commitment as a messianic believer. (Acts 8:37 is not present in the most reliable manuscripts and is most likely a later editorial insertion made by someone other than Luke.)

The area near Gaza, being desert, has very little water. However, during the rainy seasons of November through February and April/May[17] (the "latter rain" of Prov. 16:15, etc.), certain dried out creek beds, called "wadis," fill with water. The Ethiopian's ability to be baptized in the desert confirms that the feast he had attended was Passover. Of the three pilgrimage feasts of Passover, Pentecost and Tabernacles, only Passover falls within a rainy season.

Having instructed his driver to stop, the Ethiopian, accompanied by Philip, entered into the wadi and was immersed by Philip. When they came up from the midst of the water, Luke states that, by means of the Holy Spirit, Philip suddenly and miraculously disappeared. The verb *harpazō* means "to be removed, taken away, snatched, plucked," and is the word behind the doctrine of the rapture (rapture is the transliteration of *rapturo*, the Latin translation of *harpazō*). This word is used by Paul in reference to God's rescue of the church prior to the Great Tribulation (1 Thess. 4:17) and his own personal supernatural experience (2 Cor. 12:2). This sort of supernatural removal is not solely a New Testament concept, but finds precedent in the experience of the three raptured "E's" of the Old Testament: Enoch (Gen. 5:24), Elijah (2 Kin. 2:11–16) and Ezekiel (Ezek. 11:24).

Apparently, the Ethiopian took Philip's disappearance as the delightful cherry on the cake of his re-birthday. Climbing back into his carriage, he continued on his way back to the Ethiopian court, bearing the gospel and rejoicing.

After transporting Philip away from the Ethiopian, the Holy Spirit dropped him off about twenty miles away, in the city of Azotus, which in Old Testament times had been the Philistine city of Ashdod. Philip made his way north, walking another fifty miles up the coastal Via Maris highway ("the way of the sea") to Caesarea, the capital of Judea, witnessing as he went. Later on in Luke's narrative, he reveals that Philip remained in Caesarea, making it his home and raising his family there (Acts 21:8–9). Caesarea would go on to become the center of Hellenistic Jewish Christianity until the advent of the Jewish revolt against Rome in AD 66.

Conclusion

Luke did not record a great deal of detail concerning Philip or his ministry, but what was set down in Acts is top-drawer. Philip's pioneering ministry was a key component in the advancement of the church, without knowledge of which Luke's readers would be unprepared for the commission of Saul or the salvation of Gentiles.

The Samaritan's receipt of the Spirit had authenticated both the salvation of the Samaritans and the authoritative judgment of the Jewish apostles in having welcomed them as brothers. Church history records no rival sectarianism between Jewish and Samaritan believers, which had been the case between Judaism and Samaritanism. This unprecedented merger of Jews and Samaritans created a transitional bridge for the church to continue its expansion beyond Israel and the Jewish people. Now that the Samaritan community had been reached, there was only one more transitional bridge left to build—the bridge from Israel to the Gentiles.

That bridge, however, had one stop along the way to ease the transition—an African Jewish proselyte. The Ethiopian's response demonstrates that no matter where we are in the world, if we seek God, He will find us. As we willingly respond to His divine revelation, God will provide additional revelation. God has an unerring ability to track us down with His gospel. Whether a castrate and, therefore, a proselyte of the gate, or a full proselyte to Judaism, the Ethiopian would assuredly have taken much reassurance in the words of Isaiah which almost immediately follow the suffering servant passage (Isa. 56:3–8). Perhaps this passage, coupled with the suffering servant prophecy, served as the basis for the eunuch's evangelistic witness back home in Ethiopia.

Study Questions:

1. Who were the Samarians?

2. Was Simon a believer? Why or why not?

3. Why didn't the Samaritans receive the Spirit when they believed the gospel?

4. Was the eunuch a proselyte, a near-proselyte or Jewish? Defend your position.

5. Why couldn't the eunuch have been a Gentile?

5. What are the two main Jewish interpretations of Isaiah 53?

6. Summarize Isaiah's description of the suffering servant and his ministry.

CHAPTER 8

The Call of Saul
Acts 9:1–31

Preview:

This chapter contains Saul's life-changing encounter with Jesus, an event considered by Luke to be so critical to the Acts narrative that he recounted it three separate times: here in its initial narrative retelling, later as recounted by Paul before a bloodthirsty mob (Acts 21:27–40), and again by Paul before Agrippa II (Acts 26:1–23). Luke's three accounts vary slightly as one detail or another is omitted, included or emphasized, depending upon the context. Nonetheless, each of these accounts share an identical framework: Saul, while traveling to Damascus to expand the scope of his harassment of the church, has a supernatural encounter with Jesus. Each account contains a description of the blinding light, the astonishing self-identification of Jesus, and Saul's commission to preach to the Gentiles. This divine commission, foreshadowed within the ministries of Stephen and Philip, would eventually transform the complexion of the church from a Jewish sect to a worldwide movement.

Revelation on the Road to Damascus (9:1–9)

It is no exaggeration to affirm that Saul was an unusual person; a unique individual who towers over his contemporaries. His apostolic stature is rivaled only by that of the brash fisherman from Galilee, Peter. In fact, Luke presents Saul's ministry as the logical extension to Peter's ministry, linked together via that of Stephen's. Yet like Peter, Saul was a very human colossus, a man characterized by a singular mixture of admirable qualities, remarkable abilities and idiosyncratic foibles whom God chose and the Holy Spirit sanctified for His purposes. When one assembles the bare facts of Saul's life,

God's guiding orchestration becomes readily apparent in that every aspect of Saul's early biography prepared him for the distinctive ministry to which God would call him.

Sometime prior to Saul's birth, his parents had emigrated to the major Roman metropolis of Tarsus, the capital of Cilicia. At some point Saul's father (or grandfather) had been granted Roman citizenship, implying perhaps that he had either performed some service for the state or held municipal office at some point,[1] and certainly indicating that Saul's family was a member of Tarsus' upper class.[2] In fact, it is not beyond probability to assume that Saul's father or grandfather actually purchased his citizenship.[3] Alternatively, the most common method in which Jews acquired Roman citizenship was by their parents' or grandparents emancipation from slavery by masters who were citizens themselves,[4] although this seems less probable in the case of Saul's family.

Saul himself was probably born around the year AD 5/6, in Tarsus (Acts 9:11; 22:3), inheriting his father's Roman citizenship, which would prove an important asset throughout his ministry. His Hebrew name, Saul, reflects the pride of his family in the most illustrious historical member of their tribe of Benjamin, the first king of Israel. He also was given a Roman, or Latin, name, *Paulus.* Although it was common custom for Romans to be granted three names, the custom among Jews of the Roman Empire seems to have been to assign only two names.[5]

Growing up in cosmopolitan Tarsus, Saul was probably conversant with Greek since childhood,[6] but probably spoke either Hebrew or Aramaic in his home. Considering his upbringing in Tarsus and Jerusalem, his formal education, and judging from his epistles, it is clear that Saul was comfortably conversant in Greek, Hebrew, Aramaic and perhaps even Latin.

Saul, of course, was a fervent member of the Pharisees, the strictest sect of Judaism, and it is probable that Saul's father shared that affiliation. The Mishnah provides some indication of the rigorous education Jewish children (or at least, the children of Pharisees) received.[7] At the age of five, Jewish boys began their formal study of the Hebrew Scripture; being educated not only in the content, but also in the prescribed rules of biblical interpretation. At the age of ten, Jewish boys added the study of Pharisaic, or rabbinic, legal traditions. It is probable that it was at this age that Saul was sent to Jerusalem to study "at the feet of" Gamaliel (Acts 22:3), where he may have lived with family members (Saul's sister lived in Jerusalem and his family was apparently politically well connected in Jerusalem, as his nephew is able to learn of the assassination plot against Saul in Acts 23:16).

At the age of thirteen, Saul would become *Bar Mitzvah,* a "son of the commandment," which was formal recognition that he was a full-fledged, responsible participant in the Jewish community. It was in Jerusalem that Saul, like all rabbinic students, would also have been trained in a manual trade, in his particular case, that of tentmaking, although it is still debated as to whether this specifically involved working with textiles, leather or goatskin.[8]

Although church tradition ascribes to Saul a rather unimpressive appearance,[9] Luke provides no physical description in Acts to either prove or disprove this impression. From the text of Acts and Saul's epistles, one may only surmise that he possessed an unimpressive physical presence and that due to the severe punishment he received throughout his ministry, his body became horribly scarred (Gal. 6:17).

Luke now continues the account of Saul's program of persecution from where he left off in Acts 8:4. Saul is colorfully described as "breathing," or "inhaling and exhaling," *empneō*, threats and murder against the believers. He is characterized as being passionately consumed with hatred for the followers of Jesus. There certainly were multiple precedents of such godly zeal by which Saul could validate his rabid persecution and vigorous hunt of these "corrupters" of Judaism. Longenecker lists Moses' command to slay the immoral Israelites (Num. 25:1–5), Phinehas' subsequent slaying of the Israelite man and Midianite woman (Num. 25:6–15) and the Maccabees' assassination of Jewish collaborators (1 Macc. 2:23–28, 42–48).[10] Bruce adds the notable example of Elijah (1 Kin. 18:40; 19:10) to the list of God-endorsed perpetrators of holy violence.

Unable to restrict his fury to the borders of Judea, Saul approached Caiaphas, the high priest, for authorization to pursue the fugitives who had escaped to the city of Damascus. At the time of Saul' mission, Damascus had a very large Jewish population numbering in the tens of thousands.[11] It would have been a strategic city from which those who had fled the Jerusalem persecution could spread the gospel. For that reason, the fugitives needed to be located and rooted out before their corruption irreparably spread.

A treaty had been established between Rome and Judea in the intertestamental period which effectively extended the high priest's authority in Jewish communities throughout the Roman Empire (1 Macc. 15:20–24), including the right of extradition. Therefore, Caiaphas authorized Saul to enlist the leaders of Damascus synagogues in his witch hunt to assist in the identification of Jewish believers. The letters from the high priest gave Saul jurisdiction over the Jews of Damascus and authority to arrest the Christian "heretics," both men and women alike, and transfer them back to Jerusalem for interrogation and trial. Although it was rare for a Pharisee to make common cause with a Sadducee, apparently, common hatred made for "strange bedfellows," and their operative philosophy had become "the enemy of my enemy is my friend."

This ancient city lays claim to being the oldest continually inhabited city in the world. Damascus lies northeast of Israel, in Syria. Damascus is mentioned frequently in the Hebrew Bible, specifically in relation to Abraham (Gen. 14:15; 15:20) and frequently as the ally or enemy to one or another of the kings of Israel and Judah. In New Testament times, Damascus was one of the ten Roman cities comprising the Decapolis (Matt 4:25; Mark 5:20; 7:31). In addition, it was the capital and principal city of the region of Nabatea, ruled by Aretas IV (2 Cor. 11:32), king of the Nabateans from 9 BC to AD 40 and the former father-in-law of Herod Antipas (who had divorced his Nabatean wife to marry Herodias [Matt. 14:3; Mark 6:17; Luke 3:19]).

It is of interest that both at this early juncture (likely the summer of AD 35) and later on in Acts, the Christians were commonly self-designated as the followers of "the Way," *tēs hodou* (Acts 9:2; 19:9, 23; 22:4; 24:14, 22). This was a common name for the early church, probably short for "the way of Messiah" and perhaps based on Scripture passages which describe "the way of the righteous" (Ps. 1:6) and "the way of the Lord" (Is. 40:3; Luke 3:4).

Combining Luke's narrative account with the further details contained in the recollections of Saul found later in Acts 22 and 26, it is possible piece together what happened on the journey to Damascus. The road from Jerusalem to Damascus covers one hundred fifty miles and would have taken Saul and his companions approximately six days to traverse on horseback, or somewhat longer on foot. It is probable that Saul and his companions rode down that road to Damascus. On either the fifth or sixth day of their journey ("as he was approaching Damascus"), around midday, they were stopped cold and knocked to the ground by the intensity of a bright light shining from above. Saul later was to recall this as a flash of light more brilliant than the sun (Acts 26:13). The brilliance of the light was certainly intense enough to have blinded him by the time his supernatural encounter is concluded. It seems reasonable to assume that what Saul witnessed was a manifestation of God's Shekinah glory.

Perhaps the glory of God burned with greater intensity toward Saul, for while Saul was blinded, his traveling companions were not. Nor did Saul's companions see in the light He who eventually appeared to Saul, the resurrected Lord Jesus, nor could they distinguish His divine directive, though they all indistinctly heard His voice (perhaps sounding like thunder, as per John 12:29). Only Saul was able to see Jesus and hear His words clearly articulated.

Ancient rabbinic literature is replete with legendary tales of particular individuals hearing what is called the *"bat kol,"* translated literally, the "daughter of a voice"; the voice of God emanating from heaven. However, what Saul experienced was no legend; it was stark reality. Nor can it be entertained that Saul's experience was a psychological disturbance, an epileptic fit, or any other imaginative alternative to authentic historical incident. Saul's life was fundamentally turned upside down by this encounter. In the only post-ascension appearance of Jesus recorded in the New Testament (apart from John's Revelation), the risen Christ dramatically revealed Himself to Saul. This singular moment, when Saul's passion and zeal are divinely redirected from persecuting the church to propagating the gospel, is arguably the most significant event since the giving of the Spirit at Pentecost. It not only changed the course of Saul's life and career; it radically altered the destiny of the church.

It seems clear from Luke's account that Saul heard the voice of Jesus prior to actually seeing him. Accompanying the initial burst of brilliant light was a voice speaking Hebrew, addressing Saul by name. That the voice spoke Hebrew (or less likely, Aramaic) is made apparent through the change of Saul's name in form from the usual Greek *Saulos*, to the transliteration of the Hebrew, *Saoul* (there is no way to transliterate the *"sh"* sound of the actual pronunciation of *Shaoul* in Greek). This particular detail of the Hebrew pronunciation of Saul's name is repeated in the two later accounts of this encounter (Acts 22:7; 26:14). (Restraint will be exercised concerning any claim that this passage furnishes proof that God's *lingua franca* is Hebrew!) If the light had not already gotten Saul's attention, the Lord ensures it by calling Saul's name twice, following a previous pattern of heavenly address found throughout Scripture (Gen. 22:11; 46:2; Ex. 3:4; 1 Sam. 3:10).

What followed the divine utterance of Saul's name is a question, "Why are you persecuting me?" This was clearly a rebuke from God and would have caused some confusion in Saul, who both in self-understanding and by reputation was the quintessential Jew; a paragon of godly zeal and Pharisaic piety. An accusation of this sort would have been inconceivable to Saul. Why would this heavenly being accuse Saul, the energetic defender of Judaism and Torah, of divine persecution? So, brazenly but necessarily, Saul addressed the divine voice's rebuke with a question of his own, "Who are you, Lord?"

Exactly what Saul meant by this question has engendered some confusion. If Saul realized he was experiencing a *bat kol*, a divine encounter with God, why would he have asked to whom he was speaking? In addition, doesn't Saul answer his own question by directing it to the "Lord?" Some have understood the word Lord, *kurios*, in its generic courteous meaning of "sir." Yet it seems indisputable that the context of the situation called for more than mere courtesy. Saul, prostrate in the dirt and blinded by the light, surely understood that he was addressing a divine being, perhaps with the assumption that it was an angel or some member of God's heavenly host. Certainly, it should be accepted that if Saul knew to whom he spoke, he would not have asked the question.

Jesus now again accused Saul of persecuting Him. Although Saul had never had direct contact with Jesus, by persecuting the church, Saul was persecuting Jesus. The unique and organic union of Jesus with his church is a fundamental concept to Luke (Luke 10:16; Acts 1:1)[12] and is later clearly integral to Paul's theology as indicated in his epistles (Rom. 12:4–5; 1 Cor. 12:12–27; Eph. 1:22–23; 4:4–16; 5:23–30; Col. 1:18–24; 2:19).

Saul's later recollections of this event include additional conversation with Jesus, and at some point during their discourse, Jesus physically manifested Himself to Saul (Acts 9:17, 27). It is from this revelation of the risen Lord that Saul will later derive his claim to apostolic authority (1 Cor 9:1). Luke succinctly ends this monumental encounter with Jesus commanding Saul to go into Damascus as planned and await further instruction.

Luke records that Saul's companions, having seen the light but not Jesus and having heard the voice but not comprehending the words, had picked themselves up from the ground and now stood there speechless, staring at Saul. Saul, too, rose up from the ground, and although he also stared, he could no longer see anything. The intensity of the Shekinah glory had blinded him. Perhaps the horses had run off by this time, for Luke relates that the now helpless Saul was led by the hand into Damascus. There he remained, for three days, undergoing a self-imposed fast. It would seem that the Lord had successfully arrested Saul's attention.

Commissioning by Ananias (9:10–19a)

During these three days of blindness and fasting, Saul devoted himself to prayer, an understandable reaction to his new circumstances. While praying, Saul received a vision of a Jewish believer in Jesus named Ananias, who would be the instrument of his healing. Ananias was not one of the Jerusalem fugitives Saul had been pursuing, but was a resident of Damascus, demonstrating that the gospel had already made successful inroads into this strategic city (although Luke provides no details of this penetration). Ananias, noted as a man with a respected reputation in the Jewish community (Acts 22:12), also was granted a vision. When the Lord called his name, Ananias responded with the Hebrew *hineni,* "here am I," the common response to God in the Hebrew Scripture (Gen. 22:1; Is. 6:8).

The Lord directed Ananias to the house in which Saul was staying, the home of Judas on the main thoroughfare running through Damascus, Straight Street. As most city streets in the ancient world were crooked, this particular street was renowned because it was one of two that ran the length of the city in one straight line from east to west. This street still exists today, known as the "*Darb al-Mustaqim.*" Of Judas of Damascus, nothing is known. The fact that his home is on Straight Street indicates that he was a Jew of some prominence in the city, and as it seems unlikely that Saul's companions would bring him to the home of a believer in Jesus, it is most likely that Judas' home was Saul's original destination.

Of interest in Ananias' vision is that God now speaks Greek, using the Greek form of Saul, *Saulos* (Acts 9:11). This is also the first indication that Saul was a Hellenistic Jew hailing from Tarsus.

Ananias is told by the Lord that, as a result of his own vision, Saul would be expecting him. The Lord directed Ananias to lay hands on Saul, thereby restoring his vision. Ananias, however, had reasonable reservations about being in such close quarters with this potentially ferocious adversary. Ananias raised two objections to his mission of mercy. First, Saul's severe reputation had preceded him. Why heal a man who had inflicted so much *kakos*, "evil," on the church? Second, Ananias was aware that Saul's original purpose for coming to Damascus was to expand his crusade against believers. For a Jewish believer like Ananias, there was no more dangerous man in the Middle East than Saul of Tarsus. What if Saul, once healed, then arose to "bite the hand that fed him?" What if Saul were to reject his divine vision?

Acts 9:13 is the first time that the term, *hagios*, "saints" or "holy ones," is used of believers. It will eventually become the most common term for believers in the New Testament.

The Lord responds to Ananias' objections by articulating the divine mission statement of Saul. Saul is God's *skeuos eklogēs*, His "chosen instrument," His "vessel of choice" to represent Him to Gentiles, national rulers and the people of Israel. Although Saul was primarily commissioned as God's apostle to the Gentiles (Rom.11:11–14; Eph.2:11—3:6), God also chose him to witness to both Gentile and Jewish kings (notably Herod Agrippa II in Acts 26 and eventually to Caesar) and to his own Jewish people. Saul was to possess a flexible, "go anywhere" type of ministry.

Furthermore, Saul's ministry was to be characterized by an intensity of suffering for the sake of the gospel. Certainly, Saul could never accuse the Lord of leaving him unprepared or without advance notice of the tremendous suffering he would experience throughout the rest of his life on account of his witness. In what could be portrayed as "God's karma," the one who had caused such a variety of suffering would in turn experience an even greater variety of suffering (Paul provides a veritable shopping list of these personal miseries in 2 Cor.11:22–33).

In obedience to the Lord, albeit laced with a ribbon of apprehension, Ananias located the home of Judas and encountered Judas' guest, Saul. Face to face with the former archenemy of the church, Ananias accepted Saul at face value and, addressing Saul in Hebrew (again indicated by the use of *Saoul* instead of Saulos), Ananias courageously called Saul by the intimate term, "brother." He explained to Saul the mission he had been sent to accomplish; that of healing Saul and being the means by which Saul would be filled with the Holy Spirit.

There is uncertainty as to what Ananias meant by the phrase "filled with the Holy Spirit." While it is possible that Saul had not yet received the baptism of the Holy Spirit upon his initial belief in Jesus while lying prostrate on the road, and that the baptism was only now transmitted through Ananias, it does not seem likely. Unlike his account at Pentecost or with the Samaritans, Luke neither mentions Saul's receipt of the Spirit at this time nor describes any visible manifestation of Saul's filling through Ananias. The sole baptism Luke mentions is Saul's water baptism. It is more likely that Saul had indeed received the baptism of the Holy Spirit on the road to Damascus and that what Ananias referred to as the filling of the Holy Spirit was divine enablement to carry out the challenges of Saul's apostolic commission.[13] This filling of the Spirit for empowered ministry was repeatable; indeed Luke records an additional filling for Paul in Acts 13:9.

Who Was Filled with the Spirit?

Person(s)	Frequency	Reference
The twelve Apostles	two times	Acts 2:4; 4:31
Peter	three times	Acts 4:8
Seven deacons	habitually	Acts 6:3
Stephen	habitually	Acts 6:5; 7:55
Paul	two times	Acts 9:17; 13:9
Barnabas	habitually	Acts 11:24
Pisidian Antioch disciples	habitually	Acts 13:52

Ananias laid his hands on his "brother," and immediately Saul's blindness was healed. Luke describes some sort of a crusty covering, similar to fish scales, falling from Saul's eyes, resulting in complete restoration of sight. As Saul had received his spiritual sight on the road to Damascus, God now restored Saul's physical sight as well. Saul arose, and only after publicly identifying with the death, burial and resurrection of Jesus through water baptism does he finally break his three-day fast.

The Witness of Saul (9:19b-31)

Saul in Damascus (9:19b-25)

Apparently, at some point soon after his arrival in Damascus, Saul left Judas' house and stayed with fellow believers in the city for an indeterminate period (Luke's "several days.") Wasting no time, Saul immediately applied himself to his divine commission. Damascus, having a large Jewish population, had many synagogues. To the synagogues of Damascus Saul had been sent, and to the synagogues indeed, he went to proclaim Jesus to his people.

Instead of acting on his commission from Jerusalem's high priest, Saul instead began fulfilling his commission from the divine high priest. Saul confidently rose to the theological challenge for which he had trained all his life, engaging in debate with fellow Jews about Jesus. Henceforth, the greatest enemy of the gospel was to be its most passionate advocate. Saul's inexhaustible passion and zeal was now directed from the energetic persecution of the church to the vigorous proclamation of Jesus. The infamous enemy of the church was now advocating for its founder.

It is patently clear that Saul saw no contradiction between his preaching to fellow Jews and his apostolic commission to reach not only "the sons of Israel" but the Gentiles as well. Saul's entire missionary career was characterized by his depth of commitment to share the gospel first with Jews and then with Gentiles (Rom 1:16). Although the gospel would not achieve successful reception within the Gentile community for another five years (Acts 10:44), it was within the synagogue that the "God-fearers" and "proselytes of the gate," Gentiles who could be anticipated to be most receptive to the biblical concept of a promised messiah, could be found.

The reaction of the Damascus Jews to Saul's preaching was profound and immediate. Luke describes the Jewish community as being *sunechunnen*, "beside themselves," "astonished," "struck out of their senses." Saul's preaching was rocking the Jewish world; they were bewitched, bothered and bewildered. Saul was, after all, the man who had so extravagantly "ravaged," *porthēsas*, the Jerusalem community of Nazarenes and had ostensibly arrived in Damascus to continue wreaking such havoc.

This unique rabbi's theological arguments, even at this early date, were already so well developed as to be unassailable by all comers. In fact, the more Saul preached the more confused and baffled the Jewish community became. It must be remembered that this was not the first time Saul had argued with Jews as to whether or not Jesus was the Messiah. Saul already had vast experience—arguing the other side of the issue. Certainly, Saul had heard explicit gospel presentations from those believers he had arrested, interrogated, tortured and delivered for execution (Acts 26:10–11). Indeed, he had heard the words of Stephen in the synagogue and at his trial. The gospel was not an unfamiliar construct to Saul. However, it had taken his personal encounter with Jesus himself for Saul's knowledge of the gospel to become understanding and acceptance of the gospel. There can be no question that Saul had obviously absorbed and internalized Stephen's final message. It had not only been the executioners' cloaks that had been laid at Saul's feet that day. The baton of Stephen's ministry had also been dropped at Saul's feet. In Damascus, Saul picked up Stephen's fallen baton and began to run with it.

Son of God. Luke records that the focus of Saul's preaching was that Jesus was the "Son of God," *huios tou theou*. This is the only time that specific title occurs in Acts, although it is alluded to in Paul's sermon in the synagogue of Pisidian Antioch (Acts 13:33).

The term "son of God" appears in the Hebrew Scripture to denote the unique qualities of and relationship between God and Israel (Hos. 11:1), God and the king of Israel (2 Sam. 7:14) and God and the promised Messiah (Ps. 2:7).

Contrary to popularly held contemporary beliefs, in the New Testament the term, "son of God," does not refer primarily to Jesus' physical birth or supernatural lineage or whether he was in possession of divine genetic material. Rather, the designation expresses His unique relationship with God. In Greco-Roman mythology, the child of a god and a human became a sort of "half-breed," possessing semi-divine status. This is not what was meant by the term "son of God" in the New Testament.

In both Old and New Testaments, the term "son" (*ben* in Hebrew, *huios* in Greek), in addition to its commonly understood use to refer to family membership and lineage, was also a Jewish idiom used to indicate "a person's profession, his status or circumstance, or his character."[14]

For example, in the Old Testament, Amos' famous denial of being a prophet or the "son of a prophet" (Amos 7:14) was meant to show that he was not a "card-carrying" member of Israel's prophetic cohort. Another example is "sons of foolishness" (Job 30:8), which indicates people habitually characterized by stupidity.

A New Testament example, discussed earlier, is the name of Barnabas, Aramaic for "son of encouragement," which expresses his encouraging character. An additional example from the New Testament is the nickname, "sons of thunder," given by Jesus to James and John in recognition of their mutually boisterous natures (Mark 3:17). Finally, when Paul calls all Christians, "sons of Abraham" (Gal.3:7), he does not mean to indicate a miraculous transformation in anyone's physical lineage. Rather, "sons of Abraham" are believers who are characterized by the same sort of faith which Abraham exercised.

This understanding of "son" as denoting character is the reason why the Jewish people perceived full well that when Jesus claimed to be the Son of God, He was claiming essential equality with the very nature of God (John 5:18; 10:33–36). The Damascus Jews in the synagogues also had no difficulty grasping the force of Saul's argument that Jesus is the "Son of God." Wrapped up in this one weighty phrase is the entirety of Jesus' messianic identity: His birth, death, resurrection, ascension, and exaltation to co-reign at His Father's right hand. In Acts 9:22, Saul's use of the term "Son of God" is paralleled to the designation *Christos*, "Messiah," indicating Saul's synonymous usage of the two terms. It is not surprising that throughout his ministry, Saul's preaching will place him in one life-threatening predicament after another, beginning here in Damascus.

Arabia. A period of approximately two and one half years elapsed between Saul's apostolic commissioning and his escape from Damascus recounted in Acts 9:23. In Paul's letter to the Galatians, he recalls that at some point following his inaugural ministry in Damascus, he left there to travel elsewhere in the region of Arabia (Gal. 1:17). This intermission in his Damascus ministry probably occurred between Acts 9:22–23.

Many presume that Arabia refers to a vast, barren desert; a wasteland, and that following in the footsteps of numerous preceding biblical prophets, Saul sought solitary communion with God in the purifying heat of the Middle Eastern desert. However, the common assumption that Saul trekked off into the sand, Bible scrolls in hand, to spend years as a solitary hermit developing his theology, is not warranted. There are three evidentiary points that disprove this conception.

First of all, biblical Arabia does not refer to the present day arid region of Saudi Arabia. In the first century, Arabia encompassed the entire region that stretched from Damascus in the north, through what is today the country of Jordan, all the way south to the Red Sea. Although Arabia did include large stretches of desert, it was a populous region composed of many Nabatean Gentile cities. It is likely that, from the beginning, Saul sought not solitude, but to discharge his divine commission and extend his ministry of witness to the Gentiles by traveling from city to city throughout this region.

Second, Saul's total two and a half year ministry in Arabia was bracketed by two substantial residencies in Damascus. His total sojourn through the cities of Arabia need not have lasted more than a year, and potentially much less.

Third, Acts 9:20 clearly indicates that immediately following his apostolic commission, Saul "came out slugging." From the start of his ministry, he forcefully argued that Jesus is Son of God and Messiah. He takes not a minute either to navel-gaze or second-guess himself or his theological constructs. Saul is portrayed as having unmistakably "gotten it."

Saul's theology was in no need of redevelopment. On the contrary, from his fifth birthday, Saul had spent an entire lifetime absorbing the most complex, state of the art, systematic theology that had ever been developed. And having studied Pharisaic Judaism under the master rabbi, Gamaliel, Saul would have been one of the most capable rabbis of the first century.

The sole radical change to Saul's theology was the addition of Jesus as God's messianic provision. Having already spent his life laying a foundation, the gospel served as the capstone of Saul's theology. This gospel was not some odd-shaped piece which necessitated the entire reconfiguration of Saul's theological puzzle. Rather, for Saul, the gospel was the key puzzle piece that had been missing all along and, once in place, provides the "big picture" which makes sense of the whole puzzle.

Some time after Saul's return to Damascus from his Nabatean excursion, most probably in autumn of the year AD 37, a conspiracy to assassinate Saul formed between the Jewish community and the ethnarch (governor) of Damascus (2 Cor. 11:32). This was but the first of many such conspiracies, all of which would prove unsuccessful, that would erupt throughout Saul's missionary career. Saul's resignation as the chief persecutor of the church had not quelled opposition to the gospel. Rather, Saul had now become a lightening rod, attracting an intensity of hatred sufficient to incite assassination attempts. The arch-persecutor had become the locus of persecution.

However, Saul got wind of this assassination conspiracy, so while the conspirators slyly kept watch over the city gates in order to catch him outside the city walls, Saul's disciples hatched their own plot. By this time, Saul had attracted his own personal group of disciples, his *talmudim*, as was normative for rabbis. Under cover of darkness, these disciples brought Saul to a home which adjoined the city wall. There, Saul climbed into a large woven basket, of braided rope or plated reeds (suitable for carrying bales of hay, straw, cords of wood or small Jewish rabbis trying to make a getaway). As Rahab the harlot had done over fourteen hundred years earlier with the Hebrew spies she had helped escape through a window cut into the city wall of Jericho (Josh 2:15), Saul's disciples lowered him down the wall of Damascus in the basket. By this means, Saul secretly escaped his assassins, having ended his stay in Damascus almost as colorfully as it had begun. Saul entered the city as a blind man and left it in a basket.

Saul in Jerusalem (9:26–30)

Luke does not specify Saul's motive for returning to Jerusalem. Saul himself later indicates that he desired to commune with the apostles who still remained in Jerusalem, to learn from those who had known Jesus intimately (Gal. 1:18). Perhaps Saul also felt it was time to bring his ministry full circle; to return home to the scene of his crimes and attempt to make amends with the Jerusalem church. In addition, perhaps he felt it was the next logical location from which to expand his ministry. At the very least, Saul had family to visit in Jerusalem (Acts 23:16).

Although Saul had been away for almost three years, his malevolent reputation with the Jerusalem church had remained intact. Furthermore, his reputation was also intact with his old rabbinic colleagues and Pharisaic associates. To them, Saul had become a "*meshumed*," a traitor, a betrayer of Judaism and Israel. Luke makes no mention of any effort on Saul's part to reconcile with old friends and fellow students. Luke does, however, record Saul's attempts to connect with the community of believers. Their collective reaction is that of the once hunted toward their one-time hunter—pure fear. They believed that Saul was an ingenious "plant," a "mole," and that his conversion was a sham, a clever charade that was simply his latest tactic to infiltrate the community of faith in order to identify and arrest believers in Jesus.

Enter, however, Barnabas, the "son of encouragement," to intercede for Saul with the apostles. Harmonizing Luke's account with Paul's own recollection (Gal. 1:18–19), Barnabas brought Saul to the leaders of the Jerusalem church, Peter and James, the Lord's brother, who are apparently the only apostles serving in Jerusalem at this time. Barnabas explained to them how Jesus had appeared to Saul, and how He had commissioned Saul for ministry, and that Saul had boldly preached Jesus in the synagogues of Damascus. Barnabas' act of magnanimity, his willingness to step forward and "go to bat" for Saul, successfully opened the door for Saul into the Jerusalem church community. Indeed, Saul was welcomed as Peter's houseguest for fifteen days (Gal. 1:18). Between the instruction of Jesus' friend, Peter, and of His brother, James, it is certain Saul received excellent instruction concerning the life and ministry of Jesus. These apostles must have considerably "fleshed out" Saul's knowledge of Jesus during this roughly two-week period.

Accepted by the church and on intimate terms with Peter and James, Saul once again picked up the prematurely dropped baton of Stephen's ministry, not in Damascus now, but in the same synagogues in which Stephen had preached, debating with the Hellenistic Jews. One can speculate that perhaps Saul launched his Jerusalem ministry by dramatically debating in his own synagogue. Luke uses the same terminology to describe Saul's ministry as he used with Stephen's, making a clear connection between the two men. The connection between Stephen and Saul becomes even more apparent by the reaction of the Jews to Saul's arguments. As they had done to Stephen three years previously, they now attempted to do with Saul, acting upon that ancient adage, "if you can't beat them, kill them." This is the second murderous plot against Saul that Luke records.

Fortunately, however, the church community got wind of the conspiracy and, once again, Saul is forced to make an escape in order to preserve his life. It was decided that the most strategic and, perhaps, safest place for Saul would be his hometown of Tarsus, in the region of Cilicia in Asia Minor. Reading between the lines of Acts 9:30, it might appear that Saul's exit from Jerusalem was decided upon by the apostles and not by Saul himself, who may have impetuously desired to stay on. However, Saul later reveals that at this time, while praying in the Temple, he had a vision in which the Lord instructed him in no uncertain terms to depart Jerusalem immediately, for the Lord was sending him to a Gentile community (Acts 22:17-21).

The church provided Saul with a protective escort to Caesarea, the main seaport. It is probable that during the few days Saul must have spent in Caesarea waiting for a ship to Cilicia, he made then acquaintance of the church community there, including Philip, which would provide the background to the warm reception he would later experience among the Caesarian believers (Acts 21:8-14). Tarsus was Saul's home base for the next five to seven years, as he continued to discharge his divine commission by witnessing to Jews and Gentiles in the collective province of Syria and Cilicia (Gal. 1:21-23).

Tarsus. Tarsus was a major city in Asia Minor (southeast Turkey) and the capital of the Roman province of Cilicia. "No insignificant city" (Acts 21:39), it was the strategic gateway whether by land or by sea between the eastern and western segments of the Roman Empire. There had been a substantial Jewish population in Tarsus since 171 BC. Tarsus was one of three renowned university centers within the Roman Empire, along with Athens and Alexandria. While it is possible that Luke studied medicine in Tarsus, it is unlikely, since he provides not one scrap of geographical detail about Tarsus, unlike his descriptions of many other cities mentioned throughout Acts.

A Glowing Report (9:31)

Luke concludes in Acts 9:31 with a summary of the state of the church in Israel (for the first time in Acts specifically mentioning the region of Galilee). This is Luke's third of seven progress reports on the church strewn throughout the narrative (Acts 2:47; 6:7; 9:31; 12:24; 16:5; 19:20; 28:30-31). Following the departure of the controversial figure of Saul, Luke records that the entire community of faith finally was able to enjoy a period of continual peace, *shalom*. By this time, the gospel had taken firm root throughout the entirety of the land of Israel and had spread from north to south and east to west. Luke highlights that the church continued to numerically expand and grow stronger throughout this period.

Conclusion

Now that the chief persecutor of the church had become a believer and, what is more, an apostle who had quite spectacularly come face to face with Jesus, the period of persecution in which this section began was terminated. One cannot help but reflect on the ingenuity of God's sovereign plan in raising up Saul, His "chosen vessel," to expand the reach of the gospel to an international scope. Saul was uniquely qualified by lineage, temperament, training and experience to represent the Lord Jesus to "the Gentiles, kings and the sons of Israel." In every generation there are Sauls; those whom, although they may seem the least likely candidates to ever exercise faith in Christ, are the ones whom the Lord is specifically raising up for His sovereign purpose. Luke's account should rightly impassion us to pray for a plethora of Sauls to be raised up in our own generation; men and women uniquely equipped to stand on the towering shoulders of the apostles and carry on the work of the gospel.

Study Questions:

1. List ten biographical facts about Saul.

2. What did Saul hope to achieve in Damascus? What did he actually achieve there?

3. List the elements of Saul's divine commission.

4. Describe the content of Saul's gospel witness in the Damascus synagogues.

5. What is the meaning of the term "son of God?"

6. What was the reaction of the Jerusalem community to Saul's return?

7. Take a moment to pray for the salvation of the person you feel is the least likely to ever become a Christian. Consider praying regularly for this individual.

CHAPTER 9

Peter Opens a New Door
Acts 9:32–10:48

Preview:

Luke temporarily interrupts the narrative flow of Saul's biography to prepare the reader for Saul's later ministry. Now that God's apostle to the Gentiles had been commissioned, it was time for the first Gentile to receive the gospel. Although it was Saul who was called to reach the Gentiles, it was to be Peter who would actually throw wide the door of Gentile salvation and break through the barrier into that fertile new ground. Luke shows us how the rabbi would actually follow in the footsteps of the fisherman. To this point, the gospel had progressively been received by Jews, full proselytes to Judaism, Samaritans and the "proselytes of the gate." The next group to fit the divinely established pattern of response in this continually expanding circle of salvation would be the Gentile "God-fearers."

The Ministry of Peter (9:32–43)

Before Luke's narrative "rushes off" to the Gentiles, there is still important ministry to highlight among the Jews. It is now the year AD 40. Almost three years had passed since Saul left Jerusalem for Tarsus. This period of peace and absence of persecution had enabled the church to expand throughout the length and breadth of Israel. Luke picks up the narrative of Peter by joining him as he travels the circuit of churches throughout the Jewish cities of Judea and Samaria and Galilee, encouraging and building up the believers. Luke chose to highlight Peter's ministry in two Jewish cities prior to introducing Gentile salvation into the narrative. Peter will perform one spectacular miracle in each of these two cities. As portrayed by Luke, these miracles are performed by Peter in a style and manner unmistakably reminiscent of Jesus.

In Lydda (9:32-35)

The city of Lydda was known in the Hebrew Scripture as Lod (1 Chr. 8:12). This city is located twenty-five miles northwest of Jerusalem, roughly two thirds of the way between Jerusalem and the Mediterranean coast in the region Philip had traversed as he made his way up from Azotus to Caesarea almost five years earlier (Acts 8:40). Although Lydda was largely populated by Gentiles, this was still an important Jewish city, and Peter had come to visit the Jewish believers there. Perhaps this community of faith was the fruit of Philip's previous efforts.

Peter encountered a believer named Aeneas, who had become a bedridden paralytic eight years earlier, in AD 32, during Jesus' earthly ministry. Peter heals him, making certain that it is clear that the source of his immediate healing was Jesus. Not only did Peter heal Aeneas, but he commanded him to get up and roll up his own bedroll, reminiscent of the same lighthearted instructions Peter had witnessed Jesus giving to the paralytics He had healed (Matt. 9:6; Mark 2:11; Luke 5:24; John 5:8) This miracle was the means by which many of the Jewish residents of the city and the surrounding region of the plain of Sharon became believers.

In Joppa (9:36-43)

Eleven miles northwest of Lydda lay the seaport of Joppa, or in Hebrew, *Yafo* (immediately adjacent to modern Tel Aviv). The church in Joppa had learned that Peter was nearby and they sent a delegation of two believers to Lydda in order to implore him to immediately accompany them back to Joppa. A beloved member of their community had just died, a disciple of Jesus named Tabitha ("gazelle" in Aramaic), also known in this primarily Gentile region by her Greek name, Dorcas. Tabitha's life had been characterized by her habitual charity and making dresses for widows, and so, her loss was felt deeply within the community. The Joppa church was asking of Peter nothing less than that he raise Tabitha from the dead.

Yet again, this is unmistakable confirmation that in the first decades of the church age, only the apostles and their immediate associates were enabled to perform signs and wonders. The community of believers in Joppa was simply not equipped by God for miracles. It was not that they lacked faith that God could raise the dead; they exhibited their faith by summoning Peter. They knew that if there were any chance of such a miracle, they would need an apostle. The ability to perform signs, wonders and miracles was the divine validation of those with genuine apostolic authority, "the signs of a true apostle" (2 Cor. 12:12).

Time was of the essence. According to Jewish law, a dead body outside of the confines of Jerusalem may remain unburied at most for three days and nights. Once Tabitha had died, it would have taken half a day's journey to reach Peter and then another half-day's journey back. This would allow for Peter to get from Lydda to Joppa, but with no margin for delay.

Peter accompanied them to Joppa and was shown into the upper room where Tabitha's body, having been previously washed and prepared by the community according to Jewish custom, was laid. The room was filled with mourners, all widows, who displayed to Peter the clothes they were wearing which Tabitha had made for them. The women probably were displaying these garments to demonstrate to Peter that if anyone was worthy of this sort of extraordinary miracle, it was Tabitha.

Years earlier, Peter had witnessed Jesus raise a little girl (the daughter of Jairus) from the dead (Mark 5:40–41). Peter was about to do the same sort of miracle, following the example of his Teacher. As had Jesus, Peter sent the mourners out, removing all distractions. Peter, now alone with the body of Tabitha and the presence of the Lord, knelt down and, before doing anything else, prayed. Although Luke has noted throughout that Peter was a powerful miracle worker, raising the dead had not previously been part of his apostolic repertoire. On his knees, he then turned toward the body lying on the bed. Peter had heard Jesus speaking to the dead girl in Aramaic, *Talitha cumi*, "little girl, arise." Peter, changing only one letter in His teacher's phrase, uttered the words, *Tabitha cumi*, "Tabitha, arise." The corpse immediately opened her eyes, saw Peter and sat up in the bed.

Extending Tabitha a hand to help her from the bed, Peter excitedly called everyone back into the room, and presented to them a resurrected believer. As can be imagined, news of this miracle was relayed throughout the city, resulting in many Jews coming to faith in Jesus. It is interesting to notice that Luke, as writer, occasionally modifies his descriptions of people coming to faith, for example, using the phrase "turned to the Lord" in Acts 9:35 and substituting the variation "believed in the Lord" in Acts 9:42.

According to the Torah, contact with dead animals made one ceremonially unclean (Lev. 11:40). Therefore, in Jewish society, tanning, which by necessity entails continuous contact with the dead bodies of animals, was considered an unclean occupation. Tanners usually worked in or near their homes, and primarily because of the associated odor, those employed as tanners had to live a minimum of twenty-five yards outside the borders of a city. Jews ranked the occupation of tanning alongside those of prostitution, dung collecting, gambling and driving donkeys.[1]

Jews would not normally make use of the hospitality of a tanner, not wanting to run the risk of being made unclean. The fact that Peter would actually stay with a tanner, and stay for quite some length of time, is an excellent indication the Peter had already relaxed some of the stringencies of Jewish tradition. This would prepare him for what awaited him in the following passage, a key development in Luke's narrative.

Twin Visions (10:1-23a)

Cornelius' Vision (10:1-8)

Luke's readers are now introduced to a Roman centurion named Cornelius, a man of considerable social position, as indicated by his elevated rank. Centurions received double the salary of ordinary soldiers, and were non-commissioned officers who achieved their position by working their way up through the ranks by demonstration of exceptional merit. It usually took fifteen years or more of military service to attain the rank of centurion.[2] F.F. Bruce records the ancient historian Polybius' description (*History* 6.24):

> Centurions are required not to be bold and adventurous so much as good leaders, of steady and prudent mind, not prone to take the offensive or start fighting wantonly, but able when overwhelmed and hard-pressed to stand fast and die at their post.[3]

Each centurion had command of a *century*, one hundred soldiers. He and his men were assigned to a *cohort*, a group of six centurions in command of six hundred men. Luke records that Cornelius was assigned to the *Italian* cohort, six hundred men and six officers who were all natives of Italy.

Caesarea, being the Roman capital of Israel, had five cohorts stationed there, meaning that the city was teeming with thirty centurions and three thousand Roman soldiers based there. An additional cohort of soldiers was permanently garrisoned in Jerusalem in the Antonia fortress, adjacent to the Temple. Cohorts were commanded by a *tribune*. The imposing Roman legions were each composed of ten cohorts (roughly six tribunes, sixty centurions and six thousand men) commanded by an imperial *legate*.

Caesarea. The city of Caesarea Maritima, located about thirty miles north of Joppa on Israel's Mediterranean coast, is one of the most prominent of locations featured in the Acts narrative. Formerly known by the name Strato's Tower, Herod the Great renamed it in honor of Caesar Augustus following a radical renovation and enlargement of the city between the years 25–13 BC. Herod's engineers had constructed the first artificial harbor, making Caesarea a world-class seaport from which the entire Roman world could be accessed.

Herod's engineers had also constructed a thirteen-mile long, twenty-foot high Roman aqueduct to channel the necessary supply of fresh water to the city. History remembers Caesarea as one of the most impressive Greco-Roman cities in all Israel.

Caesarea was the Roman capital in Israel, and served as the center of government administration. In AD 40, it was also where King Herod Agrippa I had his palace. Although Caesarea had a significant Jewish population, the city was predominantly Gentile in character. This volatile mix of populations coexisted together more or less peacefully until AD 66, when underlying tensions between the Jewish and Gentile communities exploded into a period of violent conflict which precipitated the national Jewish revolt against Rome and would eventually lead to the destruction of Jerusalem and the Temple four years later, in AD 70.[4]

Cornelius is portrayed as devout man, a worshiper of God who had renounced the pagan gods of Rome. To Jewish eyes, his official status was as a *phoboumenos ton theon*, a "God-fearer," also known by the equivalent *sebomenou ton theon*, "worshipper of God." As previously discussed, these were not actual proselytes, converts to Judaism, or even "near converts," as were the "proselytes of the gate," but were instead uncircumcised Gentiles who worshiped the God of Israel without adopting Jewish customs or practices or initiating a formal association with the Jewish people.

Cornelius' entire household, his family and servants, also worshiped the one true God. To make plain the intensity of Cornelius' piety, Luke tells us that he was a generous benefactor to the needy among the Jewish people, and was in the customary habit of regularly and fervently praying to the God of Israel. Luke's gospel records Jesus' interaction with another centurion who likewise was a God-fearer (Luke 7:2; 23:47), and in Acts, Paul will have two positive encounters with centurions (Acts 22:25; 27:3).

One afternoon, about 3:00 PM (the ninth hour), one of the appointed hours of Jewish prayer, Cornelius received a vision of an angel bearing a message from God. Having suddenly materialized, the angel addressed Cornelius by name. Judging from the level of this battle-hardened veteran's alarm (*emphobus*, "fear"), this must have been some imposing angel. Cornelius stared at the angel and mustered a modest reply of *ti estin kurie*, "what is it, master?"

The centurion then received his orders from the angel. He was to dispatch a delegation to Joppa to summon a man named Simon to Caesarea. The angel made sure to specify that the particular Simon to bring back was the one whose nickname was Peter, and not Simon the tanner (the story would have ended differently, in that case!) Although the angel certainly could have shared the gospel with Cornelius in a most compelling fashion, that was not

God's plan for either Cornelius or Simon Peter. God desired that these two men's lives intersect, with earthshaking consequence.

The Prayers in Acts

Pray-er(s)	Content	Answer	Acts
11 apostles and others	Not specified	Not specified	1:13–14
120 disciples	Discerning God's will for Judas' replacement	Matthias chosen	1:24–25
12 apostles	Praise	Room shakes, filling with Spirit, empowered for bold witness	4:24–31
Stephen	Final words before execution	Eternal reward	7:59–60
Peter and John	For Samaritans to receive the Spirit	Samaritans received the Spirit	8:14–17
Paul	Not specified	Saul's blindness healed and filled with the Spirit	9:11
Peter	For Tabitha to raise from the dead	Tabitha is raised from the dead	9:40
Cornelius	Not specified	Vision	10:1–8
Peter	Ritual midday prayers	Vision	10:9–16
The Jerusalem Church	Peter's imprisonment	Peter supernaturally rescued	12:5, 12
The Antioch Church leadership	Not specified	Saul and Barnabas commissioned for 1st missionary journey	13:3
Paul and Barnabas	Commendation of church elders	Not specified	14:23
Paul and Silas	Their imprisonment	Supernatural rescue, salvation of jailer	16:25
Paul and Ephesian elders	Paul's farewell	Not specified	20:36
Paul	Publius' father	Publius' father healed	28:8

Peter's Vision (10:9–16)

Luke now weaves in the second and complementary vision of this chapter, that experienced by Peter. This vision would serve as Peter's preparation for what would shortly lay in store for him. It was one thing for a Gentile to invite a Jew to his home, but quite another thing for a Jew to accept the invitation. At noon on the day following Cornelius' vision, on the second day of his servants' journey from Caesarea and just prior to their arrival in Joppa, Peter climbed up on the roof of Simon's house. The roofs of most homes in Israel were flat, usually made of compressed dirt and thatch, supported by wooden beams. Noon was the optional time of midday prayer for Jewish men, and the roof would have provided a nice private area in which to pray. Alternatively, perhaps Peter simply needed to get away from the odor and breathe in some fresh sea air.

However, while up on the rooftop, Peter became intensely hungry and craved something to eat. The custom at that time was for the afternoon meal to serve as the main meal of the day, and culinary preparations must have been in progress downstairs. Many of us can relate to the distraction of sudden hunger pangs when attempting to apply oneself to a time of prayer. However, what Peter was to experience was no mere distraction. He suddenly fell into an *ekstasis*, a trancelike state, a state of standing outside of oneself. It comes as no surprise that in Peter's ensuing ecstatic vision, God uses food to make His point.

Peter saw the sky open, and being lowered down from the sky to the ground was a giant linen cloth, similar to a sheet or a sail, held by its four corners. In this sheet or sail is a miniature "wild kingdom"; a veritable menagerie of kosher and non-kosher animals (excluding fish, who would not be able to swim very well on a sheet, even within a vision). According to the kosher laws enumerated in the Torah, the only animals Jews are permitted to eat are those four-footed animals that chew the cud and have split hoofs, as well as specific kinds of birds. Every other animal is forbidden, including all reptiles (Lev. 11:1–47).

As had Saul on the road to Damascus, Peter now hears a *bat kol*, the divine voice of God from heaven. The voice commanded Peter to pick himself up, walk over to the assembled menagerie, slaughter an animal of his choice and eat it.

Peter, politely yet firmly, turned the voice from heaven down flat. Hungry as Peter was, he was not that hungry! An observant Jew, Peter maintained the laws of *kashrut*, the kosher restrictions mandated in the Torah. Most of the animals on that sheet had been forbidden to Jews by God Himself. Even permitted animals must be ritually slaughtered in the prescribed kosher manner. Peter was not hungry enough to slaughter one of these on a housetop, lacking the proper implements of slaughter. He saw no inherent contradiction in his refusal of the sovereign deity's command, and reminded God that he had never in his life eaten any unholy or unclean food. Perhaps he thought it was a divine test, another occasion to either deny the Lord (Mark 14:66–72) or affirm his love (John 21:15–17). At any rate, Peter was doggedly determined not to fail this test.

God responds to Peter's avowal by instructing that what had been divinely cleansed should no longer be considered unholy. In other words, what God has made kosher could be eaten by Peter. It is particularly significant that Mark's gospel account, which tradition affirms records Peter's recollections of Jesus' ministry, is the only gospel which contains the parenthetical statement about Jesus declaring all foods to be clean (Mark 7:19). Perhaps this vision would years later serve as the catalyst to remind Peter of that particular incident to share with Mark.

God repeats the vision twice more before drawing the laden sheet of animals back to heaven, but Peter continued to exhibit piety above and beyond the will of God. Repetition did nothing to make God's idea any less repellent to Peter. After being shown the vision three times, Peter's obstinacy would seem to thwart even a voice from heaven. It is of interest to notice that God often works with Peter in triplicate: three denials of Christ (Mark 14:66–72), three affirmations of love for Christ (John 21:15–17), and a triple vision in this passage.

Vision Application (10:17–23a)

The termination of the vision leaves Peter extremely perplexed and dumbfounded. Of course, the ultimate point of the vision and of God's statement to Peter is not about food at all, but rather that God had made Gentiles clean; that intimate contact would now be permitted between Jews and Gentiles. Reasoning from the principle of "light to heavy," or applying truth about that with lesser significance to that with greater significance, if God has declared food clean, then how much more so is this true about the Gentiles who are that much more significant than food.

There is a faction within the church, however, who even now are still stymied by this passage. It is not the application of the vision that they find bewildering; they have no problem accepting Gentiles into the church. In fact, many of them are Gentiles themselves. Their difficulty is accepting the implications of the illustration God used to prove his point, that the kosher laws no longer apply to believers in Christ. This difficulty in accepting the teaching of an abstract visual illustration is probably related to a misunderstanding of the propositional truth taught by Paul and in Hebrews that the Torah, the Mosaic Law, the ministry of death and condemnation (2 Cor. 3:6–11), has been rendered inoperative by Christ's death and the subsequent establishment of the superior New Covenant (Heb. 8:6–13). Consequently, these believers unnecessarily burden themselves (and often others) with self-imposed food restrictions, Sabbath keeping and various Mosaic minutia contained within the 613 commandments of Torah from which they select that which seems either most applicable or achievable.

This is not to say, however, that believers in Christ do not possess the freedom to participate in and apply certain aspects of the Torah to their lives. Such freedom is fundamental to both Jews and Gentiles living under grace. The problematic issue is not the exercise of a believer's freedom to live out his godly lifestyle of choice but, rather, the imposition of legal requirements to achieve either salvation or, more commonly, sanctification. This problem of pseudo-Torah observance is not a new one and will merit further discussion when Acts 15 is studied.

For now, however, we will merely deal with the refusal to accept the abrogation of the kosher laws. Aside from the fact that rejecting the face value of God's declaration in Peter's vision would seemingly make God a liar merely to make a point, logic also dictates that this passage proves that the kosher laws have been rendered inoperative. As we previously applied to the vision the rabbinic principal of reasoning from "light to heavy," if we now apply the opposite principle of reasoning from the greater to the lesser, it becomes apparent that God had unambiguously countermanded the kosher food laws. If God has cleansed the Gentiles (the greater), how much more so has he cleansed food (the lesser). What is true concerning the application must necessarily also be true about the illustration that argues the point. What is true about a point being argued must necessarily be true of the illustration utilized to make that argument. In other words, it is impossible to arrive at the conclusion that the Gentiles have been cleansed if the illustration used to prove the point, in this case that food has been cleansed, is untrue.

While Peter was still baffled over what this vision could possibly have meant (not to mention still suffering from hunger), Cornelius' delegation arrived at the gate that separated the house from the street. Luke records the detail that the men did indeed have to ask for directions to Simon's house as they traveled. However, their need to stop for directions resulted in a perfectly timed arrival, just as Peter was meditating on his perplexing vision. The men shouted out at the gate, diligently inquiring whether this was where Peter was staying as a guest. Although Peter was still outside on the roof, he was apparently so lost in thought he did not hear the commotion. The peculiar word Luke chose to describe Peter's reflection was *dienthumoumenou*, a word found only here in the New Testament, indicating Peter's fierce concentration as he kept turning the vision over and over again in his mind, pondering its ultimate meaning.

Cornelius' men informed Peter of five fast facts about Cornelius: his position as a centurion, his characteristic righteousness, his status as a God-fearer, his excellent reputation among the Jewish people, and that he had been directed by an angel to meet with Peter in Caesarea. Peter's reaction was to extend a warm welcome. As it was lunch time (and Peter still had not yet eaten!), Peter extended Simon the tanner's hospitality, inviting the Gentiles to join them inside for the meal and to stay overnight before getting an early start back to Caesarea, bringing new meaning to the phrase, "guess who's coming to dinner." Peter, as well as his host, Simon the tanner, have stepped across traditional social boundaries, although for Jews to host Gentiles was not nearly the taboo that being hosted by Gentiles was for Jews. Perhaps Peter recalled the precedent of the prophet Jonah, who though called by God to witness to Gentiles, attempted to escape his commission by fleeing from Joppa (Jon. 1:3).

Gentile Salvation (10:23b-48)

Jew Meets Gentile (10:23b-33)

The next day Peter and the Gentile delegation departed for Caesarea. Peter had also invited six other Jewish believers (the exact number is specified in Acts 11:12) to accompany them to Cornelius' home, in order to serve as witnesses to the proceedings.

Cornelius was waiting at his home's threshold to greet Peter. When the centurion saw the apostle, he fell to his knees in reverence. Perhaps, as a God-fearer, Cornelius should have known better, but this was a typical Roman response upon personally encountering a great man. Peter's innate reaction to such unfamiliar conduct was the visceral equivalent of, "Yuck! What are you doing?" Peter immediately reached down and pulled Cornelius upright, reminding him that God alone is worthy enough to receive such homage (Luke 4:8). Likely taking a deep breath, Peter, together with his host, crossed the outer threshold and entered the home. Inside, Peter found not just one or two Gentiles, but an entire packed houseful gathered together to meet him. Cornelius, understandably experiencing a sense of eager anticipation, had invited his family, friends and servants, literally Cornelius' friends, Romans and countrymen.

Peter begins his address to the assembled Gentiles by reminding them that it was common knowledge within the Gentile community that contact between Jews and Gentiles of this sort was a total cultural taboo. Jewish tradition, the Pharisaic oral law, prohibited Jews from entering the homes of Gentiles, eating with them, or from being close friends. Entering a Gentile domicile was considered to be defiling (John 18:28). As stated in the Mishnah,

"(The) dwelling places of Gentiles (in the Land of Israel) are unclean."[5] In fact, an entire tractate of the Mishnah, *Abodah Zarah*, is devoted to detailing the complex oral legislation that limited Jewish contact with Gentiles.

While some have identified this Jewish cultural exclusivity with elitism, snobbery or pride, it is more accurately recognized as a highly developed concern over theological purity. During the age of Israel's monarchy, Israel was initially enticed to sin by casual contact with neighboring Gentile nations. In the Babylonian exile, God had severely judged His people for mimicking the idolatry of the surrounding Gentile culture.

Now at last, Peter had finally perceived the point of the vision. He realized that in the vision, God had drawn an analogy between the non-kosher animals and the Gentiles. He made the connection, grasping that Gentiles were no longer to be considered off-limits. As far as Peter was concerned, the Holy Spirit had definitively spoken, and there was nothing more to be discussed. Obedience to God's directive was in order.

We must bear in mind the radical implications of this insight for a conscientious, first century Jew such as Peter as well as for the church he represented. If Jewish Christians may now be allowed to fraternize with Gentiles in their homes and even eat at the same table with them, then any additional barriers between them might not long remain in force. For other Jewish believers who, unlike Peter, had not shared in the benefit of having experienced a triple divine vision, Peter's action would prove scandalous.

Peter invited Cornelius to share his story; to relate the reason for Peter's summons. Cornelius recounted for Peter his angelic visitation, when he had been informed that his prayers had been heard by God and his charity remembered. Following the vision, which had occurred precisely four days previously to the hour (firmly setting the time for this dialogue at 3:00 PM), Cornelius had sent for Peter without hesitation, which now brought Peter up to date. Cornelius, having expressed gratitude to Peter for daring to break through his Jewish comfort zone in this unprecedented visit to a Gentile home, implored his guest to convey God's orders (Cornelius used the term *prostassō*, a military term meaning "command") to those assembled.

Peter's Witness (10:34–43)

Now that Peter perceived the point of the vision, he begins by affirming that God does not show favoritism (Deut.10:17; 2 Chr. 19:7; Rom 2:11). God accepts any individual of any nationality who fears him and demonstrates obedience to Him. Peter's use of the present tense, middle voice for the verb *katalambanō*, usually translated "perceive" or "understand," indicates that this truth is finally dawning on him. Although Peter is ready to use the keys of the kingdom to open the door of salvation to Gentiles, it will take somewhat longer for his brethren back home in Jerusalem to arrive at the same conclusion.

Peter proceeded to deliver a gospel message summarizing the ministry of Jesus of Nazareth, beginning with His baptism by John. This was familiar local history to those who had resided in Israel over the previous decade. Peter's brief outline of Jesus' life and ministry is remarkably similar to the order and scope of Mark's gospel, which, as previously noted, is claimed by church tradition to be based on Peter's personal reminiscence. In Peter's evangelistic address, he concentrated not on the teachings of Christ as much as His actions, in particular His death and resurrection, the particular components of the gospel most relevant to a Gentile audience.

For example, in Acts 10:36, Peter conveyed that "the logos" was sent to Israel, preaching peace, shalom, harmony between man and God. Of primary importance, he stressed that Jesus was the *Christos*, the Messiah, the Lord of all, Jews and Gentiles alike. In Acts 10:38, he adds that as John had baptized Jesus with water, God baptized Jesus with the Holy Spirit (Isaiah 61:1–2), divinely anointing Him with enabling power for a ministry characterized by amazing miracles, all of which were personally witnessed by the apostles.

The resurrected Christ was not revealed universally to everyone, but only to those who were *prokecheirotonēmenois* (the perfect passive participle of *procheirotoneō*, found only here in the New Testament) "hand-chosen beforehand" by God for this purpose. This verse provides the solution to the question as to why Jesus appeared to such a limited number of people. Paul records that Jesus restricted his post-resurrection appearances to approximately five hundred people (1 Cor. 15:6). For almost two millennia, Jesus' self-imposed limitation has unsettled a great many believers and raised countless cynical objections to the historical veracity of the resurrection from skeptics.

Yet Peter acknowledged that Jesus purposely did not appear before any of his opponents; not the Romans, the priests, the Sadducees or the Pharisees. One of Jesus' parables provides insight as to why He restrained Himself from so doing. To paraphrase Jesus, if His adversaries did not believe what Moses and the prophets wrote about the Messiah, they certainly would not believe in Him even if He were to rise from the dead (Luke 16:31).

Indeed, Jesus purposely did not appear in the Temple before the entire assembly of Israel. In this, the history of Israel offers perspective. As was demonstrated from the very birth of the nation of Israel, even the most spectacular of miracles could never guarantee the production of faith. No generation of Israel had witnessed a more extravagant collection of miracles than that generation which was liberated from Egyptian bondage in the Exodus. Yet as Moses recorded, despite all the unparalleled signs and wonders God had performed on their behalf, the majority of Israelites not only continued to refuse belief in God, but they actually despised Him (Num. 14:11).

Jesus appeared only to a select remnant of Israel. This was an exclusive group of Jewish men and women who would see Him, believe that He was the resurrected Messiah and obey Him. It would not have behooved Jesus to cast that most precious pearl, His resurrection, before the swine of unbelievers. No sign, even that of resurrection, would have been sufficient to sway such stiff necks and uncircumcised hearts.

Peter concludes by explaining the apostolic commission, that Christ had commanded the eyewitnesses of His ministry to preach to the Jewish people that the world would soon be evaluated by the divinely appointed Judge. Christ's judgment could only be averted by believing in Him and receiving forgiveness. Peter and his apostolic companions stood in a lengthy historical line of God's messengers who had borne witness that forgiveness of sins is available through belief in Jesus.

Peter had specifically tailored his message to communicate most effectively with a non-Jewish audience. It is an interesting exercise to compare Peter's gospel presentation to this Gentile audience with his previous presentations to Jewish audiences (Acts 2:14–36; 3:12–26; 4:8–12; 5:29–33). For example, the basic gospel that Peter relayed to the Gentiles was that that Jesus of Nazareth, an actual flesh and blood human from a Galilean village, was a prophesied miracle worker who had been anointed by God's Spirit; He had been crucified, resurrected in actual bodily form, delivers God's forgiveness from sin and has been chosen by God to be the judge of all, both in this life and in the afterlife.

Although Peter mentions that Jesus had been prophesied, he avoids quoting specific Hebrew prophecies as he had done, for instance, with the Sanhedrin and the "rejected stone" prophecy (Acts 4:11). He does not call Jesus the Son of David (Acts 2:30), or the prophet like Moses (Acts 3:22) as he had done in the Temple. He does not use an allusion from the prophets like Isaiah's "Servant of the Lord" as he had done twice previously in the Temple (Acts 3:13, 26), nor does he emphasize Jesus' betrayal and rejection by Israel (as in Acts 3:13). Perhaps to avoid confusion with the popular cult of Emperor worship, he does not refer to Jesus as prince, as he had done with both Jews and the Sanhedrin (Acts 3:15; 5:31). Whereas to Jewish audiences Peter highlights that Jesus is the promised Messiah, in a Gentile context Peter makes a strategic substitution. Although he ascribes the title of Christ to Jesus, Peter clarifies this unfamiliar term and modifies it with that of judge; a description the Romans would intuitively understand. The concept of a messiah would simply fail to communicate as much to a Gentile audience as the universally understood judge. In fact, Paul will use the same term in his sermon to Gentiles (Acts 17:31). In addition, only in this passage of Acts is Jesus called Lord of all.

Finally, Peter makes no explicit reference to the second coming as in Acts 3:20. Perhaps he would have gotten around to mentioning the second coming, had his message not been happily interrupted by God's wholesale acceptance of Gentiles into the kingdom.

Cornelius' Salvation (10:44–48)

Although Peter had not yet finished his message, apparently he had said quite enough. In the middle of Peter's presentation, the Holy Spirit fell (*epipiptō*, the same word used of the Samaritans in Acts 8:16) upon the Gentiles. Right there, in the comfort of Cornelius' own living room, he and his friends experienced their own personal Gentile Pentecost. That which the Gentiles had heard, they believed, and they therefore received salvation. That they are saved is made obvious to all when they begin to speak in tongues, the sign that they had received the baptism of the Spirit.

This is the second "echo of Pentecost". The absence of any pattern concerning Spirit baptism thus far in the Acts narrative is striking. In this instance, unlike the events of Pentecost, there is no rushing wind or fire. In addition, unlike the situation in Samaria, in this instance the Holy Spirit was poured upon the Gentiles absent any apostolic laying on of hands. All three ethnic factions to receive Spirit baptism, manifested by speaking in tongues, have done so by very different means.

The six Jewish believers with Peter were flabbergasted that the Gentiles were experiencing the exact same outpouring in the exact same fashion as had the apostles in the Temple (Acts 2:33). Yet the evidence was incontrovertible, for they were standing in a room packed full of Gentile tongues speakers! It was not the manifestation that dumbfounded the Jewish believers, it was the motivating force behind the manifestation, that God had accepted the Gentiles just as he had the Jews. Tongues served as a sign to the Jews that faith alone, trust that the resurrected Jesus forgave sins, was all that was necessary to effect Jewish or Gentle salvation. No external ritual, such as baptism, or even a visible sign of repentance was necessary. Cornelius and his friends neither raised their hands, walked an aisle nor prayed a prayer. They simply believed the gospel Peter had proclaimed.

Addressing his six thunderstruck Jewish companions, Peter asked that since the Gentiles had been Spirit baptized, if anyone objected to the new believers being water baptized as well. As phrased syntactically, the question actually requires a negative answer. If any of the believers cared to respond with reservations, he apparently kept his peace. Peter, now the ranking spiritual authority over the centurion and his company, commanded that they be baptized. Likely, the entire party headed out to the Mediterranean seaside and into the water, where Peter's companions would have baptized each new Gentile believer.

Although some find support for the practice of infant baptism in this passage, the context robustly militates against this, as does the context of every other instance of water baptism in the Acts narrative. The stress here is on baptizing those individuals who had *believed* in Jesus. Furthermore, the mention of Cornelius' *suggeneis*, "relatives," being present (Acts 10:24) in no way necessitates the presence of infants or even small children. In fact, the presence of infants at such a gathering is highly unlikely since, as described by Luke, Peter's audience seems to have been mainly composed of soldiers and servants.

Peter accepted the hospitality offered by Cornelius and stayed with him for some time in order to provide the fledgling believers a solid grounding of instruction in their new faith.

Conclusion

Two thousand years later, it is hard to imagine the cultural and theological earthquake this event represents. The first full Gentiles, the uncircumcised, have now entered the church on an equal basis with the Jews. As Cornelius had been faithful to the spiritual light God had revealed, more light had been divinely granted. Indeed, God went to a great deal of effort to ensure Gentile salvation: an angelic visitation, a triple vision accompanied by a *bat kol*, the Holy Spirit's reassurance to Peter, and, of course, the manifestation of tongues among the Gentiles. Who knows what the Jewish believers' (including Peter's!) reaction might have been had the Gentiles not broken out in tongues speaking? As it was, this was going to prove quite a controversial "test case" back in Jerusalem for years to come.

Nonetheless, some seven years after Jesus' ascension, Peter had used "the keys of the kingdom" for the final time, opening wide the door of Gentile salvation. Now the way has truly been prepared for the ministry of Saul of Tarsus. Soon Saul will ignite astonishing new advances along the trail Peter initially blazed.

Study Questions:

1. Why did the Joppa disciples seek out Peter?

2. What insight about Peter can be gleaned from his stay at the home of Simon the tanner?

3. Explain what is meant by the term "God-fearer."

4. Why was it so difficult for Peter to understand the vision?

5. Explain why the resurrected Christ appeared to such a limited number of people.

6. Compare and contrast Peter's gospel presentation to the Gentiles with those to the Jews.

CHAPTER 10

Who Let in All These Gentiles?
Acts 11:1–30

Preview:

While Peter had temporarily stayed on in Caesarea, news of what had occurred there had not. News of this magnitude travels rapidly. The church in Jerusalem, as well as the believing community throughout Israel, received word not only of Gentile salvation, but the particular circumstances surrounding the event, notably Peter's cozy association with a Roman centurion. Instead of receiving the news with joy, many met this event with apprehension. Remarkably, the immediate concern was not Gentile baptism as much as Gentile hospitality.

Peter's Defense (11:1–18)

During Peter's absence from Jerusalem, concern over the issue of his intimate connection with the Romans began to fester. When Peter finally returned to Jerusalem, a firestorm awaited him. Luke specifies that "those who were circumcised" took issue with him, which, in an all-Jewish church, simply meant everyone. For the first time, the leader of the apostles is challenged.

An accusation, fairly contemptuous in tone, is made against Peter of his having accepted Gentile hospitality. This accusation, of course, was true. Peter had not only entered a Roman's home, but had also eaten his food and slept in his guestroom! Perhaps their intense reaction can be explained by their equally intense fear that their evangelistic effectiveness in Israel was now terminated. This was potentially the end of the Jewish mission! What devout Jew would give a serious hearing to a group that indiscriminately fraternized with the uncircumcised? Of course, it was not completely out of character for Peter to act somewhat impetuously, but this latest action took the proverbial cake for recklessness. After such an extended period of peace in the church and absence from persecution from the Jewish community, what would the neighbors think?

Peter responds to these heated charges with a complete and orderly deliberation, chronologically recounting his triple vision of Acts 10:9–16 and following events of Acts 10:17–48. In relating his vision he gives careful attention to the lowered sheet and the mixture of kosher and non-kosher animals it contained, specifying "four-footed animals," "wild beasts," "creeping things," and birds. He also emphasized the instruction from *bat kol*, the voice from heaven, to kill and eat, as well as Peter's disgusted reaction and refusal, even though the voice had explained not to brand as unholy what God had cleansed.

Peter continued by detailing that it was not his own idea, but the Holy Spirit's express command, for him to accompany the delegation sent to escort him to Caesarea. While admitting to the church's charge of entering a Gentile's home, he argues his justification in so doing. Although the Holy Spirit had instructed Peter to suppress his misgivings about the venture, Peter had still taken along six other Jewish believers to cover himself. In fact, at that point in his defense, Peter likely gestured toward these six corroborating eyewitnesses, present with him in the room (*houtoi*, "these specifically" [Acts 11:12]). They were with him to serve as witnesses "for the defense." According to the Torah, two or three witnesses were sufficient to establish a matter (Deut. 19:15). Peter had brought along triple the necessary number (again demonstrating his natural affinity for things in triplicate).

Peter argued that the irrefutable proof of Gentile salvation was the pouring out of the Holy Spirit on Cornelius' household. Peter emphasized the remarkable fact that what had happened with the apostles *en archē*, "in the beginning" at the fulfillment of Pentecost, the original Spirit baptism, experienced seven years earlier on the birthday of the church (Acts 2:1–4), had now been repeated with the Gentiles. Peter archly reminded his accusers that their Spirit baptism at Pentecost fulfilled one of Jesus' final promises (Acts 1:5).

In summary, Peter defended his actions by relating his vision and its divine application, the command of the Holy Spirit to go to the Gentiles, Cornelius' divine instruction that Peter would reveal salvation, and that the evidence of God's acceptance of Gentiles was their baptism in the Holy Spirit. "Therefore," Peter concluded, "if God gave to the Gentiles the exact same gift of the Spirit as He had also given to us after believing in the Lord Jesus Christ, who was I that I could stand in God's way?" (Acts 11:17). Peter was in no position to argue with God about to whom He could or could not grant the Holy

Spirit. The Gentiles had believed, and so the Gentiles had naturally received. Salvation had been granted to Gentiles without any modification of their Gentile status.

The accusations of Peter's accusers were silenced. They had had nothing more to say or do but glorify the Lord for saving Gentiles. Although Gentile salvation was hard to believe, it was accepted as exciting news by the Jewish believers. Most of the Jerusalem church most likely considered this initial Gentile salvation to be something of an anomaly, an extraordinary circumstance not readily repeated. About this, of course, they were woefully mistaken.

As a side note and potential prophylactic correction to what potentially could be preached from this passage, it is essential to point out that just because Peter had eaten with Cornelius does not necessitate that pork chops or ham with all the trimmings was on that evening's menu. One cannot assume on the basis of Peter's vision that he instantaneously jettisoned his kosher preferences. Just because all foods were declared clean does not entail that Peter suddenly became indiscriminate in what he chose to eat. I have personally heard imaginative speculation from the pulpit that pictures Peter, like some escapee of the most restrictive of diets, merrily "chowing down" at a smorgasbord of all the forbidden foods from which he had previously been deprived all his life: pork sausage, barbequed pork, shrimp, cheeseburgers, etc.

While a delightful and humorous image, it has no basis in reality. In fact, there is no Scriptural evidence that Peter ever ate *treif* (food forbidden to Jews) at all. Just because God had said it was permissible to eat previously forbidden food does not mean that Peter found it profitable. Freedom in Christ necessarily entails freedom to either participate or abstain in particular activities such as whether or not to observe the kosher laws. Just as there are some believers who would impose kosher practices on others, so, too, there are some who, well-intentioned but misguided, would make the eating of pork, etc., the litmus test by which one judges a Jewish believer's level of devotion to Christ, to somehow prove he is no longer "under the Law" but under grace. Frankly, neither attitude is particularly graceful, in that God's grace is subverted by an ultimately uncharitable agenda.

Nevertheless, what did Peter eat while enjoying Cornelius' hospitality? The probable answer is fruits, vegetables and bread. The Torah places no restrictions on the eating of these items, even within a Gentile context (Dan. 1:12; Rom 14:2). Cornelius, as a God-fearer, would certainly have been aware of Peter's preferences and sensitive to them, having four days to prepare for his guest. At any rate, Peter certainly would have returned from his time in Caesarea more healthful!

Antioch's Witness (11:19–30)

Luke picks up the previous thread of his narrative from which he departed in Acts 8:4, doubling back past the events of the previous chapters to follow up on the immediate repercussions of Saul's persecution on the church following the death of Stephen in the year AD 37. By the year AD 40, many of the refugees from Israel had resettled throughout the surrounding region, specifically in Phoenicia, the region directly north of Israel along the Mediterranean coast, Cyprus, the sizeable island in the Mediterranean Sea situated between Israel and Asia Minor (and the homeland of Barnabas), and Antioch, the Roman capital of Syria, about three hundred miles north of Jerusalem and two hundred miles north of Damascus (Luke omitted Damascus, because he already made mention of the believers in that community). These scattered believers carried out a faithful evangelistic witness within the various Jewish Diaspora communities to which they had fled, spreading the gospel beyond the borders of Israel as had been commanded by Jesus (Acts 1:8).

In addition, Hellenistic Jewish believers from Cyprus and from Cyrene in North Africa had come to Antioch and begun to witness to the Gentiles as well. These Gentiles were presumably "God-fearers" and "proselytes of the gate," those who, like Cornelius, had some frame of reference to comprehend the gospel. Luke indicates that the evangelistic emphasis of these spiritual entrepreneurs was the Lordship of Jesus as opposed to emphasizing that he was the messiah, which as previously noted, was a Jewish concept without a Gentile context. As God was behind these evangelistic efforts, a great many Gentiles responded to the gospel.

Antioch. One of sixteen cities in the ancient world with the same name, this Antioch was often differentiated from the others by the designations "Antioch the Queen of the East," "Antioch the Beautiful," and "Antioch the Great." As it was situated in Syria, on the Orontes river, it was also called by the imaginative, "Antioch on the Orontes." With a population of eight hundred thousand, it was the third largest city in the Roman Empire, continually nipping at the heels of Rome and Alexandria for second place. Although it was predominantly populated by Gentiles, there was a significant minority of Jews, comprising about fourteen percent of the populace (almost half again as high as the Jewish population of the entire Roman Empire, estimated to be ten percent).

Antioch was the New York City of its day, at the crossroads of the Roman Empire, a bustling melting pot where East met West.[1] Like the "Big Apple," it attracted a steady flood of immigrants from all corners of the Empire, trusting that "if they could make it there, they could make it anywhere." The city also resembled New York by reputation, known as the "sin city" of its day, a major center of pagan worship, notably, the goddess Astarte.

Nevertheless, Antioch was also the home of the initial program of Gentile evangelism, as well as Gentile missions (Acts 13:3). Indeed, Antioch is often referred to as the "mother of Gentile Christianity." Antioch was to prove an important center of Christian faith and theological development for the following four centuries to come, serving as headquarters for the bishop Ignatius, the coiner of the term "catholic (universal) church,"[2] and later the renowned preacher, John Chrysostom.[3]

When the news of the mass Gentile conversions reached the mother church in Jerusalem, the apostles responded immediately. Although to this point the Jewish church had successfully absorbed Samaritans, an Ethiopian proselyte and an isolated group of Roman God-fearers, they must have been concerned about the church assimilating vast numbers of Gentiles into fellowship. After all, if enough Gentiles were added to the church, the entire complexion and nature of the church would be transformed, and then what would happen to the mission to the Jews? Seeking to avoid a potential calamity, the apostles sent their reliable and highly regarded associate Joseph Barnabas to investigate the proceedings in the Antioch church. As a Levite, a Hellenistic believer with roots in the Diaspora and a fellow apostle (of the second apostolic category, as previously discussed) who had also personally been with the Twelve since the time of Jesus' ministry, Barnabas could be trusted to represent the apostolic interests.

Barnabas reported back from Antioch to the apostles that the Gentile evangelism was indeed the authentic work of God. Luke records that Barnabas, the "son of encouragement," lived up to his name, continuously encouraging the new Gentile believers as well as the remainder of the church community. Luke characterizes Barnabas as a good-natured man, spiritually mature and habitually controlled by the Holy Spirit and faith. Barnabas was so impressed by what he witnessed in Antioch that he permanently transplanted himself there from Jerusalem to participate in God's work. Barnabas found his gifts and temperament well matched to the church's needs and proved a tremendous asset. Through his leadership, Antioch's evangelistic ministry exploded with Jews and Gentiles coming to faith. Throughout Acts, Luke regularly reports on the increasing numbers of believers. Although only twice providing specific totals of new batches of believers (the three thousand of Acts 2:41 and the five thousand of Acts 4:4) he nevertheless presents numerical growth as a positive phenomenon and unambiguous evidence of God's blessing.

After leading the Antioch church for an unspecified amount of time, likely one to two years, the ministry had become too extensive for one man's leadership. Barnabas determined that he needed a ministry partner to assist in leading this vast endeavor of Jewish and Gentile ministry. He would need the services of specialist; someone whose expertise and gifts encompassed ministry within both Jewish and Gentile cultures. At this point, Luke reintroduces Saul; last seen sailing home for Tarsus over five years earlier (Acts 9:30).

According to the biographical reminiscence contained in Galatians, Saul had hardly been sitting on his hands or twiddling his thumbs in Tarsus for five years. The divinely commissioned apostle to the Gentiles gives every indication that he had been engaged in a great deal more than tentmaking since his departure from Jerusalem. Although recorded specifics are sadly lacking, apparently Saul had engaged himself in active and distinguished (as well as unsupervised) ministry to Jews and Gentile God-fearers within the synagogues of the greater Tarsus area, the "regions of Syria and Cilicia" (Gal. 1:21–24, 2:2, 7). It is most likely during this period that Saul "suffered the loss of all things" (Phil 3:8). Whether this "loss" indicates family disinheritance, romantic rejection, loss of community standing and respect, the humiliation inherent in public synagogue thrashings (2 Cor. 11:24) or some other hardships, is unknown.

Barnabas, of course, had befriended Saul when he had taken it upon himself to advocate with Peter and James on his new friend's behalf (Acts 9:27). Barnabas had evidently seen fit to stay somewhat current with Saul, and it appears he determined that Saul was the right man to share in the leadership of the Antiochian church. Journeying one hundred miles to Tarsus, Barnabas sought out (*anazēteō*, "to diligently seek," "to hunt down") his friend, tracked him down and invited him to join the flourishing work in Antioch. Together, Saul and Barnabas discipled an innumerable amount of Jewish and Gentile believers. It must be assumed that, at minimum and in light of the great evangelistic success, the Gentiles comprised one third (and probably more) of Antioch's total population of disciples.

Christian. At this point in the narrative, Luke mentions that it was of the Antiochian believers that the term, "Christian," was originally coined. *Christianos*, probably the Greek transliteration of the Latin *christianus*, may have originally been intended to mean "partisans of Christ," "soldiers of Christ," "Christ people, "little Christs" or simply "followers of Christ." It is syntactically unclear and still debated whether it was the church or the outside community who were the first on the block to use the term. The verb *chrēmatisai*, which literally means, "doing business as," usually translated "were called," is an aorist active infinitive, and although usually understood in the passive sense, i.e., "they were called by others," it may also be understood in the middle voice, "they called themselves."[4]

Interestingly, today some Jewish believers in Jesus chafe at the title "Christian" and seek to disassociate themselves from the term. Generally, there are three basic reasons for this dissociation. For some, the appalling quantity of Jewish persecution carried out for seventeen centuries in the name of "Christianity" leaves them searching for an acceptable alternative to this emotionally sensitive designation. Although often misunderstood as separatism or elitism, this is usually motivated by emotion. For others, it is because they desire to use terminology that will effectively communicate to their unsaved Jewish friends and family, who, because of culture and history, would not intuitively understand what it means to be a Christian. For still others, it is because they have been taught that the term "Christian" was originally a derogatory term for Gentile believers, coined by Antioch Gentiles derisive of the new movement. Therefore, these Jewish believers in Jesus generally like to be called "Messianics," or more commonly, "Messianic Jews."

Yet there is no evidence within the biblical context that the term "Christian," as originally coined, was intended to be pejorative or derogatory. As Luke's record is devoid of editorial comment on the issue, one's opinion necessarily rests solely on inference. One cannot dismiss the possibility that the name "Christian" was a pagan innovation. After all, "citizens of Antioch were known for their scurrilous wit and invention of nicknames."[5] Nor can one dismiss the possibility that if it was coined by unbelievers, it may have been meant in a derogatory fashion. However, it is not necessary to conclude that it was coined by Antioch's pagan community. There is an alternative explanation.

The Jewish believers in the early church called themselves "Nazarenes" (Acts 24:5), "the Way" (Acts 9:2; 19:9, 23; 22:4; 24:14, 22), "disciples" (Acts 6:1–2, 7; 9:1, 20–26) or simply "believers" (Acts 2:32; 4:32; 5:14; 10:45; 16:1) It does not necessarily follow that they would likewise refer to Gentile believers by those same terms. It is not impossible to imagine believers, whether Gentile or Jewish, innovating a new group name for themselves; a name which would communicate who they were (and by Whom they were led) far more effectively within a new, predominantly pagan, context of Antioch.

Having a small Galilean village as namesake (Nazarene) or the ambiguous "the Way" and "believers" might have effectively expressed the group's identity within Israel proper, but certainly would not have communicated effectively throughout a worldwide mission "to the ends of the earth."[6] The term's initial coinage may simply have been recognition that the movement was outgrowing its Jewish sectarian origins and actually becoming disassociated from Judaism proper. An independent identity may have required fresh classification.

The term "Christian" appears a total of three times in the New Testament, Acts 11:26; 26:28, and 1 Peter 4:16. None of these texts reads as pejorative. To the contrary, in each instance, the term simply seems descriptive, whether used here by Luke (11:26), by Agrippa II (26:28) or by Peter himself (1 Pet.4:16). Whether *Christian* was originally coined by believers or pagans, meant derisively or not, the name certainly stuck, and most assuredly, it correctly identifies believers as partisans of Christ, the Messiah.

Whether we like it or not, in the world in which we all live, believers in Christ are universally identified as "Christians." This author's opinion is that "a rose by any other name would smell as sweet." The lively aroma of Jesus is present in all who have given themselves to Him, Jew or Gentile, no matter by which name they wish to be identified. This author gladly answers to Messianic Jew, Messianic, Jewish Christian, Jewish believer, Hebrew Christian, Christian Jew, or simply, Christian.[7] (Just don't call this author "late for dinner!")

Grammatically, if we translated *christianos* by way of its Hebrew equivalent, we would get the term, "messianic." Both terms, "Christian" and "Messianic," mean exactly the same thing and can be used interchangeably. Today, the term "Messianic' communicates a decidedly Jewish ethnic flavor. That may not hold true tomorrow, however, or the next day, as trends, fads and preferences move in and out of vogue among our community of faith.

Antioch's Generosity (11:27–30)

Approximately one year later, roughly in the year AD 44, a delegation of prophets sojourned from Jerusalem to Antioch. Prophets were those individuals gifted to receive direct revelation from God and to speak authoritatively on his behalf. The Jewish rabbis taught that the last prophet was Malachi, and with his death in the fifth century BC, prophecy formally ceased.[8] As on so many spiritual issues, the "teachers of Israel" were again mistaken. Indeed, several prophets are mentioned within the Acts narrative, including Agabus (Acts 11:27; 21:10), the entirety of the Antioch church's leadership (Acts 13:1), Judas and Silas (Acts 15:32) and Philip's four daughters (Acts 21:9).

Roman Emperors in the Period of Acts

Emperor	Years of Reign
Tiberius	AD 15–35
Caligula	AD 35–41
Claudius (Acts 11:28; 17:7; 18:2)	AD 41–54
Nero (Acts 25:11)	AD 54–68

The prophetic delegation to Antioch was led by Agabus, who delivered the first of two prophecies he would make within Acts. Agabus warned the church to prepare for imminent empire-wide famine. Later that year, this prophecy would be fulfilled when a cataclysmic series of famines began which were to continue sporadically for the next five years during the reign of the Emperor Claudius. Ancient historians, in particular, Josephus, record that the Roman Empire was beset by several severe famines between the years AD 44-49.[9]

The prophetic delegation's appeal indicates that the church of Antioch was most probably quite an affluent community in comparison to the less well-healed church of Jerusalem. By this time, evidently, the Jerusalem community had finally exhausted its supply of property and possessions to sell in support of those in need (Acts 4:34). The Antiochian church made a unified effort to systematically collect funds for the mother church's relief in preparation for the coming famine. In demonstration of the principle Paul would later articulate in his epistle to the Romans, the Gentile church reciprocated with material benefits for the spiritual blessings they had received from the Jews (Rom. 15:25-27).

The chronology of Acts 11:30 must be clarified. Luke, who is generally quite conscientious to list events in careful chronological order, seems to have inserted this verse here for thematic reasons, but chronologically it should be placed adjacent to Acts 12:25, following the events of Acts 12:1-24. Some three years later, at the height of the famine, Saul and Barnabas are sent by their church to Jerusalem with this financial aid package. This would allow sufficient time for the church in Antioch to have raised the notable benevolence collection, which Saul and Barnabas delivered to the elders leading the Jerusalem church, likely during the Feast of Tabernacles celebration of autumn AD 47.

Of interest is that the term "elder" is introduced in Acts 11:30. Apparently, sometime in decade of the 40's, the leadership of the Jerusalem church was gradually being transferred from Peter and the Twelve apostles to a council of appointed elders. This adoption of church elders in Jerusalem likely indicates that early church government was adapted from similar structures and traditions within the synagogue.

This visit of Saul and Barnabas to Jerusalem (Saul's second such visit since becoming a believer) should be correlated with the visit to Jerusalem described in Galatians 2:1-10. Properly identifying whether Galatians 2:1-10 should be correlated to Paul's second Jerusalem visit in Acts 11:30 and 12:25 or to his third visit for the occasion of the Jerusalem Council in Acts 15 is a notorious conundrum that will be taken up in detail when discussing Acts 15. Although Galatians 2:1-10 is often linked with the events of Acts 15, the evidence is slightly more compelling for identifying the Galatians visit as that recorded in Acts 11:30 and 12:25.

Conclusion

Unlike today's church, which is so often confused regarding the issue of whether a Jew may be saved and, once he is saved, how much of his Jewish culture (if any) he may still retain, the question which so greatly perplexed the early church was precisely how one goes about saving a Gentile. Indeed, there was a question as to whether seeking Gentile salvation was even a desirable activity. Although the tentative conclusion was reached that Gentiles could be saved and that, like Jews, they are saved solely through trust in Jesus apart from any other activity or belief, the exact nature of the relationship between Jewish and Gentile believers still remained to be fleshed out. How exactly were the two groups of believers to not only mingle together but also successfully blend together in affectionate coexistence? Was that even possible? Should they attempt to unite? Should they go their separate ways? How much Jewish practice did a Gentile believer need to adopt, and conversely, how much of his culture could or should he retain? These controversial issues would eventually come to a head at the Jerusalem Council in Acts 15, an astonishing nine years after Cornelius had turned to the Lord.

Study Questions:

1. Describe the nature of and the reasons for the controversy that awaited Peter upon his return to Jerusalem.

2. Explain how Peter defended himself against the accusations.

3. Do you believe Peter continued to observe the Jewish kosher laws? Why or why not?

4. What is the significance of the city of Antioch and why was Barnabas sent there?

5. Is it appropriate to continue using the term "Christian?" Why or why not?

CHAPTER 11

The Unchained Apostles
Acts 12:1-25

Preview:
Around the time that the church in Antioch was first initiating its charitable collection in preparation for the coming famine, the Jerusalem church was once again pummeled by persecution. Some nine years after Saul's initial persecution of the church in AD 35, opposition now came not from its previous source, the religious hierarchy, but rather from a new source, the recently appointed Jewish king, Herod Agrippa I.

Apostles Targeted (12:1-17)

James Executed (12:1-2)

One possible motivation for a renewed persecution at this particular time was widespread Jewish antagonism to the church's recent policy of incorporating Gentiles into their sect. Traditionally, the only way a Gentile had received an invitation to any Jewish party was through the detachment of his foreskin. The church's new cocktail of mixed Jews and Gentiles was not going down smoothly in Jerusalem, and the city was both shaken and stirred.

Herod Agrippa I. Jewish history fondly remembers Herod Agrippa I as a real "crowd pleaser." Born in 10 BC, grandson of Herod the Great and nephew of Herod Antipas, Herod Agrippa achieved a great level of popularity with his Jewish subjects during his seven-year reign. Severely insecure over his Idumean ancestry through his grandfather Herod, Agrippa went to great lengths both to please and appease his Jewish subjects, bending over backwards to generate their good will. He was especially beloved for moving the capital back to Jerusalem from Caesarea.

Agrippa was not yet four years old when his paranoid and bloodthirsty grandfather, Herod the Great, suspecting betrayal, had his own son, Agrippa's father, Aristobulus, executed in 7 BC. Thereafter, the young Agrippa was sent away from the royal household in Judea, shipped off to receive an education in Rome. Growing up as a member of the Roman Imperial court, the free-spirited Agrippa became close friends with Gaius, the man who would later become the Roman Emperor, Caligula. Caligula appointed Agrippa king of great portions of greater Israel, excluding Judea and Samaria. He proved such an excellent politician, charmer and smooth operator that Caligula's successor, Claudius, granted Agrippa sovereignty over the territories of Judea and Samaria as well. This consolidated Agrippa's complete dominion over all Israel, restoring to him control of the entirety of the territory over which his grandfather, Herod the Great, had once ruled. Agrippa's reign was one of the few periods when there was no Roman prefect or procurator looking over the shoulder of a Herodian king.

Agrippa's untimely death, at fifty-four, occurred in AD 44 (Acts 12:23). Three of Agrippa's offspring make cameo appearances in Acts: his daughters, Drusilla (Acts 24:24) and Bernice (Acts 25:13, 30; 26:30) and his son, Agrippa II (Acts 25:13—26:32).

King	Relationship to Herod the Great	Ruled	Reference
Herod the Great		37–4 BC	Luke 1:5
Herod Antipas	Son	4 BC–AD 39	Luke 3; 9; 13; 23
Herod Agrippa	Grandson (through Aristobulus)	AD 37–44	Acts 12:1–23
Herod Agrippa II	Great Grandson (through Agrippa I)	AD 44–100	Acts 25:13–26:32

It is unknown whether the new persecution against the church was actually instigated by Agrippa himself or if he merely approved the will of the Sanhedrin. Under Agrippa, the court could finally carry out a sentence of capital punishment without having to run to Rome to officially plead their case. The most likely scenario is that both Agrippa and the Sanhedrin orchestrated the persecution hand in hand. Their first action was as decisive as it was brutal. One of the Twelve, James, brother of John, one of Jesus' intimate circle of three, was arrested and beheaded. Decapitation, arguably the most merciful form of approved Jewish capital punishment (the alternatives being stoning, burning and strangulation),[1] indicates that he had been charged according to Jewish law with apostasy.[2] One of the two *boanērges*, the sons of thunder (Mark 3:17), was prematurely silenced, the first apostle to die. His brother John would be the last to die, and the only apostle to die as an old man, of natural causes. Although James and John are central figures in the gospels, Luke places them on the periphery in Acts. Aside from the list of apostles that Luke provides in Acts 1:13, this is the only other mention of James in the narrative.

Peter Imprisoned (12:3–5)

In contrast to the briefest of summaries provided concerning James, Luke is a bit more expansive in relaying the details of Peter's arrest. Realizing that the execution of an apostle was a smash hit with the Jews, Agrippa, ever the crowd pleaser, prepared an encore. Waiting for maximum impact until the combined eight day celebration of Passover and the Feast of Unleavened Bread (both terms are used interchangeably by Luke in Acts 12:3–4), Agrippa arrested Peter. Just as at Pentecost, the population of Jerusalem at Passover would swell to overflowing with Jewish worshippers from every nation in the Empire during this, the most popularly observed pilgrimage festival of the year. Clearly, the tide of the Jewish population's favorable attitude toward the church has turned. The "bloom was off the rose," no matter how many people Peter and company healed or exorcised (Acts 5:15–16). These events occurred during Passover week, AD 44, exactly eleven years following the arrest, trial and execution of Jesus. The way Luke has fashioned Acts 12:3 is an unmistakable allusion to these gospel events, firmly establishing Peter as following in the footsteps of his mentor and Lord.

This would be Peter's third imprisonment in the Acts narrative (Acts 4:3; 5:18). In light of Peter and his cohorts' notorious escape from his previous imprisonment a decade earlier, Agrippa allocates an absurd amount of security for Peter, a quantity usually only reserved for the most dangerous of prisoners. The king was taking no chances with what he hoped would prove the crowning spectacle of the holiday season and the deathblow to the Nazarene movement. Casting Peter into the Antonia Fortress, adjacent to the Temple, Agrippa assigned four squads of four soldiers each, for a total of sixteen soldiers; serving in six hour shifts per squad. Around the clock, at all hours, two guards were personally chained to Peter and two more were stationed immediately outside his cell.

It seemed inevitable that Peter would suffer the same fate as had James. Peter's days were numbered, synchronized with the conclusion of the Feast of Unleavened Bread. Luke inserts, however, that passionate and continuous prayer was being made for Peter by the church.

Peter Delivered (12:6–17)

Late on the eighth and final evening of the combined festivals of Passover and Unleavened Bread, the evening prior to Peter's execution the next morning, Luke's narrative finds the apostle soundly asleep in his cell, still flanked by the two guards to which his arms are chained, with two additional guards on the other side of the prison door. Although cognizant of his friend James' fate, Peter is evidently not too apprehensive, perhaps trusting in Jesus' promise that he would not be executed until after reaching old age (John 21:18–19). Peter had about twenty more years still coming to him.

While Peter slept, an angel suddenly materialized, accompanied by a bright light. Peter, however, was still fast asleep. Remarkably, all four guards had, by this time, either fallen asleep or into a stupor. Somewhat comically, the angel, looking down at the blissfully sleeping apostle, interrupted his slumber by giving Peter a hard push, *patassō*, "a heavy blow" (see Acts 7:24), on his side and telling him to wake up. Perhaps blinking in the bright light, Peter stumbled to his feet, his chains falling off as he arose. The angel commanded him to throw on his clothes for a swift getaway.

Luke tells us that as Peter followed the angel though the now open cell door and past the four sleeping guards, he did not appreciate that this was actually occurring in real time. He thought he was experiencing another heavenly vision, similar to his previous vision of the animals or perhaps like the angelic vision his friend Cornelius had experienced.

Having inexplicably encountered no resistance from any Roman soldiers, the iron gate leading out of the Antonia Fortress now automatically opened of its own accord for Peter and the angel. Exiting the prison into freedom, the angel escorted Peter the length of one street and then vanished as suddenly as he had appeared. Inhaling the evening air, Peter snapped out of his daze and realized that this was no dream or vision. The Lord had miraculously rescued him yet again! This of course, will be hugely disappointing to Agrippa and the Jewish populace who were enthusiastically looking forward to the apostle's execution the next day.

Realizing he would need to immediately skip town and go into hiding from Agrippa, Peter stealthily raced through the dark city streets to where he knew the believers were likely gathered. Before fleeing Jerusalem for safer territory, far from the reach of Herod Agrippa, Peter needed to inform the disciples of God's intervention.

One of the central meeting places for the Jerusalem church was the home of Mary, the mother of John Mark and cousin of Barnabas (Col.4:10). Since Peter knew exactly where to go to find the believers, it is clear that this was a regular location of assembly for at least one portion of the vast Jerusalem church membership. Tradition records the possibility that this was the home in which Jesus and the disciples had partaken of the last supper, in the upper room (Mark 14:15; Luke 22:12), and which had served as apostolic head-quarters following Jesus' death, resurrection and ascension (John 20:19, 26; Acts 1:13). Mary, apparently a widow since her husband is not referenced, must have been a member of the Levitical aristocracy to own a home in Jerusalem large enough to accommodate so many believers (not to mention having at least one servant in her employ). The local house church was gathered there that night, praying fervently and passionately for God to rescue Peter from execution the following day.

John Mark. Acts 12:12 is Luke's first mention of John Mark, who would play a supporting role in the lives and ministries of his cousin, Barnabas, Saul and Peter. It is possible that he and his mother, Mary, held Roman citizenship. Like Saul, he has a Hebrew name, *Yochanan*, "God is gracious," and also a Latin, or Roman, name, Marcus. Mark appears sporadically throughout the New Testament, both in the Acts narrative (12:12, 25; 15:37, 39) and in the epistles (Col.4:10; 2 Tim 4:11; Philem. 24; 1 Peter 5:13). Mark would later compose the gospel bearing his name, written primarily to the Gentiles, preserving the recollections and teaching of his spiritual father, Peter. Peter indicates that he was responsible for leading Mark to faith in Jesus, calling him "my son" (1 Pet. 5:13). The anonymous young man wearing nothing but a sheet, and who, naked, escaped arrest in the Garden of Gethsemane, is usually taken to be a demure self-reference (Mark 14:51–52).

Having arrived at Mary's address, Peter discreetly knocked on the outer gate to the courtyard in front of the house. The praying believers were far enough toward the back of the house that they could not immediately hear Peter's knocking, although Mary's servant, Rhoda, heard the knocking and responded. Opening the front door of the house, Rhoda peered across the darkened courtyard, unable to make out the shadowy figure standing behind the locked gate. She did, however, recognize Peter's distinctive voice. Upon hearing Peter's request for entry, Rhoda was so overwhelmed with joy that without first crossing the courtyard to open the gate, Rhoda excitedly ran back inside to inform the believers, leaving Peter still standing there.

Once back inside, Rhoda shared her thrilling news with the church. Astonishingly, the believers do not believe her, joking perhaps, that she was *mainomai*, loony, or "nuts." For a group devoting themselves to an all night prayer meeting, this reaction is, to say the least, puzzling. Undoubtedly, certain doubts had crept in to this group about what God was or was not going to accomplish on Peter's behalf, in light of God's previous failure to deliver James from similar circumstances.

Nevertheless, Rhoda continued to vigorously assert, *diischurizomai*, that Peter was outside. Finally, she was able to convince the church that there was indeed someone standing at the gate, but they steadfastly refused to believe that it could be Peter, suggesting instead that it was only Peter's angel. This reflects a common Jewish belief held at that time that each person has a guardian angel assigned to him or her (Gen. 48:16; Ps. 91:11; Matt.18:10), who, at times, may assume human appearance (Heb.13:2), occasionally of the person for whom he is guardian.[3]

Even if it were *only* Peter's guardian angel who was doing the knocking, one would expect the crowd would have run over to the door out of sheer curiosity in order to come face to face with an actual angel! This was not their response, however, and they continued to sit and have a heated discussion over who was or was not standing outside at the gate.

Simultaneous with this comical exchange, this whole time, Peter has still been knocking, waiting to be invited in to safety. Finally, either in desperation or frustration, his discreet knocking turns to increasingly insistent pounding. His persistence paid off and the assembly, taking a respite from their mini-shouting match, rush to the front door to see who is knocking so loudly in the middle of the night. Recognizing that standing there was neither a figment of Rhoda's imagination nor an angelic being, but their beloved Peter, in the flesh, they run across the courtyard, open the front gate and invite him inside.

Once safely inside, the door shut behind him, Peter signaled with his hand for the amazed crowd to silence their enthusiastic uproar. Relaying the miraculous details of his rescue from the Antonia, Peter instructs them to report this to James (the Lord's brother, not the recently beheaded brother of John!) and the other Jerusalem believers. Then Peter left their company, mysteriously disappearing back into the night, heading *eis heteron topon*, "to another place."

This episode raises the matter as to why God chose to rescue the apostle Peter but not the apostle James. This is a question that has no ready answer, accept to affirm the Scriptural record that from our perspective, God sometimes acts inconsistently and unpredictably, according to His sovereign will and purpose. One lesson that can be construed from God's dealings with both believers and unbelievers in Acts is that although God's character may be immutable, nonetheless, He refuses to be confined to a box or to one inflexible pattern of behavior.

Repercussions (12:18–25)

At daybreak, upon the change of guard at the Antonia Fortress, Peter's disappearance from his cell was discovered. Once again, this apostle, this seeming wily "Houdini," had managed to give the authorities the slip. Luke records that there was "no small disturbance among the soldiers" because of this. The guard had every right to be highly agitated, for Peter's disappearance had put their lives on the line. Agrippa was not pleased that his plans for a stunning holiday finale had been thwarted.

After conducting a systematic yet unsuccessful search for Peter, Agrippa continued his investigation by interrogating the guards. Thoroughly dissatisfied and frustrated with what little he had learned, Agrippa ordered their execution, standard procedure for any Roman soldier who proved unable to discharge his duties, in this case, the simple guarding of a chained prisoner. Their deaths were collateral damage in the wake of God's response to Agrippa's apostolic persecution. Yet in the words of Al Jolson, "you ain't seen nothing yet!" The execution of four Roman guards was only a prologue to what God had in store for Agrippa himself.

Following the disappointing denouement of Passover, Herod Agrippa left Jerusalem, returning to his palace in Caesarea to deal with an international political dispute. For some unknown reason, Agrippa had become infuriated with the leaders of Tyre and Sidon, two of the neighboring nation of Phoenicia's major cities, situated just north of Israel on the Mediterranean coastline, and had shrewdly embargoed their supply of Israel's food exports. Rome had granted Agrippa extraordinary power, and one would not have wanted to be on his bad side for very long. Battered into submission, and perhaps worried about the first possible indications of famine, Tyre and Sidon needed access to the "breadbasket" of Israel. They sent ambassadors and a huge delegation to sue for peace, having also enlisted the aid of Agrippa's close personal associate, Blastus, probably through bribery. While this happens to be one minor political squabble that no historical document corroborates, there is excellent historical verification for the manner in which this squabble was resolved.

In the summer of AD 44, on a day of festivities ostensibly honoring the Roman emperor, Claudius, the citizens of Tyre and Sidon, as well as those of Caesarea, were assembled together in the city's magnificent theater. Luke relays that Agrippa ascended to the speaker's platform and, sitting down in the seat of authority, began to make an oration. In contrast with contemporary practice, in the first century, speeches were usually presented while seated. So powerful was Agrippa's speech and so sycophantic and obsequious his audience, that the crowd reacted with worship, erupting into a chant of *theou phonē kai ouk anthrōpou*, "the sound of a god, not a man!" Evidently, Herod Agrippa's response to the worship of the crowd was not quite along the lines of Peter's modest reaction to Cornelius' misdirected homage (Acts 10:26).

Josephus also records this event in expanded, as well as graphic, detail:

> . . . (Agrippa) put on a garment made wholly of silver, and of a contexture truly wonderful, and came into the theatre early in the morning; at which time the silver of his garment being illuminated by the fresh reflection of the sun's rays upon it, shone out after a surprising manner, and was so resplendent at to spread a horror over those that looked intently upon him; and presently his flatterers cried out, one from one place, and another from another (though not for his good), that he was a god; and they added, "Be thou merciful to us; for although we have hitherto reverenced thee only as a man, yet shall we henceforth own thee as superior to mortal nature." Upon this the king did neither rebuke them, nor reject their impious flattery . . . A severe pain also arose in his belly, and began in a most violent manner . . . And when he had been quite worn out by the pain in his belly for five days, he departed this life.[4]

God reacted with swift judgment to Agrippa's acceptance of the crowd's flattery. Doubling over with intestinal distress on the speaker's platform, Agrippa is carried from the theater, dying. Agonizingly lingering on his deathbed for five days, Agrippa finally died, as Luke diagnoses, having been "eaten by worms," most likely, ten to sixteen inch-long intestinal roundworms, which feed on intestinal fluids, causing bowel obstruction, "copious vomiting of worms," and finally, death.[5] Although gruesome, it was not an atypical way to die in the ancient world. The moral of this story is that assailing God's apostles is never recommended, even for a king. Upon Herod Agrippa's untimely demise, his kingdom did not pass to his teenage son, Agrippa II. The Roman emperor, Claudius, once again appointed a Roman procurator over Israel.

Acts 12:24 contains yet another glowing summary, the fourth of Luke's seven progress reports on the church strewn throughout the narrative (Acts 2:47; 6:7; 9:31; 12:24; 16:5; 19:20; 28:30–31). With the death of Herod and the termination of the threat facing the Jerusalem leadership, the mother church once again had a chance to breathe and thrive. For the next three years, from AD 44–47, conditions in Jerusalem would be conducive to the numerical and spiritual growth of the church.

However, during those same three years, as predicted by Agabus (Acts 11:28), famine and hunger would shake the church to the core. Providentially, in what must have been their most dire hour, to the rescue came Barnabas and Saul. In Acts 12:25, Luke jumps back thematically to the Antiochian church's benevolence collection (Acts 11:30) as well as forward chronologically to Saul and Barnabas' actual delivery of the gift to the Jerusalem elders, three years later, in the autumn of AD 47.

In Paul's letter to the Galatians, he briefly mentions this visit to Jerusalem (Gal.2:1–10), which came roughly fourteen years (counting inclusively) after his conversion. Likely timing their visit with the third of the great Temple pilgrimage festivals, the autumnal feast of Tabernacles (*Sukkot*), Saul and Barnabas led a delegation from their church, which included a Gentile believer, Titus (Gal. 2:1). Conveying their much needed gift to the leadership of the church, they also took this time to privately confer with the apostles also present in Jerusalem at the time, Peter (on a return visit to Jerusalem following the death of Agrippa), John and James (Jesus' brother, not the brother of John, who had been executed).

It seems that the same issue that first arose in Acts 11 concerning the nature of Gentile salvation, surfaced yet again. Some Jewish believers had attempted to compel Torah observance on the Antiochian Gentile believers, including circumcision, essentially teaching that it was necessary for the Gentile believers to become Jewish believers in order to be saved (Gal. 2:4). This false doctrine was a radical contradiction of the grace that Saul and Barnabas affirmed in their teaching. Saul and Barnabas had come to submit their doctrine on this issue to the scrutiny of the Jerusalem leadership (Gal. 2:2). Titus, the Gentile believer, was brought along as a test case. The powwow between the leadership of the Jerusalem and Antioch churches concluded with an affirmation of Saul and Barnabas' ministry to the Gentiles and a repudiation of the divisive and aberrant doctrine (Gal. 2:9). It was incumbent neither upon Titus, nor any other Gentile believer, to be circumcised or Torah observant (Gal. 2:3). This same troublesome issue will emerge yet again in Acts 15:1–29, where it will be conclusively dealt with at the Jerusalem Council.

The Jerusalem leadership acknowledged that as the Lord had commissioned Peter to be the apostle to the Jews, so He had also appointed Saul as apostle to the Gentiles (Gal. 2:7–8). With a final exhortation from the apostles for them to continue their remembrance of the poor (Gal. 2:10), Saul and Barnabas returned to Antioch, taking with them Barnabas' cousin, John Mark.

Conclusion

This is the final section of Acts to recount Peter's ministry exploits. Luke does not specify precisely where Peter next went following his exit from Jerusalem. In Peter's absence, and in the absence of most of the other ten remaining members of the Twelve (who, by this point, have likely become itinerant), James will now assume permanent leadership of the Jerusalem church. As both apostle (of the second category) and elder, Jesus' brother will provide exceptional guidance and constancy to the original community of faith.

The New Testament epistles inform us that Peter would eventually initiate an itinerant ministry of international scope (1 Cor. 9:5). Over the next two decades, until his death in AD 64–66, Peter traveled throughout the major centers of the Roman Empire: Antioch (Gal. 2:11), Corinth (1 Cor. 1:12), Asia Minor (1 Pet. 1:1) and Babylon (1 Pet. 5:13). Church tradition also famously adds Rome. Of course, as he had previously done for a decade, Peter also continued to strengthen the churches established throughout Judea and Samaria, his beloved homeland of Galilee, as well as other regions of Israel. In addition, both the private conference of Gal. 2:1–10 discussed above, as well as the Jerusalem Council, held in autumn AD 49, two years later, will find Peter, at least temporarily, back in Jerusalem (Acts 15:1–29). With the apostle's mysterious exit of Acts 12:17, Luke's account of the adventures of Peter effectively ends; the adventures of Paul are about to begin, as the narrative now focuses on his missionary efforts to Jew and Gentile.

Study Questions:

1. Detail a biographical sketch of Herod Agrippa I.

2. Why was Peter imprisoned?

3. Where did Peter head after his rescue?

4. Why and under what circumstances did Herod Agrippa die?

5. Why do you think the issue of Gentile salvation refused to be settled?

Section 3

The Witness to the Ends of the Earth

Acts 13:1 — 28:31

CHAPTER 12

The First Missionary Journey
Acts 13:1–14:28

Preview:

The first two divisions of Acts primarily dealt with the evangelization of the Jewish people, with the witness of the apostles confined within the geographic borders of Israel. This third and final section of Acts will thrust the reader out of Israel and into the vast expanse of the Roman Empire. Luke's account commences with the first of what will be for Paul a total of three missionary journeys (13:1—14:28; 15:36—18:22; 18:23—21:14). Although within the narrative Luke does not partition these evangelistic excursions into three separate events ("missionary journeys"), they are commonly so divided for the sake of convenience of study. The Antioch church, center of Gentile Christianity and base for Gentile evangelism, will be the launching point for these missions. Antioch is "home base," and each journey originates from this city and terminates upon Paul's return, with the exception of the final journey, which concludes with his arrival in Caesarea. This initial expedition into Gentile territory will be accomplished over a period of one and a half years, from early spring 48 through autumn AD 49.

Barnabas and Saul Commissioned (13:1–3)

By March of AD 48,[1] approximately six years after Barnabas first brought Saul to Antioch from Tarsus, the church in Antioch had grown large enough that there were now five men dividing the leadership. Aside from Barnabas and Saul, Luke also lists Simeon, nicknamed *Niger*, "the Black One." The combination of his Hebrew name with his distinctive nickname indicates that he was an African Jewish believer. In addition, a Hellenistic Jewish believer is mentioned, Lucius of Cyrene, possibly one of the original evangelistic entrepreneurs of Acts 11:20. Finally, Luke lists Manaen (the Greek transliteration of the Hebrew "Menachem"), the foster brother of Herod Antipas (son of Herod the Great, uncle of Agrippa I). It is tempting to suppose that Menachem, an "insider" raised from childhood with Herod Antipas, was Luke's primary source for his gospel accounts detailing the activities of the royal court.

Luke designates these five male leaders as "prophets and teachers," with the basic distinction being that prophets were those who received direct revelation from God and teachers were those who interpreted the prophet's revelation in addition to providing instruction from the Scripture. It is possible, but not certain, that the double particle *te* in Acts 13:1 sets Barnabas, Simeon and Lucius apart as prophets, and Menachem and Saul as teachers.

While the leadership was engaged in a period of dedicated prayer (designated by Luke as "ministering to the Lord," the same phrase used in the Torah of the service of priests and Levites within the sanctuary [Ex. 28:35, 43; 29:30; 30:20; 35:19; 39:26; Num.1:50; 3:6, 31]), combined with fasting, the Holy Spirit communicated with them. Yet again, the Holy Spirit's personality is highlighted. Likely speaking through one of the three prophets, the Spirit singled out two of their number, Barnabas and Saul, for participation in a new ministry, the geographic advance of the gospel into the Gentile world. "The work" to which they had been called by the Holy Spirit likely references Saul's commission, divinely revealed thirteen years earlier in Damascus (Acts 9:15). As commissioned representatives of the church in Antioch, Barnabas and Saul were officially consecrated through their three colleagues' laying on of hands. Through these two apostles, the church in Antioch would see its ministry extend over the vast distance of seven hundred land miles and five hundred sea miles.

Early on in his recounting of this first missionary journey, Luke ceases referencing Saul's Hebrew name, choosing instead from that point on in the narrative (Acts 13:9) to use Saul's Roman name, *Paulus*, or Paul. Luke's choice indicates Paul's adoption of the tactic, "when in Rome, do as the Romans," making a strategic adjustment to facilitate his ministry within the Gentile world. Although some might assume that Saul changed his name from a Jewish one to a Christian one, this is demonstrably false. "Paul" is not a "Christian name," but a fairly common Roman *cognomen*. As a fascinating side note, Fitzmyer includes a cultural tidbit of which I had been previously unaware and which sheds additional light on Saul's choice of moniker. It seems that the contemporary first century connotation of the similar sounding Greek adjective, *saulos*, translated "loose" or "wanton," was a term used to describe "the gait of courtesans and effeminate males,"[2] making the switch to "Paul" a sensible tactic, indeed. This commentary will follow Luke's example, hereafter referring to Saul as Paul.

First Missionary Journey Itinerary
(Acts 13:1—14:28)

Location	Reference
Antioch	Acts 13:1–3
Seleucia	Acts 13:4
Salamis on Cyprus	Acts 13:5
Paphos on Cyprus	Acts 13:6–12
Perga in Pamphylia	Acts 13:13
Pisidian Antioch	Acts 13:14–50
Iconium	Acts 13:51
Lystra	Acts 14:6–20
Derbe	Acts 14:20
Lystra	Acts 14:21
Iconium	Acts 14:21
Pisidian Antioch	Acts 14:21
Pamphylia	Acts 14:24
Perga	Acts 14:25
Attalia	Acts 14:25
Antioch	Acts 14:26

The Witness in Cyprus (13:4–12)

Throughout his introduction to this journey, Luke emphasizes the Holy Spirit's active supervision of this pioneering venture, stressing His "sending forth" of the apostles to their mission field. Accompanying them was Barnabas' young cousin, John Mark, last referenced by Luke as he relocated to Antioch from his home in Jerusalem (Acts 12:25). He would serve as their *hupēretēs*, "helper," or "assistant," and perhaps, secretary, as needed. Departing from Antioch, they traveled sixteen miles west to Seleucia, the seaport, booking passage on a ship bound for the Greek island of Cyprus.

Cyprus is the third largest island in the Mediterranean, measuring approximately one hundred forty miles long by forty miles wide. Strategically nestled in the Mediterranean between Greece, Asia Minor and the Middle East, it was an important trade center. While Luke does not specify why Cyprus was designated the first stop on the apostolic itinerary, the fact that it was Barnabas' home, coupled with its substantial, well established Jewish population, made it a reasonable option. Having sailed one hundred thirty miles across the Mediterranean to the east coast of Cyprus, the missionaries reached Salamis, the largest city and main commercial center on the island. Immediately upon arrival, they headed straight for the synagogues to initiate their proclamation of the gospel to the Cypriot Jews.

To the Jew first. As did each of the Roman Empire's major cities, Salamis had a sizable Jewish community. Within every Jewish community was at least one synagogue. In fact, the Jewish population of Salamis was sufficiently extensive to require and sustain several synagogues. The synagogue served as a communal Jewish oasis in the midst of the vast Gentile world, enabling the Jewish community to remain educated in their faith and observant in their practices. In addition, the synagogue also served as a center in which interested Gentiles might investigate Judaism; an environment in which they could, as God-fearers, proselytes of the gate or full proselytes, worship the one true God. The variegated matrix of the first century synagogue would understandably prove fertile soil for responding positively to news of the Jewish messiah. Paul would capitalize on this accessible network of synagogues to strategically propagate the gospel, using the synagogues, city by city, as a strategic bridge to penetrate the Roman world.

However, Paul's recurring pattern of initially approaching the synagogues involved far more than mere missionary strategy. According to Paul's teaching, sharing the gospel with the Jews prior to approaching the Gentiles was a theological necessity, God's divinely ordained model (Acts 13:46). The gospel had particular relevance to those called by God as His chosen people, and therefore "the gospel is the power of God for salvation to everyone who believes: to the Jew first, and also to the Greek" (Rom. 1:16). To Paul's doctrinal principle must also be added overwhelming passion and unremitting concern for the salvation of his people, explicitly expressed in his letter to the Romans (Rom. 9:1–5; 10:1). Even while faithfully executing his commission to the Gentiles, Paul's motivation was transparently colored by his optimistic belief that his Gentile witness would ultimately lead to Jewish salvation (Rom. 11:11–14). Furthermore, Peter had already established that the inauguration of the coming messianic kingdom was dependent upon Jewish response to the gospel (Acts 3:19–20). Finally, Jesus Himself promised that the world would not see Him again until the moment the inhabitants of Jerusalem cry out, *"Baruch ha ba b'shem Adonai,"* "blessed is He who comes in the name of the Lord!" (Matt. 23:39).

There is no indication in either Acts or the epistles that Paul viewed following this model as incongruous or incompatible with his calling as the "apostle to the Gentiles." Throughout Paul's missionary career, he first shared the gospel with the Jews and affiliated Gentiles within the synagogue prior to directly approaching the Gentiles. Paul's commitment to this principle was so great that in the event the city's Jewish population was too small to sustain a synagogue, Paul first went instead to the Jewish place of prayer (Acts 16:11–13). It was only after the Jews in the synagogue had staunchly and overtly rejected that gospel that Paul would even attempt a direct approach to the Gentiles, even when, as in Athens, he was aggravated by the Gentiles' overt idolatry (Acts 17:16). In both word and deed, the apostle to the Gentiles was unambiguous in articulating the inherent priority of Jewish evangelism (see Rom. 1:16).

Paul Went to the Jews First

Location	Reference
Damascus	Acts 9:20
Jerusalem	Acts 9:28–29
Salamis	Acts 13:5
Pisidian Antioch	Acts 13:14
Iconium	Acts 14:1
Philippi	Acts 16:13
Thessalonica	Acts 17:1–2
Berea	Acts 17:10
Athens	Acts 17:16–17
Corinth	Acts 18:1–4
Ephesus	Acts 18:19; 19:8
Rome	Acts 28:17

Having discharged their witnessing responsibilities in Salamis (Luke does not specify whether they realized evangelistic success), the missionaries made their way across the island, traveling east to west, until they reached the capital of Cyprus, Paphos, across the island from Salamis. There they encountered two men who proved consequential to their ministry in this city. The first was the Roman proconsul of Cyprus, Sergius Paulus, a man who coincidentally shared Paul's *cognomen* (Cyprus, being a province under the custody of the Roman Senate, was governed by a proconsul instead of a prefect or procurator). Interestingly, archaeologists have found a first century inscription on Cyprus, dating from AD 52–53, which confirms both the historicity of Sergius Paulus and his status as proconsul.[3] Luke notes that this governor is a sharp cookie, calling him an *andri suneto*, "a man of understanding or perception." The missionaries had come to the attention of Sergius Paulus, and as he was evidently quite inquisitive regarding unusual spiritual issues, he summoned Barnabas and Paul to present a "command performance" of their intriguing message in person.

The second man they encountered was a Jewish false prophet and magician named Elymas, or Bar-Jesus (whose name incongruously means, "son of Jesus," or "son of salvation" in Aramaic). Elymas had previously gained the ear of Sergius Paulus and viewed the missionaries (who had invaded his turf) as undesirable competition for the affections of the proconsul. Exactly what Elymas did to oppose the missionaries before Sergius Paulus is unclear, Luke simply noting that he sought to "turn the proconsul away from the faith." As Peter had once vigorously confronted the magician Simon (Acts 8:20–24), so now Paul had a similar showdown with the magician Elymas as they battled for the soul of Sergius Paulus. Furthermore, as Peter pronounced swift judgment upon Ananias and Sapphira (Acts 5:1–11), so, too, would Paul pronounce judgment upon his opponent. Paul, empowered by the Spirit, fixed the intense gaze of a true prophet of God upon the counterfeit version standing before him. Denouncing the false prophet as a fraud who had grossly distorted the word of God, Paul derided Bar-Jesus as being *huie diabolou*, roughly the equivalent of "Bar-Devil," the "son of the devil."

Definitively settling the matter of which of them was a genuine representative of God, Paul condemned Elymas to suffer a period of temporary blindness, a condition with which Paul was all too personally familiar. As had been the case with Paul himself, spiritual blindness had once again yielded physical blindness. Unlike Paul, however, the lesson for Elymas to learn was that he who lives by the power of darkness must be prepared to live in that darkness. Immediately, "a mist and a darkness" descended upon Elymas, and defeated and humbled, he began to grope around for someone to lead him by the hand. It is impossible to know whether this outcome eventually led to his repentance. Elymas is never referenced in Scripture again.

It is said that "seeing is believing," and in this specific case, seeing the "not-seeing" Elymas led to the stunned Sergius Paulus becoming a believer. He certainly had his eyes opened to the truth of the gospel. This is the first recorded successful example of Paul's witness beyond the Jewish context of the synagogue. From this point on in the narrative, Paul, not Barnabas, will be Luke's primary protagonist.

Arrival in Pisidian Antioch (13:13-15)

Having tasted success in their missionary endeavor, the missionaries sailed one hundred eighty miles from Cyprus to Perga, on the south coast of Asia Minor. Upon reaching Perga, however, a blow is dealt to Paul and Barnabas. Their assistant, John Mark, unexpectedly left them, mid-mission, to return home to Jerusalem. Luke does not provide Mark's reason for withdrawing from the mission at this crucial point. However, it is certain that the missionaries' daunting itinerary was not for the timid, and it is not impossible to imagine several possible sources of trepidation, such as the dangers inherent in traveling through flash-flood prone, bandit-infested mountain passes or the strenuous physical difficulties entailed by such travels.[4] An alternative concern may have been the radical Gentile emphasis of the mission. Whatever the reason for John Mark's premature departure, we will later learn that Paul considered it invalid and an unacceptable abandonment of their mission (Acts 15:36-39).

Paul and Barnabas continued on alone, leaving Perga for the highlands of Pisidian Antioch, one hundred miles north of Perga. Crossing the rough and dangerous terrain of the Taurus mountain range on foot, they arrived in the cosmopolitan and architecturally impressive Roman colony of Pisidian Antioch, a hefty thirty-six hundred feet above sea level. Pisidian Antioch was actually within the province of Galatia but was so called as a result of being adjacent to the Pisidian region. This was another well-traveled city, the bustling axis of Asia Minor's east-west traffic. Not surprisingly, it also contained a large Jewish population. Following their established model of preaching the gospel to the Jew first, on the Sabbath the missionaries headed to the synagogue, taking their seats among the congregation.

Following the opening liturgical preliminaries of the service, the corporate affirmation of the *Sh'ma* (the Jewish declaration of faith based on Deut. 6:4ff, which dramatically begins "Hear O Israel! The Lord our God; the Lord is One!") and the corporate praying of the *Amidah*, or Eighteen Benedictions, the weekly portion of the Torah, the five books of Moses, was read, following an annual cycle. At the conclusion of the recitation of the Torah portion, an accompanying selection from the *Haftorah* (the Prophets and the Writings) was recited. Upon the conclusion of the reading of the Torah and Haftorah portions, a short lesson or sermon was delivered, usually, but not always, based on the contents of one of the recited Scriptures.

According to first century Jewish custom, if there was a distinguished guest present in the congregation that morning, a visiting rabbi or other Jewish authority, he might well be invited to preach as an expression of hospitality (and possibly to break the monotony of hearing from the same local rabbis week after week!)[5] That morning, Paul and Barnabas received one such invitation, which Paul accepted. Later, in Paul's letter to the Galatian church, Paul indicates that he was ill during the period of his initial preaching in Galatia, perhaps referring to the occasion of this sermon (Gal. 4:13). If accurate, it must be acknowledged that for an infirm rabbi, he preached rather well.

Paul's Witness in Pisidian Antioch (13:16–41)

A Brief Historical Review (13:16–22)

Standing up from his seat in the congregation, Paul came forward, ascending to the *bema*, the front lectern. Specifically addressing both the Jewish and the God-fearing segments of his audience, Paul called them to attention, prompting them both verbally and with an attention-commanding gesture (clear evidence that Paul spoke with his hands, as does every Jewish speaker with whom this author is acquainted). Although Luke allocates a great deal of manuscript space to this sermon, what is recorded is not the sermon in its entirety but merely the essential substance. Initially, Paul's sermon bears resemblance to Stephen's trial speech. As had Stephen, Paul briefly presents a drastically summarized review of Israel's history to reinforce his main argument, that although God had always made awe-inspiring provision for His chosen people, they, nonetheless, were often unreceptive and even scornful of that provision.

Paul's historical summary consists of the following three basic points. First, God had sovereignly chosen the Jewish patriarchs, Abraham, Isaac and Jacob, confirming with them an unconditional covenant (Gen. 12:1–7; 13:14–17; 15:1–21; 17:1–12; 26:3–5; 18:13–15). In fulfillment of promises He had made to the Jewish patriarchs, God miraculously delivered their children, the Israelites, from Egyptian bondage (Deut. 7:7–8; Ex. 6:6). However, continually scornful of their miraculous deliverance from Egypt and ungrateful for God's provision in the wilderness, the Israelites, through divine judgment, were condemned to wander for an additional forty years prior to entering the promised land, until the disdainful generation had died (Num. 14:34). Paul notes that God graciously demonstrated mercy by His "putting up" with them, *tropophoreō*, "to patiently bear with one's ill manners and foul moods" for forty years.

Second, once the period of judgment had concluded, God then granted the Israelites possession of the land of Israel as their inheritance, in fulfillment of the patriarchal promises contained in the Abrahamic Covenant. The Israelites' receipt of this inheritance entailed God's miraculous destruction, through Israelite conquest, of the seven nations previously in possession of the land of Canaan (Israel): the Hittites, Girgashites, Amorites, Canaanites, Perizzites, Hivites, and Jebusites (Deut. 7:1). Once in possession of Israel, the Lord had granted His people the extraordinary leadership of the judges, the last of whom was the prophet Samuel (1 Sam. 7:15).

450 Years. In Acts 13:19, Paul mentions that these historical events took place over a four hundred fifty year period, which would include the four centuries during which the Israelites were in Egypt, from 1846 BC through the Exodus in 1446 BC, the subsequent forty years of wilderness wanderings under Moses, from 1446 BC through 1406 BC, and the seven years it took under Joshua's leadership to conquer the land of Canaan, from 1406 BC through 1399 BC.[6] This creates a total of four hundred forty-seven years, rounded up by Paul to four hundred fifty years.

There is an alternate placement of the four hundred fifty year period in some Greek manuscript traditions,[7] linking the span not to the events of the Egyptian sojourn, Exodus and conquest referenced in Acts 13:19, but rather to the rule of the judges over Israel until Samuel, who is referenced in the following verse, Acts 13:20. While this placement is far less plausible, it has been proposed that Paul's citation of the four hundred fifty year period was meant to precisely reference the sequential chronological data offered in the book of Judges and 1 Samuel. The book of Judges contains a total of four hundred seven chronological years. To that would be added the forty years attributed to Eli's judgeship (1 Sam. 4:18) immediately prior to Samuel's ascension to leadership, for a total of four hundred forty-seven years, again rounded up by Paul to four hundred fifty years.[8]

The difficulty in accepting this proposal is that to arrive at four hundred fifty years, the chronological data in Judges must be read sequentially, not synchronously. Historically, the total possible span of time between the first judge, Othniel, in 1350 BC and the ascension of Samuel in 1104 BC, i.e., the period of the judges, cannot be more than two hundred forty-six years. The only way Paul could have arrived at four hundred fifty years is to have ignored the concurrent and overlapping chronological data in Judges, strictly adding up the furnished numbers. Presupposing Paul's awareness of the actual historical chronology, the only explanation for his citation of four hundred fifty years for the judges was that it was an accepted contemporary Jewish convention, understood by all. While this is possible, it seems simpler and more satisfactory to attribute his reference of four hundred fifty years to the period of sojourn, Exodus and conquest.

Paul continued on to explain that although God had destroyed seven nations on behalf of the Israelites, granted His people their land as an inheritance, and provided divinely appointed judges to rule over them, the people were still not satisfied with God's provision. They had one more demand, that they be ruled by a king, as were other nations (1 Sam. 8:5–6). God fulfilled their request, replacing Samuel's leadership with that of a king, Saul (1 Sam. 9:17). Saul reigned over Israel for forty years, but because of grievous sin, his dynasty was cut short with his death (1 Sam. 13:13–14).

Paul's third point was that despite the Israelites' ingratitude and dissatisfaction with God's leadership through the judges as well as the disastrous conclusion of Saul's reign, nevertheless, for His people's benefit, God lovingly appointed David, a "man after God's own heart" (1 Sam. 13:14; Ps. 89:20), to be king. Furthermore, through solemn and gracious covenant, God established the royal Davidic dynasty (2 Sam 7:16).

Paul's Gospel (13:23–37)

Therein ends Paul's history lesson. Jumping one full millennium forward in time to the present, Paul hammered home his point. Paul argued that Jesus, the promised Son of David, is the ultimate Davidic King; the prophesied Branch and Root of Jesse (Is.11:1, 10), savior of Israel. God's promise to David had entailed an eternal throne. This eternal Davidic dynasty required an eternal Davidic descendant. Through the establishment of the Davidic covenant, God had prepared Israel for the Messiah's coming. In fact, the fifteenth of the eighteen benedictions contained in the *Amidah*, corporately recited by the congregation earlier in the service, explicitly prays for the coming of this messiah, reading,

> "Speedily cause the Branch of your servant David to flourish. Exalt his horn by your salvation, because we hope for your salvation all the day. Blessed are you, O Lord, who causes the horn of salvation to flourish."

Going further, Paul cited the testimony of John the Baptist. Paul affirmed that John, as the messianic herald, had fulfilled the prophetic function ascribed in Scripture to Elijah in preparing the way of the Lord (Mal 3:1; 4:5). That John needed no introduction to Paul's audience, almost two decades after his brief ministry, indicates that he was still well known throughout the Jewish world. As the renowned prophet's mission was drawing to a climax, his foremost proclamation was that while he himself was not the promised messiah, his successor could be expected to arrive in short order.

Once again, Paul specifically acknowledged his audience of fellow Jews and the God-fearers, including both groups in his exhortation that John's expectation of the imminent arrival of the messiah to Israel had been realized in Jesus. Skipping over the earthly ministry of Jesus, Paul cut right to the death, burial and resurrection of Jesus. Correctly laying the responsibility for Jesus' crucifixion at the feet of Israel's leadership, Paul argued that although they acted in ignorance, their ignorance was no excuse. This reiterates Peter's contention to the Jews in the Temple, a decade and a half earlier (Acts 3:17). The leadership, of all people, should have been aware of the messianic prophecies contained in Scripture. As selections from the prophets were publicly read in synagogue on a weekly basis, they were without excuse. Yet again, the Israelites had scorned God's awesome provision.

Although the Sanhedrin could not substantiate their charge of blasphemy against Jesus, nonetheless, they approached Pilate and requested his execution. Ironically, their ignorant rejection and condemnation of Jesus led to the direct fulfillment of a number of these same messianic prophecies of which they were ignorant. Upon the fulfillment of the prophecies concerning the messiah's death, Jesus was taken down and buried. As previously noted with Peter (Acts 2:23; 5:30; 10:29), Paul studiously avoids using the word for cross, *stauros*, an offensive word, particularly within the context of public synagogue discourse, choosing instead the euphemism *xulon*, meaning, "tree, wood, or stake." Stirring his gospel presentation to a crescendo, Paul continued, asserting that Jesus did not remain in the tomb for long. He was resurrected, and appeared for a period of forty days to those who knew him best, five hundred people in all, including the Twelve.

Paul now provided the congregation a sampling of three messianic passages contained within the Hebrew Scripture to demonstrate the point that Jesus is the resurrected Messiah: Psalm 2:7, Isaiah 55:3 and Psalm 16:10. It is this "promise made to the Jewish fathers," that Paul calls the "good news," or gospel. As God had "raised up" David to an exalted position, that of king of Israel (Acts 13:22), so too God "raised up" Jesus to an exalted position, that of resurrected Messiah (Acts 13:30). God's exaltation of Jesus proclaims His divine Sonship and fulfills the Scripture, "You are My Son, today I have become Your Father" (Ps. 2:7) Paul's application of this Scripture to the messiah was congruent with Jewish interpretation, which had long identified this psalm as messianic prophecy.[9]

Paul continued pressing his point by linking the final two messianic scriptures together by means of a common word, a familiar rabbinic convention.[10] Powerfully combining the prophet Isaiah's record of God's promise, "I will give you the holy and sure blessings of David" (Is 55:3), together with David's own prophecy, "You will not allow Your Holy One to undergo decay," through their common Greek word, *hosios*, "holy," Paul masterfully demonstrated the necessity of Jesus' resurrection and exaltation. The "holy and sure blessings of

David" are the promises contained in the Davidic Covenant. In order for the everlasting covenant to be fulfilled, the Davidic king unavoidably had to be immortal. Furthermore, using the same argument that Peter had made at Pentecost (2:29–32), Paul reasoned that since David had died and subsequently decomposed in his tomb, his prophecy in Psalm 16:10 could not possibly apply to David but could only apply to a resurrected messiah. Therefore, the Messiah's resurrection and subsequent immortality have established the groundwork for the eventual fulfillment of the Davidic covenant when the kingdom of God is established. It would probably not be inappropriate to affirm that Jesus' glorification has launched an initial and preliminary fulfillment of the Davidic Covenant, a down payment on the day when Jesus takes his seat on David's throne in Jerusalem.

Paul's Invitation (13:38–41)

Advancing toward his conclusion, Paul now specifically addressed the Jewish segment of his audience. Whereas twice previously he had equally addressed his sermon to both his fellow Jews and the God-fearers, Paul's topic now becomes specifically relevant to his Jewish brothers (although, of course, not to the exclusion of the God-fearers). Paul revealed that forgiveness of sins is now available through Messiah, even those sins for which the Torah made no provision (Acts 2:38; 5:31; 10:43; 13:38; 26:18). Specifically, Jewish law, as contained in the Mishnah, lists thirty-six transgressions for which, if executed intentionally and defiantly, i.e., "with a high hand" (Num. 15:30), the Torah provides no means of forgiveness; for example, bestiality, incest, idolatry, blasphemy, violating Sabbath, Passover, the Day of Atonement, etc.[11] As repeatedly emphasized in the gospel accounts, the only one with the authority to forgive sin is God himself (Matt 9:5–6; Mark 2:7–10; Luke 5:21–24; 7:49), yet every condemnation in the Law of Moses can now be forgiven through the Messiah. This assertion in Acts 13:39 is Paul's unambiguous affirmation that the Messiah shares the very authority of God.

Therefore, since Jesus is superior to and more powerful than the Torah, Paul encouraged the congregation to adjust their life perspectives accordingly. He concluded his exhortation with a quotation from the prophet Habakkuk, "Behold, you scoffers, and marvel, and perish; for I am accomplishing a work in your days, a work which you will never believe, though someone should describe it to you" (Hab. 1:5), which he applied to their contemporary situation. "The work" which God had accomplished was the Messiah's resurrection, Paul was providing the "description," and the people were left with the responsibility of "believing" the message. Just as the prophet of old had warned Israel of impending disaster, so, too, Paul warned this people to prepare for imminent judgment. It was high time to break Israel's cycle of scorning God's provision.

The Reaction of Pisidian Antioch (13:42–52)

The message garnered an impressive response. As Paul and Barnabas went to leave the synagogue, the people, anxious to hear more, implored the missionaries to deliver another lecture the following week. It can be safely assumed that during the week the elders of the synagogue were furiously searching their Scriptures to investigate the claims of Paul's message. Afterward, a crowd of stragglers from the congregation, made up of Jews and full Jewish proselytes (*tōn sebomenōn prosēlutōn*, a combined construction of "God-fearer" and "proselyte," unique to this passage), surrounded Paul and Barnabas. It is possible that this crowd was composed of those who had believed Paul's message about Jesus' authority to forgive sins because the missionaries urge them to continue in God's grace. This strongly indicates that both Jews and proselytes alike had grasped that through the Messiah, one could reach God without first coming through Judaism and the Law.

On the following Sabbath, the immense impact the missionaries had made the prior week became clear. Luke reports that nearly the whole city had turned out to hear this controversial new message. Not only had the Jewish community turned out in force; the synagogue was positively spilling over with Gentiles. The Jewish community, however, was upset by the tremendous crowds of Gentiles who had chosen that Sabbath to invade their synagogue. Note that it was not the gospel that had antagonized the Jews. They were all in curious attendance to hear more of Paul's message. Rather, they felt threatened by the vast numbers of Gentiles eager to hear of God's grace. After all, if Paul was correct and God would accept the Gentiles as Gentiles, just the way they were, few would desire going though all the rigmarole of adherence to Torah and Jewish custom. Filled with jealousy, many of the Jews in attendance started heckling Paul's preaching, interrupting and contradicting him.

Paul and Barnabas did not stand there and passively accept such abuse from the Jewish community, their ostensible hosts. Amidst the heckling, the missionaries declared that they had discharged their responsibility to preach the gospel to the Jewish community prior to anyone else. The words recorded in Acts 13:46 are unmistakably clear, *humin ēn anagkaion prōton lalēthēnai ton logon tou Theou*, "it was necessary that the word of God be spoken to you first." The reason that it was necessary to first witness to the Jews is that this is God's ordained evangelistic sequence (Rom.1:16). As the gospel has particular relevance to the Jewish people, they have priority. The first opportunity to accept or reject Jesus always went to the Jew first. One could say that they had the "right of first refusal." In rejecting Jesus, the Jewish community of Pisidian Antioch had, unavoidably, also rejected God's provision of eternal life.

Therefore, the missionaries would now turn to the city's Gentile community. Quoting the mission statement of Isaiah's Servant of the Lord, "I have placed you as a light for the Gentiles, that you may bring salvation to the ends of the earth" (Is. 42:6; 49:6), Paul and Barnabas apply this divine mandate to themselves. Although this commission was initially applied in the New Testament to Jesus (Luke 2:32), the apostles claim that they, too, were participating in the Messiah's ministry by means of their close organic union with Him. In fulfillment of that commission, they would go not only to Jews with the gospel but to Gentiles as well. Paul later explains that even while evangelizing Gentiles, he is optimistic that this will result in the Jewish people becoming provoked to jealousy and thereby responding to the gospel (Rom. 11:11–14).

The Gentiles in attendance that morning responded to the reorientation of the apostle's mission with great enthusiasm. In contrast to the derision and ridicule being heaped on by the Jews, the Gentiles joyfully believed the gospel and "as many as had been appointed to eternal life believed" (Acts 13:48). It is difficult to miss the doctrine of God's sovereign election in this verse. The verb *tassō*, translated "appointed," means "to arrange" or "to assign," often in a military sense. Luke used the term here to reveal that God elects both Jews and Gentiles according to His sovereign purpose.

These "appointed" believers began spreading the gospel throughout their region of Galatia. In contrast to the activities of the newly established community of faith, the Jewish community was engaged in inciting many prominent female God-fearers who attended the synagogue to negatively influence their husbands, Pisidian Antioch's municipal leaders, against the apostles. Following a memorable period of municipally sponsored persecution, later recalled in one of Paul's letters (2 Tim 3:11), Paul and Barnabas soon found themselves formally expelled by government officials.

As Jesus had directed his apostles to do, Paul and Barnabas shook off the dust of their feet, symbolically renouncing the hospitality of the Jewish community (Matt 10:14; Mark 6:11; Luke 9:5) as well as offering a sign of coming judgment toward those who rejected the messianic message (Luke 10:11–15). Contrary to popular imagination, this ritual did not entail "shaking a leg," but rather involved removing one sandal and shaking out the dust. Hitting the road, in this case, the Via Sebaste, the apostles traveled southeast to Iconium, another eighty-five miles down the highway. Luke concludes the Pisidian Antioch segment of the narrative by noting that the newly minted Jewish and

Gentile disciples in the city's nascent church community were characterized by habitual joy and fullness of the Holy Spirit.

The Witness in Iconium (14:1-7)

The prosperous commercial city of Iconium was located at the foot of the Taurus Mountains, in the region of Galatia. The apostles' experience in this city will be the same song, different verse. Repeating their pattern of first approaching the Jewish community with the gospel, Paul and Barnabas preached the gospel in the local synagogue. Although Paul has just grandly announced that because of their rejection of the gospel, he was now through with the Jews, a few verses later, he was approaching them again. He should not be accused of inconsistency. The distinction Paul was making was that this is a fresh "batch" of Jews. It was only the community of Jews that had rejected the gospel from whom Paul had turned away.

As in Pisidian Antioch, Paul and Barnabas received a hearing in the synagogue and an excellent reception from both Jews and God-fearers. Even so, they also encountered severe antagonism to their witness. Furthermore, their Jewish opponents took steps to poison the atmosphere between the new believers and the Gentile community at large.

However, the apostles did not allow the persecution to intimidate them and spent a healthy amount of time in Iconium. Their message placed an emphasis on the Lord's grace and was buttressed by signs and wonders. Paul would later remind the Galatian church of this eruption of the miraculous in his epistle to them (Gal. 3:4-5). Note that in Acts 14:4, both Paul and Barnabas are called apostles. Luke uses this term here, not in the sense of an ordinary church missionary, nor in the technical sense of one of the Twelve, but in less restricted classification of those who had seen the resurrected Lord (1 Cor 9:1) and been specially commissioned to be his representatives. These apostles could be identified by their ability to perform "the signs of a true apostle," i.e., signs, wonders and miracles (2 Cor. 12:12). Once again, Luke is quite clear that only the apostles, and not ordinary believers, are able to do signs and wonders. Miracles were the authenticating sign from the Lord to divinely verify and validate the apostles' message and authority.

The city quickly became divided, *schizō*, in opinion as to the apostles. Finally, the opposition to the apostles among the Jews, Gentiles and municipal authorities eventually became so virulent that an attempt was made to stone them. That this attempt on their lives was incited by their Jewish opponents can be ascertained by the fact that stoning was a Jewish, not Greek or Roman, form of execution. At this juncture, the apostles evidently judged it propitious to shift their ministry to an alternative area of Galatia, the Lycaonian region, in which were the villages of Lystra and Derbe.

The Witness in Lystra and Derbe (14:8–21a)

Lystra was a small rural village, approximately one hundred miles from Pisidian Antioch and far off the main road. There was no synagogue in Lystra in which Paul could preach, as the Jewish population was not large enough to support one. Therefore, in this instance, Paul utilized a different approach to deliver the gospel to this largely provincial community. Preaching in the agora, the marketplace, Paul noticed a lame man, sitting on the ground, listening to him preach.

Perceiving that the lame man believed the message being preached, Paul thunderously commanded him to stand up on his feet. As the man had indeed believed the gospel Paul proclaimed, he obeyed and was healed. This is an unmistakable parallel with Peter's healing of the lame man at the Temple (Acts 3:1–10), down to the very phrases Luke used to describe both events. It is an inescapable conclusion that Luke is patently reminding his readers that whatever Peter was empowered to do, Paul was so empowered as well. In Luke's eyes, these two apostles are absolute equals in supernatural ability, apostolic gifting and divine commission.

More so than any sermon, no matter how compelling, this miraculous sign caught the crowd's attention. They were so enraptured by the apostles, in fact, that they began to enthusiastically shout that the gods had descended to earth in human form, erroneously identifying Barnabas as the god Zeus, the king of the Greek gods, and Paul as Hermes, the god's spokesman. The Roman author Ovid records a prominent local legend, that these two particular gods, Zeus and Hermes, disguised as men, had long ago visited the region surrounding Lystra. After searching in vain for lodging, an elderly couple were the only ones in town who offered hospitality to the disguised gods. Consequently, the elderly couple's home was transformed into a temple and the town demolished. Evidently, the Lystrans were determined not to make the same mistake as had their infamous ancestors.

As the crowd continued bellowing in their regional mother tongue of Lycaonian, neither of the apostles could understand exactly what was being proclaimed, nor could they grasp the nature of the religious preparations the townsmen began to make in their honor. It was not until the priest of Zeus began to parade his oxen, elaborately clothed in wreaths, preparatory to offering a sacrifice to them that it finally dawned on the horrified apostles exactly what was happening. Immediately and vehemently protesting the Lystrans' idolatrous initiatives, Paul and Barnabas tore their robes, an ancient Jewish sign of grief and revulsion (Gen 37:29; Est. 4.1; Job 1:20). They plunged into the crowd, attempting to quash the unfolding sacrilege. Of interest is that once again, in Acts 14:14, Luke references both Paul and Barnabas as apostles.

With these provincial pagans, Paul makes no appeal to Hebrew Scripture or Greek philosophy. The Lystrans required a more basic, less sophisticated approach. They could not be told of a Messiah while still ignorant of the One God who made the heaven and the earth, the sea and the seasons. Paul derived his argument strictly from nature, God's general revelation to humanity. He told the crowd to knock off their vain idolatry. God was not an inanimate object, a statue, but a living and creative being. His activity and creativity are abundantly apparent in nature. Although attempting to reason with the crowd from a common perspective, Paul's words had little impact in restraining their idolatrous passion. It was only with the greatest of difficulty that the Lystrans finally desisted from their preparations.

Soon after, a Jewish delegation from Pisidian Antioch and Iconium arrived, following in Paul and Barnabas' footsteps, looking to stir up trouble for the apostles. The adage proving true that nothing is as fickle as a crowd, the Lystrans, their recent lavish adoration spurned, now turned violently against Paul and Barnabas. The immediate object of their fury was Paul, whom they stoned, dragged out of the city and dumped, leaving him for dead. (Once again, the act of stoning bears the telltale fingerprints of Jewish instigation of the Gentile populace.) Paul's epistles will later reference this unforgettable experience (2 Cor. 11:25; 2 Tim. 3:11) and the enduring scars it left (Gal. 6:17). As the Lord had revealed to Ananias fourteen years earlier, it was Paul's destiny to suffer on behalf of Jesus (Acts 9:16). Ironically, Paul, who had been instrumental in the stoning of Stephen, now shared in his agony. Fortunately for Paul, however, he did not share Stephen's fate.

The Christian community gathered around the stricken apostle, undoubtedly praying for him, as he lay prone in the dirt. Astonishingly, like an apostolic Energizer bunny who "takes a licking and keeps on ticking," Paul stood up, dusted himself off and began to walk, albeit perhaps a bit on the wobbly side, back into the city. Exactly what the exchange was between the gritty apostle and those who were probably congratulating themselves on a murder well done, Luke does not see fit to record. One can only speculate whether the Greek equivalent of an exclamatory "boo!" was articulated.

The next morning, the apostles began a sixty-mile hike to Derbe, a border town on the frontier of the Roman Empire. This was, as can be supposed, not a bad showing for a fellow who had been three-quarters dead just the day prior. The apostles' mission to Lystra had not been unsuccessful. They had succeeded in establishing a small community of new believers, of whom one individual in particular would stand out later on in the narrative, a young man named Timothy (Acts 16:1). Luke tells us nothing about their ministry in Derbe, other than that they preached the gospel and made many disciples.

Return to Antioch (14:21b-28)

Having reached the eastern outskirts of the empire, the apostles retraced their steps, successively returning to the believers in Lystra, Iconium and Pisidian Antioch, strengthening the foundations they had recently laid. They were conscientious to ensure that their evangelism was followed by discipleship. Part of their program of strengthening the churches was the prayerful appointment (*xeirotoneō*, "to hand select") of a series of *presbuterous*, elders to lead the local assemblies. Paul and Barnabas preached a message of encouragement to the new believers, exhorting them that any suffering and persecution they may have and may yet experience is an expected part of the faith journey. The kingdom of God, the Messiah's reign on earth, while future, is assured, yet for most believers, entry into that kingdom will likely encompass *pollōn thlipseōn*, "many afflictions," or, "much harassment." Although discipling believers carries a lower public profile than evangelizing unbelievers, it should be noted that they were not shy in returning to each locale from which they were chased. This is an example of chutzpah, or moxie, clearly an ancient and long-standing characteristic of the Jewish people.

Thereafter, the apostles had returned to Perga, a city which had earlier received only an abbreviated visitation from the apostles (Acts 13:13). Having preached there, they hiked another eight miles to Perga's port, the city of Attalia, where they boarded a ship and returned back home to Antioch. Truly mission accomplished after some eighteen months in transit, Paul's so-called first missionary journey came to a conclusion in the autumn of AD 49. When the apostles returned, as most missionaries who are home on furlough have done throughout church history, they gathered their home congregation together to relay their adventures and particularly emphasized the response the Lord had inspired throughout the Gentile communities.

Conclusion

In the accomplishment of this pioneer missionary effort, history was made and international Gentile salvation firmly established. For the first time, Gentiles who lacked any connection to Judaism, being neither full proselytes, proselytes of the gate or God-fearers, had en masse expressed faith in the

Jewish Messiah. Over the course of this initial mission, Paul's evangelistic strategy was confirmed, a pattern he would reproduce over the next decade of ministry. Whenever possible, he would penetrate into large Gentile cosmopolitan regions, preaching the gospel to the Jewish community as first priority, thereby establishing a beachhead of Jewish and God-fearing believers, and then expand the dissemination of the gospel directly into the larger Gentile community.

Study Questions:

1. Describe the leadership of the church in Antioch.
2. Explain why Luke suddenly begins referring to Saul as Paul.
3. Did Paul follow a specific missionary strategy?
4. What is the significance of the statement, "to the Jew first"?
5. Why did John Mark abandon the mission?
6. Summarize Paul's sermon in the synagogue of Pisidian Antioch.
7. Describe the reaction to Paul's sermon in the synagogue of Pisidian Antioch.

CHAPTER 13

From Jewish Sect to Universal Church
Acts 15:1–35

Preview:

The news of the apostles' accomplishments among the Gentiles did not escape the notice of the mother church in Jerusalem. Understandably, the Jewish believers took great interest in the salvation of the Gentiles. Indeed Peter, having been the pioneer apostle of Gentile salvation (Acts 10:34–48) and having, along with John and James, publicly commended Paul and Barnabas in their mission to the Gentiles at their last meeting together in Jerusalem two years earlier (Gal. 2:9), had a personal stake in the outcome of their mission. Shortly following the missionaries' return, Peter journeyed to Antioch in order to hear in person from Paul and Barnabas of these evangelistic results, which he certainly would have received with joy.

However, in Peter's wake were other Jewish believers, who had come out of the party of the Pharisees and still had not accepted God's extension of grace and salvation to the Gentiles. Peter had, up to this point, freely associated with the Gentile Christians without limitation. Yet when this particular party of Jewish Christians arrived in Antioch, their presence somehow pressured the other Jewish believers of the Antioch church, including Peter and Barnabas, to separate themselves from table fellowship with their Gentile brethren. Paul, however, scandalized by what he observed, did not shrink from confronting his apostolic friends with their inconsistent conduct.

This episode is briefly recounted by Paul in his epistle to the newly planted Galatian churches (Gal. 2:11–21), into which this dissension had already rapidly spread. The Galatians letter, first of Paul's many epistles, was likely composed on the eve of his departure for the Jerusalem Council, the convening of which was precipitated by these thorny events.

To Circumcise or Not to Circumcise, That Is the Question (15:1–5)

That the issue of Gentile believers and their relationship to Jewish believers was still percolating and ready to unexpectedly boil over at the advanced date of late AD 49 (or perhaps even early AD 50), almost seventeen years since the birth of the church, was a major problem that threatened to throw the church into unprecedented internal crisis. In this pivotal chapter, among the most critical in the New Testament, Luke outlines the impassioned discussion surrounding this conflict and the eventual solution arrived at through the Jerusalem Council by the assembled church leadership.

Once again, as had happened two years earlier (Gal. 2:1–10), the church at Antioch was faced with a incendiary faction of Jewish believers, identified as also belonging to the Pharisee party, who had begun divisively broadcasting the necessity of Gentile circumcision. Utterly ignoring (or perhaps truly ignorant of) the conclusion arrived at by the Jerusalem church nine years earlier (Acts 11:18) when Cornelius' salvation was formally recognized, as well as the two-year old apostolic confirmation of the Antioch Gentile ministry (Gal. 2:7–10), these troublemakers came down from Judea claiming that the prerequisite for Gentile believers' salvation was circumcision.

These unauthorized teachers, or as Fruchtenbaum calls them, "these self-appointed guardians of orthodoxy,"[1] had appended the gospel of grace to include the reception of a religious rite. Not that these intimidators would have been content merely with Gentile circumcision. The phrase they used which betrayed their intentions was circumcision "according to the custom of Moses,"[2] indicating that circumcision was merely their initial requirement. This aberrant instruction was directed to the synagogue-affiliated proselytes of the gate, God-fearers and especially those Gentiles who had no previous connection with Judaism, bullying them all into believing that they first needed to become full Jewish proselytes before they could become authentic followers of the Messiah.

The teaching of these agitators hit the Antioch church like a massive theological tsunami. As Luke records, it immediately incited an enormous and pointed debate. Foremost in the fray, of course, was Paul. It apparently took a Pharisee to successfully debate a fellow Pharisee. Neither Paul nor his partner in ministry, Barnabas, could let these outrageous claims go unanswered while their church was being internally torn asunder.

Distantly gazing through the stained glass of two millennia of church history with a New Testament in one hand and a Bible commentary in the other, it is altogether too easy to stand in judgment of this faction of zealous, yet misguided Jewish Christians. On the other hand, it is difficult to ascertain the impulse behind their teaching and to appreciate how they could have so grievously misunderstood the nature of the gospel. Most of us take for granted the simple, liberating gospel truth of salvation solely by grace through faith, independent of religious ritual. We bluntly wonder what there was exactly to debate. It is tempting to portray these legalists as two dimensional villains, standing in opposition to our narrative's heroes, Paul and Barnabas. Nonetheless, more productive is an attempt to reconstruct some probable concerns and reasons which may have motivated these "self-appointed guardians of orthodoxy" to such extreme legalistic assertions.

First of all, from the legalists' AD 49 perspective, only one book of the New Testament had been written, Paul's letter to the Galatians, and that one was hot off the press, composed as a denunciation of the legalists' position! The only authoritative theological rulebook available to reference was the Hebrew Scripture. Since the Scriptural record documents that the members of God's community had always been circumcised, it would seem inconsistent to suggest otherwise within church membership. In fact, Jesus and all of the apostles had been circumcised. Perhaps it even felt it somewhat discriminatory to purposely withhold circumcision from the Gentiles.

Second, the Hebrew prophets frequently spoke of multitudes of Gentiles streaming to worship at the Temple in Jerusalem, from which the Torah would proceed (Is. 2:2–3; Zech 8:23, etc.). It was not illogical to conclude that these Scriptures would be fulfilled through massive Gentile conversion to Judaism. It is difficult to fault the legalists for not being able to accurately systematize God's prophetic plans or precisely grasp His eschatological purposes.

Third, perhaps they viewed the exponentially increasing influx of Gentiles as a threat posed to either the continued holiness of the community or the continued viability of its evangelistic outreach to Israel. They may have felt that the isolated case of Gentile salvation here or there was sufferable, but this recent massive incursion of morally flaccid pagans and salvaged idolaters into the separated community of sanctified believers was too great a risk. These ethically challenged Gentile-come-latelies could prove intolerably corrosive. Their admission should be allowed only on the basis of their accepting the holy responsibilities of Torah. Furthermore, the more Gentiles became associated with the church and the more the character of the church's ethnic composition shifted, the more difficult it would become to keep attracting Jews to the movement, even as it would become easier to attract increasingly more Gentiles.

Whatever the reasons or motivations of this faction may have been, it was determined by the Antioch church that the venue of the debate should shift to Jerusalem, there to be definitively and publicly resolved by the elders and remaining apostles. At this point in church history, the Jerusalem mother church still wielded undiminished authority in overseeing the mission of its daughter churches. The stakes could not have been higher. The ultimate question on the table was nothing less than whether the church should be identified as either the righteous remnant of Israel or a completely new and unanticipated creation which, while distinct from Israel, was composed of both a righteous Jewish remnant as well as a righteous element of Gentiles.

Paul, Barnabas and a contingent from Antioch are selected to represent the church and the gospel of grace. Following a grand sendoff, the Antioch delegation made their way to Jerusalem. As the traveled, they passed through Phoenicia, a Gentile region, and Samaria, a Samaritan region, visiting the church congregations. The missionaries enthusiastically shared stories of their success among the Gentiles, both within and apart from the synagogue during their missionary journey. The believers in both regions reacted to these results with unequivocal joy.

Once in Jerusalem, the delegation from Antioch was favorably received by the church community and its leadership. Again, the success of the first missionary journey was recounted before the assembly. In response, the legalistic opposition, here for the first time identified by Luke as Jewish believers who, like Paul, were also members of the Pharisee party, stood and succinctly stated their position. These Jewish Christian Pharisees demanded not only that circumcision was necessary to receive salvation, but also that the Gentiles must live their lives in submission to the Torah.

The Jerusalem Council (15:6–21)

Apostolic Testimony (15:6–12)

Hence, the first great church debate officially commenced among the Jerusalem leadership. Luke recounts that, aside from the delegation from Antioch and the faction of legalists, in attendance were an unspecified number of the remaining apostles, including Peter, as were the elders over the Jerusalem believers, including James, the brother of Jesus, as well as a large representation of the Jerusalem church assembly.

Just how long the controversy was discussed Luke does not indicate, recording only that a thorough inquiry had been completed and that there had been "much debate" (Acts 15:6). Undoubtedly, both sides of the controversy were given ample opportunity to state their respective cases. After the debate had raged for some time, Peter finally rose to his feet and took the floor. He referred back to the famous (and likely for some assembled, infamous) events of Cornelius' salvation, some nine years earlier, and the controversial storm which immediately followed (Acts 10:24—11:18). Peter reminded the assembly of the indisputable fact that God had specifically chosen him to unlock the door of Gentile salvation. The salvation of Gentiles had not been an innovation from Antioch or Cypress, but from Jerusalem, through the agency of the chief apostle, the "keeper of the keys." Nor was Gentile salvation a recent novelty, but a nine-year-old fact of church life.

Furthermore, God, called by Peter the *kardiognōstēs*, "heart-knower" (Acts 15:8), had authenticated Gentile salvation by granting them the baptism of the Holy Spirit, in the same fashion and measure as the Jews had experienced at Pentecost. The possession of the Holy Spirit is the indication that believers are God's children (Gal. 4:6) and is the identifying mark of a Christian (Rom. 8:11). Surprisingly or not, God had made no distinction between Jews and Gentiles and accepted both just as they were, solely on the basis of faith. Nine years earlier, the Cornelius episode had led the Jerusalem church to the unavoidable conclusion not only that Gentiles could be saved, but that the means by which they were saved was exactly the same as Jews, that is, by grace through faith (Eph. 2:8). No works or rituals had been involved. Paul echoes this same argument in Galatians (Gal. 3:2).

In light of God's undeniable choice of Gentiles and His authentication of that choice by the baptism of the Spirit, Peter charged the assembly not to test (*peirazō*, the same word he used of Sapphira just before she died [Acts 5:9]) God by challenging his authority but, rather, to trust Him in the prerogative He has exercised. He argued that demanding Gentile circumcision and their subsequent Torah observance would involve exactly such a presumptuous test.

Peter called the Torah, the Mosaic Covenant, an arduous yoke (similar to Paul's argument, Gal. 5:1), an unbearable burden which Israel, from its inception as a nation, had never been able to impeccably keep. God had established the New Covenant through the Messiah for precisely that reason (Jer. 31:31–32; Luke 22:20; Heb. 8:7). Therefore, they should not force the Gentiles to attempt what not even Jewish believers could endure. Just as Jews were saved by grace through faith alone, so too were Gentiles. If God had accepted them just as they were, the church assuredly could not do otherwise.

"Yoke" was a common rabbinic designation for the Torah, cited in the Mishnah concerning proselytes taking up "the yoke of the commandments."[3] While rabbinic literature, both ancient and contemporary, is filled with eloquent testimony to the joys and delights of keeping God's gracious gift of Torah, the average Jew has not often found this to be the case, particularly when filtered through the interpretive grid of the rabbinic oral tradition. Peter was merely stating a candid fact, one that could be bluntly reaffirmed by countless Jews throughout Jewish history.

Peter's weighty contribution to the discussion proved decisive. It is apparent just how important it had been that Cornelius and company evidenced the baptism of the Holy Spirit through the sign of tongues. This historical fact clinched Peter's argument and closed down all other dissension and debate in the Council. This is Peter's final appearance in the Acts narrative. Appropriately, these last words of the chief of the apostles serve to secure the continued ministry of the apostle to the Gentiles.

In the ensuing silence, Paul and Barnabas again took the floor, speaking unimpeded as they once again reviewed the miraculous signs and wonders which characterized their missionary journey. Taking their cue from Peter's devastating line of reasoning, their argument was that if God did not approve of Gentile salvation without qualification, He would not have supernaturally authenticated the mission.

Apostolic Verdict (15:13-21)

When the moment was finally reached when everyone who cared to weigh in on the controversy had done so and there was nothing more to be said, the chief elder of Jerusalem and president of the Jerusalem Council, the apostle James, articulated his solution.

James. More accurately, Jacob, from the Hebrew, *Ya'akov,* was the half-brother of Jesus. Interestingly, within the narrative, Luke never once clarifies that James was the brother of Jesus, evidently assuming that this fact was common knowledge throughout his readership, not requiring citation. Although he had not been a disciple during his brother's earthly ministry, James became a believer following his Jesus' death, perhaps at the moment when Jesus made an individual post-resurrection appearance to him (1 Cor. 15:7). James led the Jerusalem church for eighteen years, from AD 44–62, rising to prominence following the dispersion of most of the apostles to their respective itinerant ministries.

Church tradition remembers his nickname of James "the Just," or "the Righteous." Pious, ascetic and devout in his adherence to Torah, he was well esteemed throughout Jerusalem, respected in both Christian and non-Christian circles. Another exceptional church tradition records the detail that his calloused knees were as hard as a camel's from time spent kneeling in prayer. He was the author of the epistle of James, much of which robustly echoes the ethics of his brother's Sermon on the Mount (Matt. 5–7). The facility he demonstrates with Greek in his epistle suggests a higher level of education than is commonly assumed was possessed by Galilean craftsmen, leading many to reconsider the impact of the Greco-Roman-Galilean cultural matrix in which James was raised, as well as to revisit our perception of the educational preparation of Jesus.

Requesting the assembly's attention, James summarized Peter's (called here *Simeon*, the Aramaic form of his real name, Simon), contention of being the initial instrument of Gentile salvation. Joining the faithful Jewish remnant was now a faithful Gentile remnant, called by James, "a people for God's name." It is God's plan for His people to consist now of both Jews and Gentiles. The Gentiles were not to be considered "junior partners" within the church, but share equal status in God's sight. Indeed, this is the definition of the church Paul will later develop (Eph. 2:11–22; 3:6).

Having affirmed Peter's appeal to experience, James now adds an application from Scripture. Peter's point, that God selected from among the Gentiles a faithful remnant, a people for his name, agrees, *sumphōnousin*, "is in harmony" with the message of the Hebrew prophets. He selects a passage from Amos to support his case, although by using the plural "prophets," he indicated that if anyone objected to his use of Amos, they would find the same teaching in all the other prophets as well. His quotation is from the text of Amos 9:11–12. Although most hold that James is freely modifying a quotation from the Septuagint, the Greek translation of the Old Testament, Longenecker notes the exact correspondence with a quotation of the passage in another contemporary Hebrew manuscript found among the Dead Sea Scrolls.[4] Therefore, while some would build their interpretation of James' quotation based on his curious alterations of the Septuagint text, in light of other potential alternate contemporary manuscripts as well as the acceptable customary freedom possessed by Jewish teachers when quoting sacred Scripture, it would be better not to assign his variations too much weight and to concentrate on the essence of the original Amos passage selected by James.

The Amos passage speaks of God's restoration of the fallen ruins of the tabernacle of David during the future messianic kingdom. The tabernacle was a picture of the house of David, the Davidic dynasty, which metaphorically fell into ruin when the final Davidic king was deposed from power by Babylon (2 Kin. 25:7). Amos promised that, in fulfillment of the Davidic Covenant (2 Sam. 7:12–16), the dynasty of David would be restored to its former glory in the messianic kingdom.[5]

The Amos passage goes on to relate that when the kingdom of God is established, Gentile salvation will be normative. James was not claiming that because of the contemporary salvation of Gentiles that this prophecy was presently being fulfilled, wholly or partially. Rather, James was making a rather sophisticated present day application of a future prophecy. If Gentile salvation is to be understood as normative within the messianic kingdom, it should not be very surprising to anyone if Gentile salvation were to occur somewhat earlier. James was arguing that there was nothing unbiblical or even unanticipated concerning the salvation of Gentiles and that future Gentile salvation in no way precluded contemporary Gentile salvation. The reason James chose this particular passage from Amos is that it shows Gentiles seeking God specifically as Gentiles, and not as Jewish proselytes, masterfully settling the issue of whether circumcision was necessary. James finishes his application with a reminder to recognize that the testimony of Scripture is that the inclusion of Gentiles in God's program has always been part of His plan. Indeed, the Messiah was expected to be a light to multitudes of Gentiles (Is. 42:6; 49:6).

There are some who misinterpret James here, believing that he was arguing that this prophecy was fulfilled by first century contemporary circumstances. They erroneously suppose that the ruined tabernacle of David is the church. It is difficult to determine how they could hold this broadly spiritualized view, as David's tabernacle is described as fallen and in ruins, in need of restoration. Anyone who has read the first fifteen chapters of Acts definitely knows this description not to be true of the victorious first century church! Amos was prophesying of Israel, not of the church, which was an undisclosed mystery within the Hebrew Scripture (Eph. 3:4–5; Col. 1:26–27).

Based on the combined testimony of church experience and prophetic Scripture, James pronounced judgment. His verdict is that the Jewish believers were to cease making trouble, *parenochleō*, "to trouble or annoy," for the Gentile believers with any demand regarding their salvation other than to come to God through faith alone.

Since the matter of salvation has been definitively settled, the main issue remaining to be resolved was that of social interaction between Jews and Gentiles. On this issue, James was eminently practical, mainly focusing on food; an issue that affected the ability of Jews and Gentiles to eat together harmoniously. A letter is to be written to the Gentile community, detailing four prohibitions which, if followed, would facilitate fellowship within the church. These prohibitions were not designed to be binding commandments or absolute restrictions equally applicable in every circumstance and incumbent upon Gentile believers at all times and in all places. Otherwise, Paul's later instruction in his epistles on the subject of Christian liberty would prove directly contradictory to James' verdict (Rom. 14:1–23; 1 Cor. 8:1–10). Paul's teaching clarifies that these prohibitions were guidelines to be applied to those specific sensitive situations in which a Gentile Christian's behavior could potentially be offensive to a Jewish Christian.

The source of James' prohibitions was the Torah. He avoided mention of those particular commandments which are contained both within the Mosaic code and the Law of Christ (1 Cor. 9:21; Gal. 6:2); that is, those which reflect God's timeless moral standards and are therefore binding on all believers, Jewish and Gentile, at all times, such as the prohibitions regarding idolatry, murder or theft. The four restrictions James selected were from among the commandments that were intended to regulate behavior within the nation of Israel, yet could also prove circumstantially applicable within the church.

Some would instead locate the source of James' prohibitions within the so-called Noachide laws, the rabbinic list recorded in the Talmud of the basic, bare minimum, seven ethical requirements God has placed on all humanity since the days of Noah. These seven requirements are to practice justice and abstain from blasphemy, idolatry, adultery, murder, theft, and eating flesh or blood from a live animal.[6] While it is possible to interpret James' list as a variation on these laws of Noah, upon scrutiny there is not as much correspondence between the lists as it seems at first glance or as some would claim. Furthermore, it is by no means certain that this list had been formulated at this time. The identification, although captivating, cannot be accepted.

The first prohibition was to abstain from meat sacrificed to idols (Ex. 34:15). Invariably, it was the prime cuts that were selected for the gods' cuisine.[7] For those who realized idols were mere stone or metal and whose conscience allowed, this meat was good eating. This is one reason Paul qualifiedly allowed it (1 Cor. 8:1–10). However, if it would cause offense to a fellow believer, it was not to be eaten under any circumstance.

The second prohibition was the only one not dietary in nature, that of abstaining from fornication, *porneia*. This prohibition's inclusion on this list at first glance is troubling, as the New Testament affirms that fornication is always wrong in every circumstance. Like the child's game where "one of these things is not like the other, one of these things does not belong," fornication stands out from the other prohibitions like the proverbial sore thumb. However, the meaning of *porneia* is much broader than what we generally define as sexual immorality. In this context, fornication refers to marriages that are prohibited in the Torah such as those between close relatives, like siblings and first cousins (Lev. 18:6–18). These relationships were not uncommon in the ancient world and, although nonchalantly accepted in Gentile circles, would prove offensive to Jews.

The third prohibition was to abstain from eating meat from which the blood has not been properly drained (Lev. 17:13). When an animal is not slaughtered by having its throat cut but is instead strangled, congealed blood remains within the meat. Such meat was an offense to Jews, who were used to ritually slaughtering their meat.

The fourth and final of James' prohibitions was to abstain from drinking blood or eating food made from blood (Lev 17:10–11, 14). While certain Gentile cultures do not think twice about eating blood, enjoying foods such as blood pudding or blood sausage, such culinary delights could prove offensive to Jews.

These four prohibitions are recounted three times in the narrative (Acts 15:20; 15:29; 21:25), underlying their importance, at least within the initial century of church history. Adhering to this solution would preempt the discordant tension between Jewish and Gentile believers (and even Peter and Paul) which had arisen in Antioch from recurring in the future, enabling Gentile believers to avoid giving offense to their Jewish brethren.

Today the issue is largely irrelevant, as table fellowship and social interaction between Jewish and Gentile believers is rarely disrupted over a plate of rare roast beef, a chicken that has been sacrificed to idols, or a pair of married siblings. However, if the rare roast beef, etc., ever became an offense, then the application of James' guidelines would once again be appropriate and in order.

James concludes his verdict by reminding everyone that each church community contains Jewish believers who were potentially sensitive to offense by their Gentile brethren in these four areas. Furthermore, since Torah's ethical precepts were regularly disseminated in every synagogue throughout the Empire, these new Gentiles Christians, most of whom were God-fearers or proselytes of the gate, were already versed in the Law of Moses through their synagogue attendance. Indeed, their exposure to Torah was great enough that if they had wanted to become Jewish, they would have done so already. The church was to be satisfied that the Gentiles follow the Messiah and trouble them no further. If God laid on them no further conditions for their salvation, then neither should God's people.

The Apostolic Decree (15:22–35)

Contents (15:22–29)

The apostles, elders and the collective church, now in unified agreement, chose two Jewish envoys from the Jerusalem church to broadcast the Jerusalem Council's resolution and to authenticate the testimony of the Antioch delegation. The first envoy listed is Judas, called "Barsabbas," Aramaic for "the son of the Sabbath." Mentioned only in this passage, he was a leader in the Jerusalem church and possessed the gift of prophecy (Acts 15:32). He was likely the brother of Joseph Barsabbas (Acts 1:23). The second envoy was Silas, who, like Paul, was a Roman citizen, sometimes identified by his Latin name, Silvanus. Sharing the same credentials as Judas Barsabbas, that of Jerusalem leadership and the gift of prophecy, Silas would soon play a major supporting role within the Acts narrative, serving as Paul's partner on his second missionary journey (Acts 15:40—18:22). Paul makes mention of Silas in epistles directed to the churches they co-founded (2 Cor. 1:19; 1 Thess. 1:1; 2 Thess. 1:1). Silas was also closely associated with Peter, serving as his amanuensis (secretary) for the epistle of 1 Peter (1 Pet. 5:12).

A letter, addressed to the Gentile believers, was composed for the envoys to deliver to the churches throughout Syria, the province in which Antioch was the capital, and Cilicia, the neighboring province to the west of Syria. Paul would later also personally deliver this letter to the Galatian churches (Acts 16:4). The letter repudiated the legalists, or Judaizers, who had agitated ("unsettling your souls") the Gentile believers by promulgating their unauthorized ideas. In contrast to these illegitimate teachers, Jerusalem was now sending two men who were the "real deal," Judas and Silas, who had demonstrated their commitment to the Messiah by placing their very lives on the line. The envoys would serve to verbally confirm the letter's contents, establishing the matter by the mouths of two witnesses (Deut.19:15), according to Jewish custom. The letter designates their companions, Paul and Barnabas, as *agapētois hēmon*, "our beloved," strongly affirming that their ministry and apostleship had been publicly validated, accepted and recognized by the Jerusalem leadership.

The letter goes on to list the four essential prerequisites necessary to afford a basis for fellowship between Jewish and Gentile believers. Observing these prohibitions would go a long way in creating an atmosphere of peace, or shalom, between the two groups. The letter affirmed not only that this was the Jerusalem leadership's opinion, but went on to assert that it was also the verdict of the Holy Spirit. Having been guided by the Spirit through the decision making process, James could be confident that the Spirit was solidly in agreement with them. The letter closed with a simple "farewell," a customary, contemporary conclusion.

Delivery (15:30–35)

Following the public reading of the letter in Antioch, the Gentile believers were encouraged and rejoiced. This was followed by Judas and Silas delivering a long tag-team sermon, exhorting and encouraging the church. Staying on in Antioch for only an abbreviated period, Judas and Silas returned to

Jerusalem. Paul and Barnabas, however, stayed through the winter, but would soon be making plans to depart in the spring for their next set of missionary adventures.

(Acts 15:34 is not present in the most reliable manuscripts and is most likely a later editorial insertion made by someone other than Luke.)

Acts 15 vs. Galatians 2:1–10. By this time, it should be obvious that while many commentators have identified the events of Acts 15:1–31 with the events described by Paul in Galatians 2:1–10, this commentary does not share that opinion. Rather, as previously discussed, it is the events described in Acts 11:30/12:25 that should be identified with Galatians 2:1–10. Although, at first glance, there seem to be several surface correspondences between Acts 15:1–31 and Galatians 2:1–10, when one focuses in on the details it becomes apparent that there are fewer similarities than there are differences, some of them irreconcilable.

There are four surface similarities. First, both passages deal with the necessity of circumcision and the question of Gentile believers' responsibility toward Torah. Second, both passages arrive at the same result of Gentiles not needing to be circumcised, whereas circumcision is not at all mentioned in Acts 11:30/12:25. Third, in both passages, Paul, Barnabas, Peter and James are key figures, with Paul and Barnabas providing a report of their Gentile mission and Peter and James providing an endorsement of that mission. Finally, in both passages, Antioch and Jerusalem are the key churches.

Surface similarity however, does not require identification. There are three additional arguments for the association of Acts 15 with Gal. 2:1–10, none of which possesses sufficient heft to settle the matter. First, it is argued that to have had to deal with the issue of Gentile circumcision on two separate occasions strains credibility. This may be answered by emphasizing the immense difficulty the issue of Gentile salvation posed for the early church. It is not unreasonable to assume that a subject of this magnitude and complexity would be raised and answered on more than one occasion. Anyone who has ever served on a committee has experience with having to repeatedly address the same perplexing issues on various occasions. Furthermore, there was a two year interval between Acts 11:30/12:25 and Acts 15, plenty of time for new Jewish believers to enter to church and reprise an old issue, particularly one as thorny as Gentile circumcision.

Second, Luke's account in Acts 11:30/12:25 does not record the details of Paul's meeting with the apostles recounted in Gal. 2:1–10. This may be answered by reiterating that Luke is rigorously selective in what he includes in his narrative and that it should not prove surprising that he omits a great deal of church history. Following the authoritative verdict of the Jerusalem

Council, there was no need to record the outcome of a less momentous meeting dealing with the same subject. Third, the apostles could only have endorsed Paul as the apostle to the Gentiles following, and not prior to, his first missionary journey to the Gentiles. However, Paul already maintained a thriving ministry among the Gentiles in Antioch.

Although Luke's account of Paul's visit in Acts 11:30 and 12:25 omits the details that Paul relays in Gal.2:1–10, necessitating that one must "read between the lines," the passages should be identified as parallel for the following reasons.

First, in Galatians, Paul, providing a comprehensive listing of his visits to Jerusalem, mentions only two visits. Luke, however, mentions that the Jerusalem Council is Paul's third Jerusalem visit. If Gal. 2:1–10 corresponds to Acts 15, then one must hold either that Paul would have purposely obscured the famine visit from his argument, thus destroying his argument, or that Luke's careful reporting of Paul's activities in Acts was in error. According to both Luke and Paul, Acts 11:30—12:25 is Paul's second Jerusalem visit.

Second, the verdict of the Jerusalem Council, which would have been decisive to Paul's argument, is not at all mentioned or alluded to in Galatians, a strong indication that Paul wrote Galatians prior to the convening of the Jerusalem Council. Third, in Gal. 2:1–10, the meeting is specifically described as private, between just a few individuals, whereas in Acts 15, the meeting is manifestly public and well attended by the church. Fourth, both Acts 11:30/12:25 and Gal. 2:1–10 attribute Paul's Jerusalem visit to divine revelation. Fifth, both Acts 11:30/25 and Gal. 2:1–10 make mention of Paul's concern for the poor. Finally, it is vexing to imagine how Peter could have made the mistake of Gal. 2:11–14 following the Jerusalem Council, nor why it was that Paul neglected to remind Peter of the Council's' verdict. For these reasons, this commentary has assumed the correspondence of Acts 11:30/12:25 with Gal. 2:1–10.

Conclusion:

The Jerusalem Council, by any measure a pivotal event in church history, resulted in the complete and utter validation of Gentile Christianity. James and the Jerusalem leadership, through impassioned yet reasoned discussion, skillfully avoiding a potentially disastrous church schism and division of the church into separate Jewish and Gentile factions. From this point forward, the evangelistic program of the church was to incorporate a two-fold mission strategy, proceeding with unimpeded outreach to both Jews and Gentiles.

Somehow, for the majority of church history, that two-fold emphasis has become neglected, even obscured, but the tens of thousands of contemporary Jewish believers within the twenty-first century church are evidence that the church is, even now, reconstituting its passion toward sharing the good news with the Jewish people.

In addition, the council's action preserved the integrity of the gospel. Jews and Gentiles alike were encouraged in the definitive affirmation that salvation is solely by God's grace through faith in the Messiah. This was the point of no return for the Jerusalem church, the moment when the church was authoritatively liberated from legalism and emancipated from the rabbinic tradition.

For believers, both Jewish and Gentile, ancient and contemporary, the practical application of this historic episode is that it was recognized by the church that observance of the Law was neither necessary for salvation nor sanctification. The death and resurrection of Jesus and the inauguration of the New Covenant had made obsolete the necessity of scrupulously living according to the precepts of Torah. The Mosaic Covenant had been replaced and rendered inoperative by the Messiah's death and so was no longer obligatory (Heb. 8:13; Rom. 10:4). Both Jewish and Gentile believers were now obligated to conform to the high moral and ethical precepts of the Law of Christ (1 Cor. 9:21; Gal. 6:2), much, but not all, of which correspond to the injunctions of Torah.

However, just because Jewish believers were no longer obligated to observe Torah, it does not necessitate that they were therefore prohibited from practicing certain precepts of Torah. As the revealed, sacred standards of God, Paul confirmed that the Law retained its status as holy, righteous and good (Rom. 7:12). Furthermore, as continued members of ethnic Israel, the Torah remained the grand inheritance and heritage of the Jewish believer. In the age of the Messiah, who is the Torah's living embodiment (John 1:1) and ultimate fulfillment (Matt. 5:17), Torah observance became an issue of personal liberty and conscience. Jewish believers were completely free to observe as little or as much of the Torah as they so desired. Jewish believers had liberty in Christ to observe certain facets of the Torah as long as the practice of those particular customs did not contradict New Testament revelation (Acts 15; 16:3; 21:21–24). Nonetheless, it is the abundant testimony of the Acts narrative that the Jewish believers in the early church, perceiving no contradiction with their freedom in Messiah, freely chose to customarily and normatively continue living Torah observant lifestyles, particularly those who remained residents of the land of Israel (Acts 21:20).

Study Questions:

1. List three possible reasons why some believers wanted to impose the requirements f circumcision and Torah observance on the Gentile believers.

2. Summarize the main points of Peter's testimony at the Jerusalem Council.

3. Explain James' use of the Scripture to make his argument.

4. What were the restrictions James placed upon the Gentile believers? What reason did he have for placing any restrictions on a believer?

5. List some hypothetical examples of how you might apply James' restrictions in a contemporary situation.

6. Do you believe that the Jerusalem Council arrived at the correct conclusion? Why or why not?

7. Does the Gal. 2:1–10 account correspond to Acts 15 or to Acts 11:30/12:25? Support your conclusion.

CHAPTER 14

The Second Missionary Journey
Acts 15:36–18:22

Preview:

In this lengthy section, Luke recounts Paul's second missionary journey. In a surprise narrative twist, Luke will reveal that the long-standing partnership between Paul and Barnabas is ruptured, and a new ministry partnership is forged between Paul and Silas. Early on, an additional missionary will join them, a young man named Timothy. The journey will begin by retracing a portion of the territory of Asia Minor previously evangelized on the first journey, and then will unexpectedly lead these new partners into Europe, specifically to Macedonia and Greece. Their travels will take place over a period of two and one half years, beginning in the spring of AD 50 and concluding sometime in autumn of AD 52.

Breaking Up Is Hard to Do (15:36–41)

Not long after the delegation returned to Antioch from Jerusalem, Paul, sometime in February, AD 50, suggested to Barnabas that as soon as the weather made seagoing travel possible, i.e., within the next month, that they return to the churches they had planted in Cyprus and Galatia during their initial missionary journey to ascertain the continued status of their work there. Were the churches still there? Had they continued to thrive in the midst of Jewish opposition, or had they been overwhelmed? What had been the reaction to Paul's recently dispatched Galatian letter?

In the midst of their planning, however, the partners uncovered a difference of opinion between them. Barnabas, as on the first journey, again wanted his cousin John Mark to assist them. It is probable that the so-called, "son of encouragement," wished to provide his cousin with a second chance, an opportunity to make up for his having abandoned them midway through their mission. Paul resolutely refused Barnabas' suggestion, strongly resisting the possibility of taking along the one who had recklessly abandoned them.

Second Missionary Journey Itinerary
(Acts 15:36—18:22)

Location	Reference
Antioch	Acts 15:36–40
Syria	Acts 15:41
Cilicia	Acts 15:41
Derbe	Acts 16:1
Lystra	Acts 16:1–5
Phrygia/Galatia	Acts 16:6
Mysia	Acts 16:7
Troas	Acts 16:8–10
Samothrace	Acts 16:11
Neapolis	Acts 16:11
Philippi	Acts 16:12
Amphipolis	Acts 17:1
Apollonia	Acts 17:1
Thessalonica	Acts 17:1–9
Berea	Acts 17:10–14
Athens	Acts 17:15–34
Corinth	Acts 18:1–17
Cenchrea	Acts 18:18
Ephesus	Acts 18:19
Caesarea	Acts 18:22
Jerusalem	Acts 18:22
Antioch	Acts 18:22

The two apostles were unable to reconcile their *paroxusmos*, sharp disagreement. Evidently agreeing to disagree, at this point Paul and Barnabas severed their longstanding ministry partnership. Their friendship, however, was not severed, as later on Paul is clearly still in fellowship with Barnabas (1 Cor 9:6), although Acts 15:39 is Luke's final reference to Barnabas. This passage is also John Mark's final appearance in Acts. Paul's epistles also indicate that he later reconciled with John Mark, mentioning him with affection (Col. 4:10; 2 Tim. 4:11; Philem. 24). Luke's inclusion of this surprising rift reminds his readers that Acts is not a glossed over, airbrushed or revised history of the church's pioneer leadership but, rather, a straightforward, transparent account.

A positive outcome arose from this professional separation, as it resulted in the creation of two separate missionary teams. Barnabas, together with John Mark, sailed for Cyprus. Paul summoned his new friend Silas, the prophet who had just returned the three hundred miles to Jerusalem. Like Paul, Silas possessed Roman citizenship. As the missionaries penetrated deep within the empire, citizenship would prove a strategic asset for both partners. Accepting Paul's invitation, Silas turned back around and traveled another three hundred miles to rejoin Paul in Antioch. All that travel, from Jerusalem to Antioch to Jerusalem and back again to Antioch (some nine hundred miles!), would have been good physical preparation for the missionary journey ahead.

Sent forth with the blessing of the Antioch church, the new partners returned to the churches that Paul had planted within Syria during his ministry in Antioch and within Cilicia during his ministry in Tarsus. Their primary purpose was "to strengthen the churches," emphasizing discipleship, not evangelism. With Barnabas visiting Cyprus and Paul Tarsus, both missionary teams had returned, at least temporarily, to hometown turf.

Timothy (16:1–5)

Following their time in the provinces of Syria and Cilicia, Paul and Silas traveled by land through the Taurus mountain range, through a pass called the Cilician Gates, visiting the churches of Derbe and Lystra in the province of Galatia, planted by Paul some months prior. At this time, Paul and Silas delivered the Jerusalem Council's letter to the Galatians, who had only recently also received Paul's strongly worded epistle. In Lystra, they encountered a young believer named Timothy.

Timothy

His name, *Timotheos* in Greek, means God-honored. Mentioned seventeen times in Paul's epistles, including two letters addressed to him by name, Timothy is Paul's most frequently referenced ministry partner. Affectionately called "my son" by Paul (1 Tim. 1:18), the apostle had personally led Timothy to the Lord during his previous missionary visit to Lystra, along with Timothy's mother, Eunice, and grandmother, Lois (2 Tim. 1:5). He was the child of a mixed marriage, having a Jewish mother and a Greek father, who evidently was dead by this time as he plays no role in the narrative. Timothy's father had objected to having his baby boy receive circumcision, which Greek culture considered a disfiguring mutilation of the body. Nonetheless, Timothy had been trained since childhood in the Hebrew Scripture, likely by his Jewish mother and grandmother (2 Tim. 3:15). Although, according to rabbinic Judaism, Jewishness is traced through the mother, according to Scripture, it is generally traced through the father. Therefore, Timothy was free to choose with which heritage he wished to identify. Certainly Paul, who as a Pharisee would know a Jew if he saw one, considered Timothy to be Jewish.

Luke notes that Timothy had an excellent reputation with his home church as well as neighboring churches. Apparently, during Paul and Silas' visit, Timothy, although young (between twenty and twenty-five years of age, reckoning backward from Paul's circa AD 65 reference to him as still possessing "youth," i.e., being under forty [1 Tim. 4:12]), made such a strong impression on Paul that he recruited Timothy to join him and Silas on their mission as their assistant (the position John Mark filled on the first journey and was now filling for Barnabas). First, however, there was a sensitive matter to resolve. Timothy's uncircumcised status placed his Jewishness into question. This would limit his effectiveness in executing Paul's strategy of ministry "to the Jew first." Timothy, probably because of his status as an uncircumcised Jew, was a recognized figure within the local Jewish communities. That Timothy be taken seriously within the synagogue was crucial to the success of the mission. Paul determined that if Timothy was to minister to the Jews, he must be circumcised, befitting his standing as a true son of Abraham. As Paul would later write, "to the Jews I became as a Jew, so that I might win Jews" (1 Cor. 9:20). As far as the New Testament record reveals, once he submitted to circumcision (not an easy decision for a young man under any circumstance), Timothy's Jewish status went unchallenged within the Jewish community.

Jewish Christians Circumcised?

Was Timothy's circumcision performed merely for the sale of expediency? Aside from the practical reason Paul circumcised Timothy, was there also a theological one? The point has been made in the previous chapter that through the institution of the New (and superior) Covenant (Heb 8:7–13), a Torah observant lifestyle was no longer compulsory for Jewish Christians. Even so, the Torah's practical obsolescence as a way of life had not invalidated God's promises to the Jewish nation through His covenant with Abraham.

The Abrahamic Covenant had preceded the giving of Torah by over four centuries. This foundational covenant had not been abrogated by the New Covenant. If anything, the New Covenant upheld and more firmly established God's covenant with Abraham. Every promise God had made to Abraham, later affirmed with Isaac and again with Jacob, still securely held.

Although Jewish and Gentile believers alike, as Abraham's spiritual seed, partake of the spiritual blessings of the covenant, only Jewish believers are both Abraham's spiritual *and* physical seed, and therefore certain elements of the covenant specifically apply only to them as Jews. These same elements even apply to those Jews, as children of Abraham, Isaac and Jacob, who have not as yet recognized their Messiah. The land of Israel, given by oath to Abraham, Isaac and Jacob, continues to be the eternal possession of the Jewish people by divine right (although, for the purposes of discipline, not every generation of Jews would enjoy that privilege). Additionally, the continued existence of the Jewish people is both certain and secure (Jer. 31:35–37). An additional element of the Abrahamic Covenant still in force would be the reciprocal blessing and cursing on those who bless and curse Israel. Finally, the Jewish people continue to be a blessing to the Gentile world, both corporately as a nation and, as Paul argued, definitively through the One who personified and embodied ultimate Israel, Jesus.

With the promises of the Abrahamic Covenant still certain and in force, the covenantal obligation of circumcision is also still in force. The sign of circumcision, finding its foundation within the Abrahamic Covenant and not the Torah, is still incumbent upon all Jews, including the believing remnant of Israel within the church (John 7:22; Acts 16:3; 21:21–24; Rom. 3:1). Although circumcision had been incorporated within the Mosaic legislation, it had actually predated the legislation of Torah by over four centuries. Circumcision is not as an instrument of salvation or sanctification for anyone, as both Jews and Gentiles are saved by grace through faith alone and not by ritual (Eph. 2:8). Rather, God has ordained the sign of circumcision as the sole means of Jewish identification with His covenant with Abraham. Without circumcision, there is no identifiable Jewish identity, nor any outward sign of God's everlasting faithfulness to the children of Israel.

Therefore, circumcision was understood by the early church as a continued obligation for every Jew, including Jewish believers, the faithful remnant of Israel. Circumcision was not merely an optional issue for the church, a matter of cultural preference or practical expediency while living and ministering among Jews. The debate within the church, from Cornelius' conversion in AD 40 through the Jerusalem Council in AD 49, nine years later, was whether the Gentiles were under the same obligation to be circumcised as were Jews.

The decisive conclusion was that Gentile circumcision was not warranted. This is why circumcision was unnecessary for Titus, a Gentile believer (Gal. 2:3), but, on the contrary, quite necessary for Timothy, a Jewish believer. There was no inconsistency between Timothy's circumcision and the Jerusalem Council's verdict. Circumcision has always been essential for Jewish believers. The concept of eradicating Jewish circumcision is not contemplated in Scripture, nor would it have been imagined by Paul, Peter, James or any other member of the first century church.

A cord of three strands not being easily severed (Ecc. 4:12), the missionaries, strengthened by the addition of Timothy, revisited the churches Paul had previously established throughout the south Galatian region, specifically Pisidian Antioch and Iconium, delivering the Jerusalem Council's decree and providing guidance in facilitating intra-church Jewish/Gentile relations. Acts 16:5 contains another of Luke's periodic summaries, progress reports on the state of the church peppered throughout the narrative (Acts 2:47; 6:7; 9:31; 12:24; 16:5; 19:20; 28:30–31). For the first time, he comments on the state of the church outside of the land of Israel, reporting that both discipleship and evangelism were being vigorously implemented.

The Witness in Philippi (16:6–40)

Macedonian Call (16:6–10)

Having discipled the churches in familiar territory, the mission moved into a new phase, that of the evangelism of fresh areas of Asia Minor which Paul had not yet visited. Attempting at first to head west toward Ephesus, the missionaries were unexpectedly forced to adjust their itinerary in reaction to the guidance of the Holy Spirit, who had somehow forbidden them to go west. How and why they were forbidden to go to Western Asia Minor is not specified in the text. Paul's plan to reach Ephesus was a sound one, but evidently his timing was off, and he would not minister there for another two years (Acts 18:19). Traveling north from Galatia through Mysia toward the Black Sea and the region of Bithynia, a strategic crossroads of the Roman Empire, they were again stopped cold in their tracks by the Holy Spirit, this time designated by Luke as "the Spirit of Jesus." This particular description of the Spirit is an anomaly in Scripture, appearing only in this passage, although in his epistles, Paul uses two similar terms, "Spirit of Christ" (Rom. 8:9) and "Spirit of Jesus Christ" (Phil. 1:19). The theological implication of these interchangeable designations for the Spirit within Acts 16:6–7 is to affirm that Jesus is deity and that it is appropriate to envision that the Holy Spirit proceeds equally from both Father and Son.

Unable to push westward to Ephesus or northward to Bithynia (although Peter would soon minister there [1 Pet. 1:1]), and unwilling to go back the way they had come, they pushed on in the only open direction, northwest toward Europe. They arrived at the port city of Troas, on the coast of the Aegean Sea., ten miles from the ruins of the fabled ancient city of Troy. Troas was the main gateway harbor to Greece, the hinge linking Asia Minor with Europe.

Shortly following their arrival, Paul had a night vision in which a Macedonian appealed to him for help. How Paul perceived the man to be Macedonian is simply answered by his appeal to Paul to come help "us" in Macedonia. Free of qualm or quandary in interpreting the vision as a divine directive to evangelize Macedonia, the missionaries made immediate plans to sail from Troas to Europe. At this point in the narrative, an interesting phenomenon occurs. The pronouns suddenly change from third person plural (they) to first person plural (we), subtly indicating to the readers that Luke has joined the missionary party and is now narrating from personal recollection. This is the first of the famous autobiographical Acts "we" passages (Acts 16:10–17; 20:5–15; 21:1–18; 27:1—28:16) in which Luke is present within the story. Most probably, Luke's modesty prevented him from providing the details of his initial introduction to Paul. Perhaps Paul, as the first order of business in Troas, had gone to preach in the synagogue on the Sabbath and had there encountered a receptive Gentile God-fearer or proselyte of the gate, a physician named Luke. Whatever the specific details may have been, as the missionaries set sail for Macedonia, the trio had become a quartet.

Lydia (16:11–15)

One of Luke's idiosyncrasies in Acts is that he enjoys providing the travelogue details of their journeys. He notes the excellent time they made, sailing eighty-five miles across the Aegean the first day to the rugged island of Samothrace, at the midway point between Troas and Neapolis, and covering the remaining eighty-five miles to Neapolis on the following day. Neapolis was the port of Philippi, situated ten miles northwest up the Roman road, Via Egnatia, the Egnatian Way.

Philippi

Named after Alexander the Great's father, Philip of Macedon, Philippi possessed a rich historical heritage, being the location of the famous battle fought in 42 BC by Octavian (a.k.a. Augustus Caesar) and Marc Antony's forces against those of Brutus and Cassius during the Roman civil war which erupted after Julius Caesar's assassination. This decisive battle was the turning point that resulted in the termination of the Roman republic and the birth of the Empire. Philippi is one six cities in Acts (the others being Pisidian Antioch,

Lystra, Troas, Corinth and Ptolemais) to be classified as Roman colonies, which were intended to function as a little piece of the city of Rome, broken off and transplanted abroad. The citizens of these colonies had identical civil rights to the citizens of Rome. Philippi's greatest distinction lies in its status as the first European city in which Paul preached. Although the missionaries' stay in Philippi is a short one, Luke devotes more narrative space to the events occurring in this city than any other on this missionary journey or the next. This is perhaps a telling clue that Luke would later personally play an important leadership role in the Philippian church.

According to Paul's evangelistic strategy, it was necessary for the gospel to first be preached to the Jewish community in every city they visited (Acts 13:46). Therefore, Luke records that they first spent a few days in Philippi getting their bearings, and perhaps earning a living, while they awaited the arrival of the Sabbath, the day the Jews would congregate (Acts 6:12). Surprisingly, for a colony of Philippi's size and importance, there was no synagogue. This indicated the Jewish community was so insubstantial that it could not even sustain a *minyan,* ten Jewish men, the minimum number required to hold a synagogue service. According to Jewish custom, in the case there is no building in which to meet, the Jewish community is to congregate outdoors, preferably near a body of water to facilitate *mikvah,* Jewish ritual baptism. The missionaries made an educated supposition that the Jews would probably be meeting somewhere alongside the river Gangites and went exploring outside the city in search of the location, finding it with ease a little over a mile away.

Not only was there not a *minyan* of Jewish men, there were no men gathered there at all, only an unspecified number of women assembled to pray. The four missionaries sat down by the riverside with the women and began teaching them about Jesus. Some of the assembled women were friends, family or servants of a Gentile God-fearer (or less likely, a Jewish proselyte) named Lydia, who was a merchant originally from Thyatira, the center of the purple dye industry in the ancient world. Her trade was in highly fashionable purple fabric, a "high demand" luxury item of the time. Having listened to Paul's gospel, the Lord opened Lydia's heart to respond favorably. She, along with several of her companions, became believers in the Messiah, and were all baptized in the river. Luke does not record the reaction of the other assembled women unconnected to Lydia. Afterward, Lydia persuaded the four missionaries to accept her hospitality and use her home as their base of operations in the city. She evidently must have been quite a successful merchant to own a home spacious enough to accommodate four guests. This concludes Luke's account of how a Gentile woman, albeit one strongly sympathetic to Judaism, had the distinction of being Paul's first European convert.

Exorcism (16:16–18)

It did not take long for the missionaries to encounter antagonism. However, in the absence of a hostile Jewish community to oppose the gospel, this time the opposition came from an alternate source, the supernatural realm. Perhaps as early as the following Sabbath, the missionaries, along with Lydia and the other women, had a demonic encounter. While en route back to the riverside place of prayer, a slave girl approached them. Luke describes her as having been possessed by a "Python spirit," by which he indicated that she was in the thrall of no ordinary, run of the mill demon. In the ancient Greek world, the "Python spirit" was considered to be the supernatural force behind the famous Oracle of Delphi[1], whose priestess ("the pythoness") was the "mother of all" fortunetellers. Indeed, Luke reports that the slave girl generated a great deal of income for her owners through her demonic soothsaying ability.

Following after the missionaries, she screamed over and over that they were servants of the "most high God" (the same name for God screamed by the demoniac in Luke 8:28) and were preaching how to receive salvation. The slave girl kept up this persistent caterwauling for several days in a row, dogging Paul wherever he went to preach. The demon publicly acknowledged the missionaries' identity and their purpose, which may explain why Paul tolerated it for a time. Finally, however, Paul was sufficiently irked that he determined to put an end to this irritant, having had enough of her distracting yowling going on behind his back. Paul turned toward the girl but addressed her demonic guest. Exerting the authority he had in Christ (commanding, "in the name of Jesus Christ,") Paul instantaneously expelled the demon.

Shackled (16:19–24)

While the slave was now spiritually liberated, the exorcism did not sit well with her owners, for whom she was a meal ticket. The expulsion of the demon meant their economic desiccation. Realizing that Paul's meddling had deprived them of their source of income, they seized him, dragging him before the Philippian court of law in the agora, the marketplace. They also hijacked Silas, obviously Paul's chief partner in meddling. Luke and young Timothy remained unmolested by the slave owners, who, apparently, were content to have seized only the ringleaders.

The slave owners camouflaged their case as an issue not of pocketbook but patriotism. The accusation brought before the two *stratēgoi*, "magistrates of a Roman colony," was that Paul and Silas, being Jews, were confusing the populace of Philippi by proclaiming illegal religious customs. The anti-Semitic overtone of their charge is unmistakable. In the Roman Empire, Judaism was a licensed religion and being Jewish was no crime, although it was illegal for Jews to proselytize Roman citizens.[2] It is revealing to note that the Romans could not distinguish any difference between Christians and Jews.

A mob rapidly formed and surrounded the missionaries. Before Paul or Silas had an opportunity to proclaim their Roman citizenship, the *stratēgoi*, unquestioningly accepting the charge against the missionaries of so egregiously disturbing the peace, ordered for Paul and Silas to be stripped and severely beaten with rods. Exactly how violent this pummeling was is not detailed by Luke, who specifies only that they suffered "many blows." This is the first of three occasions when Paul will be forced to endure being beaten with rods (2 Cor. 11:25). This particular humiliating episode is cited in Paul's first epistle to the Thessalonians (1 Thess. 2:2).

Paul and Silas were summarily thrown into jail. The jailer, given strict orders (on pain of death) to secure the detainees, imprisoned them in the securest, innermost area of the prison, the windowless dungeon. Taking no chances, he also agonizingly locked up their feet in stocks.

Unshackled (16:25–34)

Midnight found Paul and Silas still awake, understandably unable to sleep, their legs cramping and knotted with pain from the stocks, their bodies battered and bruised from their beating. However, although their bodies were broken, their spirits were not. Emanating from the black depths of the dungeon that evening was the melodious sound of Hebrew chanting. Rejoicing in all circumstances and perhaps, to take their mind off their aching bodies, Paul and Silas were praying and praising God. Luke adds the detail that the prayers and praise, echoing throughout the prison, were being enjoyed by their fellow prisoners, who likely appreciated the novel sound.

Suddenly, Paul and Silas' vocalizing was interrupted by an earthquake. The magnitude of the quake was sufficient to shake the foundations of the prison, rattle open all the prison doors and unfasten every prisoner's chains. The jailer, roused from his sleep by the quake, saw only the open prison doors and assumed that all his charges had escaped. No matter the extraordinary circumstance, his superiors would consider this a dereliction of duty worthy of death. Despairing that the ultimate disaster had befallen him, that under his supervision an entire prison emptied itself, the humiliated Roman drew his short sword to his chest in preparation for committing an honorable suicide. Paul, apparently seeing the jailer's trembling silhouette through the darkness, cried out for him not to kill himself, for none of his prisoners had tried to escape. The curious fact that all of the prisoners were still present and accounted for is not explained in the narrative. After all, in the previous prison episodes, escape was the obvious course of action following a supernatural display (Acts 5:19; 12:11). One can surmise only that they were all still stunned and in awe of the powerful response that the prayers of Paul and Silas to their God had unleashed.

Calling to other subordinates, the jailer sent for torchbearers to enter the inner prison. Seeing Paul and Silas, he fell down before them as an act of worship. Bringing them out of the murkiness of the inner prison and into the light, the jailer asked Paul and Silas the single most important question in the Scripture, "What must I do to be saved?" Some wonder whether what the jailer actually meant concerned his physical salvation, i.e., avoidance of Roman punishment. That can hardly be the case, however, for with his full prison complement still intact, if not the prison itself, there was nothing for which he was liable. The jailer's query is undoubtedly concerned with how to know the God to whom he had earlier heard these remarkable men praying.

Paul and Silas replied, "Believe in the Lord Jesus, and you will be saved, and the same goes for your family" (Acts 16:31). Although this succinctly summarized the gospel, it was not the entire gospel. Later that evening, as guests in the jailer's home, Paul and Silas shared with him and his family exactly what they must believe *about* the Lord Jesus to be saved. The basic points of the gospel that Paul preached are laid out in his first epistle to the Corinthians: first, that the Messiah died for our sins, was buried and resurrected on the third day, all according to messianic prophecy contained within Hebrew Scripture, and that the resurrected Messiah appeared to witnesses (1 Cor. 15:1–8). Sometime later that night, the jailer and his family responded to the gospel. It is essential not to misconstrue the force of Paul's gospel invitation of Acts 16:31. The jailer's family (his "household") was not saved through his faith but as a result of their own. Their salvation was immediately followed by baptism, likely in a fountain outside in the prison courtyard. The jailer and his family, now brothers and sisters in Christ, joyfully gave Paul and Silas some much needed medical attention and food.

Departure (16:35–40)

The next morning, the magistrates' lackeys, the same thugs who had thrashed Paul and Silas with rods, came to the prison with orders for the missionaries' release. The jailer immediately ran back to their cell with the good news of their discharge. However, after they, Roman citizens, had endured such punishment the day before without benefit of trial, Paul was in no hurry to bid adieu to his "hoosegow hotel" just yet. The *stratēgoi* had flagrantly violated Roman laws designed to protect Roman citizens from just such foul treatment as the missionaries had received.[3] After their gross public humiliation, there was no way Paul was leaving without a very public apology and a personal escort from the *stratēgoi* themselves. Paul knew his rights as a citizen and had no qualms about exercising them.

When the magistrates received Paul's message, they understood the enormity of their error and came running to him in the prison. Issuing both apology and escort, as requested, the two *stratēgoi* repeatedly implored the missionaries to leave town. Paul and Silas agreed to move on. Before departing, they encouraged the new church of Philippian believers assembled in Lydia's home. In Acts 16:40, Luke's descriptive pronouns revert back from "we" to "they," indicating that Luke stayed on in Philippi to lead the church. Luke will later rejoin the missionaries when they again pass through Philippi (Acts 20:5–6).

The Witness in Thessalonica (17:1–9)

While most of us would have preferred taking a few days off in bed to recuperate from such a beating, Paul and Silas, along with Timothy, hit the road. They traveled westward thirty-two miles along the Egnatian Way, passing through the important city of Amphipolis. Traveling another twenty-five miles down the road, the missionaries also chose to pass through the city of Apollonia. Their destination lay another forty miles down the road, the capital of Macedonia, Thessalonica. Some have been puzzled by the missionaries' quick pass through of these two important cosmopolitan centers. Their reasoning undoubtedly lay in the fact that having spent time in Philippi, a city with a negligible Jewish population, they were eager to preach the gospel in a city containing a substantial Jewish community. Neither of the two cities they passed through met that qualification. Thessalonica, on the other hand, possessed a teeming Jewish populace among its two hundred thousand citizens. Both the city's position straddling the Egnatian Way and its harbor on the Thermaikos Gulf made Thessalonica the economic and administrative heart of Macedonia.

Upon arrival in Thessalonica, Paul immediately went to the synagogue, as was his custom (Acts 13:46; 17:2). As a visiting rabbi, albeit one who appeared a little worse for the wear (after being beaten with rods), Paul likely received an invitation to address the congregation, as had been the case in Pisidian Antioch (Acts 13:25). Luke records that on three successive Sabbaths, Paul reasoned, *dialegomai*, "to dialogue" with the Jewish community from the messianic prophecies contained within Hebrew Scripture. He explained, *dianoigō*, "to open the mind," that the Messiah had to die and be resurrected, attempting to persuade them, *paratithēmi*, "to expound, to demonstrate," that Jesus was the Messiah. Although most Jews remained unmoved by Paul's efforts, over the three week period some were persuaded, including two men who would later become Paul's companions, Aristarchus (Acts 19:29; 20:4; 27:2; Col. 4:10; Philem. 24), and Secundus (Acts 20:4). In addition, a large number of God-fearers responded to the gospel, as did a significant group of the city's female aristocracy, many of whom had been attracted to Judaism.

Luke relates few details of Paul's Thessalonian mission. Precisely how long Paul, Silas and Timothy stayed in Thessalonica is unclear, but it was far longer than the three-week period Paul spent witnessing to the Jewish community. Thankfully, Paul provides a useful biographical detail or two in his epistles. In Philippians, we learn that while in Thessalonica, he twice received financial support from the Philippian church (Phil. 4:15–16), which was one hundred miles distant, a five day journey. Paul also reveals in his Thessalonian correspondence that he and Silas primarily supported themselves in the ministry through work (1 Thess 2:9; 2 Thess 3:7–10). More significantly, he clearly indicates that the vast majority of the Thessalonian believers were Gentiles who were not God-fearers previously affiliated with the synagogue, but were instead pagans rescued from idolatry.

As had happened on Paul's first missionary journey, after awhile the Jewish community began to get its collective nose out of joint over all positive reception the missionaries were receiving among the God-fearers and proselytes of the gate. Their jealousy became manifest when they approached some loitering rabble, *andras tinas ponērous*, "some wicked, worthless men," in the marketplace. Looking for trouble and delighted to find some, this rabble was easily incited by the Jews to form a mob and create a riot. The mob surrounded the home of Jason, a new Jewish believer, and Paul and Silas' host during their stay in Thessalonica. Jason's door was broken down and the mob streamed into the house, searching for Paul and Silas, planning to drag them before the municipal courts. The search unsuccessful, the frustrated mob chose instead to snatch Jason and some other believers.

Down at the courthouse addressing the city *politarchas*, "magistrates," the mob accused Jason of harboring dangerous revolutionaries, "these men who have turned the world upside down" (Acts 17:6). Unlike the allegation at Philippi, which was related to proselytizing Roman citizens, this accusation portrayed Paul and Silas as treasonous troublemakers who proclaimed that Jesus was a rival king to Caesar. These were fairly alarming charges, particularly in light of Claudius' expulsion of every Jew from the city of Rome just months earlier (Acts 18:2) for the cause of rioting "at the instigation of *Chrestus*"[4] (a confused variant of *Christos*, "Christ.") If those preaching this Jesus could cause such turmoil in the capital of the empire, what might they do in Thessalonica? The magistrates, while disquieted, reacted more sensibly than did their counterparts in Philippi. The demanded a financial guarantee from Jason and the other believers with him that Paul and Silas would leave Thessalonica and never return. In his first epistle to the Thessalonians, Paul references both this hostile episode (1 Thess. 2:14–16) and his inability to revisit the Thessalonian church (1 Thess. 2:17–18). We also learn from Paul that, at this point, the persecution of the church in this city was only beginning (1 Thess. 2:14; 3:1–5; 2 Thess. 1:6–7).

The Witness in Berea (17:10–15)

That very evening, the Thessalonian believers quietly bid farewell to Paul, Silas and Timothy under cover of night. The missionaries made their way some fifty miles southwest to the city of Berea, which, like Thessalonica, had a sizable Jewish population. Holding to his pattern of preaching first to the Jew and then to the Greek, Paul and company entered the synagogue. As in previous synagogue visits, on the Sabbath the leaders of the synagogue would have been asked Paul, as a traveling rabbi and honored guest, to share a word of exhortation with the congregation. As seen in Thessalonica, Paul's *modus operandi* in the synagogue was to reason from Scripture, explain messianic prophecy and persuade the Jews that Jesus was the Messiah (Acts 17:2–3).

In comparison with Paul's previous reception in Thessalonica, this Jewish congregation was much more welcoming. Luke describes the Berean Jewish community as *eugenesteroi*, "more noble or open minded," for they were ready, willing and able to systematically examine the Scriptures, without prejudice, to verify the accuracy of Paul's interpretation of messianic prophecy. On a daily basis, they actively engaged with Paul's claims to see if they were true. As a result, many of the Jews became believers, among them a later companion of Paul, Sopater (Acts 20:4). In addition to the Jewish response, there was an encouraging Gentile response as well, particularly from among the men and women of the city's aristocracy. It seems clear that the one variable that set the Berean synagogue community apart from others in which Paul had witnessed was the active study of Scripture. An open-minded examination of the Hebrew Scriptures' messianic prophecies has always been and continues to this day to be an effective method of demonstrating that Jesus is the promised Messiah.

The peace of Paul's ministry within the Berean synagogue was shattered when the Thessalonian Jewish community heard that Paul was preaching in Berea. A delegation was recruited, a group motivated enough to travel fifty miles to Berea just to agitate the populace. In contrast to the Bereans' readiness to search the Scriptures with Paul, the Thessalonians were only ready, willing and able to make trouble for him. As the lightening rod on which the Thessalonians' hostility was focused, Paul left Berea in order to diffuse their opposition. He left Silas and Timothy to continue establishing the new Berean church with a directive to join him in Athens at their earliest opportunity.

The Witness in Athens (17:16–34)

Invitation to Witness (17:16–21)

It is possible that a ministry in Athens was not part of Paul's original itinerary. Having responded to the Macedonian vision, it is likely that Paul planned to make his way westward through Macedonia until he reached the opposite coast and, from there, possibly even to cross the sea and reach Rome itself. Some years later, Paul would write of his longstanding desire to go to Rome (Rom 1:13; 15:22–23) and of stymied travel plans (Rom. 1:13). At this point, however, the execution of such a plan would have been stymied both by the recent expulsion of Jews from Rome and by how dangerous Macedonia as a whole had become for Paul.[5]

Athens. Situated in the southeast of Greece, five miles off the Aegean coast, Athens has always been the preeminent city of the Greek nation, the fabled cradle of democracy. By the first century, however, Athens' glory days lay some five centuries in the past, and it was no longer the world-class city it had once been. Nonetheless, Athens remained the Roman Empire's cultural and intellectual center of philosophy, art and literature. Along with Alexandria and Tarsus, it was one of the three great "university towns" of the Roman Empire. Athens was named in honor of the goddess Athena, and her temple, the Parthenon, which contained a colossal bronze statue of Athena, perched arrestingly atop the Acropolis, the craggy hill around which the city was built.

It would be at least a week or so before Silas and Timothy would arrive from Berea. While waiting for his missionary companions to join him, Paul engaged in the time-honored activity of every first-time visitor to famous Athens and toured the city. He wandered around the city streets, rife with magnificent marble temples, columns, sculptures and statuary. These were no mere works of art to Paul, however, but an appalling plethora of idols representing pagan deities. He was hardly a stranger to Greco-Roman cities, being well traveled and a native of Tarsus. But for Paul, Athens was over the top. Luke records that the more of Athens Paul experienced, the greater became his exasperation at a city virtually dedicated to idolatry. On every corner, on every hill, on every colonnaded promenade were representations of, or dedications to, Greek gods and goddesses. Petronius, the Roman satirist, remarked, "It was easier to find a god than a man in Athens."[6]

First century Jews possessed a natural aversion to idolatry. Although ancient Israel had habitual difficulty being faithful to the first and second commandments, idolatry finally ceased being a Jewish problem as a result of God's discipline of the Babylonian captivity. Paul would later articulate his thoughts on the reprehensible foolishness of idol worship (Rom. 1:22–23). With time on his hands and much too impatient to wait for his companions, Paul determined to begin the Athenian mission without them.

According to Paul's conviction, prior to witnessing to the Gentiles he must first proclaim the gospel to the Jews and God-fearers within the synagogue. And so, on the Sabbath Paul entered the Athenian synagogue in order to reason, explain and persuade, as was his custom (Acts 17:2–3). Once his Jewish witness within the synagogue was set in motion, he then immediately plunged into a pagan witness as well. On the weekdays, he debated in the *agora* (the main marketplace, the public square and bustling city center of Athenian life). In the agora, Paul dialogued with representatives of the two main philosophical schools popular in that time, the Epicureans and the Stoics.

Epicurean. According to the followers of Epicurus' school of philosophy, the pursuit of pleasure was humanity's highest goal. Pleasure was defined not in a hedonistic way, but rather as seeking a tranquil life devoid of distress, suffering and pain. They rejected metaphysics and emphasized the material. Although acknowledging the existence of the supernatural, they believed that religion was the root source of the entire world's misery. They were practical deists, who held that if the gods existed, they were far removed from concerning themselves with man.[7]

Stoic. According to the followers of this school of philosophy, founded by Zeno (a native of Paul's hometown, Tarsus), matter was all that mattered (existed). They were pantheists, believing that the deity, or the divine spirit, saturates everything, permeating all matter. They emphasized ethics and reason. Because all destiny is dictated by fate, the goal was to achieve a deportment of apathy toward pain, pleasure, suffering or health, peacefully accepting whatever lot befell one. Because they believed that all men were suffused with the divine spark, they upheld the brotherhood of mankind.[8]

The philosophers had two main reactions to Paul's claims. Some found Paul's gospel to be unreasonable and insufficiently sophisticated, labeling him a "babbler" with nothing of importance to impart. Others completely misunderstood him, believing that he was proclaiming two new gods, whose proper names were *Iēsous* (Jesus) and *Anastasis* (resurrection), the female consort of *Iēsous*'!

According to Roman (and Athenian) law, the introduction of new religions was prohibited. In fact, it was this very accusation that had resulted in the death of Socrates, the most famous of Athenian classical philosophers. However, Luke's adds a parenthetical remark to his narrative, noting that the Athenians, like intellectual floozies, exhibited a marked propensity for loitering around the agora, eagerly awaiting the proclamation of novel ideas and new intellectual fads to discuss. The philosophers, wanting to hear more, indeed living for such stimulating opportunities, requested that Paul further explain the strange and surprising things of which he spoke. Paul was escorted (either by invitation or command is uncertain) to the Royal Colonnade in a corner of the agora. Assembled in this area was the chief judicial body of Athens, the thirty-member Council of the Areopagus.[9] The Areopagus was responsible for supervising the education (including the propagation of religion) of Athenians. The name of the council derives from *ho Areios pagos*, "the Hill of Ares," or more familiarly, "Mars Hill," the rocky hill jutting up in the shadow of the Acropolis, on top of which the council convened to adjudicate murder trials. It is to this august association that Paul is now invited to present the gospel.

Paul's Witness (17:22–34)

If Luke's Pisidian Antioch account portrays Paul as rabbi par excellence, his Athens account portrays Paul as the great Greek orator. This is the sole instance in Acts where Paul's Hellenistic education as a Tarsus native shines through. In addressing the Areopagus, Paul must temporarily remove his figurative prayer shawl and don his philosophers robe. Unable to base his evangelistic argument on the Hebrew Scripture, which would neither have been familiar nor accepted as authoritative by his audience, or even on the assumption of monotheism, Paul is compelled to an alternative point of contact from which to build a bridge of communication. Striving to find common ground between himself and the Areopagus, Paul will artfully move from creation to resurrection in a mere ten verses, all the while avoiding the presentation of Jewish concepts devoid of Gentile context. To loosely paraphrase Paul's famous statement in 1 Cor. 9:20–21, "To the Jews, I became as a Jew in order to win Jews; to the Athenians, I became as an Athenian in order to win Athenians."

In Paul's introduction, he describes the state of the Athenians as being *deisidaimonesterous* (quite a mouthful in any language), which may be translated, "very religious," with the sense of "much more religious than the average bear" or alternatively, "quite superstitious." Paul was deliberately ambiguous in his word choice, neither overtly expressing his repulsion for their idolatry nor falsely complementing it. Of course, if there had been any Jews present on the Areopagus they might have appreciated Paul's subtle *double entendre*, for the same word that is translated "religious" is understood by Jews as meaning, "fear of the demonic."

Paul notes that earlier, while as a tourist taking in the sights and sounds of the city and observing the stunning variety of objects worshiped, he happened upon an altar with the inscription *Agnōstō Theō*, "To an unknown God." That ancient Athens was chock full of many such altars addressed to unknown deities is well attested to by contemporary historical sources.[10] The reason the Athenians placed these altars in various locations around the city was as a practical safety precaution. They were an insurance policy against invoking the divine wrath of any slighted god or goddess whom, out of ignorance, they had neglected to worship. Paul affirms that the Athenians had been correct in this practice. There was indeed a God of whom they had been ignorant (and how!), who demanded their worship. Paul effortlessly sidestepped any accusation that he was illegally preaching a new religion by claiming that he was simply expounding upon a religion they were already observing and a God whom they already worshiped.

Leaving behind his introduction, Paul moved on to an elucidation of the unknown God. As he went along, he challenged a few common Greek ideas concerning deity. In contrast to the beliefs of the pantheistic Stoics, God was not some impersonal force infusing all matter but the Lord and creator of the universe. Furthermore, in contrast to Greek religion, there is only one true God and not a pantheon.

As Lord of the Universe, this God cannot be contained in handmade temples, not even a temple as magnificent as the Parthenon atop the Acropolis, elevated majestically above the city and continually visible to every Athenian. This point echoes the words of Solomon (1 Kin. 8:27) and Isaiah (Is. 66:1–2) in the Hebrew Scripture and Stephen, just prior to his death (Acts 7:48). It also remarkably represents the thoughts of the renowned classical Greek playwright, Euripides, who asked, "What house built by craftsmen could enclose the form divine within enfolding walls."[11] Paul's next point challenged the Epicureans. Not only is God unable to be contained, He is self-sufficient, having no need of offerings for his wellbeing or happiness. On the contrary, humanity desperately needs His provision, for life, breath and all else are His gifts.

Having established a few basic points about God, Paul made a few corrections to the Athenian's view of humanity. Without quoting the first chapters of Genesis, Paul nonetheless got across its basic gist, explaining that since all humanity descended from one man, all men are brothers. While the Stoics believed in the brotherhood of mankind, few Athenians would accept that its basis was humanity's common origin. The Athenians, alone among the Greeks in having no history of their ancestral immigration to Athens from elsewhere, claimed to be unique among all peoples, having sprung up whole from the soil of their region. Also taking aim at the Epicureans' deism, Paul insisted that God was firmly in control of human history and active in its affairs. The Athenians did not spring up on their own, contrary to their home-grown mythology, but God Himself determined the location and boundaries of all nations. Understandably, considering his audience, Paul neglected to elaborate that every nation's boundary was determined in relation to the population of Israel (Deut.32:8).

Paul then deftly moved to humanity's relationship with God. He highlights both God's desire that men seek him and the ease with which He may be found by those who seek Him. God is not distant and removed as believed by the Epicureans, nor does He reside upon Mt. Olympus, as did the Greek god Zeus. God is near and easy to find, if perhaps we, like the spiritually blind, would simply grope for Him. Paul masterfully punctuates his argument with quotations from two well-known Greek poets from centuries past. Epimenides of Crete, a Stoic, wrote circa 500 BC, "in Him we live and move and exist," and Aratus, another Stoic, wrote circa 250 BC, "we are His (God's) offspring."[12]

Paul transitioned to humanity's responsibility to God. Having presented basic monotheism, Paul added the thrust of Moses' first two commandments, to have no other gods and to create no engraved images. Since all men are brothers, sharing a resemblance to their divine Father, it is senseless to imagine that gods can be formed by man's craftsmanship or artistry. The worship of idols was a truly ignorant practice that must be eradicated. Although God had chosen to overlook, *hupereidon*, "wink at," such ignorance of Him in the past, this was no longer going to be the case. God now demanded repentance from all humanity. From this point on, Gentiles will be held responsible not only for natural revelation, but for specific revelation, the gospel. Paul had alluded to this with the Lystrans (Acts 14:16) and will make the same point in his Roman epistle (Rom. 3:25).

This new dispensation, this change of policy, has come about because a time is coming when God will judge the world. All humanity will be judged by one standard alone, God's righteousness. His righteousness will be personified by one man, the Messiah, who will serve as the agent of God's judgment (a point later paralleled in 1 Thess. 1:10). The certain guarantee that the future day of reckoning has been firmly set is the Messiah's resurrection.

At this point, Paul's message was interrupted by the Areopagus. Make no mistake, the council patiently stayed with him throughout his dissertation as he argued points on God, humanity and idols. However, the business about a future judgment day and a man being physically resurrected was beyond the pale, far too ridiculous for an educated Athenian to accept. Most Greeks, with the exception of the Epicureans, believed in the immortality of the soul, but no cultured Greek could but sneer at an immortal body. Some, probably the Stoics, to whom physical matter "mattered," suggested a further hearing at another time, but it seems clear that the council permanently adjourned on the matter. They perceived Paul's teaching as neither a threat to Rome or Athens and only of interest as an amusing novelty. Paul will later reflect that the wisdom of the world considers the gospel foolishness, but to those whom God calls, the gospel is both the power and wisdom of God (1 Cor. 1:21–24).

Although Paul's time in Athens is considered by some to have been a failure, Luke seems to disagree, although neither does he characterize it as a resounding success. He notes that following Paul's Areopagus address, some men joined him, *kollēthentes*, "they stuck to him like glue." While not many Athenians came to faith, some, in fact, did do so through Paul's Athenian ministry. Among the new believers was even one of the thirty members of the Areopagus, Dionysius, as well as a woman named Damaris. Furthermore, Athens was one of the few cities from which Paul left without being driven out under life-threatening circumstances!

The Witness in Corinth (18:1–18)

Ministry (18:1–11)

Sometime during Paul's brief stay in Athens, Silas and Timothy joined him from Berea (1 Thess 3:1). Having rendezvoused in Athens, the missionaries split up. Silas left to strengthen the church in Philippi (Acts 18:5). Paul, eager for information from the Thessalonian church and unable to go there himself, sent Timothy back to Thessalonica (1 Thess. 3:2). Paul departed Athens alone, never to return, bound for Corinth (Acts 18:1). As he will later reveal, the apostle was feeling discouraged, uncertain and even fearful about the future of his mission (Acts 18:9; 1 Cor. 2:3), which was approximately, at this point, at the one year mark. However, Corinth was a strategic evangelistic opportunity not to missed. Beginning in just a few weeks, in the spring of AD 51, the popular and wildly raucous biennial Isthmian Games were to be held, just outside the city. These athletic, equestrian and musical competitions would draw thousands of tourists to Corinth. Paul would also use these events to illustrate his first epistle to the Corinthians (1 Cor 9:24–27).

Corinth

A Roman colony founded in 46 BC by Julius Caesar, Corinth was the capital of the province of Achaia. Corinth is located on the northern side of the Peloponnesian peninsula, some fifty miles west of Athens, at the isthmus connecting the peninsula with the mainland of Greece. Its strategic setting on the main trade routes and its unique quality of being served by two separate harbors ensured its status as an "international crossroads of commerce and travel," a "gateway between Asia and Europe"[13] This seething melting pot ranked as one of the great commercial centers of ancient Europe and, indeed, the entire Roman Empire.

Similar to a melting pot, Corinth could get hot indeed and had an infamous reputation as the foulest, least moral city in the ancient world. The verb, "to corinthianize," meant to fornicate, and a "Corinthian girl" was a euphemism for a prostitute.[14] Not surprisingly, Aphrodite, goddess of love, was the city's favored deity. In fact, history remembers Corinth as the lascivious center of Aphrodite worship, with one thousand prostitutes (the original "Corinthian girls") employed in her temple atop the summit of the nineteen hundred foot high mountain, the Acrocorinth. During Paul's visit, there were perhaps as many as half a million residents in Corinth, including a substantial Jewish population that had recently expanded following the emperor Claudius' expulsion of the Jews from Rome some months earlier.

Upon arrival in the bustling metropolis, Paul went looking for an opportunity to ply his trade as a tentmaker (it is still a matter of debate as to whether this trade involved working with textiles, leather or goatskin).[15] Utterly alone in a new city, Paul needed money. In need of both job and friends, Paul found one job and two friends. His job hunt would have led him to the tentmakers guild, which brought him into contact with two fellow Jewish Christians, Aquila and Priscilla. How this couple had come to faith in the Messiah is not detailed by Luke, but they had evidently been believers for some time, as no mention is made of Paul introducing them to Jesus. Priscilla (or the more formal, Prisca) and Aquila had only recently arrived in Corinth, having being driven out of their home in Rome by the expulsion of the city's Jews.

Aquila was also a tentmaker and offered Paul both hospitality and the opportunity to work together in their common profession. This would mark the beginning of a lifelong friendship between this couple and the apostle, who glowingly references his friends three times in the epistles (Rom. 16:3; 1 Cor 16:19; 2 Tim. 4:19). Uniquely, in four of five New Testament references (Acts 18:18, 26; Rom 16:3; 2 Tim. 4:19), Priscilla's name often appears before that of her husband, indicating either her higher social status or that she was considered in some way more important than her husband.

In Corinth, as elsewhere, Paul gave priority of witness to the Jews. On every Sabbath, Paul was in the synagogue, reasoning with, explaining and persuading both Jew and Greek God-fearer that Jesus was the prophesied Messiah. In Acts 18:5, Silas and Timothy reenter the narrative, coming to Corinth from Philippi and Thessalonica, respectively. Silas came bearing a gift of financial support from the Philippian church (2 Cor. 11:9; Phil. 4:15), and Timothy came bearing an encouraging report on the Thessalonian believers (1 Thess. 3:6–10), although they were in need of a little clarification from Paul concerning the timing of the rapture of the church and the return of Jesus (1 Thess. 4:13—5:11). As a result of Timothy's report, Paul wrote his first letter to the Thessalonians. While still in Corinth, Paul would later author a second letter to the church in Thessalonica. The combination of the Philippians' financial gift and the unspecified but likely entrance of Silas and Timothy into the Corinthian workforce meant that Paul no longer had to expend effort engaged in tentmaking (2 Cor. 11:9). He now was able to devote all of his energy and attention to his witness within the Jewish community.

It was not long before Paul's ministry was opposed by the Jewish community. In reaction to the intensity of their resistance to the gospel and blasphemy against the Messiah, Paul flamboyantly shook out his robes to them, a solemn disclaimer of his responsibility toward them. Even more dramatically, Paul announced, "your blood is on your own heads; I am unstained by it!" Applying the imagery of the prophet Ezekiel to his ministry, Paul pictured himself as a "watchman" over the Jewish people, God's divinely appointed spokesman to warn them of coming judgment. According to the prophet, if the watchman failed to discharge his responsibility to warn the people of looming disaster, then God would hold him accountable for their deaths. However, if the watchman were to warn the people and they stubbornly refused to respond, then they would die in their sins and be liable for their own blood. In that case, the watchman would be clean of bloodguilt (Ezek. 3:17–21; 33:2–9).

The remainder of Paul's Corinthian ministry would now be focused on the Gentiles. Paul's dramatic action is not to be understood as a permanent repudiation of the Jewish people, but only a temporary one applicable to this particular community. The unvarying pattern of Paul's evangelistic strategy was to witness first to the Jews within the synagogue, ministering among that community until such time as the gospel was rejected. Upon the Jewish community's rejection, then he would concentrate his witness among the Gentiles. This was the blueprint Paul articulated in Acts 13:46 and carried out in Pisidian Antioch, Iconium, Philippi, Thessalonica, Berea, Athens, Corinth, etc. Nor is Paul's repudiation of the Jewish community meant to imply that he would give the brush to a Jewish person who wanted to dialogue with him about Jesus. He was simply shifting the focus of his ministry.

Conveniently, Paul was invited to transfer his base of operations just next door to the synagogue, to the home of Titius Justus, a new believer who had been either a God-fearer or a proselyte of the gate. His name suggests that he was a Roman citizen, and a home adjacent to the synagogue, which was sufficiently spacious to hold church meetings indicates a man of means. For the remainder of Paul's Corinthian ministry, this home would be the meeting place for the church, a continual witness to Corinth's Jewish community by its very proximity and high visibility.

In the preliminary weeks of Paul's Corinthian ministry, prior to his turning to the Gentiles, he had been moderately successful in making his case among the Jews. His epistle to the Corinthians references those initial believers whom he had personally baptized, indicating that they had come to faith prior to the arrival of Silas and Timothy. Paul mentions Stephanas whom, along with Stephanas' family, Paul calls the "first fruits" of his Corinthian ministry (1 Cor. 16:15), Gaius (1 Cor. 1:14; Rom. 16:23) and Crispus (1 Cor. 1:14). Crispus had been the leader of the synagogue, in charge of its facility and worship services. Although he would thereafter be formally relieved of his leadership responsibilities (replaced by Sosthenes [Acts 18:17]), one can imagine the impact that Crispus and his whole family becoming believers in Jesus had on the synagogue.

At some point, either immediately prior to or just after Paul transferred his ministry next door to the synagogue, Jesus ("the Lord") spoke to him in a night vision. Encouraging Paul, Jesus told him to stop being afraid. He was not to shrink from witnessing of his Messiah. In fact, Jesus had "many people in this city." There was nothing for Paul to fear; he was being supernaturally protected by the very presence of God and would not be harmed in Corinth. This was the fourth supernatural revelation Paul experienced thus far in the Acts narrative, the first being the commission on the Damascus road (9:4–6), the second the warning in the Temple, following his return to Jerusalem, to leave (Acts 22:17–18), and the third the Macedonian vision (Acts 16:9).

Following Paul's departure from the synagogue, the mission became even more fruitful. Luke summarizes the success of the Corinthian ministry in Acts 18:8, reporting that many Corinthians, having heard the gospel, believed what they heard and were subsequently baptized (the standard New Testament sequence for coming to faith). Paul would be firmly planted in Corinth for a total of eighteen months, building the church as well as planting an additional church in nearby Cenchrea (Rom. 16:1).

Trial (18:12–18)

After about a year had passed, organized Jewish opposition rose up against him. Once again, Paul was brought before a Roman court of law on the charge that he was propagating a new religion. They claimed that Christianity was not a legitimate form of Judaism but rather an unauthorized new faith.

Standing in the agora before the *bema*, the imposing elevated platform from which Roman judgment was rendered, Paul came face to face with Corinth's proconsul, Gallio.

Gallio. Possessing an eminent pedigree, Gallio was the son of the renowned rhetorician, Seneca the Elder, and brother of the famous Stoic philosopher and tutor to the Roman emperor Nero, Seneca the Younger. Celebrated for both his charm and wit, Gallio held a variety of Roman offices. Both he and his brother would be executed in AD 65 after losing favor with Nero.

A precise dating and chronology of Paul's life and ministry can prove flummoxing, to say the least. The challenge is best described as putting together a puzzle from which there are multiple missing pieces. What pieces we have come from within the Acts narrative, Paul's epistles and our general knowledge of the historical record. Of course, the key to successfully putting together any puzzle is to first identify and assemble the borders. In Paul's case, we are certain of the general time parameters surrounding his conversion (sometime between AD 33–35) and of the date of his death (sometime between AD 62–68). For everything that lies between conversion and death, we must compare the chronological sequence as laid out in Acts and the epistles with the known dates of referenced historical events. These are the death of Herod Agrippa (AD 44), the famine (AD 44–49), the expulsion of Jews from Rome (AD 49), Ananias' high priesthood (AD 42–59) and the terms of the Roman officials, Felix (AD 54?-59) and Gallio (AD 52–53).

The term of Gallio's service as Corinth's proconsul is a key historical peg on which we may hang a chronology of the second missionary journey. Fitzmyer provides a blockbuster analysis of the historical data, arguing that while Gallio's term is commonly assigned a date of 51–52, a date of AD 52–53 aligns better with the data.[16] Having taken office in late spring/early summer of AD 52, Gallio cut short his term of office, sailing from Corinth sometime between August and October, AD 52. Thus, it is viable to assign the eighteen months of Paul's Corinthian ministry the date of spring AD 51 through autumn of AD 52.

Those who appeared before the *bema* to make their defense would first place their right hand on the waist high marble "column of testimony" (archaeologists have identified both *bema* and column in Corinth. I myself have stood thus before the Corinthian *bema*!) As Paul placed his hand upon the column and began to open his mouth to defend himself from the charges that had been brought against him, Gallio cut him off. Addressing Paul's accusers, the proconsul pronounced something to the effect of, "Who are you kidding?" It was obvious to Gallio, even from a cursory glance at the rabbi from Tarsus who stood before him, that this affair was an internal Jewish matter. He explained to the accusers that it was unreasonable to expect him to adjudicate this matter since it involved neither injustice nor violent crime. There was no case to judge. They were wasting his time if they expected that he would rule on religious questions, arbitrating over words like salvation, names like Jesus or Christ, and how these all might or might not relate to the Torah. Having so forcefully dismissed the case, Gallio ventured beyond standard procedure and into the realm of anti-Semitism by ordering the Jewish accusers driven away from the *bema*.

The gathered Gentile onlookers in the agora enthusiastically took that order as an official cue to brutally assault the Jews, in particular, their leader, Sosthenes. Sosthenes had been appointed to Crispus' position following his removal as head of the synagogue. Luke tellingly records that Gallio refused to concern himself with the injustice occurring before the bema, turning a blind, anti-Semitic eye. Quite inspiring is the fact that Paul's first epistle to the Corinthians reveals that Sosthenes, this mugged synagogue leader, later became a believer and served as Paul's secretary (1 Cor. 1:1). Losing two of their synagogue leaders to their despised next-door neighbor Paul must have been particularly galling to the Jewish community.

With the church continuing to flourish, the Jewish opposition quieted, and an officially adjudicated Roman policy of toleration in place, the time came for Paul to take his leave from Corinth. In the autumn of AD 52, Paul set sail to return home to the church in Antioch. While Silas and Timothy extended their European ministry, Priscilla and Aquila accompanied Paul on the first leg of the journey, from Cenchrea to Ephesus.

Luke reports that in the port city of Cenchrea just prior to departure, Paul had a haircut, "for he was keeping a vow" (Acts 18:18). The nature of this particular vow has generated a tremendous volume of speculation. Some have taken the position that as a Christian, Paul would not possibly have taken a Jewish vow based on Torah. Of course, this objection is without merit when measured against the behavior of the Jewish Christians recorded throughout the Acts narrative. Freedom from the Law must entail freedom either to keep the Law or not, otherwise it is not true freedom. The testimony of the Acts narrative is that, under most circumstances, the early Jewish Christians chose to exercise their freedom in Christ by practicing either Torah observant or semi-Torah observant lifestyles, which includes the option of keeping a vow. Paul, in particular, the Hebrew of Hebrews (Phil. 3:5) and Pharisee of Pharisees (Acts 23:6), clearly continued the practice of Jewish customs.

Once the vow is acknowledged as a Jewish one, the task is to determine what manner of vow was meant. Luke provides neither detail nor context to answer the question decisively. It resembles the Nazirite vow, which entailed the making of a vow of dedication, at which point the hair is grown out. At the vow's conclusion, a minimum of thirty days later,[17] the head is shaved and the hair collected and burned along with prescribed offerings in the Temple (Num. 6:1–21). However, for the Nazirite vow to be valid, the head can only be shaved in Jerusalem at the conclusion of a minimum thirty-day period of purification in the city.[18] The lack of further data presents an insurmountable difficulty for the interpreter of this passage, explaining the aforementioned volume of speculation. Stern, having succinctly laid out the problem, speculates that this was possibly a "diaspora adaptation of the Nazirite vow."[19] Keener makes a complementary conjecture, asserting that Paul had taken "the less Jerusalem-centered approach of . . . Jews who had not the time or money to travel to Jerusalem very frequently."[20]

What may be decisively determined from the passage is this: At some point, perhaps following Paul's departure from the Corinthian synagogue or his trial before Gallio, he made a Jewish vow of dedication to the Lord. This entailed growing his hair out for a period of time that ended with his haircut in Cenchrea. Whether Paul's hair was collected to present in the Temple during his upcoming visit to Jerusalem (Acts 18:22), whether that visit to Jerusalem was an extended one, encompassing a thirty day period of purification, or whether Paul's hair simply fell to the floor of a Cenchrean barbershop to be swept up or blown to the winds cannot be resolved.

The Witness in Ephesus (18:19–22)

Although at the outset of the second missionary journey Ephesus had been Paul's probable goal, the city was merely a layover now for the apostle. For Aquila and Priscilla, however, Ephesus was the end of the line. They would remain in the city for several more years, finally returning to Rome prior to AD 57 (Rom 16:3). Desiring to inaugurate at least an abbreviated ministry in Ephesus, Paul parted from his friends and made a beeline for the city's synagogue. In the limited time he possessed before his ship embarked, Paul reasoned with the Ephesian Jews about their Messiah.

Ephesus. An ancient city, founded in 1044 BC, this was one of the most impressive commercial centers in the ancient world. Strategically situated on the west coast of Asia Minor, Ephesus possessed one of the few world-class harbors that existed in the Roman Empire, enabling it to serve as the intercontinental gateway linking Europe to Asia. From the fourth century BC, the city became the center of Hellenism in Asia Minor under Alexander the Great and his successors. It came under Roman rule at the end of the second century BC, as Rome began to consolidate her empire. Having become a valued jewel in the Roman Empire, this bustling metropolis became the capital of Asia Minor.

The population of Ephesus during the first century is estimated at half a million. An inordinate percentage of the population was Jewish as Ephesus had a reputation for allowing its Jews a great deal of privileges, including that of citizenship.[21] The city also had the reputation of being an axis of magical and occultic practice.

Perhaps Ephesus was most famous as the location of one of the seven wonders of the ancient word, the Artemision, the Temple of the goddess, Artemis. Artemis was the Ephesian multi-breasted goddess of fertility. Her temple was both massive in scope and breathtaking in capacity. With dimensions of 220 x 425 feet, it was four times the size of the Parthenon in Athens and was studded throughout with over one hundred twenty monumental columns, each of which was six stories high and six feet in diameter. The Artemision served as Asia Minor's greatest center of pagan worship, sacrifice and prostitution (to be expected, considering they worshiped a fertility goddess). The local economy also relied to a great extent on the merchandising of holy paraphernalia relate to Artemis worship.

The Ephesian Jews were intrigued by Paul's witness and requested that he extend his stay in the city. Paul, eager to return home, politely declined, promising to return, "if God wills," a common Jewish expression still used today, which recognizes that God is ultimately in control of every plan made by man. True to his word, Paul will return to Ephesus within a year's time (Eph. 19:8). Paul, who had booked passage not to Seleucia, the port of Antioch, but to Caesarea, probably planned to be on hand in Jerusalem for the celebration of Shavuot, the festival of Tabernacles.

Paul's ship disembarked in Israel at the harbor of Caesarea. From there, he "went up" to Jerusalem to pay his respects to James and the mother church. This is Paul's fourth recorded visit to Jerusalem since his Damascus road commission. Whether or not he had brought a pouch full of shorn hair is not specified by Luke; neither is the length of his stay in the holy city, whether thirty days or otherwise. At the conclusion of his Jerusalem visit, Paul returned home to Antioch.

Conclusion

Paul's second missionary journey saw Europe reached with the gospel, with both Jews and Gentiles responding in faith. Paul's commission as the apostle to the Gentiles in no way compromised his commitment to reaching the lost sheep of the house of Israel. This section has seen an old partnership dissolve and a new one begin, new friends and comrades added to the Acts narrative, the addition of a young protégé for Paul and, for the first time on a mission journey, an extended stay in one location. During this two and a half year odyssey, an astounding variety of individuals came to faith, including a God-fearing businesswoman, a Roman jailer, a member of the Athenian Areopagus and two synagogue leaders. Following this eminently successful mission, Paul would not be content to stay put for long in Antioch.

Study Questions:

1. Do you agree with Paul and Barnabas' decision to go separate ways? Why or why not?

2. Why did Paul have Timothy circumcised?

3. In light of Timothy's action, should Jewish believers still be circumcised today? Support your conclusion.

4. Why would Paul have expected the Jews to gather down by the riverside?

5. Compare and contrast Paul's reception from the Jews, the Greeks and the government in Philippi, Thessalonica, Berea, Athens and Corinth.

6. How did Paul's evangelistic approach differ in Athens?

7. Was Paul's Athens mission a success or a failure? Support your conclusion.

CHAPTER 15

The Third Missionary Journey
Acts 18:23–21:14

Preview:

Quickly following on the heals of his previous mission, Paul's third missionary journey will be his most protracted, extending for four years, from spring of AD 53 through spring AD 57. Just as Corinth had been the base for most of the second mission, the majority of this mission will likewise be spent in one location, Ephesus. Paul's third missionary journey was characterized not only by evangelism but by teaching, pastoring and the performance of extraordinary miracles. Among other events in this section, we will see Paul evangelize some remaining disciples of John the Baptist, pastor a growing church community and even raise the dead. Of course, Paul will again encounter the axiomatic opposition to the gospel experienced throughout each previous mission. In this instance, however, the opposition will not arise from the Jewish community but will come from a new and unanticipated source, the Gentiles.

The Witness in Ephesus (18:23–19:41)

An Eloquent Man (18:23–28)

Within six months of his return to Antioch, Paul's missionary wanderlust compelled him to set off on a third journey by the spring of AD 53, as soon as the weather was amenable to travel. The motivation behind his mission was to make good on his promise to return to the Jewish community of Ephesus, which had been receptive to his message (Acts 18:21). Ephesus had also been the initial, but supernaturally unattainable, geographic objective of the second missionary journey (Acts 16:6). This time, however, Paul traveled alone, devoid of either partner or assistant. Why he did not choose a suitable companion

from the Antioch church is not divulged, although he may have simply anticipated meeting up with his old travel mates somewhere down the road in Asia
Minor. Over the next several months, Paul strategically retraced the circuit of
his two previous missions, strengthening and confirming the churches he had
planted four years earlier in Derbe, Lystra, Iconium and Pisidian Antioch, all
the while moving ever closer to his final destination of Ephesus.

Third Missionary Journey Itinerary
(Acts 18:23—21:14)

Location	Reference
Antioch	Acts 18:23
Phrygia/Galatia	Acts 18:23–28
Ephesus	Acts 19:1–41
Macedonia	Acts 20:1
Greece	Acts 20:2
Macedonia	Acts 20:3–5
Philippi	Acts 20:6
Troas	Acts 20:6–12
Assos	Acts 20:13
Mitylene	Acts 20:14
Samos	Acts 20:15
Miletus	Acts 20:15–38
Cos	Acts 21:1
Rhodes	Acts 21:1
Patara	Acts 21:1
Tyre	Acts 21:3–6
Ptolemais	Acts 21:7
Caesarea	Acts 21:8–14

While Paul was slowly making his way through Asia Minor, the narrative
shifts to another Jewish Christian, Apollos, who had already arrived in
Ephesus sometime following Paul's brief initial ministry there. This Jewish
Christian hailed from Alexandria in Egypt, one of the foremost cities in the
Roman Empire as well as the locale of one of three of the Empire's universi-

ties (the other two being in Athens and Tarsus). With a third of its population comprised of Jews, Alexandria was the de facto center of Diaspora, or Hellenistic, Judaism. Indeed, the city had served as the location of the translation of the Hebrew Bible into Greek, the Septuagint.

Aptly, Apollos, as a product of his hometown, is portrayed by Luke as being an *anēr logios*, "an eloquent man," signifying that he was well trained in the art of rhetoric and exhibited a highly polished eloquence in his communication. In addition, Luke adds that he was thoroughly conversant, *dunatos*, "mighty" in the Scriptures, indicating that, with Apollos, there was just as much "steak" as "sizzle"; the content of his teaching matched his ability to deliver it.

Apollos is introduced in the narrative as courageously and passionately preaching about Jesus within the Ephesian synagogue, although exhibiting a glaring deficiency in his content. His teaching about Jesus was accurate, but limited. As if living in a vacuum for the previous two decades, Apollos was ignorant of the death and resurrection of Jesus. His knowledge extended only as far as John the Baptist's identification of Jesus as the Messiah and Jesus' ensuing public ministry. The response to which Apollos was calling the Jewish community was the repentance preached by John and an acceptance that Jesus was the Messiah. Perhaps, at one time, a disciple of John and subsequently of Jesus, apparently Apollos left Israel before the end/beginning of the story; the culmination, on the cross, of the Messiah's ministry.

In attendance in the synagogue and ardently listening to Apollos' call to repentance and recognition of Jesus as Messiah were Paul's associates, Priscilla and Aquila. Taking their new friend privately aside, they filled Apollos in on the essential gospel details of which he had been unaware. Luke gives no indication that Apollos received this instruction with anything other than the passion he had already expressed. This episode powerfully instructs the reader that simply recognizing that Jesus was the Messiah is insufficient, but that His death, burial and resurrection must also be acknowledged.

Whether intentionally or not, Apollos followed the reverse trajectory of Paul and left Ephesus for Greece, specifically Corinth, where the narrative finds him in Acts 19:1. The small Ephesian church wrote a letter of commendation to the church of Corinth (mentioned by Paul in 2 Cor. 3:1), and there Apollos provided both aid to the Corinthian church and a powerful witness to the city's Jewish community. Apollos had previously been a good preacher, but upon arrival in Corinth, he had become a preaching dynamo. Now that Apollos knew the complete story of Jesus, the entire message of the gospel, he became an unstoppable force. Like Paul, Apollos used the messianic prophecy of Hebrew Scripture as a powerful tool and an irrefutable means of argument to prove that Jesus was the Messiah. This is still one of the best evangelistic methods to use today within the Jewish community (providing the Jews acknowledge the authority of their own Scripture, which is too often not the case).

Apollos' ministry in Corinth successfully built upon the foundation previously laid by Paul. Paul references his colleague Apollos several times within his letters to the Corinthians and Titus (1 Cor. 1:12; 3:4–6, 22; 4:6; 16:12; Titus 3:13). Often unnoticed within the narrative progression of Acts 18:27 is the revealing phrase Luke used in reference to the church, those who "believed through grace," *pepisteukosiv dia tēs charitos*, a subtle reminder of the free gift of salvation to all those who believe the gospel.

John's Disciples (19:1–7)

While Apollos was preaching gangbusters in Corinth, Paul finally arrived back in Ephesus. As he made his way into the city, avoiding the direct route of the Roman road and instead meandering through the upper countryside, Paul encountered a dozen Jewish men who claimed to be disciples of Jesus. Evidently, after spending some time together, Paul sensed something amiss in their faith. Attempting a diagnosis, he asked the men if their salvation experience had been normative, specifically probing whether they had received the Holy Spirit upon their initial belief of the gospel. For Paul, a disciple of Jesus devoid of the Holy Spirit's indwelling was an abnormality (Rom 8:9; 1 Cor. 12:13). Of doctrinal importance is that, in relation to the receipt of the Spirit, Paul used the verb, *pisteuō*, "to believe," in the aorist active participle form, expressing contemporaneous, not subsequent action. What this grammatically demands is that the phrase must be translated "when you believed," or "simultaneously upon belief."[1] The unfortunate translation of the King James version, "since you believed," i.e., "at some later point subsequent to belief," has been the basis of a great deal of otherwise avoidable doctrinal confusion.

The men's startling reply indicated that, as with Apollos, they had not heard the entire gospel; indeed, they were aware of even less of Jesus' ministry than had been Apollos. These men are actually revealed to be disciples of John the Baptist, the forerunner of the Messiah. Having received John's water baptism of repentance over two decades earlier in Judea, they were aware only of John's identification of Jesus as the Messiah. They were completely unaware of Jesus' crucifixion and resurrection, indeed, His entire ministry. Remembering only that John had proclaimed that the Messiah would baptize with the Holy Spirit, the men were unaware that this had already occurred. They had obviously left Israel long before the extraordinary events of the Pentecost experience described by Luke (Acts 2). Paul, like a first century Paul Harvey, revealed to them the "rest of the story."

John's disciples received Paul's gospel witness and became true believers in Jesus. As they submitted to water baptism in the name of their Lord Jesus, their allegiance shifted from the forerunner of the Messiah to the Messiah Himself. Following the laying on of hands by the apostle, the Holy Spirit manifestly came upon the new believers, as verified by their breaking out in tongues and prophesying. This spiritual sign authenticated to the apostle Paul that these men had indeed become Christian believers, moving from the Old Testament expectation, preached by John, to belief in the New Testament fulfillment, accomplished by Jesus. This was the biblical culmination of a phenomenon which John himself had explained to his disciples concerning Jesus over twenty years earlier, "He must increase, but I must decrease" (John 3:30). John was only a transitional figure, not a prophet to be followed but a signpost bearing testimony to His Messiah, "the Lamb of God Who takes away the sin of the world" (John 1:36). This episode contains the final New Testament reference to John the Baptist.

This is the final "echo of Pentecost," the last mention of the phenomenon of tongues in Acts. Throughout the narrative, the purpose of tongues had been to authenticate the salvation of a new group of believers. These Jewish believers are representatives of the final group in Acts to receive a manifest baptism of the Spirit, that sub-remnant within the faithful remnant of Israel (Rom. 11:5). These were Jews who had faithfully followed John and believed his report yet were unaware of the new age that had dawned through Jesus' death and resurrection.

This passage is instructive on several levels. First, until this episode, the three transitional groups who had manifestly received the Holy Spirit, the apostles, the Samaritans and the Gentiles, had done so either directly or indirectly through Peter's involvement. This is the only instance recorded in Acts of any group of believers manifesting the Spirit with the phenomenon of tongues through the agency of Paul.

A second instruction to be gleaned from this episode is to appreciate that belief in the Hebrew Scriptures, per se, or affirming the abstract truth of messianic prophecy, is insufficient for salvation. To be accepted by God (as indicated by the receipt of His Holy Spirit) one must not only affirm the precepts and prophecies of the Hebrew Scriptures, but of necessity must recognize that Jesus is the crux of those Scriptures.

A third and final point is that all four separate cases describing the manifest receipt of the Spirit are characterized by strikingly diverse patterns. Not one episode corresponds to another in relation to order of water baptism vs. Spirit baptism or whether an apostolic laying on of hands precipitated Spirit baptism. In the case of the apostles (Acts 2), initial repentance was followed by John's water baptism, belief in Jesus and the receipt of the Spirit, in that order. In the case of the Samaritans (Acts 8), initial belief in Jesus was followed by Christian water baptism, the apostolic laying on of hands, and the receipt of the Spirit. In the case of the Gentile household (Acts 10), initial belief in Jesus was followed by receipt of the Spirit and then by Christian water baptism. In the case of John's disciples (Acts 19), their initial repentance was followed by John's water baptism, belief in Jesus, Christian water baptism, the apostolic laying on of hands and then the receipt of the Spirit.

Consequently, the book of Acts cannot be used as a guide to establish a timeless doctrine, practice or formula for the receipt of Spirit baptism. It is simply not possible to discern which one of these four examples should serve as a prototypical model for church observance. The task Luke set out to accomplish in Acts was to describe historical fact without necessarily prescribing universal doctrinal practice. Luke's' purpose, as articulated in his prologue, is to report on what happened in a particular place and time, not what must universally happen thereafter in every place and time. The unambiguous propositional instructions found in Paul's epistles are the only Scripture by which we can develop an accurate and consistent theology of Spirit baptism.

Ministry and Miracles (19:8–12)

Luke provides yet another example of Paul's unwavering commitment to Jewish witness. For three months, the Ephesian synagogue, which had so warmly received him on his previous visit, became the center of Paul's ministry. The Jewish community, having subsequently engaged in vigorous debate over the gospel with Apollos, continued to do so with Paul. The Jewish community's commitment to this dialogue resulted in Paul's longest recorded synagogue ministry. As befits an extended teaching ministry, the content of Paul's preaching is described as having advanced beyond a basic argument that Jesus was the Messiah to emphasizing the kingdom of God. It is possible that the Jewish listeners were prepared to grant the possibility that Jesus was the Messiah as a result of the combination of both Apollos and Paul's persuasive and unassailable arguments. However, the sticking point seems to have been the non-commencement of the messianic kingdom which, in Jewish expectation, was to be launched by the Messiah, the very same expectation voiced by the apostles just prior to Jesus' ascension (Acts 1:6).

After three months, however, some within the synagogue had heard enough. They became intellectually hardened and disparaging of the believers in their midst. At this point, Paul and the Jewish believers packed up from the synagogue and moved down the street to a lecture hall which they rented from their Greek landlord, Tyrannus. Of interest is that, even at this late date, Christianity is still popularly known by the designation, "the Way" (Acts 9:2; 19:9, 23; 22:4; 24:14, 22). The "school of Tyrannus" served for the next two years as Paul's mission headquarters. Tradition recalls that Paul would teach during the Ephesian afternoon "siesta," applying himself during the mornings and late afternoons to his tentmaking trade (probably alongside his former partner, Aquila). During this period, Ephesus served as "home base" for the founding of churches in the surrounding regions of Asia Minor, such as, but not limited to, Philadelphia, Laodicea, and perhaps Colossae. From Ephesus, Paul also wrote his first epistle to the Corinthians (1 Cor. 16:8). In addition, Paul's protégé, Timothy, departed Corinth to rejoin Paul (1 Cor. 4:17; 16:10–11).

Paul's Ephesian ministry was also characterized by his exercise of extraordinary miracles. As had Peter before him (Acts 5:15–16), Paul was able to perform unusual authenticating signs and wonders. These demonstrated the truthfulness of his message and established his apostolic authority. Luke records that Paul healed both directly, through the laying on of hands, and indirectly, through the application to the sick of his sweat rags and the dirty aprons used in his work as a tentmaker. In addition to the numerous healings were demonic exorcisms.

Paul's extraordinary ability to heal the sick in Ephesus was specific to the Ephesian ministry and not a permanent gifting. It is clear from Paul's own biographical epistles that he could not always heal at will (2 Cor. 12:8; Phil 2:27; 1 Tim. 5:23; 2 Tim. 4:20). It is important to notice two qualifications Luke sets forth. First, that every one of the miraculous signs and wonders within Acts was extraordinary and limited to the apostles and their immediate associates. Second, Luke was careful to emphasize that the miracles were not intrinsic to Paul, but that he was merely the instrument through whom God chose to work His power (Acts 19:11).

My Sons, the Exorcists (19:13–20)

Paul's ability to heal and exorcise demons not only made an impression on believers and those on the verge of coming to faith, but also on "the competition." Luke introduces a family of traveling Jewish sorcerers and fortunetellers, known as "the seven sons of Sceva." These were seven scions of an apostate Jewish priest, Sceva, who evidently had been exiled from Jerusalem for witchcraft, the casting of spells, or some other perversion of the Jewish faith. Jewish exorcists were respected in the Roman world as masters of the occult, commanding respect in the demonic realm through their use of powerful Hebrew invocations and the ability to pronounce the ineffable name of their God.[2]

Sceva and sons, while traveling the Asia Minor circuit, had arrived in Ephesus and, evidently, witnessed one or more of Paul's public exorcisms. Impressed by the powerful demonstration, and possibly of the mind that imitation was the sincerest form of flattery, Sceva's sons decided to help themselves to what they assumed was Paul's incantation formula. Luke provides an amusing account of their attempt at one such exorcism using their newly lifted Pauline methodology. Having entered the home of a demon-possessed man, the seven sons commanded the demon, "by Jesus, the specific one of whom Paul speaks." Sceva's boys quickly realized that they were playing with fire; the name of Jesus was no magic incantation.[3] Instead of submissively obeying their command, the demon spoke back, replying that while he knew (*ginōskō*) Jesus and was familiar (*epistamai*) with Paul, he wanted to know whom these presumptuous men thought they were to try to cast him out! The demon-possessed man sprung upon them and, exhibiting supernatural strength, overpowered all seven exorcists. The sons of Sceva were forced to flee the possessed man's house, naked and traumatized (*traumatizō*, "to wound").

The news of this humiliation circulated widely throughout Ephesus, and the citizenry realized that when it came to effective exorcisms, they could accept no substitutes for "the real deal." The Lord was magnified in the eyes of unbelievers, who developed a sudden, newfound respect for the name of Jesus. In addition, the new believers were strengthened in their faith. They were so profoundly affected by this episode that any vestiges of the new believer's remaining occult practices were now purged from the nascent Ephesian church. Nullifying the power of their spells and incantations through a public confession of them, the believers repudiated their former lifestyles, corporately destroying fifty thousand days' wages worth of occult literature, resources and amulets in a great bonfire.

What a Riot (19:21–41)

In AD 56, as winter began to yield to spring, Paul determined that his unqualifiedly successful Ephesian ministry was drawing to a close. Not only had Ephesus been evangelized, but so had every major city in Asia Minor. In addition, the churches in Macedonia and Greece were also thriving. In a mere decade, Paul and his comrades had borne witness of Christ within every strategic region throughout the northeastern sector of the Roman Empire. He began planning his fourth missionary journey. As Paul revealed in his Roman epistle, he desired to unearth fresh sectors to evangelize, those cities which still remained unplowed by other missionaries' endeavors, "not building on another man's foundation" (Rom. 15:20–23). Paul set his sites on reaching the northwestern quarter of the Empire. Paul had desired to minister to the existing Roman church for some time (Rom. 1:10, 15; 15:23). Planning to use the church of Rome as his home base of support, from there he could reach westward, to the very edge of the Empire (Rom. 15:24).

However, prior to attempting such an ambitious mission, there were three locations that took priority on Paul's itinerary. The first location was Macedonia, where he planned to strengthen the churches he had planted (with the exception of Thessalonica, where he was forbidden to return [Acts 17:9]). The second location was the region of Achaia, specifically Corinth, to strengthen that church. In addition, Paul determined to collect from these churches an offering to deliver to the mother church in Jerusalem, his third location (1 Cor. 16:1–4). Paul determined to remain in Ephesus a short while longer to tie up the loose ends of his two and a half year ministry (1 Cor. 16:8–9). Nevertheless, in advance of his European visit, Paul sent Timothy and another coworker, Erastus to Macedonia. Erastus was a prominent and wealthy citizen of Corinth, having served as its city treasurer (Rom. 16:23; 2 Tim. 4:20). A large stone plaza, dating to AD 50, has been uncovered in Corinth, on which an inscription was found specifying that an "Erastus" had personally sponsored its construction at his own expense.[4]

Although Paul planned to extend his stay in Ephesus, God had alternative plans. As eventually happened in previous ministry locations, intense opposition to the gospel arose. This time, however, the opposition arose from an unexpected quarter, the Gentiles. Luke describes this episode as "no small disturbance," which, being translated, means "a big, fat Ephesian riot." Again. as evidenced in Acts 19:23, as elsewhere (Acts 9:2; 19:9, 23; 22:4; 24:14, 22), "the Way" is one of Luke's preferred terms for the church.

Luke identifies a rabble-rouser named Demetrius as the troublemaking ringleader of the riot. His livelihood as a silversmith involved the manufacture of silver idols of the goddess Artemis and reduced scale models of her Temple. The Ephesian goddess Artemis is not to be confused with the goddess Artemis of the Greek pantheon or the alternate Roman version, Diana, the beautiful, virginal goddess of nature. Artemis of the Ephesians was the ugly and misshapen, multi-breasted goddess of fertility, the "Great Mother." Her temple at Ephesus was one of the seven wonders of the ancient world, and the worship of Artemis generated enormous revenue for the city, in particular for its craftsmen and artisans. However, as more and more Ephesians became followers of Jesus, the pool of Artemis worshipers began to shrink noticeably. This deeply cut into the business of those whose livelihoods, like Demetrius', depended on goddess worship.

Demetrius, likely the leader of the local crafts guild, called a union meeting of his fellow artisans of idolatry. In one of the few recorded speeches of an

unbeliever in Acts, Demetrius first informs his colleagues that, "It's the economy, stupid." This Paul fellow had gone too far, turning away hordes of former
Artemis worshippers who now worshiped his invisible god. His influence was
cutting into their business. This was not a religious issue but an economic one.
Paul represented a threat both to the craftsmen's personal livelihood and to the
Ephesian municipal economy. The context of Paul's preaching against idolatry
can be discerned from Demetrius' diatribe. As a biblically literate Jew and
exceptionally well-educated rabbi, Paul would have quoted extensively from
the prophet Isaiah's denunciation of idolatry (Is. 44:9–17).

Unfortunately for Demetrius and company, they could not wait another
few centuries when silversmiths and goldsmiths could forevermore sustain a
living designing lovely silver or gold crosses, crucifixes, and assorted Christian
medallions. If only Paul, with all his visionary prowess, could have foreseen
the Christian jewelry industry, he could have provided a whole new stream of
revenue for Ephesus, thus averting a riot and threat to his life. Had the wearing of religious jewelry even been conceivable to the first century church, the
renowned Ephesian artisans could have innovated a completely new product
line, perhaps including a cross cleverly inserted within a Jewish star to serve
their new Jewish Christian customers. (This is neither condemnation of nor
diatribe against contemporary Christian fashion, but merely an observation
for us all, myself included, to ponder. I do, however, vividly recall my late
great aunt, Hilda Koser, a missionary to the Jews for forty years, who when
asked why she personally disapproved of religious jewelry, replied that since
Jesus was not crucified on a cross of gold, neither would she wear one.)

Demetrius then added a complaint against the Christians which, building
upon his economic grievance, sent the crowd over the edge, filling them with
rage. Appealing to the Ephesians' religious pride and municipal patriotism, he
accused Paul of devaluing their great goddess Artemis in the eyes of the world.
Although she was the most popular goddess of the ancient world, she would
be dethroned from her preeminence in the pantheon once the word circulated of her humiliation at the hands of a lowly Jewish rabbi. Demetrius succeeded in whipping his audience into a frenzy, and they began continuously
crying out the religious mantra, "Great is Artemis of the Ephesians." As a riot
began, the city became flooded with chaos and confusion.

Unable to locate the source of their fury, Paul, the crowd instead snatched
up two of Paul's companions, Gaius (Rom. 16:23; 1 Cor. 1:14) and Aristarchus
(also referenced in Acts 20:4; 27:2; Col. 4:10; Philem. 24) and dragged them
into the great theater of Ephesus. Centrally located near the agora and the
courts of law, built on the side of a hill just off the colonnaded avenue that led
to the harbor, the theater could hold up to twenty-four thousand spectators.

This theater, like much of ancient Ephesus, has been excavated and can be explored by contemporary tourists.

From Luke's account, we can see that the mob occupied the theater for several hours. With a good percentage of the city now up in arms and gathered within the theater, total chaos and confusion reigned as multiple slogans were chanted. Much of the mob had been propelled into the theater and was not even aware of the ostensible grounds of the riot. During this time, Paul wanted to boldly face the masses head on. However, he was restrained him from going to the theater by the Ephesian believers (likely including Priscilla and Aquila) and by Paul's friends among the Ephesian municipal leaders, via messenger. These leaders, properly designated by Luke as "Asiarchs," were culled from the Ephesian aristocracy and presided at athletic events and religious festivals. It was a prestigious office, also involving the collection of mandatory taxes supporting the worship of the emperor. That Paul had friends among the Asiarchs indicates that, in contrast to the common populace, the Roman government did not perceive Christianity as a threat.

Within the theater, the Ephesian Jewish community must have been somewhat uptight, to say the least. Although comprising some ten percent of the population of the Roman Empire, the Jewish people's status was always an uneasy one. Being a monotheistic minority living amidst a passionately polytheistic majority, the Jews were never entirely secure in their societal position and were ever subject to the whims, mistrust and prejudices of not only the Roman Emperor, but also every petty municipal authority in every Roman city. (This societal insecurity is indicative of the experience and perception of the Jewish community throughout their history, in every nation and state in which they have lived, with the exception of Israel.) Although the Jews of Ephesus possessed Roman citizenship, their community's recent expulsion from Rome through Claudius' imperial decree was still fresh in their minds. Therefore, the Jewish community made an attempt at a preemptive defense to the mob. Knowing that many of the Christians, especially the leaders, were Jewish, the Jews likely planned to declare that Paul and his ilk did not represent the Jews; in fact, he had been thrown out of the synagogue. A Jewish leader, Alexander, was put (pushed!) forth to make that case. He waved his hand to quiet the mob.

Whatever defense Alexander had planned on making, he never got to deliver the message. When the mob realized that Alexander was Jewish, it fueled their pagan rage all the more. The idolaters had no patience for discerning the differences between monotheistic religions. To their mind, every group that had rejected "the Great Mother" was as repugnant as another, and they continued shouting in adoration of their goddess for another two hours.

Paul makes mention of this Alexander in his second letter to Timothy (2 Tim. 4:14), noting that he was a coppersmith and had done Paul much harm in opposing the gospel. As a coppersmith, perhaps Alexander though he would be heard and respected by his fellow artisans and guild members. One would hope that poor Alexander was not too disappointed by the rejection of his Gentile peers.

Finally, the *grammateus*, the "town clerk," the most important Ephesian civil executive, successfully calmed the crowd down. The *grammateus*, by virtue of his office, commanded attention and respect, even from an irrational mob. In yet another recorded speech of an unbeliever in Acts, he assuaged the mob's fears that the goddess Artemis, her reputation or her temple was threatened by anyone. Ephesus was well known as the "Warden of the Temple,"[5] the keeper of the Artemision and guardian of the image of the goddess which "fell from the god's abode" (this most likely refers to a lumpy meteor, which the pagan mind assumed to be a multi-breasted fertility goddess).

The *grammateus* underscored that neither Gaius nor Aristarchus was a temple thief or goddess blasphemer, and sagely reminded the crowd that if they had an authentic grievance, their irrational mob violence should give way to appropriate legal procedures. Indeed, if anyone wanted to draft a lawsuit, they were welcome to do so as the courts were open for business. Furthermore, if the courts proved insufficient to address their grievances, the Roman proconsuls were available to adjudicate offences of the greatest magnitude. The Roman government viewed all such riotous assemblies with the deepest of suspicion, and no one in the crowd that day would want to be called upon to provide an explanation for their illegal rioting to "Uncle Caesar's" crew. The mob's anger now diffused, the *grammateus* formally and officially dismissed and dispersed the assembly.

Up to this point in Acts, the vast majority of opposition the church had experienced derived from the Jewish community, in particular, their leadership. In Ephesus, for the first time we see passionate, mobilized Gentile opposition, emanating not from the leadership but from the grassroots. As the gospel was to be proclaimed to both the Jew and the Gentile, it had become clear to the church that double-barreled opposition to the gospel would also come from both Jews and Gentiles.

There were additional Ephesian adventures and dangers which Paul notes in his epistles but Luke choose not to record, such as Priscilla and Aquila risking their lives to save Paul (Rom 16:3–4); Paul's fighting wild beasts, whether literally or metaphorically (1 Cor. 15:32); Paul's facing many adversaries (1 Cor. 16:9), and his encountering afflictions so severe that he was, "despairing even of life" (2 Cor. 1:8–10).

Return to Israel (20:1–21:14)

The Witness in Macedonia and Greece (20:1–5)

Paul took the riot as his cue to depart Ephesus. After encouraging the Ephesian believers, Paul made his way to Troas, planning to rendezvous with his colleague Titus to receive from him the latest news of the Corinthian church. Too impatient to remain in Troas, Paul moved on to Macedonia, where he finally caught up with his friend (2 Cor. 2:12–13; 7:5–6). Having received heartening news from Corinth, Paul took several months to travel east to west through Macedonia, encouraging and strengthening the Macedonian churches. During this Macedonian ministry, Paul wrote the second epistle to the Corinthians in preparation for his impending visit. As wintry weather approached, curtailing travel, Paul crossed the border into Greece, where he spent three months of winter AD 56–57 with the community of believers in Corinth. That winter, he wrote his letter to the Roman community of believers, informing them of his plans to visit them in the following year (Rom. 15:23–24) on his planned fourth missionary journey.

In March of AD 57, as the inhospitable winter winds gave way to the more favorable seagoing climate of spring, Paul planned to return to Jerusalem in order to present the monetary support he had been collecting from the daughter churches to their mother church (Rom. 15:25–31; 1 Cor. 16:1–4; 2 Cor. 8:1–7) as well as to celebrate Passover in the holy city (Acts 20:6; Rom. 15:25). Paul would not be returning to Jerusalem alone. Luke recounts that Paul traveled in the company of eight representatives, a mix of Jewish and Gentile believers, from several of the primarily Gentile churches in which he had ministered. Joining Paul from the Macedonian church of Berea was Sopater, and from the Macedonian church of Thessalonica were both Aristarchus (also referenced in Acts 19:29; 27:2; Col. 4:10; Philem. 24) and Secundus. From the Galatian church of Derbe was Gaius, and from the Galatian church of Lystra was Timothy. Representing the Asian churches were Tychicus and Trophimus (also mentioned in 2 Tim. 4:20). Paul's final traveling companion, representing Philippi, the original Macedonian church, was Luke himself. Having been left behind by Paul during the second missionary journey to provide leadership to the Philippian believers (Acts 16:40), Luke rejoined Paul at this time and reinserts himself into the narrative beginning in Acts 20:5. Luke's presence as Paul's companion is felt throughout the next portion of the narrative, studded throughout with references to "we" and "us" (Acts 20:5–15; 21:1–18).

While gathered in the port city of Cenchrea, awaiting a vessel to carry them across the Aegean to Troas and from there to the province of Syria, they uncovered a Jewish assassination conspiracy against Paul to be implemented aboard ship, while at sea. Possessing this piece of intelligence made necessary the alteration of Paul's itinerary. Taking Luke with him for safety and companionship on the road, Paul set out from Corinth to Troas via the lengthy land route back through Macedonia. Paul's seven other companions, against whom there was no plot, set sail to Troas as planned, where they would wait for Paul and Luke to catch up with them. This inconvenient yet essential schedule modification resulted in Paul missing the Jerusalem Passover celebration. Rather than enjoying Passover in the holy city, Paul and Luke spent the eight days of Passover (called in Acts 20:6 by its alternative designation, the Feast of Unleavened Bread) in Philippi. Paul would, however, arrive in Jerusalem in time for the next great pilgrimage festival, Pentecost, or Shavuot, seven weeks later.

The Witness in Troas (20:6–12)

At Passover's conclusion, Paul and Luke traveled another five days to Troas, linking up with their traveling companions. The New Testament mentions two previous visits of Paul to Troas, both of them abbreviated. The first was when Paul received the Macedonian vision (Acts 16:8–10), and the second was an aborted ministry visit due to Paul's preoccupation with Titus's absence and the lack of news from Corinth (2 Cor. 2:12–13). On both of those occasions, Paul made a hasty departure from Troas. This time, Paul and his eight companions stayed in the city for a full week, strengthening and encouraging the church of Troas. On their final evening together with the Troas believers, "the first day of the week," Paul and company met together with the congregation to corporately "break bread," i.e., to formally share a communal meal.

Acts 20:7 is often incorrectly employed as Scriptural justification for the practice of holding Sunday morning church services. While I personally enjoy attending church services on Sunday mornings (and strongly affirm the freedom of each local congregation to set its own worship day and time), it must be emphasized that this verse does not provide an example of a local first century church's' Sunday morning service. (There is no such example in the New Testament of a Sunday morning church meeting. Of course, the absence of a Scripture passage from which to model Sunday morning worship does not preclude the contemporary church choosing to meet on Sunday mornings, Sunday evenings, midweek or any other time deemed appropriate.)

Rather, what Acts 20:7 does provide is an unambiguous example of the local church meeting on Saturday evening. Luke specifies that the congregation of Troas' believers gathered "on the first day of the week." According to the Jewish calendar, the first day of the week always indicates Sunday. Furthermore, according to Jewish reckoning, days do not begin and end at midnight, but at sundown. In other words, the first day of the week extends from Saturday evening's sunset through Sunday evening's sunset. It is clear from the context of the verse that the meeting time is Saturday evening, subsequent to the *havdalah* candle-lighting ceremony that traditionally marks the departure of the Sabbath.

Following the meal, Paul began to preach a message to the several dozen believers crowded together in this large third floor upper room. Paul's intent was to depart the next morning, Sunday, a normal "work day" (the two-day weekend having not yet been innovated!). Perhaps because he was conscious that this would be the last opportunity for them to receive his instruction, Paul's preaching went a bit longer than was usual. In fact, Luke specifies that Paul taught the disciples until midnight. (Those who desire to see a Sunday morning service in this passage must envision a veritable filibuster of a sermon, with Paul preaching this windy blockbuster from just after breakfast all the way through to the midnight hour!)

Due to the lateness of the hour, a young fellow named Eutychus was struggling to stay awake. Although Luke notes that there was plenty of light from the multitude of burning oil lamps, the smoky lamps would also have suppressed the air flow in such a crowded enclosure. The need for ventilation in the room made essential the opening of every window. Eutychus, sitting in the open windowsill, was in a precarious position but was too drowsy to realize it. His proximity to fresh air could not keep Eutychus awake. As Paul's loquacious preaching continued, this sleepy fellow quietly nodded off, lost his balance and fell to his death three stories below.

Eutychus' descent was noticed immediately by those sitting adjacent to him. One imagines that this would normally place quite a damper on the atmosphere of such a gathering. As the believers all rushed down two flights of stairs to respond to the emergency, their worst fear was confirmed. Eutychus was dead. Luke the physician would certainly have been able to identify a genuine dead body.

An anguished Paul (perhaps feeling somewhat responsible for the mishap) fell upon the body and sorrowfully embraced the dead man. Luke does not provide any insight into Paul's psyche at this point or record any prayers, but the apostle's behavior is reminiscent of that of the prophets Elijah and Elisha, both of whom, on two separate occasions, raised the dead with just such an embrace (1 Kin. 17:21; 2 Kin. 4:32–37). Achieving the same miraculous result as had the Hebrew prophets before him, Paul declared to the encircling mourners that Eutychus was alive.

Now all quite alert and awake, everyone made their way back upstairs, rejoicing and "greatly comforted" (Acts 20:12). It seems that there is nothing like resurrecting the dead to wake up a sleepy crowd or to stimulate the appetite. They decided to continue the meeting, pausing first, however, for a "midnight snack," after which Paul got his second wind and continued teaching them into the wee hours of the morning.

Paul's Farewell Address (20:13-38)

At daybreak, Paul and his companions departed from Troas for Assos, a distance of twenty miles. Curiously, for this one-day journey they split up, with the apostle traveling via the land route and his friends traveling via the sea. Luke does not record why Paul chose to hike the Roman road while his friends sailed to the same destination. However, Luke does provide a detailed travelogue of their journey to Jerusalem. Paul joined his friends aboard ship at Assos. From there they sailed thirty miles to Mitylene, on the island of Lesbos. Over the next two days, they sailed past the Greek islands of Chios and Samos, respectively.

On the following day, they arrived at Miletus, on the mainland of Asia Minor about thirty miles south of Ephesus. Luke explains that this itinerary was a direct route bypassing the port of Ephesus. They had chosen such a route not to avoid Ephesus per se, but in order to hasten their arrival in Israel, as Paul was eager to celebrate Pentecost in Jerusalem. As it was, there would be no time to waste. The delays they had already experienced would make their itinerary tight. Note again that Luke records the observance of Jewish custom by a Jewish Christian at face value, without criticism or comment. Paul's desire to celebrate one of God's appointed holy days at the Temple was a wholly anticipated and acceptable desire for any Jew, messianic or nonmessianic. Paul's Christian faith did not encroach on his freedom in Christ to observe a holy precept of Torah, the Mosaic Law.

With their ship docked in the port of Miletus for three or four days to unload and load cargo, Paul summoned, via messenger, the elders of the Ephesian church to rendezvous with him. While a messenger could have covered the thirty miles from Miletus to Ephesus in one day, once summoned, it would have taken the Ephesian elders no less than two days before they could reach Paul's location. When the elders arrived at Miletus, Paul had a few final thoughts to impart to them. This "farewell address" is the only recorded sample of Paul's preaching to his fellow Christians. In this address, these leaders are referenced using three titles, that of *presbuterous*, "elders" (Acts 20:17), *episkopous*, "bishops" (Acts 20:28) and those with responsibility to *poimainō*, "shepherd" (Acts 20:28). Paul neither differentiates between the designation of elders, bishops and pastors nor delineates between their responsibilities to lead, oversee and shepherd the church. Some interpret this as an indication that each term references the same clerical office.

In his introduction, the apostle recounted his Ephesian ministry, from his initial arrival in Ephesus four and a half years earlier through his roughly two and a half years pastoring the Ephesian church. He characterized his behavior as an example for the elders to follow, citing his energetic teaching and discipleship training (Acts 20:20) as well as his humble service and bold evangelistic witness in the midst of Jewish opposition to his ministry (Acts 20:19, 21). Paul reminded the elders that the thrust of his gospel message was the necessity of "repentance toward God and faith in the Lord Jesus Christ" (Acts 20:21) and to actively turn toward God and accept that His sole provision for the salvation of both Jew and Gentile is Jesus' death and resurrection.

Paul transitioned from the past example that he had set for the Ephesians to his present example. He explained that the Holy Spirit was currently compelling his return to Jerusalem, although once there, Paul's destiny was far from certain. Without providing any specific details, the Holy Spirit had repeatedly prepared Paul that suffering ("bonds and afflictions") inevitably awaited him in Jerusalem. It was, after all, a city with a proven track record of assassinating God's prophets (Matt. 23:37). Paul's objective, however, was not the avoidance of personal suffering or even death (2 Cor. 4:7–12; Phil. 1:20). Rather, Paul's ambition was to discharge his divine calling to ministry and his charge to witness of the Messiah, that he received twenty-two years earlier on the Damascus road.

Paul then moved back to his past example of ministry in order to provide a final exhortation to his protégés. He testified to them that he was innocent of the blood of all men. In stating this, he was not minimizing his former leading role as the arch-persecutor of the early church or his involvement with the suffering and even death of believers such as Stephen. Rather, he is harkening back to the warning God gave the prophet Ezekiel to faithfully broadcast God's program to His people. The prophet's responsibility had been properly discharged whether the response to his witness was positive or negative; whether or not it resulted in repentance and faith. Therefore, the prophet could be considered innocent of their blood (Ezek. 3:17–21; 33:2–9). Paul had made the same allusion to Ezekiel upon leaving Corinth's synagogue (Acts 18:6).

Believing that perhaps he would not survive his visit to Jerusalem and that these were indeed his final words to the Ephesian leadership, Paul entrusted them with a solemn charge. Paul was mistaken about his longevity, however. He did return later to Ephesus, as noted by plans to do so (1 Tim 1:3; 3:14; 4:13), as well as to Troas [2 Tim. 4:13] and Miletus [2 Tim. 4:20]). Paul charged the elders to guard against opposition and to stand fast in keeping their own divine appointments. The Holy Spirit had chosen them as church elders and they were to conscientiously pastor their congregation. Their motivation for such vigilant leadership is that the Lord Jesus purchased the church with His own blood. The church is the Messiah's personal possession. It is crucial not to miss how Paul equated the shed blood of Jesus with God's own blood, expressing Jesus' deity and incontestably equating Jesus with God (Acts 20:28).

Paul soberly warned the Ephesian leadership that their church would need protection from false teachers imminently arising from both without and within their congregation. Not long afterward, Paul's warning would be realized. Writing to Timothy (who would serve as the Ephesian pastor) from Rome some years later, Paul referenced these false teachers at length (1 Tim.1:3–7, 19–20; 4:1–7, 6:3–5; 2 Tim 1:15, 2:16–18; 3:1–9). Decades afterward, by the time the apostle John authored his Revelation, these false teachers had been successfully vanquished from the Ephesian church (Rev. 2:2–3). Paul advised his protégés to follow the example of constant vigilance he had set for them throughout his twenty-seven month Ephesian ministry. (In Acts 20:31, Paul referenced three years as his time in Ephesus according to Jewish reckoning, which customarily considered any part of a year as counting for the whole).

Closing his message with an exhortation, Paul commended the elders to God and to the Scripture, "the word of His grace." Paul's view of the Scripture was that it possessed the power to build up and provide an inheritance equally shared by all of God's "holy ones." He reminded them that he was not in the ministry for the money but, rather, supported himself by employment in his tentmaking trade. By following Paul's example, the leadership would be able to ensure that the needs of the poor in the community were provided. Paul illustrates his point with a quotation from Jesus which is not found in the gospels, "It is better to give than to receive" (Acts 20:35). This statement was likely one of many of Jesus' teachings passed down to Paul through Peter or another of the apostles.

Having knelt together in prayer (note the particular posture of prayer in Acts 20:36, also demonstrated by Jesus [Luke.22:41], Peter [Acts 9:40] and Paul and company [Acts 21:5]), the Ephesian elders, with tears, hugs and kisses, accompanied Paul to the ship and bid him farewell. The apostle was dearly loved by his protégés and would be sorely missed. As the gathering is specifically affirmed to be comprised of the elders, one small application that can seemingly be drawn from this passage is that real men are not afraid to express their emotion.

Return to Caesarea (21:1–14)

Luke straightforwardly records the sailing itinerary of the missionaries. Having "torn themselves away" from the elders in Miletus, they sailed directly to the island of Cos, a distance of approximately forty miles. From Cos, they sailed the next day to the urbane and cosmopolitan island of Rhodes. Rhodes was the site of another of the seven wonders of the ancient world, the Colossus of Rhodes, the great lighthouse built as a ten-story high bronze statue of the god Helios, whose right arm held aloft a torch and left arm a javelin, and whose legs were reputed to be planted bestride each side of the harbor. From Rhodes they sailed east to Patara, in Asia Minor, where they changed from their small ship offering only coastal "local service," to a larger, cargo ship offering an "express route" directly to Phoenicia, just north of Israel, a five-day open voyage across the Mediterranean sea.

The ship put in at the port of Tyre for a week to discharge its cargo. Paul and his eight friends disembarked to seek out the hospitality of the city's believers for the duration of their layover. Paul had some indirect responsibility for the founding of the Phoenician church, as it had initially resulted from the dispersion of the Jewish believers ensuing from his great persecution (Acts 11:19).

Luke records that the disciples of Tyre ardently warned Paul "through the Spirit not to set foot in Jerusalem" (Acts 21:4). The Spirit's message to the disciples was consistent with the revelation previously given to Paul that danger awaited him in Jerusalem. In light of this danger, the disciples prevailed upon Paul to change his plans and avoid Jerusalem. The phrasing of Acts 21:4 has caused confusion for some readers. Luke presents the disciples, through the Spirit, as directing Paul not to go to Jerusalem. However, what is meant by the phrase, "through the Spirit," is the disciples' apprehensive reaction to the Spirit's revelation and not the specific directive of the Spirit. This verse in no way supports the conclusion that Paul disobeyed the Holy Spirit's directive to avoid Jerusalem. In fact, the Spirit issued Paul no such command and had merely provided a preparatory warning of what awaited Paul upon arrival in Jerusalem. Indeed, it is later confirmed that it had been God's will for Paul to go to the holy city (Acts 21:14).

At the end of the week, after kneeling together in prayer on the beach with the families of the church of Tyre, Paul and company returned to their ship. They sailed twenty-five miles south along the Mediterranean coast to the Roman colony of Ptolemais, the Old Testament city of Acco (Judg. 1:31). Once again, the ship had cargo to unload, but this time only enough to require an overnight layover. Paul and company once again disembarked and looked up the city's believers, both to pay their respects and enjoy their hospitality.

The apostle and his companions departed the next morning on the final leg of their journey, sailing thirty miles further down the Mediterranean coast to the magnificent Herodian port of Caesarea. In Caesarea, Luke reintroduces his readers to an individual who had been out of sight for thirteen chapters,

Philip the deacon, last seen preaching in the region of Caesarea (way back in Acts 8:40). His witness must have been both successful and potent, for Luke now calls him Philip "the evangelist." Philip had made Caesarea his home, settling down and raising a family. His family included four virgin daughters (it is unclear whether this implies that they had consecrated themselves to remain unmarried) who possessed the gift of prophecy (called "prophetesses" by Luke in Acts 21:9).

Apparently, the weary travelers had made good time on their journey, arriving in Caesarea at least a week in advance of the onset of Pentecost (May 29, AD 57).[6] Therefore, not needing to rush to Jerusalem to attend the feast, they enjoyed the hospitality of Philip and his family for the next several days. It is unknown whether Paul and Philip had been previously acquainted, but this was certainly Luke's first introduction to the evangelist. Their relationship undoubtedly proved a rich resource of recollection for Luke to tap in the process of compiling material for his church history.

While staying in Caesarea, Paul was reacquainted with the prophet Agabus, absent from the Acts narrative since his brief entrance (Acts 11:28) to deliver a prophecy to the church in Antioch. Agabus had come down in person from the province of Judea to deliver a prophecy to Paul. Taking Paul's belt, Agabus dramatically tied the lengthy material around his own hands and feet, using this symbolic action to reinforce the weight of his prophecy. To ensure absolute clarity that he was now voicing the word of God and not his own opinion, Agabus prefaced his prediction with a formula of identical weight to the Hebrew Scriptures' familiar "thus saith the Lord." Agabus declared, "this is what the Holy Spirit says." The Spirit was the source of Agabus' prophecy, not the prophet's own imagination. The Holy Spirit's message was that as Agabus had been bound, Paul, too, would be bound by the Jews and consigned to Gentile custody.

Some have mistakenly reasoned that Agabus' prophecy was inaccurate. They allege that Agabus somehow got the Holy Spirit's message wrong, distorting it in the transmission since it is the Romans and not the Jews who bind Paul, and because Paul, rather than being handed over by the Jews is rescued from them by the Romans.[7] However, this allegation cannot be supported from the text. Paul later affirms the accuracy of Agabus' prophecy, stating that he had been "delivered from Jerusalem into the hands of the Romans" (Acts 28:17). Paul understood that the Jews were responsible for his arrest. One would be hard-pressed to demonstrate a more explicit confirmation of Agabus' prophecy.

Furthermore, the emphasis that Agabus placed on his words being a direct quotation from the Holy Spirit prohibits accusation of error or distortion in transmission. If the prophecy were inaccurate, the responsibility would lay not with the prophet but with the Holy Spirit. The fidelity of the entire Scripture is compromised if the Spirit cannot be trusted to superintend the accurate transmission of His messages. Finally, there are other biblical examples of responsibility being attributed to the party who had provoked an action rather than to the direct agent who carried out the action. For example, John wrote as if Pilate, as the responsible party, had scourged Jesus, even though it was his soldiers who were the direct agents of the scourging (John 19:1). In addition, Peter spoke as if the Jews had crucified Christ, even though the Romans were the direct agents of the crucifixion (Acts 2:23). Agabus was not mistaken in his assertion that the Jews would be responsible for Paul being bound and remanded to the Gentiles.[8]

Agabus' prophecy came as no surprise to Paul and only served to confirm what the Lord had already revealed. Again, those who contend the Paul was disobedient in going to Jerusalem must contend with the fact that the prophecy contains no such prohibitions whatsoever. Paul could no more avoid his destiny in Jerusalem than could Jesus, and just like Jesus, neither would Paul have wanted to do so. Paul's entry into Jerusalem would open up incalculable opportunities to fulfill his divine commission of witnessing of the Messiah to "Gentiles, kings and the sons of Israel" (Acts 9:15). It would also provide the occasion to ultimately realize the accompanying suffering God had promised (Acts 9:16).

As other disciples had previously done upon hearing this foreboding message, the Caesarean disciples, as well as even Luke himself (the "we" in Acts 21:12), attempted to dissuade Paul from his Jerusalem plans. In an intimate glimpse into Paul's psyche, he reproved his friends for "weeping and breaking his heart" (Acts 21:13). Their persuasive attempts were softening his will and breaking down his determination. However, as had Jesus before him, Paul remained resolute, ready to face his fate, come what may. As his Lord had done some twenty-five years earlier, Paul "steadfastly set his face toward Jerusalem" (Luke 9:51). In service to His Lord, Jesus, Paul affirmed that he was prepared not only to be arrested, but crucified as well. All those present fell silent, recognizing that it was God's will for Paul to stand in the shadow of Jesus to meet his destiny in the holy city of Jerusalem.

Conclusion

With Paul's arrival in Israel, the third missionary journey came to a conclusion. In contrast to the two previous journeys, Luke's account of the third mission reveals less action and less evangelism but offers a much more revealing glimpse into the heart and motivation of the apostle Paul. If on the previous two missions Luke tends to broadly paint his hero as "bigger than life," in these chapters Luke portrays the apostle as a man; an emotional, pastoral, courageous, headstrong, three-dimensional human being who just happened to God's chosen instrument to evangelize a vast portion of the Roman Empire.

Study Questions:

1. Why was it necessary for the disciples of John to receive a manifest baptism of the Spirit?

2. Broadly review the itinerary of Paul's third missionary journey.

3. Describe the riot in Ephesus, explaining both its cause and resolution.

4. List the reasons that the Troas church meeting was held on a Saturday evening and not a Sunday morning.

5. Summarize Paul's farewell address. What does its content reveal about the apostle's concerns?

CHAPTER 16

Paul in Jerusalem
Acts 21:15–23:30

Preview:

This section recounts the events which transpired with Paul's return to Jerusalem. We will see Paul reaffirm both his commitment to Israel and to God-given ancestral Jewish customs. In the midst of so doing, however, Paul's mere presence in the Temple precipitates a riot of such violent magnitude that he must be rescued by the Roman army. Paul will be arrested by the Romans and, as had Peter and the apostles, will stand trial before the Sanhedrin. Finally, to escape a plot against his life, Paul will be forced from Jerusalem and sent to the Roman procurator in Caesarea.

Request from Headquarters (21:15–26)

After staying the better part of a week with Philip, Paul's party, together with a contingent of believers from Caesarea, made the two-day journey up to Jerusalem for the festival of Pentecost. Lodgings for Paul and companions were provided by Mnason, a Hellenistic Jewish believer whom Luke notes had come to faith in the early days, probably as one of the three thousand saved at Pentecost (Acts 2:41) or the five thousand saved as a result of Peter's later Temple sermon (Acts 4:4). At the home of Mnason, Paul and his companions received a warm reception.

On the following day, likely two days before Pentecost, Paul and his delegation called on James, the brother of Jesus, and the elders, the leadership of the Jerusalem church. By this date, May AD 57, the remaining apostles were no longer in Jerusalem but were dispersed in itinerant ministries. The mother church was now led solely by James and an unspecified council of elders. The visit of Paul and his friends was anticipated as indicated by the assembly of the entirety of Jerusalem's leadership. It had been almost five years since Paul had last seen James (Acts 18:22). Paul related, in great detail, the events of the latest missionary journey to James and the elders. The Jerusalem leadership responded to the news of God's work among the Gentile nations with joy and worship. At this time Paul delivered the European and Asian churches' financial contribution to the Jerusalem church (Acts 24:7), in fulfillment of James' (and Peter and John's) decade old admonition to "remember the Jerusalem poor" (Gal. 2:10). Whatever doubts Paul may have had about the Jerusalem church accepting his support (Rom. 15:31) were evidently dispelled by their grateful acceptance of his gift.

Acts 21:18 is the last time Luke will write in the first person plural ("we") until he reinserts himself into the narrative in Acts 27:1. His shift in tenses notwithstanding, there is no reason to doubt that Luke was not a personal witness to the majority of events he describes in Acts 21:19—26:32.

During their time together, the Jerusalem leadership broached a sensitive issue with Paul. They highlighted the vast numbers (*muriades,* "tens of thousands") of Jewish Christians who were in Jerusalem to celebrate Pentecost. Taking *muriades* (from which the word "myriads" is derived) at face value, this indicates that there were a minimum of thirty thousand Jewish believers in Jerusalem. (Of course, over two decades earlier, during the first few years of the church, there were almost that many Jewish believers already living in Jerusalem [Acts 2:41; 4:4].) James qualified *muriades* with *posai,* "many," meaning there were more than just two sets of ten thousand. Therefore, it is quite possible that there were as many as forty or even fifty thousand Jewish believers in Jerusalem that week for Pentecost. Although a portion of them were Jews of the Diaspora making pilgrimage for the feast, most of them were residents of Israel. By any reckoning, this was a weighty assemblage of believers.

James calls these Jewish Christians "zealots for the Torah" (Acts 21:20), underscoring their passionate commitment to the observance of the Torah. That these first century Jewish believers still conformed to the precepts of Torah even though no longer under obligation to do so (Rom. 10:4; 2 Cor. 3:6–11; Gal. 3:10–25; Heb. 8:1–13) demonstrates the strong connection between Torah, the nation of Israel and Jewish identity. To Jewish residents of Israel, Torah observance was not just a theological commitment but also a national and cultural one. To abandon the Torah would have not only been disloyal and unpatriotic, but was tantamount to the discarding of Jewish identity.

Two scandalous rumors, which James and the elders knew to be false, had been circulating about Paul among the Jewish believers. There had been allegations made which claimed that Paul taught the Jews of the Diaspora to abandon (*apostasia*, "apostasy, rebellion") the Law of Moses and to discard circumcision. Ironically, the narrative of Acts reveals Paul's actions to be precisely the opposite of that of which he was accused. Paul was so committed to the idea of circumcision that he had Timothy, a grown man, circumcised (Acts 16:3). Furthermore, the most casual perusal of Acts reveals how Paul lived as a Jew when among Jews (1 Cor. 9:20). Paul's life simply does not read as that of an apostate Jew. There can be no doubt that the source of this gossip mongering was the faction of Jews visiting from Ephesus who will shortly propel Paul's life in a chaotic direction (Acts 21:27ff).

James and the elders conceived a plan to enable Paul to proactively dispel the false rumors. Considering Paul's well known, nearly infamous, reputation in Jerusalem, it would simply be impossible for him to keep a low profile during the holiday. The best strategy to deal with the perception of apostasy was to be seen, very publicly, as complying with Torah in a particularly virtuous fashion. Paul must be seen as "walking orderly," in other words, not "out of line" with Torah. Taking this action would prove that there was no substance to the rumors. Paul voiced no objections to the recommendation of the Jerusalem leaders. Paul could later affirm that he was innocent of offense against Torah or Temple (Acts 25:8) or the Jewish nation or their customs (Acts 28:17).

There were four Jewish believers who had recently taken a Nazirite vow of consecration during which they were growing out their hair, abstaining from grapevine products and avoiding ritual defilement (Num. 6:1–21).[1] Paul was to publicly associate himself with these believers through a magnanimous defraying of their expenses for the variety of Temple offerings associated with the vow's termination. To be offered in the Temple along with each man's hair clippings was one male lamb for a burnt offering, one female lamb for a sin offering, a ram for a peace offering, one basket of matzah for a grain offering and container of wine for a drink offering, per vow. This was a costly strategy, but a worthwhile one if it served to alleviate the concerns of the faction of zealots. Paul's generosity would be considered by the Jews to be a *mitzvah*, a good deed.[2]

In order to carry this plan out, Paul would need to undergo a week-long purification process, as his almost five year long absence from Israel had ritually defiled him.[3] This purification did not entail taking on a Nazirite vow himself, however.[4] The next day Paul and the four men entered the Temple. Paul began his seven-day purification period, and in order to insure the timely preparation of the offerings, also informed a Temple priest of the completion date of the Nazirite quartet's vows.

As the leaders had requested Paul to publicly affirm Jewish freedom to keep the Law, James now reaffirmed Gentile freedom not to keep the Law.[5] He reiterated the Jerusalem Council's decision that Gentiles had no obligation to Torah other than the four practical restrictions to facilitate fellowship between Jewish and Gentile believers. Holliday provides perspective, noting that, "These 'Torah-zealous' Jewish Christians are not trying to make gentile Christianity Jewish; they are trying to keep Jewish Christianity from becoming gentile."[6]

A Riotous Time in the Temple (21:27–36)

Well over a million Jews from Israel and every corner of the Diaspora were gathered together in Jerusalem to celebrate Pentecost. The city was teeming with Jewish pilgrims, many of whom had arrived weeks before the holiday's advent and would stay weeks afterward to worship in the Temple, peruse the holy city's wealth of shops or to otherwise take in the splendid magnificence of the holy city. Following the celebration of Pentecost, Paul would have routinely continued to frequent the Temple courts during the remainder of his purification period, joining the lingering post-holiday throngs of Judean residents and Diaspora pilgrims. On one such visit to the Temple, toward the conclusion of his week of purification, Paul was recognized by a hostile group of Ephesian Jews. These long-time opponents of Paul had noticed him earlier in the week while walking the city streets in the company of the Gentile believer Trophimus, whom they also recognized from Ephesus (Acts 21:29).

At this point the Ephesian Jews, although seeing no companions presently accompanying Paul within the Temple, in their enmity for the "apostate rabbi," jumped to the mother of all conclusions. With outraged shouts of alarm and distress, the Ephesians shattered the poised sanctity of the Temple, crying out that Paul had defiled the Temple by bringing a Gentile into the inner courts. The primary accusation was that Paul had brought a Greek past the *Soreg*, the four and one half feet high stone wall barrier that encircled the inner perimeter of the Court of the Gentiles, serving to separate the outer court from the remaining interior courts.[7] Just beyond the *Soreg* were the steps ascending to the elevated terrace surrounding the outer wall of the Court of Women, the first of the Temple courts strictly reserved solely for Jewish access. Archaeologists have discovered examples of the large stone plaques which adorned this balustrade, each inscribed in both Greek and Latin with a warning that, "No foreigner may enter within the barricade which surrounds the temple and enclosure. Anyone who is caught trespassing will bear personal responsibility for his ensuing death."[8] These warnings posed no idle threat. The Jews' preoccupation with safeguarding the Temple's sanctity was a matter that the Roman government formally acknowledged; the Jews were authorized to practice capital punishment in the case of Temple defilement.[9]

The Ephesian Jews added three other inflammatory accusations in addition to that of bringing a Greek beyond the forbidden boundary. These accusations are strikingly similar to those leveled against Stephen by his Hellenistic Jewish contemporaries over two decades earlier (Acts 6:13–14). They accused Paul of broadly propagating antagonism toward the Jewish people, toward the Torah and the Temple. Each one of their accusations was completely without merit. First, while Paul had been seen publicly around the city in the company of Trophimus, it was an unwarranted conclusion that he had escorted Trophimus or any other Gentile past the *Soreg,* up the steps to the terrace and through the grand "Corinthian" Gate into the inner Temple courts. Second, there is no evidence within Acts or Paul's epistles of any anti-Semitic teaching. Paul is constant and firm in upholding the essential role and continuing importance of the Jewish nation in God's program (see Rom. 9–11 to start). Third, Paul was never antagonistic toward the Torah, recognizing it as holy, righteous and good (Rom. 7:12), God's tutor pointing the way to the Messiah (Gal. 3:24). However, his doctrine that the Torah was no longer binding on believers (1 Cor. 9:20) has often been misconstrued as teaching against Torah. Fourth, Paul spoke not a word against the Temple. His teaching that God's presence could not be confined within the Temple walls (Acts 17:24) was not to be construed to mean that God could not be found within the Temple walls at all!

Although false, these outrageous accusations aroused the attention of the gathered masses, stirring up vast confusion and considerable commotion. The crowd, who mere moments ago had been engaged in worship, prayer, study or the transaction of other sacred business, now became an incensed mob. Their religious passions aroused, they focused holy outrage and pious indignation upon Paul in a brutal attack. Their ferocity, however, was not unbounded but tempered with calculated premeditation. As bloodshed would defile the inner courts, the mob dragged Paul from the Court of Women and manhandled him down the steps to the Court of the Gentiles, where they could permissibly beat him to death. To safeguard the holiness of the Temple's inner sanctum from violence, once Paul was thrown down to the lower level, the Temple guard immediately shut all the gates to the inner courts.

Overlooking the northwest corner of the Temple and connected to it via an adjacent wall was the Antonia Fortress. This was the Roman garrison in Jerusalem, positioned strategically to enable the Roman forces to observe the daily goings-on in the center of Jewish life and affairs and to rapidly intervene when necessary. During the over five decades of their occupation of Israel, the

Romans had learned to be particularly hyper-vigilant in the volatile days surrounding the major Jewish holidays like Passover and Pentecost. Indeed, the Temple tumult that day did not proceed unnoticed by the eagle eye of Rome. While Paul was being brutalized, word was sent to Claudius Lysias, the tribune or *chiliarchos*, commander of the roughly one thousand Roman soldiers garrisoned in the Antonia Fortress, that murder was about to be committed. Springing into action to prevent the riot from getting any further out of hand, the tribune immediately dispatched two *centuries*, two groups of one hundred soldiers apiece, each commanded by a centurion, to accompany him into the Temple to settle down the uproar. Hastening down the double flight of steps that linked the Antonia to the Temple, the Roman soldiers entered the Court of the Gentiles and plunged into the fray. This simple flexing of Roman power put an immediate halt to both the thrashing of Paul and the riot.

Based upon the crowd's ferocious conduct, Claudius Lysias judged Paul to be a violent criminal. Taking Paul into custody, the tribune ordered that Paul be bound with a chain on each wrist to two flanking soldiers. Attempting to ascertain from the crowd who this criminal was and what crime he had committed, Claudius Lysias could not get a straight answer from the frenzied crowd. Realizing the futility of seeking reasonable answers from an enraged pack of overwrought hotheads, the tribune ordered Paul removed to the Antonia for interrogation. When the crowd realized that Paul was being taken from their midst, they violently pressed against the contingent of soldiers in a last ditch attempt to break through them and get to Paul. Ferociously screaming, "Away with him!" the mob echoed the lethal rejection of Jesus at his trial before Pilate (Luke 23:18). Rapidly exiting the Temple, the soldiers picked Paul up and began carrying him up the double staircase leading into the fortress.

Self-Defense (21:37–22:21)

An Audacious Request (21:37–40)

Paul, while battered in body, was still courageous in spirit and keen of mind. In the midst of being borne up the staircase by two Roman soldiers to whom he was chained, accompanied by one hundred ninety-eight other soldiers, two centurions and a tribune, Paul nonetheless astutely recognized that this ignominious situation presented an unparalleled opportunity to bear witness of Christ to multitudes of rapt Jews. Wanting to act on that opportunity, Paul asked the tribune for permission to address the crowd.

Claudius Lysias was surprised to hear Paul speaking in Greek, for he had mistaken Paul for an infamous wanted criminal, an Egyptian agitator. Three years earlier, this Egyptian Jew, claiming to be a prophet, had attracted some thirty thousand followers. He led them to the Mount of Olives in preparation for capturing Jerusalem, for he had promised that at his command the city's walls would miraculously crumble. A delegation of Roman troops rapidly put a bloody end to this fantasy, but the Egyptian had escaped.[10] The tribune also incorrectly linked the Egyptian with another band of Jewish criminals that had recently arisen, the *Sicarii*, "dagger-men," a group of Jewish assassins of the pro-Roman Jewish aristocracy, who had recently dispatched the former high priest, Jonathan.[11]

Paul reassured the tribune that he was Jewish, not Egyptian, and hailed not from Egypt but the great metropolis of Tarsus, in Cilicia. Remarkably, Paul was granted permission to speak. Using the staircase as an elevated stage, flanked by a bevy of Roman soldiers, Paul audaciously quieted the mob with his hand. Further arresting their attention, he spoke to them in Hebrew, the language of the Temple courts and comprehensible to every Jew present, Judeans, Galileans and Jews of the Diaspora (although probably unintelligible to the Roman soldiers).

Resume and Testimony (22:1–16)

Having simmered down the mob's uproar, Paul offered his defense. This will be the first of a total of five defenses Paul is forced to make between Acts 22:1 and 26:29. He began by addressing them with the respectful yet familiar, "brothers and fathers," the same phrase used by Stephen in his defense before the Sanhedrin (Acts 7:2). Now that he had their attention, his concern was to repudiate the charge that he was an apostate Jew, and to demonstrate instead that he was an exceptionally obedient one. He lays out his biographical resume as a Tarsus-born Jew, raised in Jerusalem since early adolescence. He reminds them of his personal training in Pharisaic Judaism and instruction in the Torah's minutia by none other than the most revered rabbi of the day, *Rabban* Gamaliel. His point seems to be that there was none in the Temple crowd that day whose passion for Torah or zeal for God could have rivaled that of Paul's. Paul's dedication to Judaism led him to engineer an intense program of persecution against the followers of Jesus. Paul had imprisoned men and women without distinction and had been directly responsible for the deaths of many believers in Jesus. Yet again, the designation, "the Way," is used of the Christian movement (Acts 9:2; 19:9, 23; 22:4; 24:14, 22). That this was the most familiar contemporary term for the church is indicated by Paul's usage here without qualification. The crowd had no difficulty understanding to which group Paul referred. Paul emphasized that what he was recounting was not imaginative embellishment but historical fact. The high priest at the time, Josephus Caiaphas, and many members of the Sanhedrin were still alive and could easily verify Paul's former hatred of the Way as well as the authorization he had received from them to arrest the Jewish believers in Damascus and extradite them to Jerusalem.

For the second of three times within Acts (9:1–19; 22:6–16; 26:12–18), the narrative is recounted of Paul's Damascus road encounter with the resurrected Messiah and subsequent commission. This account varies little from Luke's initial explanation, although unlike Luke's earlier third person account, this one has the benefit of coming directly from the mouth of Paul himself, tailored for the occasion. Paul described the blinding brilliance of the Shekinah glory and his conversation with the voice from heaven, whose words were intelligible to no one else in Paul's party. The voice twice called Paul's Hebrew name, *Saoul*, and asked the question, "Why are you persecuting me?" Paul, the energetic defender of Judaism and Torah, the self-proclaimed quintessential paragon of godly zeal and Pharisaic piety, had been confused by the rebuke and brazenly asked the speaker to identify himself. The heavenly speaker shockingly identified Himself as Jesus the Nazarene. Through his persecution of the church, Paul had been attacking Jesus as well. Jesus commanded Paul, now blind, to go into Damascus for further instruction.

Providing details omitted in Luke's previous account, Paul relayed how in Damascus he had encountered Ananias, a believer in Jesus, recognized as a pious and conscientious observer of Torah by the city's entire Jewish community. Paul shared how Ananias, his new brother in faith, after having miraculously restored his vision, conveyed Paul's divine apostolic appointment to bear witness of having seen the resurrected Messiah. Jesus is designated here as, "the Righteous One," (from the Hebrew *Tzaddik*), a messianic title derived from Isaiah's Suffering Servant prophecy (Is. 53:11). Having both restored Paul's sight and delivered his commission, Ananias charged Paul as a new believer to without hesitation carry out his responsibility to identify himself publicly as a follower of Jesus through baptism.

Acts 22:16, like the Acts 2:38 text on baptism, has been used in some quarters to argue that water baptism is necessary for the forgiveness of sins, i.e., salvation. The argument based on Acts 22:16 rests on interpreting Ananias' statement to mean that baptism was the time when Paul's sins were to be "washed away." In addition, the act of baptism is equated with the "calling on the name of the Lord." Although this position maintains the grace of God accomplished by Christ's death on the cross in salvation, nevertheless, in this view, salvation can only be activated upon the new believer's obedience in baptism. This interpretation must be rejected as it directly contradicts the numerous passages elsewhere in Acts, the gospels and the epistles that straightforwardly affirm that salvation derives solely by faith that Jesus is the Messiah (Acts 3:19; 5:31; 8:22; 10:43–44; 11:19; 13:24; 17:30; 19:4; 20:21;

26:18–20; John 3:16, 36; Rom. 11:6; Eph. 2:8–9). Furthermore, Paul's personal encounter with Christ on the Damascus road, coupled with the fact that Ananias had called Paul a "brother," strongly suggests that Paul had already become a Christian prior to baptism.

Ananias' linking of baptism with the washing away of Paul's sin is best interpreted not as a theological proposition of doctrine, but rather as evocative and potent Jewish imagery, relevant only to those who, like Paul and the Temple audience to whom he was relating the story, were familiar with the various forms of *mikvah*, Jewish ritual self-baptism, carried out for purposes of ceremonial cleansing, conversion, and repentance (e.g., John's baptism). For Jews especially, baptism could be characterized as "calling upon God's name," in the sense that it was a public identification of the believer with Jesus and the church community, a mandatory pledge of allegiance to the Messiah (see Acts 2:38 for further discussion).[12] As Fruchtenbaum maintains, "While baptism is not essential to salvation, it is essential to obedience and discipleship."[13]

Temple Vision (22:17–21)

Paul's commission was confirmed in Jerusalem three years after the Damascus encounter. This event transpired sometime during the period covered in Acts 9:26–30, but is recorded only in this passage. While praying in the Temple, Jesus once again appeared to Paul in a vision. The Lord commanded Paul to "get out of Dodge." Jerusalem was not a safe locale for the apostle as there was no shortage of aspiring assassins waiting for an opportunity to kill him. Jesus warned Paul that Jerusalem would prove vehemently unreceptive to his gospel witness. Paul disagreed (!), countering with an assumption that his renowned former role as arch-persecutor of the church, particularly as a willing participant in the murder of Stephen, would immunize him from molestation. Jesus knew, however, that as Jerusalem had rejected Stephen, they would reject Paul in the same violent fashion. Jesus has the final word, instructing Paul that he would be sent "far away to the Gentiles." As interesting as it is to note previously undisclosed details of Paul's commission, of equal significance are the details purposely omitted by Paul in this retelling. In his Temple defense, Paul specifically excluded mention of the two other demographic groups (specified in Acts 9:15) to whom he was to bear witness, "kings" and "the sons of Israel," only mentioning the Gentiles.

Under Arrest (22:22–29)

It may have been Paul's intent in his Temple defense to justify his activity among the Gentiles through demonstrating his obedience to a pair of heavenly visions. That the crowd listened respectfully thus far was an indication that he was beginning to make his case. However, at the mention of the inflammatory term, "Gentiles," the crowd lost its composure, reminded of Paul's apostasy of teaching Gentiles about God apart from Judaism. Enthusiastically screaming for Paul's death, they threw off their outer cloaks and began tossing Temple dust into the air.

Seeing their blood thirst, Claudius Lysias had enough. He ordered that Paul be brought into their custody within the Antonia Fortress, terminating this explosive scenario. Having not comprehended Paul's Hebrew speech, still having no understanding of what had provoked such tumult, the tribune was determined to expeditiously determine the underlying cause of this crisis through whatever means would prove necessary. He ordered the interrogation of Paul through scourging. Evidently, in his quest for satisfactory answers, Claudius Lysias' preferred tactic was torture.

The Roman scourge, or *flagellum* in Latin, was a wooden baton to which was attached an array of leather strips studded with jagged bone or metal chunks. In the right hands, it was one of the empire's most formidable and injurious instruments of torture. Jesus had been forced to endure scourging prior to his crucifixion (Matt. 27:26; Mark 15:15; Luke 23:16; John 19:1). As the soldiers stood Paul between two pillars and stretched out his arms to tie them with thongs, moments away from experiencing unimaginable agony, Paul asked the supervising centurion if it was lawful to scourge a Roman citizen who lacked even benefit of trial, thereby somewhat caustically informing the centurion of Paul's citizenship. Horrified at the capital crime for which he was about to be responsible, the centurion halted the scourging preparation and rushed to his commander, Claudius Lysias, to forcefully alert him of the news.

Incredulous at the possibility that this Jewish delinquent could possess Roman citizenship, the tribune hustled to Paul's side, asking for personal confirmation of the report he had received. At Paul's confirmation of his legal status, Claudius Lysias revealed that he had been forced to purchase his own citizenship at a great price, the inference being that citizenship must have cost Paul an even heftier bundle of drachmas. Paul coolly replied that bribery played no part in his status, but that citizenship had been his birthright.

Before the Sanhedrin (22:30–23:11)

The next day, Claudius Lysias, still ignorant of the factors precipitating the Temple riot, ordered the high priest and the entire body of the Sanhedrin to convene within the Antonia for a special investigative session. The matter in question was clearly of a religious nature, and the tribune anticipated that the Supreme Court of Israel would be able provide him the necessary illumination. Paul was brought before the Sanhedrin, composed mainly of Paul's contemporaries, who, under different circumstances, could have been his colleagues. Absent the grace of God, Paul would have been sitting there among them. Staring intently into the faces of the Council, sizing up those who gathered in judgment of him, Paul's opening statement avowed his clear conscience before God regarding his lifestyle. This was as far as Paul's opening statement was allowed to proceed, for his first remark had already infuriated Ananias, the high priest.

Ananias commanded his servants to rap Paul across the mouth. This was illegal treatment, as Paul had yet to be even charged with a crime. Stunned by this flagrant violation, Paul indignantly retorted that God Himself would likewise strike Ananias. Paul called the high priest a "white-washed wall," a colorful metaphor that referenced the common practice of applying a fresh coat of paint to disguise a decrepit, ramshackle wall. Paul condemned the hypocrisy of being judged according to Torah while at the same time being brutalized in violation of Torah.

Paul's condemnation of Ananias was perceptive. The high priest from AD 47–59, Ananias was notorious for his greed, corruption, and pro-Roman policies.[14] The Talmud remembers him for regularly appropriating the sacred temple sacrifices for his own use.[15] Following his deposal from office, he maintained power by using the wealth he had accumulated during his twelve year tenure as high priest to bribe his successor to the high priest's office as well as the Roman procurator.[16] Hated by many for his cozy collaboration with Rome, Ananias was hunted down by Jewish zealots at the outbreak of the revolt against Rome in AD 66. After his mansion was burned down by the zealots,[17] the former high priest was found cowering in an aqueduct. He was dragged from his hiding place and summarily dispatched.[18]

Although no one batted an eyelash at Ananias' command to strike Paul, Paul's harsh rebuke to Ananias succeeded in shocking the Sanhedrin. They admonished Paul for speaking to the high priest with such disrespect. Paul gave an apology (of sorts), replying that he was unaware that it was the high priest to whom he had spoken. He quoted Torah's prohibition of speaking evil of Israel's leaders (Ex. 22:28), in recognition that the office of high priest commanded respect regardless of the qualifications of the particular individual holding the office.

There are two possibilities to explain Paul's ignorance of Ananias being high priest. First, Paul may well have recognized the high priest but was sarcastically commenting that Ananias' boorish and inappropriate action had rendered him unrecognizable as high priest. The alternative explanation, however, is more likely. As this was a specially convened session held within the Antonia, there is no reason to believe that Ananias would have been wearing his high priestly garments or anything to indicate his status as anything other than a simple priest or scholar. As an infrequent visitor to Jerusalem, Paul would have previously seen Ananias only a few times, and then at a distance. Considering that the room was filled with heavily bearded Jewish men of a certain age, it is not surprising that Paul was unable to recognize Ananias as high priest.

Realizing that he was not going to receive a fair hearing before this group, Paul did not care to wait patiently for the next round of physical abuse. Having sized up the composition of the Sanhedrin, weighing the ratio of Pharisees to Sadducees, Paul shrewdly took matters into his own hands. Taking his best shot, he threw out the most inflammatory barb in his arsenal. He cried out that he was a Pharisee, a descendent of Pharisees, who had received an education within an academy of Pharisees. The reason he was on trial was his belief in the resurrection of the dead, a theological conviction common to all Pharisees. It was not necessary for Paul to specify that the particular resurrection in question was that of Jesus, since absent the Messiah's resurrection, no further resurrections could take place (1 Cor. 15:23).

With stunning accuracy, Paul's rhetorical grenade exploded in the midst of the assembly. Raising the controversial concept of resurrection created an immediate division between the Sanhedrin's Pharisees, who believed in a future resurrection and Sadducees, who rejected the notion. Abruptly, a heated argument on the issue erupted, (*kraugē megalē*, "a great uproar"), the latest chapter of a century-old running theological disagreement between the two sects. With one deft oratorical move, Paul succeeded in playing one side of the Council against the other.

Paul himself rapidly became a mere sideshow to the main attraction: a room full of priests and rabbis arguing theology amongst themselves. Doubtless seeking to provoke the Sadducees further, several Pharisees widened the argument to encompass other areas of theological disagreement, broaching the possibility that Paul had received supernatural revelation from an angel or spirit! Anyone who has been witness to a meeting of the modern Israeli Knesset (parliament) can attest to the "liveliness" of the proceedings when a roomful of passionate Jewish big shots begin to fervently argue the issues of the day. Fingers point, hands are waved in the air and epithets fly across the room (as does the occasional chair).

Claudius Lysias found himself plunged into the middle of yet another tumult and still frustrated in his quest for answers concerning his prisoner.

Fearing for Paul's safety, the tribune removed Paul from the proceedings, leaving the Sanhedrin to continue their argument among themselves.

Three noteworthy observations can be discerned from Paul's divide and conquer stratagem. First, even after having been a Christian for over two decades, Paul still considered himself to be a Pharisee. Although Paul had added the identification of Jesus as Messiah to his theological matrix, he still held the same basic theological beliefs as every Pharisee: the resurrection of the dead, immortality of the soul, eternal reward and punishment, angelic and demonic activity, divine sovereignty balanced against human responsibility, and the divine authority of the entire Hebrew Scripture.

Second, while Pharisees could become Christians and still remain (modified) Pharisees, Sadducees could not become Christians without rejecting their party affiliation. Christians could not reject, as did Sadducees, the doctrines of resurrection, angelic or demonic beings, eternal reward or punishment and the immortality of the soul. Nor could Christians accept only the Torah and reject the Hebrew Prophets as the divinely authoritative word of God.

Third, knowing that he possessed only one opportunity to witness before the Sanhedrin, the assembled company of the greatest Jewish minds and teachers of his day, Paul thrust directly to the essential heart of the faith, resurrection. The resurrection of Jesus is the bottom line ultimately underlying every objection to Christianity. The Christian faith rises or falls on the historical veracity of the account of Jesus rising from the tomb (1. Cor 15:16–17). This is the central evidence of His messiahship. There is no Christianity without a resurrected Christ. Without Jesus' resurrection, Christianity is a theological system fit only for fools and slackers; a faux Judaism for those too morally flaccid to handle the heavy legal requirements of the genuine article.

On the following evening, Jesus appeared to Paul, the fourth such appearance in the Acts narrative (Acts 9:5; 22:17–21; 18:9–10; 23:11). Jesus provided Paul with divine assurance of His presence. Complimenting His apostle for his Jerusalem witness, Jesus told Paul to take courage for his safety was secure and his witness destined to continue in Rome.

Yet Another Murder Conspiracy (23:12–30)

The next morning, more than forty unnamed Jewish zealots formed a conspiracy to murder Paul. Placing themselves under a solemn oath, *anathematize*, "to curse," "to devote to destruction," they committed to abstain from eating or drinking until Paul was dead. Approaching the high priest and his associates, the zealots reported their vow, seeking to enlist the entire Jewish leadership in their murderous conspiracy. The Sanhedrin was a necessary component in their plan to extricate Paul from the Antonia into the open where he would be vulnerable. The Sanhedrin was to notify Claudius Lysias that the court wanted to continue their investigation of Paul. This time, however, the inquiry would not be held in the Antonia Fortress but in the judgment chamber of the Sanhedrin. Tucked away within the security of the Antonia, Paul was inaccessible, but the assassins could strike as the Roman guard transferred their charge from the Antonia to the Sanhedrin's chambers. This was not a strategy designed to avoid casualties. That the ambush of a Roman guard would invariably result in the deaths of most of the band of forty conspirators reveals the depths of their shared commitment to Paul's elimination.

Knowing in hindsight that the conspirators did not succeed in their plot and that Paul would not be executed for another decade or so, and then by Roman, not Jewish hands, we need not imagine that these zealots kept their oath and starved to death. Rabbinic law was extremely lenient in providing for the release of vows under extenuating circumstances. Almost any circumstances (vows made based on erroneous information, or in the heat of the moment, or due to opening a big mouth, or that proved too difficult to fulfill) could be considered sufficiently extenuating.[19]

However, somehow privy to the murderous conspiracy was Paul's nephew. This is Luke's sole mention of Paul's relatives, and no other information about this nephew is revealed in either Scripture or church tradition. It is possible only to speculate whether the nephew was a fellow zealot and present with the conspirators when the plot was originally hatched, or if he was informed through means of his family's political connections. Regardless of how Paul's nephew learned of the plot, he came to his uncle in the Antonia to warn him about the intended ambush. Paul immediately sent his nephew to report the conspiracy to the tribune.

Claudius Lysias sprang into action. It was clear that Paul was not safe in Jerusalem and that sooner or later Paul's enemies would prevail. Therefore, Claudius Lysias took decisive steps to ensure that the prisoner was quickly transferred out of the tribune's jurisdiction and handed over to the procurator in Caesarea. Taking no chances with security, he commanded two centurions to prepare with due haste a task force, comprised of nearly half of the Antonia's garrison, to escort Paul from Jerusalem. Under cover of night, at roughly nine o'clock that evening, Paul, along with his escort of two hundred infantry, two hundred auxiliary troops and seventy cavalry, departed for Caesarea. Paul was not to see Jerusalem again.

Accompanying the military delegation was a hastily dispatched letter to Felix, the procurator, in Caesarea. Claudius Lysias summarized his rescue of Paul from the Temple riot (and stretched the truth a bit by reporting that he had effected the rescue having learned of Paul's Roman citizenship [Acts 23:27]). In his opening address to Felix, the tribune used the term *kratistos*, "most excellent," which was a formal Roman designation of honor. This is the same term Luke uses of his patron, Theophilus, to whom the books of Luke and Acts are addressed (Luke 1:3). The tribune finished the letter with his conclusion that the issues against the prisoner were of a religious, not civil, nature, and regarded Jewish law. Therefore, as far as the he was concerned, Paul was innocent of any crime under Roman law. However, for the prisoner's safety, he was being transferred to the procurator's jurisdiction.

Conclusion

Antonius Felix served as procurator of Judea from AD 52–59, a period of dramatically increasing tensions between the Jews and their Roman occupiers. Originally a slave, Felix had a good friend in the emperor Claudius, who granted him his freedom and later appointed him to the oversight of Samaria in AD 48[20] and soon after to the office of Judea's procurator. Evidently, Felix had charm to spare, for this former slave married into Jewish royalty. One of his three wives was Drusilla, the daughter of Herod Agrippa I and sister of Herod Agrippa II, (a genuine Jewish princess) who divorced her husband for Felix. (Felix and Drusilla's son would later be killed when Vesuvius erupted over Pompeii in AD 79.[21]) No matter the extent of his facility in political and romantic flirtation, history remembers Felix more for the corruption, cruelty and lust that characterized his tenure. The historian Tacitus records that Felix exercised the power of a king with the instincts of a slave.[22] Felix will play an significant role in the next two years of Paul's life as we shall see in the following section.

Study Questions:

1. List the accusations made against Paul which precipitated the riot in the Temple. Provide a defense of Paul's innocence on each charge.

2. Explain the rumors circulating in Jerusalem among the Jewish Christians about Paul and James' plan to dispel them. Should Paul have consented to James' plan? Why or why not?

3. What was the significance of *the Soreg*?

4. How did Paul's Roman citizenship make a difference in the outcome of the events described in this section?

5. What strategy did Paul employ when brought before the Sanhedrin?

CHAPTER 17

Paul in Caesarea
Acts 23:31–26:32

Preview:

In this section, covering a two-year period, from summer AD 57 through summer AD 59, the stage will be set for Paul's journey to Rome. Having already delivered, in the previous section, a defense before the Jewish mob and another before the Sanhedrin, Paul will again be forced to defend himself before two Roman procurators and a Jewish king. Luke's narrative here follows the straightforward pattern of Jewish charges being presented against Paul, his defense against those charges, and the resulting Roman reaction to Paul's defense. This pattern will play out three times, between Paul and Felix, Paul and Festus, and Paul and Agrippa II.

Paul's Defense before Felix (23:31–24:27)

Transfer to Caesarea (23:31–35)

Traveling rapidly and under cover of night, Paul and his military escort covered some thirty-five miles to arrive in Antipatris by morning. Having escorted Paul a considerable distance away from the Jerusalem conspirators, it was safe for the four hundred foot soldiers to return to the Antonia. Paul and his remaining escort of seventy Roman cavalry continued on the additional twenty-seven miles to Caesarea. Arriving at their destination, Herod's palace, the Roman procurator's headquarters, Paul was presented to Felix along with the letter from Claudius Lysias. Felix, having read the letter, inquired of Paul whether he was from a province requiring the consultation of an additional local ruler, just as Pilate had done in first sending Jesus to Herod Antipas, ruler of Galilee (Luke 23:7). As Paul was from Cilicia, the buck with whom his case stopped was Felix. Paul was imprisoned in the palace to await the procurator's adjudication.

Jewish Accusations (24:1–9)

The next day, specified by Luke as being five days after Paul's Temple arrest, Ananias and a select delegation from the Sanhedrin arrived in Caesarea to bring legal indictment against Paul. To ensure that they effectively made their case against Paul, they hired Tertullus, a slick Gentile lawyer familiar with Roman law. Notably absent from the group are the Ephesian Jews who had made the initial accusations and the band of forty conspirators. Assembled together before Felix, Tertullus began his accusation. In an address dripping with florid rhetoric and gratuitous flattery, the lawyer praised Felix for the peace he had established and the reforms he had initiated in Judea. (Of course, the reality was that Felix' rule was characterized by an abundance of both violence and corruption.) Once again, we see the use of the honorific, *kratistos,* "most excellent."

Tertullus brings three charges against Paul. First, Paul is accused of being a public pest, a nuisance with a worldwide track record of inciting sedition and rebellion. Second, Paul is a ringleader of the "Nazarenes," an early designation of the Jewish Christians (similar to the contemporary Hebrew word for Christians in general, *"Notzrim"*). Note that at this point the Jews still considered the followers of Jesus to be Jewish. The Nazarenes were merely one more aberrant, demented Jewish sect among many. The final charge was Paul's alleged profaning of the Temple, a capital crime. Luke notes that Tertullus' oratory was cheered on in hearty agreement by his employers.

(Acts 24:6b-24:8a is not present in the most reliable manuscripts and is most likely a later editorial insertion made by someone other than Luke.)

Paul's Defense (24:10–21)

Paul, receiving permission from Felix to defend himself, launched a vigorous rebuttal. In contrast to Tertullus' flattery, Paul simply acknowledged that he anticipated a fair hearing as Felix was no newcomer to Israel, having ruled as procurator for over five years. Answering the charge of inciting rebellion, Paul argued that having been in Jerusalem a mere twelve days, three of which were spent locked in the Antonia, he would have been hard pressed in a little over a week to have fermented any sort of insurrection. The accusation of sedition was insupportable, as he had not been seen to be plotting sedition or causing riots in the Temple, the synagogue or anywhere else in Jerusalem. In fact, Paul had been diligent to keep a particularly low profile in light of the concerns of James and the elders of the Jerusalem church (Acts 21:20–24).

Moving on to the accusation of his being a leader in the Nazarene sect, Paul freely admitted to membership in "the Way" (yet again the term is used of Christianity, see also Acts 9:2; 19:9, 23; 22:4; 24:14, 22). However, contrary to the optimistic aspirations of Ananias and his colleagues, belonging to the Christian "sect" of Judaism was not (yet) a criminal offense under Roman law. In fact, the apostle presented Christianity as the truest representation of Judaism, the ultimate fulfillment of everything written in the Torah and Prophets, the Hebrew Scripture. Going further, as he had done before the Sanhedrin, Paul again identified the actual underlying opposition as originating in his faith in the resurrection of both righteous and unrighteous (Dan. 12:2; John 5:29), even though those with Ananias who were Pharisees also held to this doctrine. In view of his anticipation of the coming resurrection, Paul emphasized his maintenance of a blameless conscience before both God and men, the same basic affirmation Paul made before the Sanhedrin, which resulted in his being rapped across the mouth by Ananias' lackeys (Acts 23:1–2).

Paul next protested the most serious accusation, the capital crime of profaning the Temple. He explained how less then two weeks ago he had returned to Jerusalem after an almost five year absence with benevolence, not insurrection, in mind, bearing charity for the Jewish nation (without specifying that it was specifically for the church) and an financial offering with which to celebrate Pentecost. While in the Temple, alone and going about his own ritualistic business, some Ephesian troublemakers with a grievance saw him and instigated a riot. Paul noted that these "hit and run" Ephesian Jews were conspicuously absent from the proceedings, probably already home in Ephesus. In fact, there was not a single witness present who could substantiate any of the charges against Paul. His implication, therefore, was that the entire investigation was a colossal abuse of Rome's time and energy. Furthermore, Paul pointed to the high priest and the Sanhedrin delegation who had personally conducted their own investigation one day prior. They had found Paul guilty only of believing in the resurrection of the dead, a controversial issue to Jews, but a non-issue to Romans.

Felix Passes the Buck (24:22–27)

Felix, having been in Israel for nine years, five of them as procurator, could not help but possess an acquaintance with the basic beliefs of Christianity. Consequently, he most assuredly realized that the charges against Paul were of a religious, not civil, nature. However, instead of outright dismissing the case and setting Paul free, Felix instead deferred the matter, seeking to avoid offending the Jewish leadership. Ostensibly, the delay would only persist until Jerusalem's tribune, Claudius Lysias, could personally testify before Felix.

However, in actuality, Felix had no intention of sending for Claudius Lysias, whose presence was rendered unnecessary by the letter he had sent in which he had rendered his opinion of Paul's innocence. Placing Paul in protective custody, Felix granted his "guest" the full rights of visitation befitting an innocent and salubrious Roman citizen.

Some time later, Felix, along with his young wife, the Jewish princess Drusilla, wishing to learn more about Christianity, sent for Paul. Their "theologian-in-residence" bore faithful and significantly bold witness of what was entailed in exercising faith in Jesus Christ. Luke records that Paul spoke candidly to his captors of living a life of self-control that reflected God's righteous standards, in light of the future judgment to come with the establishment of the messianic kingdom. Evidently, Paul struck a sensitive nerve in the ethically lax procurator. Felix became frightened by Paul's teaching on future moral accountability and prematurely terminated the lesson, putting Paul off for another time.

This must have been the sole time Felix lost his composure with Paul, as the procurator would frequently summon his pet prisoner for conversation. Apparently, Felix had been impressed with Paul's ability to raise the money brought to the Jerusalem church. Indeed, the procurator was eager for Paul to reprise his fundraising efforts to secure his release from Felix's custody with a bribe. However, no bribe was ever forthcoming from the apostle.

Felix's charade with Paul continued for some two years, until Felix was recalled to Rome for employing too heavy a hand in quashing a rebellion of Caesarea's Jewish community. To make up for his treatment of the Jewish citizens of Caesarea, Felix did the Jewish leadership a favor before leaving office. He left Paul to languish in prison. It was within this two-year period of time that Luke, assuredly Paul's steadfast companion during this period, collected the numerous personal testimonies that he would later collate as the basis of his gospel and the book of Acts.

Paul's Defense before Festus (25:1–12)

Felix' successor as procurator was Porcius Festus. History tells us nothing about this procurator except that he was appointed circa AD 59 by Nero to replace Felix and that Festus served until dying in office in AD 62. The political situation in Judea was volatile enough that Festus took only three days to settle in to his new headquarters before meeting with the Jewish leadership in Jerusalem. Upon making the acquaintance of the high priest (a new one, Ishmael) and his colleagues, Festus was immediately set upon with a renewal of the charges against Paul. In contrast to his predecessor, Festus was completely ignorant of Christianity, and the Jewish leadership prevailed upon their new procurator for a favor. They requested that Festus have Paul transferred to Jerusalem for trial. However, the leadership secretly planned, in a revival of the two-year old murder conspiracy, to ambush their enemy while on the road to the holy city.

Festus saw no reason for Paul to be transferred from his current imprisonment in Caesarea, although he invited the Jewish leadership to accompany him back to Caesarea to reopen Paul's trial. After having spent a little over a week in Jerusalem, Festus returned to his palace in Caesarea, accompanied by the Jewish leadership. One day after their arrival, Festus convened yet another trial for Paul. The Jewish leadership, this time minus their slick lawyer, once again brought a pile of two-year old charges against Paul, none of which they could prove.

Paul responded in turn to each major charge, avowing his innocence of offending the Torah, the Temple or Roman law. Yet again, Paul argued that the underlying, essential issue of contention was Jesus' resurrection (Acts 25:19). Festus was at a loss as to how to overcome the impasse between Paul and the Jerusalem delegation. The novice procurator was fully aware of Paul's innocence, yet lacked the courage to risk offending the Jews with an acquittal for lack of evidence. He decided to act on the Jewish leadership's request for a favor, inviting Paul to change the trial's venue and stand trial before Festus in Jerusalem's Antonia Fortress.

However, Paul was no fool. Deprived of justice after enjoying two years of the indifferent hospitality of two separate procurators, he realized that that there was no chance he would receive justice in Jerusalem. In the unlikely event that he was able to avoid assassination prior to his arrival in Jerusalem, Paul estimated that the likelihood was high of ending up again before the Sanhedrin. The odds of surviving a second confrontation with that august body were not at all favorable. It could be safely surmised that Festus was either too weak or too inexperienced to safeguard Paul. Therefore, the apostle refused Festus' offer to transfer trial venues to Jerusalem. Furthermore, Paul admonished Festus for abdicating his responsibilities by trying to pass him off to the Jewish authorities.

A drastic measure was called for. If Festus, literally sitting on the Roman judgment seat, would not exercise his authority to adjudicate, then Paul would go over Festus' head to demand Roman justice from the highest possible authority. Paul invoked his right as a Roman citizen and appealed to Caesar for justice. Since 23 BC, Roman citizens throughout the empire had the right to request trial in Rome with their verdict to be decreed by the emperor himself.[1] In appealing to Caesar, Paul was not so much entrusting his fate to the whim of Nero as to the care of the Lord. Jesus himself had promised that

Paul would witness in Rome. Yet two whole years had already passed while Paul remained immobilized in Caesarea. At fifty-four years of age, he was not getting any younger. It was high time for Paul to act while he could to assist the Lord in fulfilling His promise.

After conferring with his advisors, Festus realized that his hands were tied. Paul would be sent to Rome. However, it was now Festus' thorny responsibility to navigate through strange and unfamiliar Jewish religious issues in order to formulate substantive charges against Paul for which he could be sent to the imperial court for trial. In this task, Festus would enlist the aid of a colleague better educated and more experienced in Jewish matters, the Jewish king, Herod Agrippa II.

Royal Consultation (25:13–22)

Several days later, the ruler of the neighboring territory to the north, King Agrippa II, along with his sister, Bernice, paid a social call on the new procurator.

Agrippa II

Born in AD 27, Agrippa II was the grandson of Herod the Great and son of Herod Agrippa I, who had murdered James the apostle fifteen years earlier (Acts 12:2). He was also the brother of Felix' wife Drusilla. Only seventeen years old in AD 44 when his father died, Agrippa II was considered too young to inherit his father's vast domain. Judea, therefore, reverted back to the administration of a Roman procurator.[2]

Six years later, Agrippa II was finally granted a modest kingdom, and from AD 50–56, Caesar gradually expanded the size of the young king's realm to finally encompass most of the region of greater Galilee, north of Judea. Agrippa II was also granted oversight of the Temple, with the authority to appoint and dismiss the high priest, a power that he frequently exercised. This did not endear him to the Jewish people. Educated in Rome and sympathetic to Roman policies, he was viewed by most Jews as little more than a Roman puppet. After the Jewish revolt's disastrous conclusion in AD 70, Agrippa II returned to Rome until his death toward the turn of the century. With Agrippa's passing, the famous/infamous Herodian dynasty came to an end.[3]

Bernice

Born one year later than her brother, Agrippa II, history has granted Bernice a memorably flamboyant reputation. After being widowed at an extremely young age, Bernice married her uncle, (yet another) King Herod of Chalcis.[4] Unfortunately, this husband died as well, and in AD 48, she moved in with

Agrippa II. Rumors abounded of the brother and sister's unnaturally intimate relationship.[5] It is during this period of cohabitation that this royal duo is introduced into the Acts narrative.

Four years later, in AD 63, with the intent to dispel the rumors surrounding her and her brother, Bernice entered into her third matrimonial venture, this time to the king of Cilicia. The king, for his part, married Bernice for her money. Their partnership was short-lived, and three years later Bernice returned to her brother. Soon afterward, in the days leading to war with Rome, Bernice, in her capacity as queen, interceded with the Roman government on behalf of her people, putting her own life at great risk[6] Later in life, after the destruction of Jerusalem, Bernice was to find fulfillment as the mistress of the architect of that city's destruction, the Roman general then emperor, Titus.

During Agrippa and Bernice's extended visit to what had once been their father's palace, Festus enlisted the expertise in Jewish law of his royal house-guest. Soliciting Agrippa's opinion on the matter of Paul's appeal, Festus brought the king up to date on the apostle's case. The procurator summarized his meeting with the Jewish leadership, at which time they had renewed their charges against Paul, and the subsequent trial he had convened in Caesarea. Festus expressed his surprise at the nature of the charges the Jews had brought against Paul. Based upon the vitriolic hostility of the Jewish leaders, Festus had been led to expect accusations of heinous villainy and flagrant defiance of Roman law, not charges concerning Jewish religious sensitivities. As far as he could understand, the whole debate hinged upon the non-issue of whether or not a dead man, Jesus, had come back to life.

Festus recounted how he had asked Paul to stand trial before the Sanhedrin. Concealing from Agrippa his true motivation in asking Paul to go back to Jerusalem (the desire to do the Jewish leadership a favor [Acts 25:9]), instead he attributed the request to his lack of familiarity with Jewish law. Concluding his summary, Festus noted that Paul, having objected to being tried in Jerusalem and subsequently exercising his Roman right of appeal to Caesar, was therefore still in custody, awaiting transfer to Rome. As Agrippa expressed enthusiasm in personally hearing from Paul, Festus promised his guest an audience with the controversial prisoner on the following day.

Paul's Defense before Herod Agrippa II (25:23–26:1–32)

The next day, King Agrippa and his queen, Bernice, entered the palace auditorium with great pageantry. Accompanying them, in a parade of pomp, was Festus, the most prominent (predominantly Gentile) citizens of the city, and Festus' five military tribunes, each one a commander of one thousand troops garrisoned in Caesarea. Lastly, in an absence of pomp but a considerable amount of circumstance, Paul entered the auditorium, shackled in chains. Festus, addressing the king and other prominent guests assembled to hear Paul, again reviewed the circumstances leading up to Paul's appeal to the emperor. Finding nothing under Roman law of which Paul was guilty, the procurator was enlisting the aid of Agrippa and the assembly to determine the charges to include in the report to Caesar. It would be absurd to send a prisoner to Rome without an accompanying accusation of wrongdoing. Furthermore, a report sent to the imperial court that did not include specific charges against the prisoner would not reflect well on Festus.

Resurrection on Trial (26:1–8)

The fifth and final defense delivered by Paul in Judea serves as the oratorical climax of the book of Acts. By any measure, it is the apostle's virtuoso evangelistic *tour de force*. Gathered in one location were all three of the people groups to whom Paul was divinely commissioned to witness: gentiles, kings and the sons of Israel (Acts 9:15). In fact, this would be Paul's first occasion to preach to a king. The apostle capitalized on this rare opportunity. Addressing Agrippa, whom Festus was allowing to preside over this inquiry, Paul shared his enthusiasm to bear witness before such an educated authority in Jewish religious affairs. He then requested the patient indulgence of the king, as Paul planned to take his time in making his case.

As there were no actual charges under Roman law from which Paul needed to defend himself, he instead used to public forum to disclose his personal testimony. Paul conscientiously demonstrated that his Christian faith did not arise in a vacuum, but was a logical and natural result of his commitment to Judaism. Beginning with his biographical background, Paul noted that whether referencing his childhood in Tarsus or his later years in Jerusalem, his life had always been an open book. Paul had been no mere "blip" within the Jewish nation, but a rather prominent member. In fact, there were many individuals who could testify to Paul's strict adherence to the rigorous lifestyle and scrupulous beliefs of the Pharisees. One particular doctrine held by every Pharisee and by which every Pharisee was known, was that of resurrection. Yet again, Paul brought his current plight back to the essential issue of the Christian faith. Paul referred to the resurrection as the universal (with the exception of the sourpuss Sadducees) Jewish hope in the promise God had made to their ancestors; a promise to which Israel's twelve tribes, through their faithful service to their Creator, hoped someday to attain. Therefore, in light of this commonly held doctrine of future resurrection, it should not seem remarkable to anyone if God had already chosen to raise someone from the dead.

Under this criterion, God's resurrection of the Messiah should be considered the most Jewish of all beliefs!

Of interest in Paul's presentation is his casual mention of the twelve tribes of Israel. This passage, along with others in the New Testament (Matt. 19:28; Luke 22:30; James 1:1; Rev 21:12) should put to rest the myth of the so-called "ten lost tribes of Israel." Despite the Assyrian destruction of the northern kingdom in 722 BC and subsequent dispersion of a majority of Israel's population, neither tribal identity nor tribal integrity had been compromised for any of Israel's tribes. In the first century, the Jewish nation was still comprised of an identifiable twelve tribes.

What's a Nice Jewish Boy Doing in a Place Like This? (26:9–23)

Of course, no one could understand Jewish objections to Jesus' resurrection better than could Paul himself. He admitted how, as a devout Pharisee, he had felt compelled by duty to vigorously oppose the followers of Jesus of Nazareth. Therefore, backed by the authority of the high priest and the twenty-four chief priests, he had launched his own personal "holy war" against the Jewish believers in Jesus. Although not a member of the Sanhedrin, as the arch-persecutor of Christians, Paul had not only beaten and imprisoned many of their number, but had also in some cases consented to their execution. In addition, Paul admitted to attempts at compelling the believers to blaspheme. This admission meant that Paul either strove to get them to renounce Jesus in order to avoid punishment, or to get them to commit a capital offense to justify their execution. In his fury, Paul had traveled from synagogue to synagogue, energetically hunting the believers down. The boundaries of Jerusalem and Judea were too small to contain Paul's hatred, and he compiled a target list of foreign cities to which the believers had fled.

It was while Paul was en route to the first of those cities, Damascus, that he came face to face with the risen Messiah. This is the third and final time within the Acts narrative (Acts 9:1–19; 22:6–16; 26:12–18) that Paul's Damascus road encounter with Jesus and his subsequent commission is relayed. Its triple inclusion reveals how critical Luke believed this event to be in the scope of his narrative argument. Suiting his testimony to his audience, Paul excluded reference to his own blindness and healing as well as to Ananias' vital role in the events. Concentrating on the elements demonstrating the Messiah's resurrection, Paul related how he and his "posse" had been surrounded by the blinding light of the Shekinah glory and fell to the ground. Paul does reveal, however, a new conversational detail not previously disclosed by Luke in either of the preceding accounts. After hearing a Hebrew speaking voice twice calling his name, "Saul, Saul," and being accused by the voice of persecution, Paul adds that the voice admonished him with the phrase, "It is hard for you to kick against the goads' (Acts 26:14). According to Longenecker, this was a well-known Greek idiom for opposition to deity.[7] In opposing the church, Paul had been opposing the very will of God Himself. Furthermore, because of the supernatural union that exists through the Spirit between Jesus and his people, it was as if Paul had been persecuting Jesus personally.

Paul concluded the testimony of his Damascus road experience with a summary statement of the commission he had received, both from Jesus directly and later through Ananias, relaying God's promise of supernatural deliverance from the machinations of those who would seek his life, whether Jews or Gentiles, and Paul's appointment to bear witness of the Messiah. The results of his apostolic witness would be enlightening with spiritual light those immersed in spiritual darkness; in other words, turning them from submission to Satan's power to God's power in order to receive divine forgiveness of sins and an eternal inheritance from God alongside all of His people. As he had done in his Pisidian Antioch sermon (Acts 13:47), Paul again identifies his commission with that of Isaiah's servant of the Lord. Having been (both spiritually and physically) blind himself, Paul had now been called to become a light to the nations to heal their blindness (Is. 42.6–7) so that God's salvation might reach to "the ends of the earth" (Is. 49:6).

As a pious Pharisee, Paul could not have been disobedient to this divine vision. Like John the Baptist (Luke 3:8), Paul called for repentance accompanied by a lifestyle in keeping with turning to God through His son. Paul's witness of the resurrected Messiah began immediately with the Jews of Damascus, continued in Jerusalem and then extended to the Gentile nations. It was specifically because of his preaching to Gentiles that the Jewish leadership had tried to kill him. With God's protection, however, their murderous efforts had failed, which is why Paul stood before the assembly that day, testifying to both the prominent and the common, the distinguished as well as the undistinguished. Everything Paul testified to was in strict accord with the ancient promises of Moses and the prophets contained in Hebrew Scripture of how the Messiah would suffer and die and as the first fruits of the resurrection (1 Cor. 15:23) would spiritually enlighten Jews and Gentiles alike. One need not look further than Isaiah's description of the suffering servant of God to locate the Scriptural origins of Paul's assertion (Is. 52:13—53:12).

Royal Reaction (26:24–32)

All this supernatural mumbo-jumbo proved too much for Festus. Unable to endure one more moment of Paul's whimsical babble, the procurator interrupted the presentation by loudly declaring that Paul's advanced education in the Hebrew Scriptures had made him some kind of maniac. To this practical Roman administrator, Paul's endurance of prison, multiple trials and murder attempts over such a non-issue seemed insane. Paul respectfully disagreed with his "host," assuring Festus of the truth and gravity of the gospel. In fact, Paul implied that even if his arguments had been over the head of the procurator, they were certainly grasped by King Agrippa. Every one of the events Paul had related were a matter of public knowledge. Jesus had been a well-known figure in Israel, and the Christian movement, replete with Judean adherents, was already close to three decades old. Jesus' corpse had never been produced, his empty grave never adequately accounted for and the meteoric rise of the church never explained aside from the resurrection.

Going on the offensive for once, Paul asked Agrippa whether he believed the prophecies of Scripture. Before the king could open his mouth in reply, Paul had already answered for him in the affirmative. It was unthinkable for such a renowned expert in Judaism, the warden of the temple and its high priesthood, not to take seriously the Hebrew prophets. Moreover, for Paul, the messianic prophecies spoke so clearly of Jesus that to believe them would invariably lead to the recognition of Jesus as their fulfillment.

Whatever Agrippa's private opinion, the king deftly sidestepped Paul's implication, ironically wondering aloud whether Paul thought that he could make Agrippa a Christian in such a short amount of time. Paul's earnest response was that it was his prayer that whether in a brief or lengthy amount of time, the king and all assembled that day to hear him would become just as he was, with the exception of the shackles dangling from his wrists, adding irony of his own.

With that exchange, the hearing concluded. Later that day, in private consultation, Festus and Agrippa agreed that Paul was completely innocent of any crime under Roman law. In fact, Agrippa concluded, if only Paul had not appealed to Caesar, he could have been a free man.

Conclusion

As Jesus had faced both Roman prefect, Pilate, and Jewish king, Herod Antipas (Luke 23:8–12), so too, Paul faced a Roman procurator, Festus, as well as a Jewish king, Herod Antipas' great-nephew, Herod Agrippa II. This intriguing parallel serves to demonstrate Paul's faithful following in the footsteps of his Lord, no matter where they led. However, whereas Jesus' encounter with the authorities led to his crucifixion, Paul's encounters will carry him "to the ends of the earth." Despite the opposition and accusations of the Jewish leadership, Luke's continued emphasis throughout this section has been Paul's innocence in the eyes of Roman government. Nonetheless, it was Paul's destiny to go to Rome. Jumping out of the frying pan and into the fire, Paul will exchange his chances with the Judean procurator, Festus, for the infamous emperor of Rome, Nero.

Study Questions:

1. Provide evidence from this section that Christians were still considered to be Jewish.

2. Why was Paul imprisoned in Caesarea for two years?

3. Compare and contrast Felix, Festus and Agrippa II.

4. Compare and contrast Paul's three defenses in this section.

5. Why did Festus enlist Agrippa's consultation?

CHAPTER 18

Apostolic Adventures En Route to Rome
Acts 27:1-28:10

Preview:
Very late in the summer of AD 59, Festus gave the order for Paul to be transported from Caesarea to Rome. The description of this voyage contains a remarkable amount of detail and is indisputably the result of Luke's eyewitness testimony. In Acts 27:1, Luke, who had been in Judea throughout Paul's imprisonment (most likely hard at work constructing his gospel and the first half of Acts), now reinserts himself into the narrative. This is the lengthiest of Acts' four "we" sections (Acts 16:10–17; 20:5–15; 21:1–18; 27:1—28:16).

Adventure at Sea (27:1-44)

Setting Sail (27:1-8)

Overseeing Paul's transfer to Rome was Julius, one of the ten centurions assigned to the Augustan cohort. Luke provides no additional information concerning this centurion other than the exceptional courtesy and deference he exhibited to Paul throughout the journey (Acts 27:3, 43). Although Julius and his soldiers were also responsible for the transfer of several other prisoners, Paul's status as a Roman who had appealed to Caesar would have made him particularly notable. In addition to Luke, also traveling with Paul was Aristarchus, Paul's Thessalonian friend who had accompanied him to Judea (Acts 19:29; 20:4; Col. 4:10; Philem. 24).

Apparently unable to locate a ship sizable enough to travel across the open Mediterranean Sea, Julius and his party embarked from the harbor of Caesarea aboard a small ship that would travel along the coast of Asia Minor. By the second day of their voyage, they had covered seventy miles, reaching Sidon, just north of Israel. During this stopover, the centurion graciously allowed Paul, undoubtedly chained to a soldier, to visit the believers in Sidon.

Following their departure from Sidon, the weather began to gradually increase the voyage's level of difficulty. Owing to the force of the northwestern wind blowing from the same direction as the ship was headed, the leg from Sidon to Myra in Asia Minor was particularly protracted. Unable to sail directly across the open sea, the ship was compelled to navigate between the island of Cyprus and the sheltering land mass of Asia Minor. Myra was the main midway port of call for grain ships traveling between Egypt, the breadbasket of Rome, and Italy. In Myra, Julius transferred his party to one of these larger grain cargo ships. In addition to holding its vast cargo, this ship was large enough to accommodate a combined complement of two hundred seventy-six crew and passengers (Acts 27:37).

Continuing their voyage in a larger ship, however, did not make the sea passage any less arduous. With great difficulty, they battled the contrary wind as they sailed northwest along the Asia Minor coastline the one hundred forty miles from Myra almost to Cnidus, at the extreme southwest corner of Asia Minor. Having come to the end of Asia Minor and, therefore, running out of shelter from the northwestern wind, the ship was incapable of making it safely to the port of Cnidus. The ship consequently diverted from its westward course and, seeking an alternative buffer from the wind, headed south to sail underneath the island of Crete, placing another land mass between itself and the wind. Finally, they were able to take shelter at the harbor of Fair Havens, midway along the southern coast of Crete. There they disembarked, determining to wait for the wind to subside before continuing their voyage

Storm (27:9–26)

They spent a considerable amount of time in Fair Havens waiting for more favorable weather. However, the longer they waited, the more dangerous their eventual voyage became. Sailing the Mediterranean Sea was known to be particularly hazardous from September 14 through November 11; no ships sailed at all from November 12 through February 7. It was clear that it was no longer possible to make Italy before the seas closed, so the remaining question was whether Fair Havens was a secure enough harbor in which to spend the winter. Luke records that while they were harboring in Fair Havens, *Yom Kippur*, the Day of Atonement ("the Fast," *tēn nēsteian*) had already come and gone.

In AD 59, *Yom Kippur* fell on October 5. This places the travelers solidly within the dangerous sailing season.

The Day of Atonement is the holiest date on the Hebrew calendar, the one day of the year when the High Priest was allowed to enter into the innermost sanctum of the Temple, the Holy of Holies, to make atonement for sins not confessed by the nation or forgiven by God throughout the previous year. Unlike Passover, Pentecost and Tabernacles, the Day of Atonement was not one of the great pilgrimage festivals when every male was commanded to worship in Jerusalem. Rather, the Day of Atonement was commemorated with a solemn fast by Jews wherever they were. Christians believe that Jesus, through his death and resurrection, has become our atonement in his dual identity as both ultimate high priest and perfect sacrifice.

Paul, voicing opinion and not divine revelation, advised not to embark under such hazardous conditions. Based upon his previous experience of three separate shipwrecks (2 Cor. 11:25) and obviously desiring to avoid shipwreck number four, Paul warned of the possible loss of cargo, ship and lives. However, the centurion took the advice of the captain and pilot of the ship who, concerned about the inadequacy of the Fair Havens harbor to shelter their ship through winter, decided to navigate westward another forty miles to the more secure harbor of Phoenix on the southwestern corner of the island.

A favorable alteration in the wind seemed to confirm their decision to press forward. Hugging the southern coast of Crete, they embarked on what they optimistically hoped would be a mere day's journey. Unfortunately, without warning, the gentle wind was suddenly displaced by a draft sweeping down the island from the northeast, a typhoon so infamous and notoriously violent that it possessed the nautical designation, *Euraquilo* "east/north wind." Caught in this tempest, the ship was thrown off-course and was borne along by the wind twenty-five miles southwest to the island of Clauda. At this point, the crew was able to regain enough control of the ship to position themselves in a buffer zone south of the island. Not knowing how long this window of opportunity would last, the crew took the opportunity to secure the ship's hull with rope and, through exerting great effort, hoisted up the waterlogged lifeboat, which had been dragging behind the ship, out of the sea. In addition, fearful of being driven so far south that they would run aground on the sandbars of the Syrtis off the African coast, they slowed their momentum by lowering the sea anchor.

Over the next three days, still violently tossed around by the tempest, the crew was forced to lighten the ship by jettisoning their cargo and the ship's tackle. However, these actions did nothing to alleviate the desperation of their situation. After being battered by the storm for a full two weeks and powerless in the unremitting darkness to navigate by the stars or even to determine their position, all but one of the two hundred seventy-six voyagers began to abandon all hope of survival.

Paul, the sole remaining hope bearer, delivered a message of comfort to his desperate shipmates. Although unable to resist saying, "I told you so," by reminding them of his warning not to leave Fair Havens, Paul encouraged them with a supernatural revelation he had received from an angel on the previous evening. To ensure that the idolaters whom he addressed recognized the source of the supernatural revelation, the apostle identified the angel who had appeared to him as representing the specific God to whom Paul belonged, whom he served and in whom he believed (Acts 27:23, 25). They were to take courage, for although the storm would claim the ship, not one life would be lost. The ship would run aground on an unknown island. Paul's shipmates were being graciously preserved through God allowing them to ride the coattails of His plan for the apostle. Paul was under supernatural protection, at least until he fulfilled his commission to stand trial before Caesar.

Shipwreck (27:27–44)

Around midnight that same evening, as they continued to be blown across the Sea of Adria (the central portion of the Mediterranean between Greece, Rome and north Africa) the crew heard the ominous sound of land approaching. They immediately took two soundings to determine the depth of the water in which they sailed. The first reading indicated a depth of one hundred twenty feet and a second warned of a current sea depth of merely ninety feet. Fearing, in the darkness, that they would soon be wrecked upon the inevitably approaching rocks, the crew dropped four anchors from the rear of the ship to halt their momentum until the penetration of daylight allowed them to get their bearings.

Believing that to stay aboard ship was suicidal, a faction of sailors plotted to escape in the lifeboat. Although pretending to lay out anchors from the front of the ship, the sailors were actually lowering the ship's dinghy into the sea. However, their duplicitous action did not escape the eagle-eyed apostle's notice, and Paul hastily alerted the centurion of the sailor's scheme, telling Julius that it was necessary for all hands to remain on board if everyone's' life was to be preserved. The situation was too grave for Julius to risk once again disregarding his prisoner's sage advice. He ordered his soldiers to cut away the lifeboat, letting their only ostensible avenue of escape from the ship crash into the sea.

Paul then exhorted his shipmates to keep up their strength by taking food. For two weeks, the unrelenting force of the storm, likely combined with accompanying perpetual nausea, had impeded opportunities for the consumption of food. Paul, again repeating the divine promise that everyone aboard would be preserved, also emphasized that they would all need nourishment for the final ordeal to come. Grabbing a loaf of bread, Paul loudly and publicly gave thanks to God for His provision by reciting the *b'rakhah*, the traditional blessing made by Jews before eating bread, "Blessed are you, O Lord, our God, king of the universe, who brings forth bread from the earth. Amen." As is Jewish custom subsequent to this blessing, Paul broke off a hunk from the loaf and took a bite. Paul's example encouraged his two hundred seventy-six shipmates to follow his advice.

When everyone had eaten sufficiently, they threw out the remainder of their wheat cargo into the sea to lighten the ship. This would cause the ship to float higher up in the water, allowing them to get as close as possible to land before being run aground. When daylight came, an unfamiliar land mass appeared. No one could realize that they had been driven four hundred seventy-six miles off course to Malta, sixty miles south of Sicily, a modest island measuring eighteen miles long by eight miles wide. Distinguishing both bay and beach in the distance, they decided to sacrifice the ship by running it directly into the bay, getting as close to the beach as possible before the ship was run aground. To gain the necessary speed, they disconnected the ship's anchors, loosened the rudder controls and hoisted up their sail to the wind.

As the ship gathered momentum on its headlong dash toward the beach, however, it prematurely ran aground on a sandbar. With the front of the ship stuck fast in the mud and clay, the rear of the ship began to disintegrate in the pounding force of the waves. With the ship breaking apart beneath them, the Roman soldiers, accountable with their own lives for their prisoners, planned to prevent their charges' escape by means of a makeshift mass execution.

However, Julius, wanting to save Paul's life, quashed their plan, taking the risk that any escapees could be rounded up later. The centurion commanded everyone who could swim to abandon ship and make for the beach. Those who could not swim were to make their way to land by floating on wooden planks or whatever pieces of wreckage to which they could latch themselves. The power of Paul's God was consequently manifest when all two hundred seventy-six shipwreck victims arrived safely on shore.

Adventure on Land (28:1–10)

When the survivors staggered out of the pounding surf and onto the beach, they were greeted by a welcoming party of hospitable Maltese. Although in Acts 28:1, Luke refers to the Maltese as *hoi barbaroi*, "barbarians," he did not mean to imply that they were primitive, unsophisticated natives. "Barbarian" was simply a term used by Greeks and Romans to denote a foreigner who spoke neither Greek nor Latin. The Maltese's native tongue was a variation of Phoenician. While few of the shipwrecked survivors may have been facile in Phoenician, their soggy, exhausted and near hypothermic state would have spoken for itself. For their part, the Maltese communicated with the universal language of hospitality, receiving their sodden guests with a welcoming bonfire on the beach.

Following such a taxing ordeal, it might be expected that a man of Paul's age (fifty-four) might have collapsed into a spent puddle on the sand. However, Luke describes Paul doing his part to keep the fire going. Having collected a bundle of sticks to throw on the blaze, Paul had inadvertently also gathered up a viper, mistaken for a stick because it was stiff from the cold. Once added to the fire, however, the viper, in a panic, sprung to life and latched onto the apostle's hand.

The Maltese, observing Paul standing there with a viper dangling by its fangs from his hand, assumed that he was a murderer with whom the goddess *Justice* (*he dike*) had finally caught up. Although this man had somehow cheated death by surviving the sea, he was now receiving his just desserts for his crimes. The Maltese kept their eyes on Paul, waiting for him to keel over. Paul casually shook the viper off into the fire and went about his business. The Maltese's opinion of Paul soon changed when with great astonishment they observed that, contrary to their expectations, not only was Paul still breathing, but he also seemed completely unaffected by the poison. Seeing that not even Paul's hand so much as swelled up or turned a different color, they concluded that he was a god. Although this humorous episode is reminiscent of the reaction of the Lystrans to Paul (Acts 14:11–19), there is no indication that the Maltese attempted to worship the apostle.

However, their estimation of Paul's supernatural stature was probably what led to the subsequent event described by Luke, for it is difficult to otherwise explain how Paul, a Roman prisoner, came to be welcomed into the home of Publius, the governor of Malta (*prōtō tēs nēsou*, "first man of the island"). Paul and his friends Luke and Aristarchus were invited as Publius' guests on his estate for three days. Publius' father was suffering from *Malta fever*, an illness, similar to malaria, characterized by recurrent fever and dysentery, caused by a microbe in the milk of indigenous goats.[1] Paying a visit to the sickbed of Publius' father, Paul prayed, laid hands on him and instantaneously healed him of his debilitating illness. Once word of this miracle circulated around the island, Paul's social calendar rapidly filled with a steady stream of miracle seekers. Luke records that Paul healed everyone who came to him over their three-month residence on Malta. While Luke curiously does not describe the evangelistic result of all this extraordinary activity, he does portray the continued generosity of the Maltese as well as the high level of esteem in which they held Paul and his companions throughout their stay.

As throughout Acts, Luke's description in Acts 28:8–9 of miraculous healing is yet again depicted as being performed only by means of an apostle. While Paul's companions, Aristarchus and Luke were both believers, neither of them was God's chosen instrument of healing (although certainly Luke's medical knowledge must have proven useful in substantiating the healings). This supernatural activity powerfully authenticated Paul's message of salvation to the Maltese.

Conclusion

This episode provides a measure of narrative high adventure, particularly after the lengthy account of Paul's sedentary two-year prison term. However, Luke's purpose in detailing these events was not to "shake things up a bit," but to emphasize God's faithfulness in carrying out his promise to conduct Paul safely to Rome. Although Paul faced seemingly insurmountable obstacles that place him in peril of fulfilling his destiny, God's purpose for the apostle could not be frustrated. Whether facing shipwreck, a makeshift execution attempt or a poisonous snakebite, Paul overcame all life threatening dangers. The reader is left in no doubt that Paul will stand trial before the emperor of Rome.

Study Questions:

1. Compare and contrast the behavior of Paul, Julius, the soldiers and the crew throughout the voyage.

2. Explain why Paul's voyage to Rome ended in disaster.

3. Examine a map of the Mediterranean Sea and trace the course of this disastrous voyage.

CHAPTER 19

To the Ends of the Earth
Acts 28:11–31

Preview:
In this final section, Luke charts his hero's voyage to Italy and climactic arrival in Rome. With the recounting of Paul's presence and ministry in the capital of the Roman Empire, the purposes of Luke's narrative have been achieved and the book can conclude on a triumphal note. This brief section will cover two years, from February, AD 60 through early AD 62.

Arrival at Rome (28:11–16)

With the arrival of winter, sea navigation was impermissible. The shipwreck survivors had no choice but to remain on Malta for the next three months, November through January. With the arrival of weather that once again permitted safe seafaring navigation in the second week of February, AD 60, the centurion, Julius, for the third time booked passage for himself, his soldiers and their prisoners on a ship bound for Rome. As was their second, ill-fated ship, this too was an Alexandrian grain ship, but this time, Julius went an "extra measure" to assure their safe voyage. Luke ironically notes that the figurehead on the ship that Julius had engaged was a carved representation of Castor and Pollux, twin sons of Zeus and patron gods of sailors.

Sailing from the island of Malta, the ship sailed north eighty miles to the main port of Sicily, Syracuse. Remaining in port for the next three days, either loading/unloading cargo or, more likely, awaiting calmer weather, the ship then sailed another eighty miles due north to the port of Rhegium on the "toe" of Italy. In Rhegium, they were forced to wait one day for a favorable wind strong enough to allow them passage through the treacherous straights between Sicily and Italy's toe and then up to the western coast of Italy. Sailing for two days and one hundred eighty miles on this final leg of their voyage, the ship put in at its final destination, southern Italy's main seaport, Puteoli, nestled in the Bay of Naples.

Disembarking from their ship, Julius, who apparently had some business to attend to, allowed Paul, with Luke and Aristarchus, to enjoy the hospitality of the church in Puteoli for a full week, although under the supervision of a Roman guard. With the conclusion of the stopover in Puteoli, the final leg of Paul's journey began, a one hundred forty mile trek to Rome. Julius, his soldiers and their prisoners, along with Paul's two friends, set out along the Appian Way, the straightest and most venerable of Roman roads.

The church in Puteoli had earlier sent word to the Roman believers that the apostle Paul was bound for Rome. Enthusiastic representatives from the Roman church came out to meet Paul at two resting points along the Appian Way, the first at the Market of Appius, forty-three miles southeast of Rome, and the second at the Three Inns, another ten miles further along the road. Perhaps Paul's old friends Aquila and Priscilla were among the welcoming party. The personal escort into Rome provided Paul by these Roman believers caused him to both thank God and to take courage for what lay ahead.

In Acts 28:16 Paul finally entered Rome, at last fulfilling his long-term desire to visit the capital of the Roman empire (Rom. 15:22–24, 28–29). Rather than being sent to prison, Paul received permission to live in his own rented quarters, albeit with a liberty somewhat curtailed by the continuous turnover every four hours of Roman guards chained to his wrist.

Rome. Capital of the vast Roman Empire, the so-called "eternal city" was, in the first century AD, an incomparable cornucopia of brilliant marble monuments, polished columns, dazzling temples, imposing palaces, panoramic parkland and extravagant stadiums. Not only was the architecture of Rome unique; the population was an exceptional blend of wealthy aristocracy, middle class, the poor and a population of slaves that comprised at least half the city's population of over two million residents. Within this population was a substantial Jewish community of at least forty thousand, large enough to necessitate several dozen synagogues.

The Witness in Rome (Acts 28:17–29)

To the Jew First (Acts 28:17–24)

Under "house arrest" and therefore unable to leave his apartment, Paul was, however, allowed to receive visitors. Three days after his arrival in Rome, being unable to visit the synagogue, he invited the leaders of the synagogue to pay him a house call, in accord with his longstanding theological conviction of witnessing to the Jews prior to approaching the Gentiles (Acts 13:46; Rom. 1:16).

Warmly addressing the assembly of Jewish community leaders as his brothers, Paul summarized the events that led to his presence in Rome as a prisoner. He explained to them that although he was innocent of any violation of Torah or offense against Israel, he nonetheless was consigned by Jerusalem's leadership into the custody of the Romans. Although they conducted a meticulous investigation, the Romans could not attribute any punishable crime to Paul. The Roman authorities were inclined to have released Paul, but did not act on that inclination in response to the intimidation of the Jewish leadership. His hand being thus forced, Paul appealed to Caesar in self-defense. He now awaited trial before the highest court in the empire. Paul was particularly diligent to assuage the Roman Jewish leadership's concern that he might now bring countercharges against the Jewish community in Rome or against the Jerusalem leadership. The apostle emphasized his continued identification with the Jewish people. Israel is designated by Paul as "my nation" and the Jewish people continue to be his people (Acts 28:19).

Flamboyantly indicating his unwieldy bracelet as well as the Roman guard to whom he was linked, Paul concluded with his familiar claim that his situation was ultimately due to his belief in *tēs elpidos tou Israēl*, "the hope of Israel" (Acts 28:20). For Paul, the "hope of Israel" is the resurrection (Acts 23:6; 24:15; 26:6–7), specifically the resurrection of Jesus, who as the Messiah and the first fruits of resurrection personifies God's resurrection power and incarnates every messianic promise within the Hebrew Scriptures.

Surprisingly, the Roman Jewish leadership responded that they had received no communication or instruction about Paul from the Jerusalem leadership, either in person or by letter. Furthermore, they expressed personal interest in learning more about Paul's side of the story. To say that Christianity was infamous within the Roman Jewish community would be gross understatement. It was, after all, due to riots over the issue of Jesus Christ (called "*Chrestus*" by Suetonius[1]) that the Jewish community had been expelled from the city in AD 50 (Acts 18:2). The Jewish community had only recently been allowed to return, in AD 54, six years prior to Paul's arrival in Rome. It would be beneficial for the Jewish leadership to be addressed directly by one of the most prominent leaders of the Nazarene sect of Judaism.

An appointment was made with Paul, and on the scheduled date the Roman Jewish community came to hear him in great numbers. In order to accommodate this influx of inquirers, Paul's apartment must either have consisted of one large room or else he led them outside his quarters to some sort of courtyard. Whether in or out of doors, Paul's daylong seminar on the gospel was filled to capacity. From morning until evening, Paul marched his guests through the messianic matrix of Hebrew prophecy, using Moses and the Prophets to testify and persuade them concerning Jesus' identity.

During this passionate debate, Paul also was forced to answer one of the most basic of Jewish objections to Jesus being Messiah, that of the delay of the promised messianic kingdom. To this day, Jews continue to stumble over the concept of a messianic king with no accompanying kingdom. Nonetheless, the consistent teaching of the New Testament is that the kingdom of God is a future certainty and will be inaugurated upon Christ's return (Matt. 5:20; 6:10; 7:21; 8:11; 26:29; Mark 14:25; 15:43; Luke 1:33; 11:2; 13:28–29; 14:15; 19:11; 21:31; 22:16–18, 29–30; 23:42, 51; Acts 1:3–6; 14:22; James 2:5; Rev 11:15; 12:10). In the book of Acts, Luke portrays teaching on the kingdom as being presented alternately to the church as well as Jewish and Samaritan unbelievers. Interestingly, Luke never cites anyone teaching unbelieving Gentiles about the kingdom, most likely because among non-Christians, only Jews and Samaritans had a developed context for understanding the concept of a messianic kingdom.

And Also to the Gentile (Acts 28:25–31)

The result of Paul's effort was that some Jews believed his apostolic witness. Regrettably, the majority thoroughly rejected the gospel. There is an old adage that where there are two Jews there are three opinions, and the Jewish community was likewise greatly divided over Paul and his highly controversial message. When Paul realized that his witness had penetrated as deeply as it was going to that evening, he neatly terminated the hubbub and debate with a dramatic announcement.

As previously done in numerous examples strewn throughout the Acts narrative, although most dramatically and explicitly at Pisidian Antioch (Acts 13:46) and Corinth (Acts 18:6), Paul publicly announced the discharge of his duty in witnessing to the local Jewish community and his intent to focus his future attention on Gentile evangelism. To this end, Paul quoted Isaiah 6:9–10. Noting both the Holy Spirit and Isaiah's dual authorship of this scripture, Paul applied this prophecy of Israel's obtuseness and blindness in recognizing God's plan to the Roman Jews. Three decades earlier, Jesus had made the same application of this passage to his unresponsive audience (Matt 13:14–15; Luke 8:10). Just as Luke commenced his record of Jesus ministry with a quotation drawn from the prophet Isaiah (Is. 61:1–2; Luke 4:17–19), Luke likewise concludes his record of the apostle of Jesus with another passage from the same prophet.

Since the Jewish community of Rome had been given opportunity to understand and respond to the gospel, Paul now announced his freedom to witness to the Gentiles. This statement is often grossly mischaracterized as a final denunciation and repudiation of Jews everywhere and at all times for having rejected the gospel. However, this dismal interpretation could not be further from the truth. Indeed, this was not even a final denunciation or repudiation of the Roman Jews. Paul's announcement was nothing more than what we have seen Paul do throughout his ministry within every community: preach first to the Jews and, upon the Jewish majority's rejection of the gospel, carry his witness to the Gentiles.

It was decidedly not that the totality of the Roman Jewish community had rejected the gospel; indeed, a remnant of Paul's company that day had believed the gospel. The enthusiastic response of the Jewish remnant to the Messiah, God's sole provision for salvation, was the pattern repeated throughout the entirety of Paul's ministry. Paul deals at length with the theological phenomenon of a continued faithful Jewish remnant in Romans 9–11, in which he instructs that the spiritual blindness to Jesus experienced by the vast majority of Jews has not taken God by surprise. Rather, Jewish rejection of the gospel is an opportunity to invite Gentiles to respond to God's grace. Furthermore, it will be the Gentile response to the gospel that will eventually provoke the Jews to jealousy and allow them at last to perceive their Messiah with clarity (Rom. 11:1–11). God is far from through with the Jews! Part of Paul's motivation in faithfully executing his commission to the Gentiles was the conviction that his successful Gentile witness would ultimately secure greater Jewish salvation (Rom.11:12–14).

One of the most frequently asked questions concerning Jewish evangelism is why such a small percentage of Jews have responded to the gospel. The companion question that should always be immediately asked is why such a small percentage of Gentiles have responded to the gospel. The bottom line is not that so many more Gentiles than Jews receive Jesus; it is that there are so many more Gentiles than Jews, period. It is probably not inaccurate to estimate that, solely on a percentage basis, the number of Jewish and Gentile Christians achieves rough parity. It seems that God prefers to work primarily with remnants, both of Jews and Gentiles.

(Acts 28:29 is not present in the most reliable manuscripts and is most likely a later editorial insertion made by someone other than Luke.)

In the final two verses of Acts, Luke concludes his epic narrative with a summary of Paul's ministry in Rome. Far from idle during the two years of his housebound imprisonment, from March 60 through the first portion of AD 62, the apostle entertained a steady stream of guests, boldly preaching about the kingdom of God and teaching about the Messiah Jesus, the hope of Israel and Lord of all. Remarkably, Paul's evangelistic ministry was unhindered by Roman interference. In fact, he remarked in one of his epistles how the entire imperial guard, through their intimate proximity to the apostle, chained to him as they were in a succession of rotating four-hour shifts, had been rapidly and thoroughly familiarized with the details of the gospel (Phil.1:12–13).

Also during this time, Paul composed his letters to the churches of Ephesus, Philippians and Colossae, and also dropped a personal note to a Colossian believer, Philemon. These letters reflect his optimistic expectation of impending acquittal (Phil 1:19, 25–26; Philem. 22) and express his plans to initiate a "fourth missionary journey" that would carry the apostle back to Macedonia (Phil. 2:24), Colossae (Philem. 22), and Ephesus (1 Tim. 3:14).

While on the surface it appears that Luke has left Theophilus and other readers hanging by not fully concluding Paul's life story, it must be remembered that if Acts was indeed composed in AD 62–63, Paul's life would not conclude for another five years or so! Furthermore, Luke's purpose in writing Acts was not solely that of a biographical account. The eventual outcome of Paul's trial before Caesar is not the climax of Acts; rather, it is Paul's bravura arrival in Rome to carry out his divine mandate. In addition, Luke successfully traced the triumphal, three decade long geographic advance of the gospel as it extended from Jerusalem to Judea, to Samaria and on through to the ends of the earth.

Furthermore, Luke conclusively established that Christianity was primarily a religious movement, not a political one, with a profound connection to Israel and the Jewish nation. Although Jewish opposition to Christianity grew to a crescendo in the narrative, the official Roman response had constantly been fairly benign. Finally, Luke traced the definitive broadening of God's salvation through the Messiah to now include both Jews and Gentiles. Neither group has replaced or excluded the other in God's program. Both now possess equality of access to God and impartiality in status before him through the simple action of placing their faith in His Messiah.

Conclusion

With the conclusion of Acts, our awareness of subsequent church history becomes much more tenuous. Nonetheless, by combining accepted church tradition with certain events mentioned by Paul in his letters that cannot be fit into the chronology of Acts, we can design a reasonable outline of the remainder of the apostle's life. Upon receiving back his liberty in AD 62, Paul embarked on his fourth journey. It had long been his desire to reach Spain (Rom.15:23-29), which represented the western limits of the empire, and there is a tradition which confirms the apostle's ministry there.[2] Following his visit to Spain, Paul's travels can be traced through the details strewn throughout his final letters. He mentions ministry in Crete (Titus 1:5), Nicopolis (Titus 3:12), and a return to the familiar territories of Troas (2 Tim. 4:13), Corinth (2 Tim. 4:20) and Miletus, where Paul left his sick friend, Trophemus (2 Tim. 4:20). Presumably, Paul also returned. as planned in his epistles, to Macedonia (Phil. 2:24), Colossae (Philem. 22), and Ephesus (1 Tim. 3:14).

In Paul's absence from Rome, the climate for Christians had dramatically changed. The tolerance exhibited by Roman officials throughout the Acts narrative was eliminated and severe persecution, instigated by Nero himself, had broken out against Roman Christians from AD 64. In late AD 67 or early AD 68, Paul returned to Rome, where he was rearrested and subjected to a more rigorous imprisonment and trial than he had previously experienced. The harsh condition of his second Roman imprisonment is documented in his second letter to Timothy (2 Tim 2:9). Unlike his earlier experience of house arrest, Paul was imprisoned, and the optimism which had accompanied his earlier captivity had been replaced with a realistic expectation of impending execution (2 Tim 4:6-8). Church tradition records that Paul was brought to trial and convicted. In early AD 68, he was beheaded outside of Rome on the Ostian Way.[3]

In AD 70, four decades after Jesus' crucifixion, the divine judgment that had been impending throughout Acts finally fell upon Israel. God removed from the Jews their Temple and their land. In the twentieth century, God began orchestrating the return of the Jewish people to the land of Israel and in 1967 once again granted them control of Jerusalem, their holy city. Yet today, in our generation, when the land of Israel, including the holy city of Jerusalem, is once again in Jewish hands, the Jewish people are experiencing the greatest imaginable apostasy. In a time and an era when one would expect great sweeping revival as a result of the realization of Judaism's 1900 year old national and religious aspirations, we are instead witnessing the wholesale abandonment of religious commitment, spiritual apathy and rebellion on a near suicidal level. Among contemporary Jews, belief in God is purely optional, and obedience to Him is déclassé, even intolerable. The latest surveys reveal that fifty percent of ethnic Jews in America not only do not identify with the Jewish religion, they actually repudiate it. Something is desperately wrong. Absent the Messiah, the center of Judaism will not hold and is imploding from within.

The opportunity that God is presenting to His church is abundantly clear to all who have eyes to see and ears to hear. It took an astonishing seven years after the ascension of Jesus before the first Gentile, Cornelius the centurion, was saved in AD 40. It would be almost a decade after that epochal event, AD 49/50, before Gentiles were universally accepted as full members within the church. However, by that time, the vast majority of the Jewish believers had been convinced of the necessity of Gentile evangelism. Acts documents how the Jewish church made Gentile evangelism their passionate priority, resulting in the church's taking the Roman Empire by storm.

How times have changed. This is a moment in history when the Jewish people are more receptive to the gospel than they have been at any time since the first century. Yet the evangelism of the Jewish people is rarely an emphasis in the contemporary church. Furthermore, churches are largely devoid of the powerful Jewish context that proved so characteristic of the church that Luke described in Acts. Today's church, overwhelmingly composed of Gentiles, now possesses the opportunity to turn full-circle and return the favor shown Gentiles by the earliest Christians by making Jewish evangelism their passionate priority. When this paradigm shift occurs, and the church once again ardently seeks out the faithful Jewish remnant, spoken of by Paul, in order to successfully provoke them to jealousy over their Messiah (Rom. 11:11), it would not be surprising if Christians might once again be accused of turning the world upside down.

Study Questions:

1. What encouraged Paul on the final leg of his journey into Rome?

2. For whom did Paul immediately send upon arriving in Rome and why?

3. What was the Jewish response to Paul's summary of his imprisonment?

4. What was the Jewish response to Paul's gospel presentation?

5. Why did Paul quote the Isaiah passage to his audience?

6. Explain why Acts does not teach that the gospel should no longer be presented to the Jewish people.

Speeches in Acts

As becomes obvious on first reading, a vast portion of Acts (roughly one third) is composed of various sermons and speeches, primarily those of Peter, Paul and Stephen. Indeed, based on the percentage of narrative content dedicated to the speeches, perhaps Acts should have been assigned the more precise title, *Selected Acts of a Few Apostles and a Large Assortment of their Sermons.*

It is in the record of these speeches that Luke's qualitative faithfulness to his historical sources shines through. Luke's usual method is to quote a portion of the original speech and then summarize the remainder using his own words. There is every reason to attribute the quoted text of these speeches to either some sort of written record (although the presence of an on-scene "stenographer" is unlikely) or the personal reminiscence of the speaker himself or a member of his original audience. Most of these speeches were delivered on what, admittedly, must be described as "memorable occasions," which likely burned the content into the consciousness of speaker and listeners alike. This would have been particularly true in a culture like Israel's, which so highly valued the memorization and oral transmission of the instruction of valued and beloved teachers.[1] In addition, the Holy Spirit must have been influential in the preservation and recall of these messages.

Each speaker in Acts has his own distinctive voice: Peter, Paul, Stephen and James all qualitatively read very differently from one another, even when addressing the same broad themes or making reference to identical Old Testament prophecies. Furthermore, each speech is tailor-made for the particular audience to which it is addressed. Peter addressing the Sanhedrin is not identical to his addressing Cornelius. Paul addressing the synagogue reads very differently than when addressing the Athenians.

While is doubtful that it would have been possible for Luke, decades after the fact, to accurately reflect the exact word-for-word text of every speech, it is not at all improbable that he accurately reflected the substance of each speech as originally delivered. In other words, we can be confident that what was eventually recorded was the substantial gist of what was originally spoken. It must be reiterated that Luke claimed to be a conscientious reporter of history and not a creative writer of fiction.

Reference	Speaker	Audience	Content
Acts 1:16–22	Peter	Believers	Apostolic replacement
Acts 2:14–36	Peter	Jews	Evangelism
Acts 3:12–26	Peter	Jews	Evangelism
Acts 4:8–12	Peter	Sanhedrin	Answering accusations
Acts 4:24–30	Apostles	God	Prayer
Acts 5:29–33	Peter	Sanhedrin	Answering accusations
Acts 5:35–39	Gamaliel	Sanhedrin	Cautious council
Acts 7:2–53	Stephen	Sanhedrin	Indictment of leadership
Acts 10:34–43	Peter	Gentiles	Evangelism
Acts 11:4–17	Peter	Believers	Gentile evangelism
Acts 13:16–41	Paul	Jews	Evangelism
Acts 14:15–17	Paul	Gentiles	Evangelism
Acts 15:7–11	Peter	Believers	Gentile inclusion
Acts 15:13–21	James	Believers	Gentile inclusion
Acts 17:22–31	Paul	Gentiles	Evangelism
Acts 19:25–27	Demetrius	Gentiles	Inciting a riot
Acts 19:35–40	Town Clerk	Gentiles	Calming a riot
Acts 20:18–35	Paul	Believers	Farewell speech
Acts 22:1–21	Paul	Jews	Personal Defense
Acts 24:2–8	Tertullus	Felix	Accusation
Acts 24:10–21	Paul	Felix	Personal Defense
Acts 25:6–11	Paul	Festus	Personal Defense
Acts 25:14–21	Festus	Agrippa II	Soliciting advice
Acts 26:1–29	Paul	Festus, Agrippa II	Personal Defense
Acts 27:21–26	Paul	Gentiles	Encouraging shipmates
Acts 28:17–28	Paul	Jews	Evangelism

The Five Transitional Circuits in Acts

Acts is a unique component within the NT corpus. It is only the book of Acts that recounts the historical record of the church's first three decades. The evolution from small Jewish sect to universal movement was not always smooth. The history of apostolic activity serves as a transition between the resurrection of Christ and our own post-apostolic era. Acts serves as the bridge over the following five transitional pathways, or circuits.

First, there is a *historical transition* as the repercussions of Jesus passing over the mantle of His ministry to His closest followers are traced. The book of Acts records the developing apostolic application of the ministry of Jesus.

Second, there is a *cultural and geographic transition* as the church developed from its initial Jewish milieu to its eventual expanded, international scope. It was a long road from Jerusalem to Rome, and Acts records the essential elements of that journey.

In Acts, we see the circumstances by which the door to the original Jewish community of believers is unlocked to Gentiles. We learn how spiritual equality was established and recognized between Jews and Gentiles within the broadened community of faith. In Acts, we are privy to the theological difficulties and the very practical obstacles to Gentile equality with which the Jewish community needed to wrestle and ultimately overcome.

In Acts, we also see the paradox inherent in such a specifically Jewish message being rejected by the majority of Jews, yet accepted so willingly by Gentiles who lacked any biblical background or education.

There is also an *evangelistic directional transition*, with the nation of Israel evolving from the point of terminus in finding God to its serving as the point of departure. In the Hebrew Scriptures and the gospels, a *centripetal* ministry is modeled, where Israel is the center of God's activity, and one who seeks Him must necessarily come through the Jewish people. In Acts, God's activity diffuses, and the rotation of outreach has reversed to one of *centrifugal* force, where representatives from Israel spin out into the world, bringing God to the nations. The narrative traces a steady progression outward from Jerusalem, through Israel and to the nations. This was not always a natural or willing transition, and circumstances often provided the catalyst to make this transition.

In addition, there is a ***theological transition***, which moves the church from the personal presence of Jesus to the personal and internal presence of the Holy Spirit. As Jesus directed his apostles throughout His earthly ministry, Acts records the Spirit's direction and guidance of the church. With 2000 years difference between the twenty-first century and the first century, it is sometimes difficult to appreciate just how radical it was for this movement to succeed without the physical presence of its founder and leader. There is a major difference between Jesus being among believers and the Holy Spirit dwelling within believers. Acts records the unprecedented genesis and consequence of this divergence.

In addition, Acts records the movement away from the Law as a way of life and means of relating to God, to that of grace. Following the resurrection and exaltation of Jesus, the Mosaic Law has been abrogated (Acts 15:1–29).[1] A new dispensation had dawned, characterized by the law of Christ, not Moses (1 Cor. 9:21; Gal. 6:2). Almost from the beginning, the early church was accused of preaching that, in some fashion, the Law had been nullified as a way of life (6:11–14; 18:13; 21:21).

The ramifications of Jesus' resurrection and exaltation as Messiah and the subsequent creation of a new entity, the church community, would force what had begun as a Jewish sect to necessarily make the painful break away from the Jewish religion. Acts traces the church's break with Judaism from original fracture (4:1–2) to gaping chasm (25:2–3).

While the church broke from Judaism as a system, it did not break from Israel as a nation. As the Acts narrative concludes, the church is still heavily Jewish in character. The abrogation of the Law does not imply that the early church abandoned the Law wholesale or ceased observing Jewish customs and traditions (Acts 21:20). The early church regularly attended Temple (2:46; 3:1) and synagogue (13:14), observed the Sabbath (15:21) and circumcision (16:3), and performed ceremonial vows (18:18; 21:24).

Only gradually, over its first decade and a half, did the church as a whole begin to realize that the Law of Moses was no longer operative as the standard way of life for believers. This revolutionary transition slowly came to be understood with the incorporation of Gentiles into the church (11:1–18). Gentiles did not need to become Jews prior to becoming Christians.

The Mosaic Law, however, did not cease to be recognized by the early church as Holy Scripture, God's divine revelation. It continued to be their central basis of instruction, guidance, and source of messianic prophecy. In fact, the Law's greatest purpose for the early church was in its prophetic testimony of the Messiah. It contains the promises of the Messiah, now fulfilled in Jesus (Acts 3:13, 22–23; 24:14; 26:22–23).

Finally, there is a *Christological transition*, which moves Israel and the world from an anticipated messiah to a returning messiah. With the death and resurrection of Christ, God's expectations of His people Israel and of the nations undergo a radical adjustment. Although, from the beginning, salvation has ultimately always been by grace through faith, the specific content of that faith develops over time with each new revelation. Since the dawn of the church age, following the resurrection and ascension of Jesus, salvation is solely through faith in Him. Acts records the passion of the apostles as they energetically broadcast the new requirements for the salvation of Jew and Gentile alike.

This relates to the final aspect of Acts' Christological transition, the generation of devout Jews and God-fearing Gentiles whose lives spanned the period prior to and following Christ's resurrection. Similar to the generational torch which passed during Israel's forty year wilderness sojourn, there was a transitional period of apostolic activity which roughly extended until the death of the final member of the generation which came of age prior to Christ's resurrection.

What Was Preached about Jesus in Acts

Content	Preacher	Audience	Reference
Christ	Peter	Jews	Acts 2:31
	Paul	Jews	Acts 9:22; 17:3; 18:5
	Paul	Agrippa II and Festus	Acts 26:23
	Apostles	Jews	Acts 5:42
	Philip	Samaritans	Acts 8:5
	Apollos	Jews	Acts 18:28
God's Christ, your Christ	Peter	Jews	Acts 3:18; 3:20
Jesus Christ; Christ Jesus	Peter	Jews	Acts 2:38
	Peter	Aeneas	Acts 9:34
	Peter	Cornelius	Acts 10:36,48
	Paul	A demon	Acts 16:18
	Paul	Felix	Acts 24:24
	Philip	Samaritans	Acts 8:5,12
Jesus Christ the Nazarene	Peter	Jews	Acts 3:6
	Peter	Sanhedrin	Acts 4:10
Crucified One	Peter	Jews	Acts 2:23,36
	Peter	Sanhedrin	Acts 4:10
	Peter	Cornelius	Acts 10:39
	Paul	Jews	Acts 13:28
	Stephen	Sanhedrin and the mob	Acts 7:52

Content	Preacher	Audience	Reference
Deliverer from Sin	Peter	Jews	Acts 2:38; 3:19
	Peter	Sanhedrin	Acts 5:31
	Peter	Cornelius	Acts 10:43
	Paul	Jews	Acts 13:38–39
Disowned One	Peter	Jews	Acts 3:13
Exalted One	Peter	Jews	Acts 2:33
	Peter	Sanhedrin	Acts 5:30–31
	Angels	Apostles	Acts 1:11
God's Anointed	Peter	Cornelius	Acts 10:38
	Apostles	God	Acts 4:27
Holy One	Peter	Jews	Acts 2:27; 3:14
	Paul	Jews	Acts 13:35
Hope of Israel	Paul	Jews	Acts 28:20
Jesus the Nazarene	Peter	Jews	Acts 2:22
Jesus of Nazareth	Peter	Cornelius	Acts 10:38
	Paul	Agrippa II and Festus	Acts 26:9
Judge	Peter	Cornelius	Acts 10:42
	Paul	Gentiles	Acts 17:31
Lord	Paul	Jews	Acts 9:28; 22:19
Lord Jesus	Peter	Jewish believers	Acts 1:21; 15:11
	Paul	Gentile jailer	Acts 16:31
	Paul	church	Acts 20:24,35
	Paul	church	Acts 21:13
	Stephen	Sanhedrin and the mob	Acts 7:59–60
	Philip	Samaritans	Acts 8:16
	Ananias	Saul	Acts 9:17
	Church at Antioch	Gentiles	Acts 11:20
Lord Jesus Christ	Peter	Jewish believers	Acts 11:17
	Paul	Jews and Gentiles	Acts 20:21
	Paul	Gentiles	Acts 28:31
Lord and Christ	Peter	Jews	Acts 2:36
Lord of All	Peter	Cornelius	Acts 10:36
Man	Peter	Jews	Acts 2:22
	Paul	Gentiles	Acts 17:31
Miracle worker	Peter	Jews	Acts 2:22
	Peter	Cornelius	Acts 10:38

Content	Preacher	Audience	Reference
Prince of Life; Prince	Peter	Jews	Acts 3:15
	Peter	Sanhedrin	Acts 5:31
Prophesied One	Peter	Jews	Acts 3:24
	Peter	Cornelius	Acts 10:43
	Paul	Jews	Acts 11:23,33–37; 17:3; 28:23
	Paul	Agrippa II and Festus	Acts 26:22
Prophet Like Moses	Peter	Jews	Acts 3:22
Rejected Stone	Peter	Sanhedrin	Acts 4:11
Resurrected One	Peter	Jews	Acts 2:24,32; 3:15
	Peter	Sanhedrin	Acts 4:10
	Peter	Cornelius	Acts 10:40
	Paul	Jews	Acts 11:30; 17:3
	Paul	Gentiles	Acts 17:18,31
	Paul	Agrippa II and Festus	Acts 26:23
Returning One	Angel	Apostles	Acts 1:11
	Peter	Jews	Acts 3:20
Righteous One	Peter	Jews	Acts 3:14
	Paul	Jews	Acts 22:14
	Stephen	Sanhedrin and the mob	Acts 7:52
Savior, Only Savior	Peter	Sanhedrin	Acts 5:31; 4:12
	Paul	Jews	Acts 13:23
Sent by God	Peter	Jews	Acts 3:26
	Paul	Jews	Acts 13:23
Servant of the Lord	Peter	Jews	Acts 3:13,26
	Apostles	God	Acts 4:27,30
	Philip	Ethiopian	Acts 8:35
Son of David	Peter	Jews	Acts 2:30
	Paul	Jews	Acts 13:33
Son of God	Paul	Jews	Acts 9:20; 13:33
Son of Man	Stephen	Sanhedrin and the mob	Acts 7:56
Suffering One	Peter	Jews	Acts 3:18
	Paul	Jews	Acts 17:3
	Paul	Agrippa II and Festus	Acts 26:23

Bibliography

Alexander, Joseph A. *A Commentary on the Acts of the Apostles*. London: Banner of Truth, 1963.

Bauckham, Richard, ed. *The Book of Acts in Its First Century Setting*. Vol. 4. Grand Rapids: Eerdmans, 1995.

Blaiklock, E. M. *The Acts of the Apostles*. Tyndale Commentary Series. Grand Rapids: Eerdmans, 1976.

Bock, Darrell. "A Theology of Luke-Acts," in *A Biblical Theology of the New Testament*, eds. Roy Zuck and Darrell Bock. Chicago: Moody Press, 1994.

Bruce, F. F. *The Book of Acts*, rev. ed. Grand Rapids: Eerdmans, 1988.

Couch, Mal, ed. *A Bible Handbook to the Acts of the Apostles*. Grand Rapids: Kregel, 1999.

Johnson, Luke Timothy. *The Acts of the Apostles*. Vol. 5 in Sacra Pagina. Collegeville, MN: The Liturgical Press, 1992.

Longenecker, Richard. *Acts*. Vol. 9 of The Expositor's Bible Commentary, ed. Frank Gaebelein. Grand Rapids: Zondervan, 1981.

Polhill, John B. *Acts*. New American Commentary. Nashville: Broadman Press, 1992.

Stott, John R. W. *The Message of Acts*. Downers Grove, IL: InterVarsity Press, 1990.

Toussaint, Stanley. "Acts," in *The Bible Knowledge Commentary: New Testament*, eds. John Walvoord and Roy Zuck. Wheaton, IL: Victor Books, 1986.

Notes

Foreword

1. Craig S. Keener, *The IVP Bible Background Commentary: New Testament* (Downers Grove: InterVarsity Press, 1993), Acts 1:1.

Introduction—Background of Acts

1. Donald Guthrie, *New Testament Introduction* (Downers Grove: InterVarsity Press, 1970), 354.

2. Ibid., 354.

3. Mal Couch, ed., *A Bible Handbook to the Acts of the Apostles* (Grand Rapids: Kregel, 1999), 369.

Chapter 1—Beginning in Jerusalem

1. Flavius Josephus, *The Works of Josephus: Complete and Unabridged* (Peabody: Hendrickson, 1996), Apion I 1.

2. P.W. Barnett, "Apostle," in Gerald F. Hawthorne and Ralph P. Martin, eds., *Dictionary of Paul and His Letters* (Downers Grove: InterVarsity Press, 1993), 45–50.

3. Flavius Josephus, *The Works of Josephus: Complete and Unabridged* (Peabody: Hendrickson, 1996), Ant. XVIII, v 2.

4. A comprehensive discussion of baptism in the NT is contained in Richard E. Averbeck, "The Focus of Baptism in the New Testament," *Grace Theological Journal* (Grace Seminary, 2:2, Fall 1981) 266-301.

5. *Mishnah*, Sotah 5:3.

6. Arnold Fruchtenbaum, *Messianic Christology* (Tustin: Ariel, 1998), 153–154.

7. Oskar Skarsaune, *In the Shadow of the Temple: Jewish Influences on Early Christianity* (Downers Grove: Intervarsity Press, 2002) 40-42. See also the extensive and enlightening discussion in Richard A Horsley, Archaeology, History and Society in Galilee: The Social Context of Jesus and the Rabbis (Valley Forge: Trinity, 1996), 157-171.

Chapter 2—Birth of the Church

1. Philo, *The Works of Philo: Complete and Unabridged* (Peabody: Hendrickson, 1996), Decalogue 46.

2. S. Lewis Johnson, "A Symposium on the Tongues Movement; Part II: The Gift of Tongues and the Book of Acts," *Bibliotheca Sacra* (Dallas Theological Seminary, 120:480, Oct. 1963), 309ff.

3. Richard Bauckham, "James and the Jerusalem Church," in Richard Bauckham, ed., *The Book of Acts in its First Century Setting, vol. 4: Palestinian Setting* (Grand Rapids: Eerdmans, 1995), 417-419.

4. Walter C. Kaiser, Jr., *The Uses of the Old Testament in the New* (Chicago: Moody Press, 1985) 91 as well as Richard N. Longenecker, *Biblical Exegesis in the Apostolic Period, second edition* (Grand Rapids: Eerdmans, 1999), 70-71.

5. Darrell L. Bock, "A Theology of Luke-Acts," in Roy B. Zuck and Darrell L. Bock, eds., *A Biblical Theology of the New Testament* (Chicago: Moody Press, 1994), 142.

6. Walter C. Kaiser, Jr., *Hard sayings of the Bible* (Downers Grove: InterVarsity, 1997), 514.

7. A thorough discussion of the grammatical interpretive options is laid out in Lanny Thomas Tanton, "The Gospel and Water Baptism: A Study of Acts 2:38," *Journal of the Grace Evangelical Society* (Grace Evangelical Society, 3:1, Spring 1990), 27-52. See also Luther B. McIntyre, Jr., "Baptism and Forgiveness in Acts 2:38," *Bibliotheca Sacra* (Dallas Theological Seminary, 153:609, Jan. 1996), 53–62.

8. F.F. Bruce, *The Book of the Acts, revised edition* (Grand Rapids: Eerdmans, 1988), 70.

9. For example, this is the position tentatively set forth by Charles Ryrie in his *Ryrie Study Bible* (Chicago: Moody Press, 1978).

10. Daniel B. Wallace, *Greek Grammar Beyond the Basics* (Grand Rapids: Zondervan, 1996), 370.

11. F.F. Bruce, *The Book of the Acts, revised edition* (Grand Rapids: Eerdmans, 1988), 69-70.

12. Stanley D. Toussaint, "Acts" in John F. Walvoord and Roy B. Zuck, eds., *The Bible Knowledge Commentary: New Testament* (Wheaton: Victor: 1986), 359.

13. Brad H. Young, *Paul the Jewish Theologian* (Peabody: Hendrickson, 1997), 55.

Chapter 3—Miracle in the Temple

1. Flavius Josephus, *The Works of Josephus: Complete and Unabridged* (Peabody: Hendrickson, 1996), Ant. XIV, iv 3.

2. Everett F. Harrison, "The Attitude of the Primitive Church Toward Judaism," *Bibliotheca Sacra* (Dallas Theological Seminary, 113:450, April 1956), 130ff.

3. Alfred Edersheim, *The Temple: Its Ministry and Services* (Grand Rapids: Eerdmans, 1965), 47.

4. *Mishnah*, Middot 1:3

5. Alfred Edersheim, *The Temple: Its Ministry and Services* (Grand Rapids: Eerdmans, 1965), 43.

6. John A. McLean, "Did Jesus Correct His Disciples' View of the Kingdom?" *Bibliotheca Sacra* (Dallas Theological Seminary, 151:602, April 1994), 224.

7. Philo, *The Works of Philo: Complete and Unabridged* (Peabody: Hendrickson, 1996), The Special Laws, I 65.

Chapter 4—Those Irrepressible Apostles

1. Flavius Josephus, *The Works of Josephus: Complete and Unabridged* (Peabody: Hendrickson, 1996), Apion II 8.
2. David A. Fiensy, "The Composition of the Jerusalem Church," in Richard Bauckham, ed., *The Book of Acts in its First Century Setting, vol. 4: Palestinian Setting* (Grand Rapids: Eerdmans, 1995), 221.
3. Flavius Josephus, *The Works of Josephus: Complete and Unabridged* (Peabody: Hendrickson, 1996), Ant. XIII, x 6.
4. Ibid., Ant. XVIII, i 4.
5. Ibid., Wars II, viii 14.
6. Ibid., Ant. XVIII, i 4.
7. *Mishnah*, Sanhedrin 1:6.
8. Ibid., Sanhedrin 1:6.
9. Flavius Josephus, *The Works of Josephus: Complete and Unabridged* (Peabody: Hendrickson, 1996), Ant. XX, x 1.

Chapter 5—Opposition from Within and Without

1. Ibid., Ant. XVII, ii 4.
1. David A. Fiensy, "The Composition of the Jerusalem Church," in Richard Bauckham, ed., *The Book of Acts in its First Century Setting, vol. 4: Palestinian Setting* (Grand Rapids: Eerdmans, 1995), 216-218.
2. Arnold Fruchtenbaum, *Acts*, cassette series.
3. Ibid.
4. For example, "The Shekinah rests only on a man who is brave, wealthy and sensible" (*Talmud*, Shabbat 92).
5. *Mishnah*, Sotah 9:15.
6. Flavius Josephus, *The Works of Josephus: Complete and Unabridged* (Peabody: Hendrickson, 1996), Ant. XVIII, i 3.
7. *Mishnah*, Avot 1:1.
8. Flavius Josephus, *The Works of Josephus: Complete and Unabridged* (Peabody: Hendrickson, 1996), Ant. XVII, ii 4.
9. This is not the Theudas whom Josephus mentions, for his rebellion occurred in AD 44, nine years after the events of Acts 5. See Flavius Josephus, *The Works of Josephus: Complete and Unabridged* (Peabody: Hendrickson, 1996), Ant. XX, v 1.
10. Ibid., Ant. XVIII, i 1.
11. Ibid., Ant. XIII, x 6.
12. *Mishnah*, Makkot 3:10-14.
13. Flavius Josephus, *The Works of Josephus: Complete and Unabridged* (Peabody: Hendrickson, 1996), Ant. XX, ix 1.

Chapter 6—The Witness of Stephen

1. Rainer Reisner, "Synagogues in Jerusalem," in Richard Bauckham, ed., *The Book of Acts in its First Century Setting, vol. 4: Palestinian Setting* (Grand Rapids: Eerdmans, 1995), 205.
2. Flavius Josephus, *The Works of Josephus: Complete and Unabridged* (Peabody: Hendrickson, 1996), Ant. XIV, vii 2.

3. *Mishnah*, Sanhedrin 6:4.

4. *Mishnah*, Makkot 1:5.

5. J. Julius Scott, "Stephen's Speech: A Possible Model for Luke's Historical Method?" *Journal of the Evangelical Theological Society*, (The Evangelical Theological Society, 17:2, Spring 1974), 91.

6. 4QExEd.

7. Howard Clark Kee, *To Every Nation Under Heaven* (Harrisburg: Trinity Press International, 1997), 97.

8. Flavius Josephus, *The Works of Josephus: Complete and Unabridged* (Peabody: Hendrickson, 1996), Ant. II, ix 6.

9. Philo, *The Works of Philo: Complete and Unabridged* (Peabody: Hendrickson, 1996), On the Life of Moses, I 20-24.

10. Arnold Fruchtenbaum comments in typically deadpan fashion: "Burning bushes are not unusual in the Sinai desert; however, a bush that continues to burn without being consumed is unique. One from which the voice of the Lord proceeds is exceedingly unique," *Acts*, cassette series.

11. F.F. Bruce, *The Book of the Acts, revised edition* (Grand Rapids: Eerdmans, 1988), 152

12. The mediation of the Torah by angels was an ancient Jewish belief, indicated by the Septuagint reading of Deut. 33.2, and affirmed here by Stephen as well as in Gal. 3:19 and Heb. 2:2. Also Jub.1:27-29.

13. *Mishnah*, Sanhedrin 6:3.

14. Ibid., Sanhedrin 6:4.

15. Walter Bauer, William F. Arndt and F. Wilbur Gingrich, *A Greek-English Lexicon of the New Testament and Other Early Christian Literature* (Chicago: University of Chicago Press, 1979), 534.

16. *Mishnah*, Sanhedrin 6:2.

17. B.L. Blackburn, "Stephen," in Ralph P. Martin and Peter H. Davids, eds., *Dictionary of the Later New Testament and its Developments*, electronic edition (Downers Grove: InterVarsity Press, 1997).

18. *Mishnah*, Sanhedrin 6:6.

19. Flavius Josephus, *The Works of Josephus: Complete and Unabridged* (Peabody: Hendrickson, 1996), Ant. XIII, x 6.

Chapter 7—The Witness of Philip

1. Ibid., Ant. XVIII, ii 2.

2. Joseph A. Fitzmyer, *Acts of the Apostles*, The Anchor Bible, vol. 31 (New York: Doubleday, 1997), 405.

3. F.F. Bruce, *The Book of the Acts, revised edition* (Grand Rapids: Eerdmans, 1988), 166-167.

4. Joseph A. Fitzmyer, *Acts of the Apostles*, The Anchor Bible, vol. 31 (New York: Doubleday, 1997), 401.

5. Yohanan Aharoni and Michael Avi-Yonah, The Macmillan Bible Atlas, revised edition (New York: Macmillan, 1978), 152

6. Gerhard Kittel, *Theological Dictionary of the New Testament*. (Grand Rapids: Mich.: W.B. Eerdmans, 1985), 2:766.

7. Richard N. Longenecker, "Acts" in Frank E. Gaebelein, ed., *The Expositor's Bible Commentary*, vol. 9 (Grand Rapids: Zondervan, 1981), 363.

8. The New International Dictionary of New Testament Theology vol. 1, ed., Colin Brown. "eunuch" pg. 560 (Grand Rapids: Zondervan, 1975)

9. Richard N. Longenecker, "Acts" in Frank E. Gaebelein, ed., *The Expositor's Bible Commentary*, vol. 9 (Grand Rapids: Zondervan, 1981), 363.

10. The late rainy season of April/May is the only time following a pilgrimage feast that the desert wadis of Gaza would likely hold sufficient water to perform a baptism. In addition, the tight chronology adapted for AD 35 requires this event to have occurred early in that year. See Table 2.

11. "Falashas," *Encyclopedia Judaica* (Jerusalem: Keter, 1990), 6:1143ff

12. Flavius Josephus, *The Works of Josephus: Complete and Unabridged* (Peabody: Hendrickson, 1996), Ant. VIII, vi 5.

13. "Falashas," *Encyclopedia Judaica* (Jerusalem: Keter, 1990), 6:1151ff.

14. The New International Dictionary of New Testament Theology vol. 1, ed., Colin Brown. "eunuch" pg. 560 (Grand Rapids: Regency, 1975)

15. F.F. Bruce, *The Book of the Acts, revised edition* (Grand Rapids: Eerdmans, 1988), 175.

16. Arnold Fruchtenbaum, *Messianic Christology* (Tustin: Ariel, 1998), 54.

17. J.M. Houston, "Rain," in D.R.W. Wood et al, eds., *New Bible Dictionary*, third edition (Downers Grove: InterVarsity Press, 1996), 1000.

Chapter 8—The Call of Saul

1. R. Alan Cole, "The Life and Ministry of Paul," in Frank E. Gaebelein, ed., *The Expositor's Bible Commentary*, vol. 1 (Grand Rapids: Zondervan, 1981), 563.

2. Mal Couch, ed., *A Bible Handbook to the Acts of the Apostles* (Grand Rapids: Kregel, 1999), 103.

3. Arthur A. Rupprecht, "The Cultural and Political Setting of the New Testament," in Frank E. Gaebelein, ed., *The Expositor's Bible Commentary*, vol. 1 (Grand Rapids: Zondervan, 1981), 487.

4. Simon Legasse, "Paul's Pre-Christian Career According to Acts," in Richard Bauckham, ed., *The Book of Acts in its First Century Setting, vol. 4: Palestinian Setting* (Grand Rapids: Eerdmans, 1995), 372.

5. Ibid., 371.

6. Ibid., 374.

7. *Mishnah*, Avot 5:21.

8. Simon Legasse, "Paul's Pre-Christian Career According to Acts," in Richard Bauckham, ed., *The Book of Acts in its First Century Setting, vol. 4: Palestinian Setting* (Grand Rapids: Eerdmans, 1995), 378.

9. R. Alan Cole, "The Life and Ministry of Paul," in Frank E. Gaebelein, ed., *The Expositor's Bible Commentary*, vol. 1 (Grand Rapids: Zondervan, 1981), 557-558.

10. Richard N. Longenecker, "Acts" in Frank E. Gaebelein, ed., *The Expositor's Bible Commentary*, vol. 9 (Grand Rapids: Zondervan, 1981), 368-369.

11. Flavius Josephus, *The Works of Josephus: Complete and Unabridged* (Peabody: Hendrickson, 1996), Wars VII, viii 7.

12. Timothy J. Ralston, "The Conversion of Paul and its Theological Significance," *Bibliotheca Sacra* (Dallas Theological Seminary, 147:586, April 1990), 213.

13. Mal Couch, ed., *A Bible Handbook to the Acts of the Apostles* (Grand Rapids: Kregel, 1999), 138.

14. S. Herbert Bess, "The Term 'Son of God' in the Light of Old Testament Idiom," *Grace Journal* (Grace Seminary, 6:2, Spring 1965), 17.

Chapter 9—Peter Opens a New Door

1. David A. Fiensy, "The Composition of the Jerusalem Church," in Richard Bauckham, ed., *The Book of Acts in its First Century Setting, vol. 4: Palestinian Setting* (Grand Rapids: Eerdmans, 1995), 223.

2. G.L. Thompson, "Roman Military," in Craig A. Evans and Stanley E. Porter, eds., *Dictionary of New Testament Background: A Compendium of Contemporary Biblical Scholarship*, electronic edition (Downers Grove: InterVarsity Press, 2000).

3. F.F. Bruce, *The Book of the Acts, revised edition* (Grand Rapids: Eerdmans, 1988), 202.

4. Martin Hengel, "The Geography of Palestine in Acts," in Richard Bauckham, ed., *The Book of Acts in its First Century Setting, vol. 4: Palestinian Setting* (Grand Rapids: Eerdmans, 1995), 56.

5. *Mishnah*, Ohalot 18:7.

Chapter 10—Who Let in All These Gentiles?

1. Richard N. Longenecker, "Acts" in Frank E. Gaebelein, ed., *The Expositor's Bible Commentary*, vol. 9 (Grand Rapids: Zondervan, 1981), 399.

2. John P. Meier, "Antioch, "in P. J. Achtemeier, ed., *Harper's Bible Dictionary*, first edition (San Francisco: Harper & Row, 1985), 34.

3. Chrysostom also has the unfortunate distinction of being a great propagator of anti-Semitism. His vitriolic ranting about Jews have been well preserved and documented.

4. Joseph A. Fitzmyer, *Acts of the Apostles*, The Anchor Bible, vol. 31 (New York: Doubleday, 1997), 478.

5. Ibid, 475.

6. It is precisely this same desire to facilitate awareness of Jewish Christian group identity among their our unsaved brethren which motivates the increasing popularity of the term "Messianic Jew."

7. For a candid and insightful discussion on the whole "controversial" issue of Messianic Jew vs. Hebrew Christian, see David H. Stern, *Jewish New Testament Commentary: A Companion Volume to the Jewish New Testament*, first edition (Clarksville: Jewish New Testament Publications, 1992), Acts 11:26.

8. Flavius Josephus, *The Works of Josephus: Complete and Unabridged* (Peabody: Hendrickson, 1996), Apion I 8.

9. Ibid., Ant. XX, ii 5.

Chapter 11—The Unchained Apostles

1. *Mishnah*, Sanhedrin 7:1

2. Ibid., Sanhedrin 9:1

3. Tobit 5:4–5.

4. Flavius Josephus, *The Works of Josephus: Complete and Unabridged* (Peabody: Hendrickson, 1996), Ant. XIX, viii 2.

5. Richard N. Longenecker, "Acts" in Frank E. Gaebelein, ed., *The Expositor's Bible Commentary*, vol. 9 (Grand Rapids: Zondervan, 1981), 413.

Chapter 12–The First Missionary Journey

1. The first week of March was the commencement of the navigation season. Prior to that week, rough winter seas would prohibit travel by sea. See Merrill F. Unger, "Archaeology and Paul's Tour of Cyprus," *Bibliotheca Sacra* (Dallas Theological Seminary, 117:467, July 1960), 229.

2. Joseph A. Fitzmyer, *Acts of the Apostles*, The Anchor Bible, vol. 31 (New York: Doubleday, 1997), 503.

3. Merrill F. Unger, "Archaeology and Paul's Tour of Cyprus," *Bibliotheca Sacra* (Dallas Theological Seminary, 117:467, July 1960), 233.

4. Merrill F. Unger, "Archaeology and the Cities of Paul's First Missionary Journey, Part II: Pisidian Antioch and Gospel Penetration of the Greek World," *Bibliotheca Sacra* (Dallas Theological Seminary, 118:469, Jan. 1961), 48.

5. J. Julius Scott, Jr., *Customs and Controversies* (Grand Rapids: Baker, 1995), 142.

6. Harold W. Hoehner, "The Duration of the Egyptian Bondage," *Bibliotheca Sacra* (Dallas Theological Seminary, 126:504, Oct. 1969), 306ff.

7. Specifically, the *Textus Receptus*, or *Majority Text*, on which the KJV and NKJV translations are based.

8. Eugene H. Merrill, "Paul's Use of 'About 450 Years' in Acts 13:20" *Bibliotheca Sacra* (Dallas Theological Seminary, 138:551, July 1981), 246.

9. Arnold Fruchtenbaum, *Messianic Christology* (Tustin: Ariel, 1998), 80.

10. F.F. Bruce, *The Book of the Acts, revised edition* (Grand Rapids: Eerdmans, 1988), 260.

11. *Mishnah*, Keritot 1:1.

Chapter 13–From Jewish Sect to Universal Church

1. Arnold Fruchtenbaum, *Acts*, cassette series.

2. The laws and techniques of circumcision was set down and codified not in the Torah, but in the Jewish oral law, considered by Pharisees to carry the authority of Moses' own words. *Mishnah*, Shabbat 19:1–6; Nedarim 3:11.

3. *Mishnah*, Berakhot 2:2.

4. 4QFlor, Richard N. Longenecker, "Acts" in Frank E. Gaebelein, ed., *The Expositor's Bible Commentary*, vol. 9 (Grand Rapids: Zondervan, 1981), 447.

5. Mal Couch, ed., *A Bible Handbook to the Acts of the Apostles* (Grand Rapids: Kregel, 1999), 421.

6. *Talmud*, Sanhedrin 56a.

7. F.F. Bruce, *The Book of the Acts, revised edition* (Grand Rapids: Eerdmans, 1988), 299.

Chapter 14–The Second Missionary Journey

1. Mal Couch, ed., *A Bible Handbook to the Acts of the Apostles* (Grand Rapids: Kregel, 1999), 97.

2. Joseph A. Fitzmyer, *Acts of the Apostles*, The Anchor Bible, vol. 31 (New York: Doubleday, 1997), 587.

3. The lex Valeria, which prohibited the striking of a Roman citizen and the lex Porcia which prohibited the scourging of a Roman citizen for any reason. See Merrill F. Unger, "Archaeology and Paul's Campaign at Philippi," *Bibliotheca Sacra* (Dallas Theological Seminary, 119:474, April 1962), 159.

4. Suetonius, *Claudius* 25:4.

5. Richard N. Longenecker, "Acts" in Frank E. Gaebelein, ed., *The Expositor's Bible Commentary*, vol. 9 (Grand Rapids: Zondervan, 1981), 472.

6. Petronius *Sat.* 17, cited in J.R. McRay, "Athens," in Craig A. Evans and Stanley E. Porter, eds., *Dictionary of New Testament Background: A Compendium of Contemporary Biblical Scholarship*, electronic edition (Downers Grove: InterVarsity Press, 2000).

7. "The Epicureans," in A.B. du Toit, ed., *Guide to the New Testament, Vol. II: The New Testament Milieu.* (Halfway House: Orion, 1998), 7.10.

8. "The Stoics," in A.B. du Toit, ed., *Guide to the New Testament, Vol. II: The New Testament Milieu.* (Halfway House: Orion, 1998), 7.11.

9. J. Daryl Charles, "Engaging the (Neo) Pagan Mind: Paul's Encounter with Athenian Culture as a Model for Cultural Apologetics (Acts 17:16-34)," *Trinity Journal* (Trinity Evangelical Divinity School, 16:1, Spring 1995), 52.

10. J.R. McRay, "Athens," in Craig A. Evans and Stanley E. Porter, eds., *Dictionary of New Testament Background: A Compendium of Contemporary Biblical Scholarship*, electronic edition (Downers Grove: InterVarsity Press, 2000).

11. Euripides, *Fragments*, 968, cited by Richard N. Longenecker, "Acts" in Frank E. Gaebelein, ed., *The Expositor's Bible Commentary*, vol. 9 (Grand Rapids: Zondervan, 1981), 476.

12. Aratus, *Phainomena*, 5.

13. J.R. McRay, "Corinth," in Craig A. Evans and Stanley E. Porter, eds., *Dictionary of New Testament Background: A Compendium of Contemporary Biblical Scholarship*, electronic edition (Downers Grove: InterVarsity Press, 2000).

14. F.F. Bruce, *The Book of the Acts, revised edition* (Grand Rapids: Eerdmans, 1988), 346.

15. Simon Legasse, "Paul's Pre-Christian Career According to Acts," in Richard Bauckham, ed., *The Book of Acts in its First Century Setting, vol. 4: Palestinian Setting* (Grand Rapids: Eerdmans, 1995), 378.

16. See Fitzmyer's comments. Joseph A. Fitzmyer, *Acts of the Apostles*, The Anchor Bible, vol. 31 (New York: Doubleday, 1997), 620-623.

17. *Mishnah*, Nazir, in which the guidelines for Nazirite vows are spelled out in painstaking (and eye-straining) detail.

18. Ibid., Nazir 3:6.

19. David H. Stern, *Jewish New Testament Commentary: A Companion Volume to the Jewish New Testament*, first edition (Clarksville: Jewish New Testament Publications, 1992), Acts 18:18.

20. Craig S. Keener, *The IVP Bible Background Commentary: New Testament* (Downers Grove: InterVarsity Press, 1993), Acts 18:18.

21. Flavius Josephus, *The Works of Josephus: Complete and Unabridged* (Peabody: Hendrickson, 1996), Ant. XIV, x 13.

Chapter 15—The Third Missionary Journey

1. Fritz Rienecker and Cleon Rogers, *Linguistic Key to the Greek New Testament* (Grand Rapids: Zondervan, 1980), 312.
2. F.F. Bruce, *The Book of the Acts, revised edition* (Grand Rapids: Eerdmans, 1988), 368.
3. Mal Couch, ed., *A Bible Handbook to the Acts of the Apostles* (Grand Rapids: Kregel, 1999), 99.
4. J.R. McRay, "Corinth," in Craig A. Evans and Stanley E. Porter, eds., *Dictionary of New Testament Background: A Compendium of Contemporary Biblical Scholarship*, electronic edition (Downers Grove: InterVarsity Press, 2000).
5. B.W.R. Pearson, "Civic Cults," in Craig A. Evans and Stanley E. Porter, eds., *Dictionary of New Testament Background: A Compendium of Contemporary Biblical Scholarship*, electronic edition (Downers Grove: InterVarsity Press, 2000).
6. F.F. Bruce, *The Book of the Acts, revised edition* (Grand Rapids: Eerdmans, 1988), 387.
7. Wayne A. Grudem, *The Gift of Prophecy in the New Testament and Today* (Westchester: Crossway, 1988), 96-100.
8. Robert L. Thomas, "Prophecy Rediscovered? A Review of *The Gift of Prophecy in the New Testament and Today*," *Bibliotheca Sacra* (Dallas Theological Seminary, 149:593, January 1992), 91.

Chapter 16—Paul in Jerusalem

1. *Mishnah*, Nazir 6:1.
2. Mal Couch, ed., *A Bible Handbook to the Acts of the Apostles* (Grand Rapids: Kregel, 1999), 117.
3. *Mishnah*, Ohalot 2:3.
4. Joseph A. Fitzmyer, *Acts of the Apostles*, The Anchor Bible, vol. 31 (New York: Doubleday, 1997), 694.
5. Arnold Fruchtenbaum, *Acts*, cassette series.
6. Carl R. Holliday, "Acts" in James L. Mays, ed., *Harper's Bible Commentary* (San Francisco: Harper & Row, 1996), *electronic edition*, Act 21:27.
7. Flavius Josephus, *The Works of Josephus: Complete and Unabridged* (Peabody: Hendrickson, 1996), Wars V, v 2.
8. F.F. Bruce, *The Book of the Acts, revised edition* (Grand Rapids: Eerdmans, 1988), 409.
9. Flavius Josephus, *The Works of Josephus: Complete and Unabridged* (Peabody: Hendrickson, 1996), Wars VI, ii 4.
10. Ibid., Wars II, xiii 5; Ant XX, viii 6.
11. Ibid., Wars II, xiii 3.
12. A most extended and helpful discussion on the interpretive options for Acts 22:16 is in Lanny Thomas Tanton, "The Gospel and Water Baptism: A Study of Acts 22:16," *Journal of the Grace Evangelical Society* (Grace Evangelical Society, 4:1, Spring 1991), 23–40.
13. Arnold Fruchtenbaum, *Acts*, cassette series.

14. P.W. Barnett, "Revolutionary Movements" in Gerald F. Hawthorne and Ralph P. Martin, eds., *Dictionary of Paul and His Letters* (Downers Grove: InterVarsity Press, 1993), 815–819.

15. *Talmud*, Pesachim 57a.

16. Flavius Josephus, *The Works of Josephus: Complete and Unabridged* (Peabody: Hendrickson, 1996), Ant XX, ix 2.

17. Ibid., Wars II, xvii 6.

18. Ibid., Wars II, xvii 9.

19. *Mishnah*, Nedarim 3:1.

20. B.M. Rapske, "Roman Governors of Palestine" in Craig A. Evans and Stanley E. Porter, eds., *Dictionary of New Testament Background: A Compendium of Contemporary Biblical Scholarship*, electronic edition (Downers Grove: InterVarsity Press, 2000).

21. Flavius Josephus, *The Works of Josephus: Complete and Unabridged* (Peabody: Hendrickson, 1996), Ant XX, vii 2.

22. Tacitus, *History of the Empire After Marcus*, 5.10 as cited in B.M. Rapske, "Roman Governors of Palestine" in Craig A. Evans and Stanley E. Porter, eds., *Dictionary of New Testament Background: A Compendium of Contemporary Biblical Scholarship*, electronic edition (Downers Grove: InterVarsity Press, 2000).

Chapter 17—Paul in Caesarea

1. Charles F. Pfeiffer, and Howard F. Vos, "The Apostle Paul in Italy," in *The Wycliffe Historical Geography of Bible Lands* (Chicago: Moody Press, 1967) electronic edition.

2. Flavius Josephus, *The Works of Josephus: Complete and Unabridged* (Peabody: Hendrickson, 1996), Ant XIX, ix 2.

3. "Agrippa II," in A.B. du Toit, ed., *Guide to the New Testament, Vol. II: The New Testament Milieu.* (Halfway House: Orion, 1998), 11.2.6.

4. Flavius Josephus, *The Works of Josephus: Complete and Unabridged* (Peabody: Hendrickson, 1996), Ant XIX, v 1.

5. Ibid., Ant XX, vii 3.

6. Ibid., Wars II, xv 1.

7. Richard N. Longenecker, "Acts" in Frank E. Gaebelein, ed., *The Expositor's Bible Commentary*, vol. 9 (Grand Rapids: Zondervan, 1981), 552.

Chapter 18—Apostolic Adventures En Route to Rome

1. F.F. Bruce, *The Book of the Acts, revised edition* (Grand Rapids: Eerdmans, 1988), 499.

Chapter 19—To the Ends of the Earth

1. Suetonius, *Claudius* 25:4.

2. 1 Clement 5.7.

3. Eusebius, *Ecclesiastical History* 2.25.7–8.

4. Flavius Josephus, *The Works of Josephus: Complete and Unabridged* (Peabody: Hendrickson, 1996), Ant XX, ix 1.

5. Eusebius, *Ecclesiastical History* 2.23.3–18

6. Andre LeMaire, "Burial Box of James the Brother of Jesus," *Biblical Archeology Review* (Biblical Archaeology Society, 28:6, Nov./Dec. 2002), 24–33.

Appendix 1–Speeches in Acts

1. The entire complex corpus of Jewish oral law is built on this memorization and oral transmission from one generation of rabbis to the next. This corpus of oral customs, traditions, edicts and verdicts was not committed to writing until the second century AD, following the destruction of Jerusalem and the Temple, and the majority of the Jewish people's exile from the land of Israel.

Appendix 2–The Five Transitional Circuits in Acts

1. Darrell L. Bock, "A Theology of Luke-Acts," in Roy B. Zuck and Darrell L. Bock, eds., *A Biblical Theology of the New Testament* (Chicago: Moody Press, 1994), 138.

About the Author

Steven Ger grew up in a Jewish family in New York and New Jersey, where he was educated in both church and synagogue due to his distinctive heritage as a Jewish Christian. He is the founder and director of *Sojourner Ministries*, an organization dedicated to *exploring the Jewish heart of Christianity*. The name of the ministry is derived from the Hebrew meaning of Steven's surname. In Hebrew, the word *"ger"* means *sojourner* or *wanderer*. This particular "wandering" Jew's faith journey has led him to the conviction that Jesus is the Messiah who was foretold in the Hebrew Scriptures. Steven's life is dedicated to helping people see their Messiah more clearly—through Hebrew eyes.

Steven has led eleven tours to Israel, with extensions to Egypt, Greece, Jordan, Turkey and Germany. He has lectured at *Dallas Theological Seminary* and at *Tyndale Seminary*. He earned a BA in psychology and interpersonal communications from Trenton State College and a ThM from Dallas Theological Seminary. Steven lives in the Dallas area with his wife, Adria, and their son, Jonathan Gabriel.

About the General Editors

Mal Couch is founder and president of Tyndale Theological Seminary and Biblical Institute in Fort Worth, Texas. He previously taught at Philadelphia College of the Bible, Moody Bible Institute, and Dallas Theological Seminary. His other publications include *The Hope of Christ's Return: A Premillennial Commentary on 1 and 2 Thessalonians, A Bible Handbook to Revelation,* and *Dictionary of Premillennial Theology.*

Edward Hindson is professor of religion, dean of the Institute of Biblical Studies, and assistant to the chancellor at Liberty University in Lynchburg, Virginia. He has authored more than twenty books, served as coeditor of several Bible projects, and was one of the translators for the New King James Version of the Bible. Dr. Hindson has served as a visiting lecturer at Oxford University and Harvard Divinity School as well as numerous evangelical seminaries. He has taught more than fifty thousand students in the past twenty-five years.